THE ENGLISH NOVEL
Volume II

Smollett to Austen

Edited and Introduced by

RICHARD KROLL

LONGMAN
LONDON AND NEW YORK

Addison Wesley Longman Limited
Edinburgh Gate
Harlow, Essex CM20 2JE
England

and Associated Companies throughout the world

Published in the United States of America
by Addison Wesley Longman Inc., New York

First published 1998

ISBN 0 582 09969–2 Paper
ISBN 0 582 09968–4 Cased

British Library Cataloguing-in-Publication Data

A catalogue record for this book is
available from the British Library

Library of Congress Cataloging-in-Publication Data

The English novel / edited and introduced by Richard Kroll.
p. cm. — (Longman critical readers)
Includes bibliographical references and index.
Contents: v. II. Smollett to Austen
ISBN 0–582–09968–4 (v. II). — ISBN 0–582–09969–2 (pbk. : v. II)
1. English fiction—History and criticism. I. Kroll, Richard W.
F. II. Series.
PR823.E57 1998
823.009—dc21 98–13802
CIP

Produced by Addison Wesley Longman Singapore (Pte) Ltd.,
Printed in Singapore

Contents

General Editors' Preface

The outlines of contemporary critical theory are now often taught as a standard feature of a degree in literary studies. The development of particular theories has seen a thorough transformation of literary criticism. For example, Marxist and Foucauldian theories have revolutionized Shakespeare studies, and 'deconstruction' has led to a complete reassessment of Romantic poetry. Feminist criticism has left scarcely any period of literature unaffected by its searching critiques. Teachers of literary studies can no longer fall back on a standardized, received methodology.

Lecturers and teachers are now urgently looking for guidance in a rapidly changing critical environment. They need help in understanding the latest revisions in literary theory, and especially in grasping the practical effects of the new theories in the form of theoretically sensitized new readings. A number of volumes in the series anthologize important essays on particular theories. However, in order to grasp the full implications and possible uses of particular theories it is essential to see them put to work. This series provides substantial volumes of new readings, presented in an accessible form and with a significant amount of editorial guidance.

Each volume includes a substantial introduction which explores the theoretical issues and conflicts embodied in the essays selected and locates areas of disagreement between positions. The pluralism of theories has to be put on the agenda of literary studies. We can no longer pretend that we all tacitly accept the same practices in literary studies. Neither is a *laissez-faire* attitude any longer tenable. Literature departments need to go beyond the mere toleration of theoretical differences: it is not enough merely to agree to differ; they need actually to 'stage' the differences openly. The volumes in this series all attempt to dramatize the differences, not necessarily with a view to resolving them but in order to foreground the choices presented by different theories or to argue for a particular route through the impasses the differences present.

The theory 'revolution' has had real effects. It has loosened the grip of traditional empiricist and romantic assumptions about language and literature. It is not always clear what is being proposed as the new agenda for literary studies, and indeed the very notion of 'literature' is questioned by the post-structuralist strain in theory. However, the uncertainties and obscurities of contemporary theories appear much less worrying when we see what the best critics have been able to do with them in practice. This series aims to disseminate the best of recent criticism and to show that it is possible to re-read the canonical texts of literature in new and challenging ways.

RAMAN SELDEN AND STAN SMITH

The Publishers and fellow Series Editor regret to record that Raman Selden died after a short illness in May 1991 at the age of fifty-three. Ray Selden was a fine scholar and a lovely man. All those he has worked with will remember him with much affection and respect.

Editor's Preface

As I have said in my preface to the companion volume in the Longman Critical Readers Series, these anthologies of essays have the virtue of directing (or redirecting) attention to the eighteenth century as a literary field. This particular volume has the virtue of showing that – as the general editors point out – there is an enormous variety of critical and theoretical approaches facing the student of literature: almost no essay in the following collection agrees entirely in its method or approach with any other. This might indicate an era of critical confusion or alarming choice, almost a complete inability to agree about literature as such, let alone the validity of different approaches to it, but paradoxically what I think we can also see here is a renewed sense of the power and sophistication of political analysis, especially as it applies to the later eighteenth-century novel. It is my personal belief that political analysis has been a presiding strength in the criticism of neoclassical literature, which is ironically one of the reasons why it has remained for so long the poor relation of literary study, yet one of the reasons why it has so much to teach those fields which have traditionally championed the stability of largely a-political, aesthetic categories.

This turn is particularly evident in the criticism of the later eighteenth-century novel. Whereas the 'realist' novel, so called – a term often applied to the great early eighteenth-century novels – tends to encourage a referential and thus obviously characterological, ethical, and political reading of the individual's relations with the world, the representational and affective modes associated with the age of sensibility and the gothic have resisted such thematics. Critics have thus had to translate the sensational, spectacular, grotesque, fragmentary, and often phantasmagoric rhetoric of the later eighteenth-century novel into a symbology approximating political motives of various kinds. Generally speaking, this critical movement has – among other things – legitimated a recourse to political philosophy, such that debates about the conflict between virtue and the transformation of Britain into a commercial and imperial nation weave in and out of many of the essays that follow. The political languages intensify or gain in immediacy, obviously, as the century draws to a close, most especially as the promise of the French Revolution begins to turn into what many saw as a nightmare. We finish with Jane Austen debating the significance of the revolutionary option in *Northanger Abbey*, which may have been written as early as 1794.

I repeat my gratitude to the many colleagues who – some years ago – were willing to provide ideas about books and essays that they found seminal: Paul Alkon, Paula Backscheider, Eve Tavor Bannet, John Bender, Michael McKeon, Max Novak, Ruth Perry, John Richetti, Peter Sabor, and William Warner. My jobs at Princeton and UCI have also provided superb colleagues in my field: Margaret Doody and Earl Miner; Homer Brown, Bob Folkenflik, and Ann Van Sant; as well as Fred Keener during my visiting year at Hofstra. It is a measure of those individuals' caliber that I have, in good conscience, been able to include their work in what follows. Carol Kay, whose work I have found newly inspirational for this project, has remained a friend of heart and head. Most of the preliminary footwork was done with flair and intelligence by Diana Secker. Finally, I have found rigorous readers in Steve Barney, Fraser Easton, Brean Hammond, Fred Keener, Allison Kroll, Jayne Lewis, Mark Phillips, and Victoria Silver. I recognize that there are many fine pieces of criticism I have omitted from this anthology, and that all errors in fact or judgment remain mine.

Irvine, California, 1998

Publisher's Acknowledgements

We are grateful to the following for permission to reproduce copyright material:

Cornell University Press for the essay '*A Sentimental Journey*: Purposeful Play' from *Political Constructions: Defoe, Richardson, and Sterne in Relation to Hobbes, Hume, and Burke* by Carol Kay, pp. 246–63. Copyright © 1988. Cornell University; the author, Robert Folkenflik for his essay 'Self and Society: Comic Union in *Humphry Clinker*' from *Philological Quarterly* 53 (Spring, 1974), pp. 195–204; The Johns Hopkins University Press for the essays 'The Comic Sublime and Sterne's Fiction' by Jonathan Lamb from *ELH* 48 (1981) and 'Time and Family in the Gothic Novel: *The Castle of Otranto*' by Ian Watt in *Eighteenth Century Life* 10 (1986); Novel Corp. for 'Mary Wollstonecraft: The Gender of Genres in Late Eighteenth-Century England' by Mary Poovey from *NOVEL: A Forum on Fiction*, vol. 15, No. 2, Winter 1982. Copyright NOVEL Corp. © 1982; Oxford University Press for 'The Juvenilia and *Northanger Abbey*' from *Jane Austen and The War of Ideas* by Marilyn Butler (1975) © Oxford University Press 1975; Routledge for 'A Diffused Picture, An Uniform Plan: Roderick Random in the Labyrinth of Britain' from *English Literature in History, 1730–1780: An Equal Wide Survey* by John Barrell (Hutchinson, 1983); Studies in English Literature 1500–1900 for the article 'Rhetoric, History, Rebellion: *Caleb Williams* and the Subversion of Eighteenth-Century Fiction' by Donald Whers from *SEL*, 28, 3 (Summer 1988); The University of Chicago Press for 'The Juvenilia and *Northanger Abbey*: The Authority of Men and Books' from *Jane Austen: Women, Politics, and the Novel* by Claudia Johnson (1988); University of Oklahoma Press for '"Only a Boy": Notes on Sentimental Novels' by George Starr and 'Deserts, Ruins and Troubled Waters: Female Dreams in Fiction and the Development of the Gothic Novel' by Margaret Anne Doody from *Genre* 10 (1977); The University of Wisconsin Press for 'Cecilia: Money and Anarchy' from *The Iron Pen: Frances Burney and the Politics of Women's Writing* by Julia Epstein © 1989.

1 Introduction

This is the second of two volumes anthologizing a series of previously published critical essays and book chapters about the eighteenth-century British novel. The first covers the period from 1700 to the end of Fielding's career; the second covers the period between mid century and Jane Austen's earliest novels, so that we conclude this volume with two essays on *Northanger Abbey* which debate Austen's relationship to the revolutionary climate of the 1790s.[1]

My intention is to present both volumes, with their introductions, as a pair. The first introduction is the more 'literary' of the two, focussing on the rich historiography about the 'rise of the novel,' discussing some of the most successful attempts to describe the novel's cultural role in the eighteenth-century, and concluding with three attempts to place early women novelists into either or both of those frameworks.

In this introduction, I approach the historiography of the later eighteenth-century novel by a different, but I hope complementary, route. My reading of both the novels and the criticism is governed by what I see as two salient facts. First, the kinds and varieties of authors, of interests, and of narrative techniques greatly expand after mid century. Second, unlike the criticism of the earlier period, the criticism of novels and novelists in the later eighteenth century is itself varied, and responds to no dominant critical canon. This is in marked contrast to the substantial literature on Defoe, Richardson, and Fielding, as well as criticism on the early novel in general, all of which it seems must, at some point or another, engage with Ian Watt's classic *The Rise of the Novel: Studies in Defoe, Richardson and Fielding* (1957).[2] My first introduction therefore orients the student by showing how criticism has used or departed from Watt. And it describes some models for thinking about the nature of the eighteenth-century novel as a whole, as well as its relation to questions of gender.

In the absence of the framework provided by Watt, my purpose here is to emphasize how the later eighteenth-century novel is engaged in a number of cultural and historical debates which are distinct to this period. I cast the issues in historical rather than literary terms, not least because the essays that follow provide the literary applications. And I describe three different, but closely related, arenas of discussion, all of which seem especially animated because they seem so closely to reflect our current uncertainties about how we are to revise or confirm conventional modes of political identity and organization.

First, historians have focussed on the question of how the individual can continue to act virtuously in the context of an increasingly commercial society. Neil McKendrick – along with John Brewer and J. H. Plumb, in a joint volume – has famously proposed that the last quarter of the eighteenth century experienced a consumer revolution.[3] This literature has been greatly expanded by a series of almost epic collections, edited by John Brewer and others, elaborating on the extent and breadth of eighteenth-century consumerism, which resulted from and was associated with Britain's rapidly increasing role in world trade.[4] Indeed, we could treat Britain's experience through the course of the century as marked by a series of stages in the expansion of her mercantile reach and power. For political theorists, the accompanying changes in people's status and the way they could proclaim it seemed to herald potentially destructive changes in traditional modes of social deference and obligation. They became the explicit occasion for heated debates about how the subject was to imagine and execute his or her role in the polity, since these changes called into question the stability of individual personality, and consequently, conventional ways of picturing its obligations to others. Already quite early in the eighteenth century – especially after the establishment of the national debt and the new economic order it denoted – Britons were exercised by the problem of how the possession of money and goods might erode people's sense of moral connectedness.

Second, historians and critics alike have developed an interest in the public sphere. This idea serves as a means to typify distinctively eighteenth-century modes of rationality and sociability, which, on this view, encouraged certain literate styles of speech and self-representation. As we will see, for Jürgen Habermas, its main modern exponent, this notion is also associated with new ideals of civic conduct, and with the kinds of *bürgerlich* clubbishness and conversational codes promulgated by the coffee houses, first established in London in the late 1650s, and rendered into a systematic social protocol by such journals as Addison's *The Spectator*, first published in 1711.

Finally, I link these discussions to the interest in sentimentalism, about which there is currently some vigorous disagreement. I argue that the conventional habits of thinking about the later eighteenth century, which associate that period with the ideals of sentiment and the rhetoric of sensibility, are in fact well founded. But by contrast to a slightly circular tradition of defining the period by an appeal to sensibility and vice versa, I also want to propose that sentiment and the gothic, as literary styles, describe novelistic attempts to mediate a series of political and ethical pressures that characterize political – as well as literary – history after 1746.

The expansion of novelistic authorship

I have mentioned both a growth in the numbers of novelists writing in the later eighteenth century, and a corresponding proliferation of critical approaches to the material. These facts are registered in the wide range of approaches informing the following essays, and the large number of different, and in some cases fairly minor, novelists they discuss. It would hardly be an exaggeration to say that the period after 1750 witnesses an explosion in the number and kinds of authors that turn their hand to writing novels, and this is especially true after about 1780 or so, a point I also elaborate below.[5] Significantly, the numbers have received the closest scholarly attention in the case of women authors. Where in the early period we are talking about a handful of novelists of any kind, including women such as Aphra Behn, Delarivière Manley, and Eliza Haywood, the later eighteenth century experiences a notorious rise in the sheer number of women authors, a rise that sometimes led to the (misleading) view that women now dominated novelistic production. Cheryl Turner's *Living by the Pen: Women Writers in the Eighteenth Century* (1992) shows that there was a brief rise then decline in women's writing between 1725 and 1740, a gradual and continuous rise thereafter, and finally a spectacular rise in the last quarter of the eighteenth century.[6] (We must however avoid the assumption that the novel was the most popular reading form by the end of the century. In fact, sermons remained the single most popular genre.) This rise certainly contributed to the prejudice against the novel as a form which, being so easily consumable, relaxed the reader's vigilance and enervated his or her (usually her) morals.

This expansion in production produces its own interpretative problems. Many critics believe that the increasing success of women novelists produced a paradox. Mary Poovey for one has pointed out that, as writing achieved greater respectability, it also became a more concentrated source of social anxiety for women, since to publish was improperly, even imprudently, to enter the public forum, the domain of masculine prerogative.[7] Moreover, in response to the dangers stemming from such public exposure, women novelists after mid century strove to distance themselves from what they saw as the indecorous interests and themes in earlier writers such as Behn and Haywood, whom we now value precisely because they explore female desire. William Warner partly ascribes this shift to the moralizing atmosphere surrounding Richardson and his circle, in which what was approved if not invented was an ideal of female virtue, so that the culture associated with novel-writing and novel-reading became, with the success of *Pamela* (1740) and *Clarissa* (1747–48), explicitly dedicated to the preservation of piety and morality.[8]

These features of the literary landscape create particular challenges for a certain tradition of Anglo-American feminism. I would stress that they exemplify the larger problems of how we are to approach later eighteenth-century novelists in general. The desire of later eighteenth-century writers to avoid the moral taint of a supposedly more licentious age makes it impossible to argue – as Elaine Showalter famously does for the Victorians – that eighteenth-century women created a seamless literature of their own.[9] It is only by limiting the time-line – typically to the last decade of the century – that a coherent genealogy of this kind can emerge. Thus Mary Poovey's *The Proper Lady and the Woman Writer* (1984) discusses Mary Wollstonecraft, Mary Shelley, and Jane Austen; while Claudia Johnson's *Equivocal Beings: Politics, Gender, and Sentimentality in the 1790s* (1995) discusses Wollstonecraft, Ann Radcliffe, Frances Burney, and Austen.[10] In the wake of the French Revolution, with its promise of a more egalitarian dawn, the 1790s undoubtedly intensified the debate about whether and how women could claim a share in the body politic. And it is therefore possible to see something of an unusual concentration of interests among certain types of writers animated by the political climate. Consequently, we are faced with the odd situation that – apart from Sterne criticism – the most canonical traditions of interpretation to have developed in recent years surround the writers of the 1790s, both because almost all the most powerful writers are women, and because the fate of contemporary critical politics is perceived to hinge on how we interpret their views of the French Revolution and new forms of eighteenth-century feminism. Our concluding pair of essays on Austen is animated by precisely such concerns.

Pocock and Habermas

Many books about later eighteenth-century literature – indeed about the period as a whole – engage with two very influential general models for reading eighteenth-century intellectual and cultural history. J. G. A. Pocock's *The Machiavellian Moment: Florentine Political Thought and the Atlantic Republican Tradition* (1975) and *Virtue, Commerce and History: Essays on Political Thought and History, Chiefly in the Eighteenth Century* (1985) represent the most schematic and influential accounts of traditional ideas of individual virtue, and the challenges to that ethic represented by Britain's success as a commercial society.[11] Jürgen Habermas's *The Structural Transformation of the Public Sphere: An Inquiry into a Category of Bourgeois Society* (1962; trans. 1989) is by now the established starting point for discussions of eighteenth-century sociability and rational debate, and their productive relationship to a new urban phenomenology, especially the world of the coffee houses.[12] Although they have very different interests, both writers believe that the debates they describe make the eighteenth century distinctive. In some ways they both assume that these discussions become increasingly marked aspects of life as the century progresses. For the purposes of this introduction, I would argue that this is indeed the case. Pocock describes an attitude that has an ancient genealogy, and coffee houses as an institution predate even the Restoration. But the codes that each writer lays out become increasingly assumed frames of reference – both for contemporary Britons and for modern critics – especially when, as I argue below, national anxieties after about 1750 turn from constitutional and dynastic to more ethical and micropolitical issues. Sustaining one's virtue in the face of larger and more impersonal social forces, or cultivating proper modes of social deportment and conversation (both central criteria of value for Austen), can be said to belong to the culture of sentiment in general, even if they anticipate it, and even if they do not define it.

Pocock's view of virtue and commerce and Habermas's notion of the public sphere also affect how we are presently to perceive the genealogy and health of the Anglo-American liberal tradition, and the extent to which it can contribute meaningfully or effectively to political arrangements at the end of the twentieth century. In this connection, the debate is partly about usable history, one already richly at play in the eighteenth century itself. In some ways, all parties assume that modern capitalism and modern varieties of liberalism derive from the period of the long eighteenth century, with much of the stress lying on interpretations of the Glorious Revolution in 1688. But the questions that remain include the extent to which constitutional liberalism depends on or is inevitably engrafted into a defence of *homo economicus* – the possessive individual described almost mythically by C. B. Macpherson's *The Political Theory of Possessive Individualism: Hobbes to Locke* (1962).[13] On textual and historical grounds, Macpherson's reading of Hobbes and Locke has largely been disproved. But Macpherson's model has nevertheless enjoyed a remarkable afterlife, both because the phrase 'possessive individualism' rolls so easily off the tongue, and because his Marxist critique of liberalism encapsulates an ongoing discomfort about liberalism in general. Put simply, his thesis argues that the liberal defence of political rights is enmeshed in a defence of acquisitive market practices: individual political rights depend on the individual owning property. The stakes are all the higher for the later eighteenth century, since classical economics is the child of the Scottish enlightenment. Adam Smith's *The Wealth of Nations*, published the year of the American Revolution, can seem to argue that the market produces its own self-regulating economy, and that it is a good in itself, not fully accountable to traditional debates in ethics and politics.[14] Was Smith celebrating a kind of amorality of the marketplace that before the fact justified the worst excesses of *laissez-faire* economics? (This fear received contemporary encouragement from Mandeville's sardonic celebration of acquisitive instincts in *The Fable of the Bees* [1714–29] under the rubric *'Private Vices, Publick Benefits.'*) Or can the force of the marketplace remain indebted to a broader definition of political economy, which might explain Hume's receptiveness to the civilizing force of the forum – in all its senses – and Smith's own career and status as a moral philosopher? For Hume and Smith, one could argue, 'commerce' retained the broad ethical register it has in Locke's *Essay concerning Human Understanding* (1690), where it mediates among several senses, the primary ones describing the way the mind negotiates with the world, and the way individuals consort in society.

For a number of reasons, the novel is very much implicated in these various cross-currents. Whatever its precise genealogies, it is usually seen as the most distinctive literary product of the eighteenth century, most responsive, since Defoe, to the psychology of market relations, and most focussed on the extent to which market relations mediate social bonds.[15] It is also the clearest symptom of the extent to which (after Dryden) literature in general owes its existence to a literary marketplace, not least in its connections to journalism. And finally, it is increasingly produced by women authors, and increasingly stresses affective relations as the century wears on. It therefore raises vexing questions about the relationship between the market and gender ideology. Is it proper for women to expose themselves to the potentially brutalizing conditions of the market, in which they risk becoming more visibly commodities than the marriage market already makes them? Or is it possible that their presence in this forum, like their presence in the new consumer environment, might have a softening and civilizing effect on society at large? That is, what are the precise connections between expanding consumerism and new forms of sociability, symbolized for many in coffee-house culture, coffee itself epitomizing the connection between exotic imports and new modes of social comportment? Or, alternatively, if women are part of a rapidly expanding consumer culture, could their presence on the scene confirm the fact that luxury has effeminated the polity, a fear that has a strong classical pedigree?[16]

These concerns took time to intensify or become coherent. In a loose sense, they belong to the entire century, so that it is important to understand how they developed before 1750. The period after the Glorious Revolution was affected by what P. G. M. Dickson calls 'the financial revolution in England.' After 1688, a national debt was incurred as a result of King William's wars on the continent, the Bank of England was founded (1694), and the government also relied increasingly on systems of credit made possible through the East India and the South Sea Companies.[17] The development of public credit produced a storm of argument about whether it put the nation on a more or less secure footing.[18] The uncertainties about what this system might entail for the nation and for the lives of ordinary English men and women seemed disastrously confirmed with the crash of stocks held in the South Sea Company in 1720, known as the South Sea Bubble.

The psychic consequences of this crash were profound, and remained of almost obsessive concern to Pope and Swift, as well as providing an occasion for one of Defoe's strongest novels, *A Journal of the Plague Year* (1722). The circumstances by which the nation was seen to be rescued propelled Robert Walpole into a position of power that he occupied until 1742. An apocryphal but indicative belief was that Walpole's maneuverings in the wake of the Bubble earned him a fortune. The story gained credit because Walpole subsequently so used the Whig party machine with a determination, ruthlessness, and effectiveness as to ensure his control of parliamentary processes for over twenty years. The 'Robinocracy,' as it is called, was the occasion of some of the greatest imaginative literature of the century. In *Gulliver's Travels* and *The Dunciad* respectively, Swift celebrates the career of Henry St. John, Viscount Bolingbroke, during the reign of Anne as a contrast to the supposed corruption and pettiness of the Walpole regime, and Pope prophesies the collapse of civilization as such. Part of the *Dunciad*'s attack is on the tyranny not only of fashion, but of the commodification of culture in general, with which Pope explicitly associates the novel.

Further, in Pocock's account at least, Bolingbroke's opposition politics in *The Craftsman* and *The Idea of the Patriot King* revived the classical republican opposition to corruption, to empire, to luxury in favor of a pure ideal of civic virtue. The value of real property was opposed to mobile property, especially credit, as much funny money then as it is today, and more terrifying because so new, and so morally and epistemologically volatile. This line of thinking Pocock denominates 'neo-Harringtonianism.' It valued property only insofar as it endowed the individual with an integrity flowing from his self-possession.[19] Though the possessor of property, the self-possessed individual is to be radically distinguished from Macpherson's possessive individual, because in owning land especially, he could resist the blandishments of corrupt politicians, and preserve the athletic ideal of the classical-republican farmer-soldier.

Several features of the second half of the eighteenth century intensified and ramified the debate about the relationship between commerce and ethics.[20] First, already by the end of the seventeenth century London was the largest city in Europe, ten times larger than any other town in Britain, and incorporating a far higher percentage of the nation's total population than, for example, Paris. This itself raised the question of how urban life could be or remain urbane in the most cultivated sense. Second, by the middle of the century, we can detect elements of what has come to be called, retrospectively, the industrial revolution, though modern historians are quick to point out that this did not necessarily entail the elements of advanced industrial capitalism. And finally, if Neil McKendrick is right, the last quarter witnessed 'the birth of a consumer society.' McKendrick goes to some lengths to defend the choice of the term 'birth,' because although presumably there have always been consumers, the scale of the change during the reign of George III (1760–1820) was such that it qualitatively eclipsed all analogous forms of behavior in Europe.[21] If these were distinct, and distinctly British, dimensions of experience especially after mid century, the question was, of course, how they were alternatively to be defended or criticized. There is also a good case to be made that the Scottish determination to be included in the polity from the 1740s on explains Hume's and Smith's embrace of the relationship between a more heavily inflected consumer culture and the celebration of politeness, manners, and conversation. These could be read as modes of intercourse which had sublimated the recourse to violence associated with the seventeenth century and the Stuart clan, not to mention Scottish tribalism.[22] Thus by the 1760s, sentimental transactions in *A Sentimental Journey* are rhetorically confused with a traffic in objects such as snuff boxes or coins, whereby genuineness of feeling seems secured by a king of commodity exchange. It is easy to see Austen as belonging to this line, since what remains unquestioned in her novels is the institution of conversation as the guarantee of civility in general, and a regard for the political vulnerability of women in particular.

Both Pocock and Habermas present useful introductions to different aspects of these concerns, as well as elements of the languages in which they were couched. Nevertheless, I think it is fair to say that, in their very different ways, their interpretations are elitist in implication, and accordingly limited as accounts of the eighteenth century. On the one hand, Pocock preserves the discourse of classical republicanism from all other forms of eighteenth-century dissent. This has several payoffs. First, it attaches the eighteenth century firmly to the classical and humanist tradition described in *The Machiavellian Moment*, and gratifies the modern historian by allowing him or her to arbitrate classical forms of knowledge. Second, it secures a language of dissent already purged of the insidious materialism of eighteenth-century celebrations of consumerism, commerce, and sociability. Third, it does double historiographical duty because it steers clear of Macpherson's version of liberalism (combining political rights for the individual with the individual's rights to property),[23] while also abjuring its Marxist alternatives. Pocock consistently opposes the myth of the Roman republic to that of the early empire. The former assumes an agrarian base, in which the ideal self-possessed actor serves the polity because his freedom permits the cultivation of *virtu*, the expression of which realizes his true nature as a political being.[24] By contrast, the latter is oligarchic, jurisprudential in tenor, conceiving the individual as an actor endowed with rights based on law, and whose relations with others and the state are mediated through the acquisition of things.[25] And finally, to treat the complex of commercial and political languages as perennially opposed by 'the unspecialized agrarian ideal of the patriot' is a means of interpreting the American Revolution as the last and perhaps most conclusive expression of classical republican rejections of parliamentary corruption and placemen.[26]

On the other hand, Habermas's argument goes in very different directions. It is at root a celebration of the peculiar texture of English (or British) eighteenth-century liberalism and an elegy for its difficulties or even its betrayal by advanced capitalism from the late nineteenth century on.[27] The structural transformation to which his title refers has little to recommend it – it is an attack on twentieth-century continental statism and the dictatorship of advertising culture over the independent life of the mind – and he is frank in calling for a revival of the forms of critical rationality he associates with the public sphere.[28] Habermas's book was written immediately in the wake of the Second World War. It is easy to see that he refers at once to the forms of state intervention characterizing German political culture after Bismarck and to fears that the new Germany (reconstructed under the Marshall Plan) and the new world order will perpetuate the way that statist public policy subverts vigorous, public, and rational debate.

Whereas Pocock's view of political languages is strictly oppositional – the republican language only running *in parallel* with the alternatives, to use his image – Habermas's view is more genuinely dialectical, since he embraces the association between commercial and liberal culture in the eighteenth century. Because the middling classes (Habermas uses the German term *bürgerlich*, tendentiously translated as 'bourgeois') were property owners on a roughly equal footing, the conditions of their engagements, domestic, social, and conversational, assumed the virtual parity of all involved.[29] Just as the laws of commerce operated irrespective of personal interests, the forms of rationality developed by the commercial or property-owning classes gathered in social spaces (the public sphere) permitted a kind of disinterestedness that always operated in critical relation to power itself.[30] Yet because the business of state depended on the assent of those very classes (in part because the trade economy arose with state encouragement[31]), the conduct of the polity could never proceed without being first subjected to full critical scrutiny.[32] That is, the governing rule of debate supposed the contractual equivalences required in the exchange of goods in the marketplace, and restaged in the exchange of news, such that – in opposition to Pocock – it is essential to Habermas's model that the debaters participate in the emerging world of eighteenth-century commerce.[33] In a peculiar way, indeed, Habermas celebrates the extent to which being commercial agents allowed individuals something like the self-possession Pocock reserves exclusively for agrarian republicanism.[34] A great deal rests on this equivalence. According to Habermas's model, it permitted groups of individuals to remain unbeholden to (or 'emancipated from'[35]) the state, since their legitimacy had been independently earned, and was sustained by the numerous protocols of sociability mentioned above.

Further, and centrally, these individuals were literate. Their literacy remained the gymnasium within which the protocols of rational debate were developed and refined – the medium of knowledge was the theater, the museum, the concert hall, and most importantly the newspaper and the novel, which re-enacted the world that the newspaper assumed and described.[36] Habermas consistently opposes the value of horizontal relationships to the coercion associated with hierarchical relationships – imposed earlier by feudal and court culture, and later by the industrial state. Although, as in Walter Benjamin, art has lost its aura, it becomes the vehicle through which critical reasoning and debate is realized: Habermas takes the commodification of art as the condition of its answerability to a new public forensic. It must submit to the forum of public opinion which habitually tested its claims by rational debate; and for this process to occur, knowledge of all forms depends on a new kind of 'publicity.'[37] Moreover, the kinds of literate gatherings epitomized in the coffee houses model a special kind of critical-rational debate which mediates between the intimacies of family life and the purely public purposes of the state, allowing individuals to emerge from the intimate space of the bedroom to the semi-intimate spaces of the salon and the coffee house, both of which remained at an architectural and ideological remove from state power.[38]

And, of course, of all the literary forms it is the novel which is most obviously produced by the culture Habermas describes and which most clearly remains a primer for the kinds of sociability that guarantees ongoing membership in it: 'the psychological novel fashioned for the first time the kind of realism that allowed anyone to enter into the literary action as a substitute for his own, to use the relationships between the figures, between the author, the characters, and the reader as substitute relationships for reality.'[39]

Habermas expresses a profound appreciation for the fragility of the social, political, and literate economy he associates with a brief moment in European (mainly British) history. For, according to his account, by 1873, a different configuration of interests, of state power, and of capitalist relations conspired to destroy the independence and integrity of the public sphere. The emergence of proletarian consciousness created a demand that the state itself intervene to regulate interests in the polity; and state planning and control increasingly rendered impotent the space mediating between the state and family intimacy (the classical public sphere). State policies were no longer subject to scrutiny via vigorous public debate. The state became the sole instrument forging and executing such policies. What remained of the intimate sphere became privatized and excluded from political discussion.[40] Policy became a matter of party-political interests promulgated by and on behalf of apparatchiks Simultaneously, the public became a mere passive consumer of culture, not the forum in which culture was debated; and the mass media increasingly responded to the demands of advertising.[41] What often looks like debate in this regime is in fact only the display of debate for mass consumption, such that even intellectuals have in effect become institutionalized into a bureaucratic elite: publicity now belongs not to a critical but to a manipulative atmosphere. In short, *epideixis*, or a purely celebratory rhetoric, subverts the primacy of deliberation in liberal argumentation.

Habermas and Pocock are obviously constructing allegories of the eighteenth century for their own more immediate purposes, although Habermas is more direct about his motives than Pocock. The differences between them are, however, significant. First, they reveal how highly charged this phase in Western debates about commerce, about money, and about acquisition is, since both Habermas and Pocock see that the response of the eighteenth century to these issues carries with it profound ethical and political implications for us. Habermas is particularly relevant to this volume because he sees the novel as an essential medium within which the debate was pursued. Pocock is almost exclusively interested in political theory, and this might paradoxically confirm Habermas's point. For Pocock's general evasion of the literate dimensions and conditions of the debate seems to accompany his apparent disdain of all things associated with commerce, with law, and with empire: for all his methodological pronouncements about language, his actual analysis seems largely unembarrassed by the complexities of literary mediation. For Habermas, by contrast, the mediations of the literary are precisely one of the guarantors of critical rationality in political discussion.

Like many others, both thinkers share a general discomfort with modernity. But in their different ways, Habermas and Pocock want to rescue the possibility of rational and critical inquiry from the general malaise. Pocock's answer is essentially thematic, implicitly prescribing a return to a classical republican past. Habermas's is more genuinely methodical, finding in the activity of a certain kind of sociability and the culture which sustained it an alternative to the soullessness and conformity of late-twentieth-century state planning.

These two models can be usefully compared with Michel Foucault's reading of the eighteenth century in many of his works, but most influentially at present in *Discipline and Punish*, which I also mention in my first introduction.[42] Foucault treats the development of the eighteenth century as a movement towards Jeremy Bentham's designs for prisons which empower the authorities to observe and regulate the prisoners' every motion. This image of incarceration serves as an allegory of the regulated nature of modern state power, because on this account eighteenth-century rationality renders transparent the relation between the state and its subjects. But Foucault's view is finally disturbingly nihilistic. Since he argues that modern 'disciplinary regimes' (as he calls them) saturate society as a whole, including the individuals within it, Foucault seems to deny what Pocock and Habermas want to preserve, namely the efficacy of rational debate or languages permitting dissent from hegemonic forms of power. In Foucault's account, we are trapped in endless prisons of our own making.

Whatever their differences, all three thinkers seem to miss something about the kind of pleasure that supplies an ongoing topic of discussion in the later eighteenth-century novel. Although the final givens of society are not ultimately questioned or exploded, the hero's or heroine's capacity to read comprises a unique pleasure and supposes two crucial facts about the world. As Hume and Burke point out, we are largely constituted by the institutions around us, whether imagined as novels, the family, society, or conversation. And we can and should read them interpretatively. As the experience of Catherine Morland, heroine of *Northanger Abbey*, shows, the process of reading does not open a window onto some scene of unhindered rational discussion, since Catherine's interlocutors are all influenced by their relations to the various institutions that make conversation possible; but, no more than for Emily in Radcliffe's *The Mysteries of Udolpho*, Catherine's reading does not merely reinscribe woman's oppression. To learn to read aptly – however painfully, and there is pain involved – gives both Emily and Catherine the ability to understand what they see, to name it. And understanding, however contingent, is a kind of power.

Sentimentalism and the gothic

In this section, I will argue that sentimentality, sensibility, and the gothic are legitimate means to approach the distinctive literary concerns and methods of the later eighteenth-century novel. This is a well-established view of how to divide eighteenth-century literary history. Nevertheless, I believe that there are specific political and cultural reasons why sentimentalism is a useful way to think about the novel's relation to the wider world after the middle of the century: this is the point of the opening essays by G. A. Starr and Margaret Doody, who implicitly disagree with Leo Braudy's notion that the history of sentimentalism runs parallel to the history of the English novel as such.[43] I stress the specificity of the idea because the recent appearance of G. J. Barker-Benfield's *The Culture of Sensibility: Sex and Society in Eighteenth-Century Britain* (1992), which is large and comprehensive, reveals the importance of the term 'sensibility' both to literary critics and to historians.[44] Barker-Benfield in effect argues that sensibility is the prime means to understand the development of British culture from at least the late seventeenth century on. According to him, sensibility flows from and amplifies a number of different features that are of central interest to critics of the novel, not to mention political and cultural historians such as Habermas, Pocock, McKendrick, or Brewer. These include changes in theories about how humans apprehend the physical and social world; changes in ideas about how men and women are different, and, in significant ways, alike; changes in the extent of consumer culture; and a corresponding change in how humans interpret their relations to objects, especially as objects mediate relations between persons. (Or, as Carol Kay puts it below, changes in how the arts of politeness are shaped.)

One of the central subjects of debate is the question of how the individual recognizes and fosters social instincts in himself or herself; whether women model more appropriate social instincts than men, unless men become softened in their dealings with the world; and whether, because people are allowed to channel their competitive and potentially destructive energies into the marketplace, commodities also play a correspondingly socializing role.[45] But the student must approach this book with some caution. For the weakness of Barker-Benfield's description is that it does treat virtually every major aspect of British life and thought from the middle of the seventeenth century until the end of the eighteenth as equivalent. Barker-Benfield's purpose may be to unearth the genealogy of sensibility. But it does not serve to analyze change in the course of the eighteenth century, and so does not help to sensitize the reader to how literature in the Restoration or early eighteenth century may respond to social and political realities somewhat differently from the literature that succeeded it.[46]

By contrast, R. F. Brissenden's *Virtue in Distress: Studies in the Novel of Sentiment from Richardson to Sade* (1974) and John Mullan's *Sentiment and Sociability: The Language of Feeling in the Eighteenth Century* (1988) both emphasize how sentiment occurs as a general cultural shift, one (according to Mullan especially) clearly remarked in Hume's ethics.[47] It is important to recognize that this shift does not occur as a purely 'literary' or 'novelistic' phenomenon. To restrict the question to literary history would be to endorse the pre-romantic reading of the period, which has tended to treat the literature after mid century as somehow less political and more purely aesthetic and affective in its motives than Dryden, Pope, or Swift. Rather – much like Carol Kay's *Political Constructions: Defoe, Richardson, and Sterne in Relation to Hobbes, Hume, and Burke* (1988) – I would argue that the literature of sensibility and the gothic represent new ways of debating what remain unequivocally political questions.[48] It is just that the economy of the issues and the angles from which individuals approach it have changed.[49]

We should consider several features of the scene. All the literature we are describing in this volume was published after the collapse of the 1745 rebellion. Historians generally agree that this comprised a political and ideological watershed, since the bloody defeat of the Jacobite cause finally destroyed lingering doubts about the legitimacy of the Hanoverian regime. As J. C. D. Clark puts it, most political questions before this date were inflected with deeply constitutional, what he calls 'dynastic,' anxieties.[50] These insecurities we could date at least to 1649 (the execution of Charles I), or even 1603 (the accession of James I), and they emerge regularly thereafter: 1660 (the Restoration), 1679 (the Exclusion Crisis), 1685 (the accession of James II), 1688 (the Glorious Revolution), and 1714–15 (the accession of George I and the 1715 rebellion). Thus, Restoration and early-eighteenth-century literature between the beginning of Dryden's career and the deaths of Pope and Swift is often clearly occasional, responding to some distinct macropolitical, constitutional, or dynastic crisis, whether real or perceived. Even with a figure like Defoe, the issues are often contractarian or vaguely Hobbesian at root, where the question concerns how individuals – imagined as uniformly motivated political and psychic agents – participate in the construction of a viable polity. It is as if apparent social insecurities stand in for a much more troubling obsession with whether the institutions that can guarantee political continuity are settled or might any moment collapse. Thus for Dryden or Pope, bad writing, which we could interpret as a local ethical or mere technical flaw, almost always seems to threaten the state and civilization as such.

It seems that a change in literary culture does take place after 1746. This is not a purely organic change, generated from within literary tradition, though convention takes the deaths of Pope (1744) and Swift (1745), and subsequently Fielding (1754) and Richardson (1761), to mark an internal transformation of the literary system. Rather, the defeat of the '45, in finally exorcizing a series of powerful ghosts (though how powerful is a matter of some debate), had a number of important consequences for the nature and style of ethical deliberation thereafter.[51] Whereas earlier the body politic had been defined by the problem of its very survival and continuity, the stakes were hitherto less dire. (Folkenflik's essay in Chapter 5 below also suggests that this may partly be owing to the Act of Union, which united England and Wales with Scotland in 1707.) New energies shifted to a related but different question. Given that we now largely agree that political institutions are secure, what kinds of individuals and what kinds of ethos are most proper for the society we actually inhabit?

Here the difference between Hobbes's and Locke's scepticism (on the one hand), and Hume's scepticism (on the other) is instructive. The former employ the virtues and court the dangers of appealing to a state of nature, however much that idea operates as a purely heuristic device: for both, the state of nature represents some epistemological or moral ground zero from which their arguments can start. The latter, by contrast, systematically doubts that we might ever have a view of such a state. The proper role of philosophy, so epistemologically circumscribed, is to turn its attention to what *can* be known: human nature, with all its particularities, fluctuations, eccentricities, and variations in taste. Hume consequently makes the ethical project more difficult for himself. The philosopher must now try to determine under what sets of circumstances individuals – who tend to become isolated in a world of their own ideas and associations – might meaningfully participate in society as such.[52] He cannot, like Hobbes or Locke, treat the individual as a political and cognitive given: Hobbes can think indiscriminately of all individuals as political atoms driven by fear and desire; Locke, of all individuals as made by God, and constituted universally by sensation and reflection.

As Mullan demonstrates, the equivocations within the Humean project are intense. The focus on the moral and physiological constitution of the individual invokes the very real possibility that he or she is only that – trapped within the flux of sensations and habits that divide him or her from others.[53] The implication is that the period after 1746 intensifies a kind of phenomenological paradox. Whereas the larger political structures appear less threatened than before, the individual feels increasingly alone, and increasingly anxious about which of his or her sensations might secure contact with another person. (The dilemma of solitude is the motif of John Sitter's *Literary Loneliness in Mid-Eighteenth-Century England* [1982].)[54] The extent to which this is a general paradox emerges further if we accept the view that some time before 1746, British politics had been transformed from a series of violent altercations between Whigs and Tories into an altogether less heated debate between Court and Country sensibilities, where the elite as a whole generally rested secure in its claims to power.[55] It is as if, now that the grand issues of state have been settled, a more finely tuned discussion about the individual's apprehension of the wider world comes to the fore.

Broadly speaking, we could say that earlier political and ethical arguments are contractarian or constitutionalist in tenor, whereas after mid century the interest shifts to how society rests more indistinctly on trust, habit, and custom.[56] The former view demands constant debate about the epistemic and social grounds of knowledge and behavior; the latter view pays greater attention to the world as we find it, and the customs and institutions that facilitate civil conduct (though this doesn't of course obviate epistemological inquiry). It is of course in this context that the questions foregrounded by Pocock and Habermas achieve a particular relevance, focus, and clarity, since they bear so directly on the issue of how individual forms of behavior serve a specific vision of social and ethical relations. Further, in their general books about the course of eighteenth-century history, both J. C. D. Clark and Linda Colley emphasize a similar tension in the texture of politics after the accession of George III in 1760.[57] The new king benefited from a new cult of the stability of the monarchy, matched by the increasing homogeneity of the ruling elite. But this was also a time when the party-political arrangements that characterized the middle of the century were eroding.[58] In the poetry of mid century and after, two words begin to garner a special cultural resonance: 'anxious' and 'conscious.' Both terms seem to respond to a shift from contractarian to affective ways of thinking about social bonding, since they both depict the sensations of the mind thrown back uncomfortably on itself. Similarly, though there are complicated exceptions such as *Clarissa*, earlier novels tend to move towards the making (or unmaking) of society; later novels tend to show individuals trying to negotiate social relations, whose necessity remains unquestioned.

The equivocations built into sensibility, and later the gothic, also stem from another source. That is, writers themselves hail from increasingly dispersed regional and class origins, whose connection to London, the literary center, was by no means automatic. I have mentioned the rise in the numbers of women writers. But the 1740s on witness the rapid development of Scottish intellectual culture. Hume is accompanied and followed by a whole slew of writers who profoundly influence the ethical debates that occur in the novel: Adam Smith, Hugh Blair, Adam Ferguson, Alexander Gerard, Francis Hutcheson, Henry Home (Lord Kames), James Burnett (Lord Monboddo), and Thomas Reid.[59] With some exceptions, the conventional canon of later eighteenth-century literature makes a similar point: apart from Smollett and Sterne, most of the major novelists are women; the first acknowledged gothic novelist was a homosexual; like Boswell after him Smollett was a Scot; and Sterne was from Yorkshire, almost like Smollett a North Briton. Like Sheridan, Burke was an Irishman; Gibbon preferred a life on the continent. The communities from which all these individuals derive, or their personal inclinations, stand in some complex and potentially dissenting relation to the centers of cultural and political power, perhaps epitomized in the most charged way by Horace Walpole. It should not entirely surprise us that the energy, excitement, and formal experimentation we associate with early-eighteenth-century political satire becomes redirected into a no less political though sentimental depiction of the individual's relation to himself or herself and to others.

To speak of the 'gothic' as a subset of the sentimental is to recognize that later eighteenth-century literary history responds to a series of stages in political history after 1750, each of which intensifies the ethical concerns at the heart of the sentimental enterprise. Brissenden recurs immediately to the French Revolution as one such stage in the intensification of political sensibilities. He is correct inasmuch, for example, as Burke's organicism is indebted to Hume's and Smith's emphasis on the necessarily social conditions of human life. But that is to overlook the tremendous political changes that occurred between the '45 and 1789. The accession of George III coincided with a newly fractious parliamentary culture, such that the hegemony of political elites that marked the reign of the earlier Hanoverians was not as unquestioned. And the period between 1760 and the French Revolution experiences a rise in a number of radicalisms, the most politically visible being John Wilkes's manipulation of crowds for political ends.[60]

The 1760s also marked the end of the Seven Years War, which had at first caused tremendous anxiety, and then, after 1759, left Britain in control of most of North America and India. Linda Colley argues that this war was one of a series of engagements in which 'British' identity was increasingly forged in opposition to French power, the first such major engagement and series of successes being of course earlier in the century, with the Duke of Marlborough's victories during the War of the Spanish Succession. Colley writes too that the forging of British identity in opposition to France, which culminated at Waterloo, also helped draw previously marginalized groups into the experience of the nation as a whole. Her most powerful example is the Scots, who rapidly came to play a very significant role in Britain, especially in the wake of the '45. At the accession of George III, the king's favorite minister was a Scot, Lord Bute; and the emergence of Scottish genius was partly responsible for Wilkes's violent attacks on Scottish interests in *The North Briton*. The symbolic tension between Bute and Wilkes is re-enacted in the ambiguous nature of sentimental rhetoric, where anxiety about isolation vacillates with a tremendous urge for social coherence. That ambivalence is repeated, if we are to believe Colley, in the wake of the Seven Years War, for the British had no conception of what winning the war against the French might entail.[61] Finding themselves suddenly in possession of vast tracts of the globe intensified British anxieties about the world around them. And it may be partly that anxiety which fuelled the hagiography around the death of General Wolfe.[62] Colley writes:

> it is not too much to say that from this point on until the American Revolution and beyond, the British were in the grip of a collective agoraphobia, captivated by, but also adrift and at odds in a vast empire abroad and a new political world at home which few of them properly understood.[63]

And of course the events leading up to the American Declaration of Independence and the eventual defeat of British forces in 1782 involved all the trauma of what was effectively a civil war of sorts, as well as the first unqualified defeat in the series of wars initiated by William III. The American Revolution inevitably stimulated radical discussion about the nature of the British constitution and the need for different forms of representation, since that issue was expressly at the heart of the colonists' gripes against central control. But without downplaying the trauma and the internal divisions that the crisis engendered, I suspect Colley is right to emphasize that the nation recovered with a new sense of coherence rapidly thereafter. The anti-Scots sentiment that Wilkes had been able to exploit now evaporated, since Britons – including very much the Scots – could map themselves against the lost American colonies and their French allies, an opposition which was dramatically rehearsed with the onset of the French Revolution only seven years later.[64]

As we know, the Revolution encouraged the revival and refashioning of various forms of radicalism, which found expression for example in the Jacobin novel. Modern liberal and radical sentiment is often keen to respect the highest motives of the Revolution, whatever became of it by early 1792 or so. So it is tempting to assume that such sentiments went deeper than they actually did. Arguments about the meaning of the Revolution are largely what fuel the critical interest in the novels of the 1790s; and the implication is that good literary politics tend to favor Revolutionary answers to social problems. However, H. T. Dickinson argues that, although at its best the nature of radical argument was intellectually profound and in the long run effective on utilitarian grounds, for the British the radical appeal was in fact fairly limited. It was faced by a hostile government; it had little popular support; and, one might add, it was the occasion for the pre-eminence of the most powerful political thinker of the age, namely Burke. Dickinson points out too that for all their dissatisfaction, the radicals would never have suggested a violent revolution on the French model, which again encourages the impression that the fundamental continuities of British life remained unquestioned.[65] What does seem to have happened between the American Revolution and the Napoleonic Wars is that the terms by which society functioned came ever more severely under scrutiny. Geoffrey Holmes and Daniel Szechi argue that once Wilkes had raised the specter of reform, it became a staple of politics, though not, until the early nineteenth century, a central one. For this very reason, one could see the gothic as an intensified means of exploring the tensions embedded in the sentimental tradition. The gothic characteristically affirms the patriarchy, but on the way thrusts its characters into physical and psychological extremes in which the patriarchy appears purely oppressive or enfeebled. In *The Mysteries of Udolpho* and *Northanger Abbey*, the re-established patriarchy is associated in any case with second sons (Valancourt; Henry Tilney) rather than fathers or their direct heirs.

The novel and the body

Finally, the distinctions I have been sketching have potentially important consequences for the current critical interest in the body. As with Barker-Benfield's approach to sensibility, much of this criticism proceeds as if the analytical category of the body were epistemologically stable and historically uniform. Appeals to the body as an idea often assume that we already know what the body denotes. It is as if, on the one hand, ordinary language represents potentially uncontrollable semantic or rhetorical slippages, or the conceptual logic associated in some cases with a patriarchal system of value. The body, on the other, serves to anchor knowledge in material reality, a particularized, three-dimensional world serving as a permanent rebuke to linguistic universals. By extension, it can represent a world of feminized and sensate coherence set against the alienated consciousness of masculine abstraction.

Of course, more anthropologically aware approaches assume more or less the reverse: the meanings supplied by somatic behavior can be as culturally specific as any other symbolic order. Along these lines, Mullan and Ann Jessie Van Sant show how one crucial aspect of the cult of sensibility derives its force from the language of eighteenth-century physiology. This discipline attempts to determine how the human body responds to and calibrates the miriad of sensations that bombard it from moment to moment – a calculus that governs the rhetoric of *A Sentimental Journey*.[66] In this context, the body is and means something different from what it means in Hobbes and Locke, or in Defoe, Dryden, Pope, or Swift. In the earlier authors, the body serves as the physical corollary to the political atom, the physical given which the individual actor is and inhabits. There is little to differentiate one body from the next. In Hobbes's political philosophy, we are bodies driven by fear and desire; in his literary psychology, we are bodies capable of receiving, combining, and reproducing images. In Locke, we are all equally bodies made by God, and bodies whose applied labor makes property with use value. As Kay argues, Defoe's political calculus develops along similar lines. It is not as if Robinson's or Moll's sensational life is eccentric relative to other humans. What makes their experience particular is the sum of accidents that comprises their story, during which they succeed in making a political economy by their exertions. In some ways, that is also true of Fielding and Richardson, certainly the Richardson of *Pamela*. There is no effort to suggest that Pamela's corporal life is anything more than a platform from which she observes the world around her, including Mr. B's attempted assaults on her. And Dryden, Pope, and Swift find much that is grotesque and unusual about the human body, but those grotesqueries are what mark the human condition as such, fascinating and repellent as it is.

In the later literature, it is as if the eye is turned inward. The body is not the ground from which experience is measured. It supplies rather the primary reflexes from which the individual infers his or her standing in the world. Since those reflexes are by nature utterly local and unpredictable, the individual cannot be entirely secure in himself or herself, and cannot always be sure of his or her connections with others. Smollett recognizes how those uncertainties can signify the parlous state of political minorities of one kind or another, especially when the body creates or receives pain or distress.[67] Sterne treats them comically. And many women writers recognize that these instabilities and uncertainties are powerful tools by which to expose the complex relations that bind and divide individuals in the family, since, as I have been arguing, the evacuation of macropolitical or dynastic argument after mid century funnels a corresponding energy into a consideration of that micropolitical or domestic entity.

Notes

1. Thanks are due to a number of readers of early drafts of this introduction: Allison Kroll, Jayne Lewis, Mark Phillips, Steve Pincus.
2. Ian Watt, *The Rise of the Novel: Studies in Defoe, Richardson and Fielding* (1957; rpt. Harmondsworth: Pelican, 1976).
3. Neil McKendrick, John Brewer, J. H. Plumb, *The Birth of a Consumer Society: The Commercialization of Eighteenth-Century England* (London: Europa, 1982).
4. See, for example, John Brewer and Roy Porter (eds), *Consumption and the World of Goods* (London: Routledge, 1993).
5. The range is suggested by the number of novels mentioned or discussed in the essays below. These include: *The Man of Feeling, A Sentimental Journey, Evelina, Humphry Clinker, The Italian, Love Intrigues, The Female Quixote, The History of Miss Betsy Thoughtless, The Recess, Cecilia, Tristram Shandy, Camilla, Emmeline, Maria, Desmond, The Castles of Athlin and Dunbayne, A Sicilian Romance, The Mysteries of Udolpho, The Monk, Roderick Random, The Castle of Otranto, Caleb Williams, Love and Friendship, Northanger Abbey.*
6. Cheryl Turner, *Living by the Pen: Women Writers in the Eighteenth Century* (London: Routledge, 1992).

7. Mary Poovey, *The Proper Lady and the Woman Writer: Ideology as Style in the Works of Mary Wollstonecraft, Mary Shelley, and Jane Austen* (Chicago: University of Chicago Press, 1984), 35.
8. William Warner, 'Licensing Pleasure: Literary History and the Novel in Early Modern Britain,' in John Richetti *et al.* (eds), *The Columbia History of the British Novel* (New York: Columbia University Press, 1994), 1–22.
9. Elaine Showalter, *A Literature of their Own: British Women Novelists from Bronte to Lessing* (Princeton: Princeton University Press, 1976).
10. Mary Poovey, *The Proper Lady and the Woman Writer: Ideology as Style in the Works of Mary Wollstonecraft, Mary Shelley, and Jane Austen* (Chicago: University of Chicago Press, 1984); Claudia Johnson, *Equivocal Beings: Politics, Gender, and Sentimentality in the 1790s: Wollstonecraft, Radliffe, Burney, Austen* (Chicago: University of Chicago Press, 1995). See also Terry Castle's introduction to Jane Austen, *Northanger Abbey, Lady Susan, The Watsons, and Sanditon*, ed. John Davie (Oxford: Oxford University Press, 1990).
11. J. G. A. Pocock, *The Machiavellian Moment: Florentine Political Thought and the Atlantic Republican Tradition* (Princeton: Princeton University Press, 1975); and *Virtue, Commerce and History: Essays on Political Thought and History, Chiefly in the Eighteenth Century* (Cambridge: Cambridge University Press, 1985).
12. Jürgen Habermas, *The Structural Transformation of the Public Sphere: An Inquiry into a Category of Bourgeois Society* (1962; trans. Cambridge, MA: MIT Press, 1989).
13. C. B. Macpherson, *The Political Theory of Possessive Individualism: Hobbes to Locke* (London: Oxford University Press, 1962).
14. For the classic exploration of this issue, see Albert O. Hirschman, *The Passions and the Interests: Political Arguments for Capitalism before its Triumph* (Princeton: Princeton University Press, 1977).
15. See Colin Nicholson, *Writing and the Rise of Finance: Capital Satires of the Early Eighteenth Century* (Cambridge: Cambridge University Press, 1994); and Sandra Sherman, *Finance and Fictionality in the Early Eighteenth Century: Accounting for Defoe* (Cambridge: Cambridge University Press, 1996).
16. See John Sekora, *Luxury: The Concept in Western Thought, Eden to Smollett* (Baltimore: The Johns Hopkins University Press, 1977). Pocock characterizes the view: eighteenth-century economic man 'was seen as on the whole a feminised, even an effeminate being, still wrestling with his own passions and hysterias and with interior and exterior forces let loose by his fantasies and appetites, and symbolized by such archetypically female goddesses of disorder as Fortune, Luxury, and most recently Credit herself' (*Virtue, Commerce and History*, 114).
17. P. G. M. Dickson, *The Financial Revolution in England: A Study of the Development of Public Credit, 1688–1756* (London: Macmillan, 1967).
18. Isaac Kramnick, *Bolingbroke and His Circle: The Politics of Nostalgia in the Age of Walpole* (Cambridge, MA: Harvard University Press, 1968).
19. See Caroline Robbins, *The Eighteenth-Century Commonwealthman: Studies in the Transmission, Development and Circumstance of English Liberal Thought from the Restoration of Charles II until the War with the Thirteen Colonies* (Cambridge, MA: Harvard University Press, 1959).
20. As Paul Langford puts it, 'Within a framework of continuing mercantilism, overseas trade and colonial development were displaying new features, the

full significance of which became clear only in the 1750s and 1760s' (*A Polite and Commercial People: England, 1727–1783* [Oxford: Clarendon Press, 1989], 124).

21. See Neil McKendrick *et al.*, *The Birth of a Consumer Society*, 4–5.

22. Thus Pocock writes, 'The social psychology of the age declared that encounters with things and persons evoked passions and refined them into manners' (*Virtue, Commerce and History*, 49). A thorough exposition of the development of this ideology is Lawrence E. Klein, *Shaftesbury and the Culture of Politeness: Moral Discourse and Cultural Politics in Early Eighteenth-Century England* (Cambridge: Cambridge University Press, 1994).

23. Thus, liberalism does not define persons 'as possessing a personality adequate to participation in self-rule.' Pocock also writes that the liberal and republican traditions always 'remained incommensurate' (Pocock, *Virtue, Commerce and History*, 45; 47).

24. Thus: 'the affirmation of classical republicanism has something which is humanist about it; it entails the affirmation that *homo* is naturally a citizen and most fully himself when living in a *vivere civile*, and humanist techniques of scholarship and reschematization of history are mobilized around this affirmation whenever it is made' (Pocock, *Virtue, Commerce and History*, 39).

25. '. . . since law is of the empire rather than the republic, its attention is fixed on *commercium* rather than *politicum*'; 'jurisprudence can be said to be predominantly social, concerned with the administration of things and with human relations conducted through the mediation of things, as opposed to a civic vocabulary of the purely political, concerned with the unmediated personal relations entailed by equality and by ruling and being ruled' (Pocock, *Virtue, Commerce and History*, 43; 44). A rhetorician might notice something of a nostalgia here for an unmediated universe of human relations, and ask (especially given Cicero) whether that is possible, or even desirable.

26. Pocock, *Virtue, Commerce and History*, 110.

27. 'Our investigation is limited to the structure and function of the *liberal* model of the bourgeois public sphere, to its emergence and transformation' (Habermas, *Structural Transformation*, xviii).

28. See Habermas, *Structural Transformation*, 210, where Habermas calls for a return to 'rationalization.' This opposition can be traced to the specifically Hegelian and German tradition of opposing the state to civil society, a tension that inhabits Marx's attempt to conceptualize the relation between the state and the individual. The issue is finely discussed in Louis Dumont, *From Mandeville to Marx: The Genesis and Triumph of Economic Ideology* (Chicago: University of Chicago Press, 1977), 120ff.

29. Actually, Habermas writes at one point of the 'fundamental parity among owners of commodities' (*Structural Transformation*, 75).

30. Habermas, *Structural Transformation*, 24–25; 54; 56.

31. Habermas, *Structural Transformation*, 19.

32. Habermas, *Structural Transformation*, 27–28.

33. 'In a certain fashion commodity owners could view themselves as autonomous. To the degree that they were emancipated from governmental directives and controls, they made decisions freely and in accord with standards of profitability. In this regard they owed obedience to no one and were subject only to the anonymous laws functioning in accord with an economic rationality immanent, so it appeared, in the market' (Habermas, *Structural Transformation*, 46).

34. In classical terms, Habermas argues, precisely, that *polis* depends on *oikos*: 'it was . . . their private autonomy as masters of households on which their participation in public life depended' (Habermas, *Structural Transformation*, 3).

35. Habermas, *Structural Transformation*, 74.

36. Habermas, *Structural Transformation*, 38–43.

37. '. . . the same process that converted culture into a commodity . . . established the public as in principle inclusive' (Habermas, *Structural Transformation*, 37).

38. Habermas, *Structural Transformation*, 44–46.

39. Habermas, *Structural Transformation*, 50.

40. '. . . the family lost power as an agent of personal internalization' (Habermas, *Structural Transformation*, 156).

41. 'The culture of harmony infused into the masses per se invites its public to an exchange of opinion about articles of consumption and subjects it to the soft compulsion of constant consumption training' (Habermas, *Structural Transformation*, 192).

42. Michel Foucault, *Discipline and Punish: The Birth of the Prison* (New York: Vintage, 1979).

43. See Leo Braudy, 'The Form of the Sentimental Novel', *Novel*, 7 (1993), 5–13.

44. G. J. Barker-Benfield, *The Culture of Sensibility: Sex and Society in Eighteenth-Century Britain* (Chicago: University of Chicago Press, 1992).

45. For the role of commerce in human relations, see Kay's essay below.

46. There are other problems with Barker-Benfield. He relies very heavily on secondary sources; and where he does use primary sources, and those sources are novels, he treats literary characters and themes as if they were transparent representations of social actualities. This last weakness he inherits from Lawrence Stone's hugely influential *The Family, Sex and Marriage in England, 1500–1800* (New York: Harper and Row, 1979).

47. R. F. Brissenden, *Virtue in Distress: Studies in the Novel of Sentiment from Richardson to Sade* (London: Macmillan, 1974); John Mullan, *Sentiment and Sociability: The Language of Feeling in the Eighteenth Century* (Oxford: Clarendon Press, 1988). See also James P. Carson, 'Enlightenment, Popular Culture, and Gothic Fiction,' and John Mullan, 'Sentimental Novels,' in John Richetti (ed.), *The Cambridge Companion to the Eighteenth-Century Novel* (Cambridge: Cambridge University Press, 1996), 255–76; 236–54.

48. Carol Kay, *Political Constructions: Defoe, Richardson, and Sterne in Relation to Hobbes, Hume, and Burke* (Ithaca: Cornell University Press, 1988). For a fuller discussion of Kay, see my Introduction to *The English Novel Volume I: 1700 to Fielding* (London: Longman, 1998); and also my review in *Eighteenth-Century Studies* 23 (1989): 103–07.

49. For the idea that sensibility is an historically specific phenomenon, see Paul Langford, *A Polite and Commercial People*, esp. 463ff.

50. See J. C. D. Clark, *English Society, 1688–1832: Ideology, Social Structure and Political Practice during the Ancien Regime* (Cambridge: Cambridge University Press, 1985).

51. On the effects of the '45, see Clark, *English Society*, 131; Linda Colley, *Britons: Forging the Nation, 1707–1837* (New Haven: Yale University Press, 1992), 119–24;

W. A. Speck, *Stability and Strife: England, 1714–1760* (London: Arnold, 1977), 249–51. Geoffrey Holmes and Daniel Szechi write, 'Jacobite hopes were not finally extinguished, realistically, until they lay amid the carnage on Culloden's field in 1746' (*The Age of Oligarchy: Pre-Industrial Britain* [London: Longman, 1993], 330).

52. Mark Phillips points out that, as a corollary to the shift I describe, Adam Smith breaks with a tradition of seeing most classical history as driven by the need to define public political values, and turns more toward a history of private life and sentiment. See 'Adam Smith and the History of Private Life: Social and Sentimental Narratives in Eighteenth-Century Historiography,' in Donald Kelley and David Sacks (eds), *The Historical Imagination in Early Modern Britain: History, Rhetoric and Fiction, 1500–1800* (Cambridge: Cambridge University Press, 1997), 318–42.

53. Mullan writes, 'the novel of sentiment in the eighteenth century, committed as it might be to the celebration of fellow-feeling, elaborates pathos from exactly the disconnection of special experiences of sympathy from dominant patterns of social relationship' (*Sentiment and Sociability*, 34).

54. John Sitter, *Literary Loneliness in Mid-Eighteenth-Century England* (Ithaca: Cornell University Press, 1982).

55. Speck writes, for example, 'The process by which the friction of two power elites was transformed into the rule of a governing class was one of the most crucial developments of eighteenth-century England' (*Stability and Strife*, 147).

56. Thus Clark writes that under the Hanoverians Providential Divine Right became less embodied in the person of the King and more in the body of society as a whole (*English Society*, 184).

57. See Clark, *English Society*; and Colley, *Britons* (note 50).

58. Clark, *English Society*, 194–95; Colley, *Britons*, 229–36.

59. For comments on Hume's (as well as Smollett's) position after 1745, see Pocock, *Virtue, Commerce and History*, 250; 252.

60. H. T. Dickinson writes, for example, 'From the 1760s the campaign of criticism levelled at the Whig establishment began to undergo significant changes. Under the first two Hanoverians the Country opposition had been directed from within parliament or by spokesmen with very close ties with the parliamentary classes. Starting with the Wilkite petitioning movement of the late 1760s however the most important and vociferous opposition to the establishment was extra-parliamentary and was directed by men who were not among the parliamentary elite' (*Liberty and Property: Political Ideology in Eighteenth-Century Britain* [New York: Holmes and Meier, 1977], 195). For an excellent discussion of Wilkes and reform, see Holmes and Szechi, *Age of Oligarchy*, 315–24.

61. See also Langford, *Polite and Commercial People*, 617–21.

62. See Simon Schama, *Dead Certainties (Unwarranted Speculations)* (New York: Vintage, 1992).

63. Colley, *Britons*, 105.

64. Pocock argues that in many ways the American Revolution was a reflex of the fundamental stabilities of British institutions. See *Virtue, Commerce and History*, 83; also 81.

65. See H. T. Dickinson, *Liberty and Property*, 263; also Pocock, *Virtue, Commerce and History*, 74; 276. This is also very much the drift of Marilyn Butler's work

on the 1790s and the Revolutionary period. See *Jane Austen and the War of Ideas* (Oxford: Clarendon Press, 1975), from which we reprint a chapter below. Holmes and Szechi write, 'The overwhelming majority of the political nation, and probably the nation at large, were indifferent or hostile to grand schemes of reform' (*Age of Oligarchy*, 315).

66. See Mullan, *Sentiment and Sociability*; Ann Jessie Van Sant, *Eighteenth-Century Sensibility and the Novel: The Senses in Social Context* (Cambridge: Cambridge University Press, 1993).

67. For an excellent appraisal of Smollett along these lines, see Aileen Douglas, *Uneasy Sensations: Smollett and the Body* (Chicago: University of Chicago Press, 1995).

Part I

General Essays: The Sentimental and the Gothic

2 'Only a Boy': Notes on Sentimental Novels

George Starr

George Starr, one of the most distinguished critics of Defoe, argues that there are meaningful connections between earlier eighteenth-century novels – such as *Colonel Jack* – and the habits and tendencies of sentimental novels such as *The Man of Feeling*. Starr argues that the defining formal features of the sentimental novel are that it opposes or resists the movement of the classic *Bildungsroman*, by which a protagonist is inducted into a mature engagement with his personal and social obligations. Defined in part by a linguistic scepticism, the sentimental hero resists maturation of this sort, finding refuge in a strangely effeminized rejection of society at large, which is altogether too articulate, and by the same token, morally untrustworthy.

I

This paper is concerned partly with the form of the sentimental novel, partly with its relation to the society from which it springs, and partly with the responses that the sentimental novel seeks to elicit. The form of the sentimental novel, I shall suggest, is best understood as that of an anti-*Bildungsroman*. Instead of a progress toward maturity, the sentimental novel deals sympathetically with the character who cannot grow up and find an active place in society. Its ideal is stasis or regression, which makes for episodic, cyclical narratives that finally go nowhere or back where they began. My chief contention about the genesis of such novels is that, owing to different social assumptions about masculinity and femininity, the sentimental heroine can figure in conventional novelistic plots that end with wedding bells, since her role conforms to the popular sense of what a young lady should be; the sentimental hero poses an implicit challenge to accepted notions of masculinity, and cannot be assimilated into the world represented in the novels. As a consequence, sentimental novels tend to become satires on 'the world,' but satires in which the hero himself cannot usually take part because of his naivete, good nature, and general childlikeness. As to the reader's response, I shall suggest that the sentimental novel affects us in ways often associated with the pastoral. Most of my discussion will focus on four texts: Defoe's *Colonel Jack*, Mackenzie's *Man of Feeling*, Sterne's *Sentimental Journey*, and Burney's *Evelina*.

The sentimental novel often deals with the same portion of life as the typical *Bildungsroman*, adolescence, but does not chronicle an attainment of maturity: in one way or another the onset of adulthood, the goal of the *Bildungsroman*, is obstructed, evaded, or undone. The sentimental novel shows change stopped or reversed – and often time along with it. The *Bildungsroman* treats time respectfully, as not only measuring but fostering the processes which it celebrates. In the sentimental novel time becomes a major enemy, the agent of feared or despised changes. Various strategies are devised to arrest or fragment its ongoingness, and to retrieve or redeem moments which seem to stand outside time or otherwise defy it. One such strategy is to break down the linear, causal, sequential flow of narrative into discrete episodes; another is to arrange episodes in non-chronological order (as Sterne does), or to introduce digressions (as Sterne and Mackenzie both do), or to posit gaps (as Mackenzie does with his 'lost' chapters), all tending to disrupt temporal continuity. If the sentimental novelist is to free his hero from the ordinary effects of time, drastic tactics are called for, since narrative is always threatening to imply progress simply by unfolding in time. Such tactics as Sterne's and Mackenzie's, sometimes regarded as experimental departures from the realistic conventions of the 'standard' novel, or as attempts to get beyond the 'literary' artificiality of inherited narrative modes, are especially appropriate to the sentimental novel because of the significance attached to time. What is most benign about time in the *Bildungsroman* – its efficacy as agent of growth and development – becomes in the sentimental novel its most malign feature: the power of time to transform boys into men and sons into husbands is the very thing that the sentimental novel seeks to elude or deny.

The jargon satirized in Huck Finn's account of Emmeline Grangerford's taste in literature is what one tends to think of as the language of sentimentalism. Yet what is characteristic of sentimentalism is not the set of terms with which it originally sought to vivify and extend the inherited language of emotion, for these terms quickly dwindled into equally rigid, lifeless set phrases, but rather a fundamental skepticism about the adequacy of language itself as a medium of expression or communication. The distinctive sentimental attitude toward language is to be discovered not in the shibboleths of its pioneers but in the conviction of sentimentalists in each generation that language, like the world that uses it, is profoundly debased – better suited to self-disguise than self-revelation, more often employed to exploit than enlighten, something ideally to be avoided but at all events to be used (if used it must be) with mistrust. Sentimental writers have responded to this impasse with two centuries of narratives in which articulateness is associated with villainy,[1] and true heroism is always more or less tongue-tied. Twain's own practice in *Huckleberry Finn*, for example, is to assign the gift of gab to those who manipulate language (and other people) for selfish or sinister purposes, like the Duke and the Dauphin and Tom Sawyer; the halting, non-standard English of Huck and Jim not only becomes a sign of their relative freedom from the moral and intellectual contamination of polite culture, but also proves more genuinely expressive than the idiom of civilized (i.e. corrupt) society.

A similar attitude toward language characterizes many nineteenth-century novels more commonly regarded as sentimental. In *Hard Times*, for instance, those who speak easily and authoritatively – Gradgrind, Bounderby, Harthouse, Slackbridge – all prove deceived or self-deceived, and facile utterance is a major symptom of their folly or tool of their knavery. Those who are 'no clackers' – Stephen Blackpool, Sleary – are barely articulate, and speech impediments, bizarre dialects, and a fundamental diffidence about verbal communication are stigmata attesting the validity of what they do manage to say. Sentimental figures tend to be babes linguistically (as in other ways), out of whose mouths comes much odd-sounding sense.[2]

The sentimental view of language may be clarified further by contrasting Smollett's treatment of Winifred Jenkins in *Humphrey Clinker*. 'Cette dislocation comique de la langue,' asks Professor Boucé, 'n'est-elle pas l'ultime refuge de l'individu qui se sent menacé par les pressions de la société et, sous le couvert d'un idiolecte, tente de conjurer son propre néant et la mort d'une civilisation? . . . Le comique verbal de Smollett dans *Humphry Clinker*, et celui de ses successeurs modernes, apparaît donc comme volonté de détruire, mais aussi de créer pour se protéger d'un néant inéluctable par une dernière incantation aux forces de la vie.'[3] Smollettesque wordplay is far too active a response to the *pressions de la société* to afford ultimate refuge to the menaced sentimental hero, who yearns for silence and the 'pure' expressiveness of pre-verbal gesture. True, he may seldom reach this state – Mackenzie's Harley comes closer than most – and there may be something inherently paradoxical about the very attempt to represent it in words. All the same, Harley and his brethren prefer childish prattle to adult Babel, and the splash of a single tear is the next best thing to the perfect stillness of womb and tomb.

The humor of a Win Jenkins depends partly on the assumption that between words and their meanings there is an arbitrary but straightforward relationship, to be mastered as one of the burdensome yet necessary parts of growing up. Win's escape from the toils of correct usage is a buoyant, exhilarating suspension of lexical norms to which Smollett, his reader, and *Humphry Clinker* as a whole are nevertheless committed. This sense of freedom, of local and temporary exemption from obligations sensed as irksome but just, is distinctively comic; what it gratifies is a will less to destroy than to circumvent or hold in abeyance constraints half-resented yet accepted. From a holiday or truancy like Win's there is an inevitable return, as social standards (including customary patterns of speech) resume their sway.

The sentimental hero, however, denies the desirability as well as the necessity of mastering language. Shunning forbidden knowledge – and to him there is no other kind – he naturally repudiates the word, which is its key. He is disturbed less by the arbitrariness or artificiality of a system of verbal signs, which he finds equally in other social institutions, than by the enormities of adulthood to which language-learning is a kind of forced initiation. What makes his project of escape from the word so desperate and pathetic is that far from trying to *conjurer son propre néant*, he welcomes it with open arms. Win Jenkins may belong to a tradition of wise fools, who utter truths greater or other than those they intend, but the sentimental hero belongs rather to a tradition of saintly fools,[4] whose most eloquent testimony to truth is often garbled or mute.

The heroes of most sentimental novels are humorless, nor is this simply a matter of their not having the time or inclination to dry their tears before the next bout of weeping. The image of the outside world in a sentimental novel is that found in satire: most people prove to be self-serving, callous, hypocritical, and so on. Moreover, the narrators of sentimental novels are capable of considerable irony, as in *The Man of Feeling*. But the sentimental hero himself is generally lacking in irony and devoid of wit, and one reason for this is probably the authorial realization that wit is itself a form of control, a way of ordering, judging, and thus mastering one's world – which would run contrary to the helpless, passive, victimized posture of most sentimental heroes.[5]

I am not the first to regard sentimentalism as embodying an essentially negative response to the world as it is. Both Ronald Paulson, in his fine study of *Satire and the Novel in Eighteenth-Century England*, and R. F. Brissenden, in his stimulating recent work on the novel of sentiment, maintain that sentimentalism tended to displace traditional modes of satire as a vehicle for the expression of discontent with existing society.[6] But the historical as well as the generic aspects of the satire–sentimentalism relationship remain somewhat problematic, owing partly to different scholarly conceptions of the mood or spirit of sentimentalism.

Some have seen sentimentalism as springing from a basic optimism that renders satire unnecessary (men are naturally good, and need to be reminded of their latent goodness rather than their manifest shortcomings); or ineffectual (men's natural goodness can be elicited better through sympathetic tears than scoffing laughter); or immoral (satire indulges impulses in its author and readers just as base as those it purports to chastise). On this view, later eighteenth-century literature exhibits a gradual moderating – some would say a blurring and emasculating – of the rigorous Augustinian or Augustan visions of man and society on which the satire of Swift, Pope, and Johnson had been based. This somber, demanding ethos is supposed to have given way to a bland faith in progress – a confidence that though the world was not yet all it might be, philanthropy and forbearance would bring it around, since its defects lay more in reformable institutions than in human nature itself.[7]

Others have seen sentimentalism as the expression of a pessimism so thorough-going that one can scarcely hope to improve society, but at most to escape from it. The idea of progress is not only an illusion but a snare, tempting man to linger in a city of destruction that he had better flee, even if flight inward (or backward) is the only route open to him. On this view, too, individual man may be inherently good, but society turns him into a predatory beast, and its customs and institutions are so incurably vile that the good man must be an exile or a victim – never the active, socially engaged hero of traditional epic or comedy, even in their novelistic forms. In either case, sentimentalism is seen as having rejected the Calvinist notion of man's innate depravity. But drastically different inferences about the relation of the individual to society can be drawn from the assumption that man is naturally good. The positions that I have somewhat baldly summarized as 'optimistic' and 'pessimistic' appear to have stemmed from the same conviction of man's native goodness, and to be equally entitled historically to the epithet 'sentimental,' which may help to explain critical disagreement over the compatibility of sentimentalism and satire.[8]

The sentimental hero tends to have a child's-eye view of the world, which occasionally gives way not to an adult's but a giant's. In sentimental fiction, it is true, heroes seldom experience straightforwardly the exhilarations of giantism, such as the uninhibited self-assertion of putting out a Lilliputian fire. Instead, they discover that an obliteration or virtual extinction of self can paradoxically produce the same sensations of release, transcendence, and power.

The sentimental victim can reduce his oppressors to the same helpless insignificance they have imposed on him by enlarging his frame of reference; the result is not only instant pygmification of one's enemies, but an expansion of the sense of self through empathetic contemplation of infinitely vast forces in nature. Ellena, the heroine of *The Italian*, is shut by her persecutors in a monastic cell, but it has a splendid view, and Radcliffe declares that:

> Here, gazing upon the stupendous imagery around her, looking, as it were, beyond the awful veil which obscures the features of the Deity, . . . dwelling as with a present God in the midst of his sublime works; with a mind thus elevated, how insignificant would appear to her the transactions, and the sufferings of this world! How poor the boasted power of man, when the fall of a single cliff from these mountains would with ease destroy thousands of his race assembled on the plains below! . . . Thus man, the giant who now held her in captivity, would sink to the diminutiveness of a fairy; and she would experience, that his utmost force was unable to enchain her soul. . . .[9]

Here we have literal identification of the oppressor as a giant, made to dwindle at a stroke to 'diminutiveness.' In characteristic sentimental fashion, Goliath is struck down, but not by the hand of David: the 'easy' destruction of thousands of 'his' (not 'our') race is imagined with relish, but it is God's doing, or Nature's, not the heroine's. Ellena's musings turn the tables on her persecutors in typical sentimental fashion; since it is wholly imaginary, this triumph has a completeness and an innocence seldom manageable in reality. The formerly puny one becomes the giant, but far from making away with the giant or even wishing to supplant him, has been 'elevated' through humbling herself.

The complex psychology of the sentimental Sublime cannot be dealt with here in any detail,[10] but one further passage may help to illustrate what I take to be its distinctive pattern. Samuel Clemens writes from Carson City, Nevada:

> I said we are situated in a flat, sandy desert – true. And surrounded on all sides by such prodigious mountains, that when you gaze at them awhile, – and begin to conceive of their grandeur – and next to *feel* their vastness expanding your soul like a bladder – and ultimately find yourself growing and swelling and spreading into a giant – I say when this point is reached, you look disdainfully down upon the insignificant village of Carson, and in that instant

> you are seized with a burning desire to stretch forth your hand, put the city in your pocket, and walk off with it.[11]

Like Radcliffe, Clemens manages to convey a good deal of aggressiveness toward 'his race assembled on the plains below,' although he takes somewhat different precautions against the stigma of misanthropy. *He* is not its agent – all this is what 'you' feel, what anyone would feel – nor is its object fellow human beings but an insignificant village. Disdain is harmless – a matter of a look, no more damaging than your stare is to a mountain – and the innocuous goal of burning desire is to pocket and walk off with some portable property, not to 'destroy thousands.' And of course touches of bathos ('like a bladder') and bombast ('growing and swelling and spreading') help to make this mock-heroic giant playfully unthreatening, oversized yet benign.

All the same, Clemens' brush with Western sublimity has the same basic contours as Ellena's in the Appennines. Absorbed 'gazing' (each uses the term) leads to identification with enormous objects perceived initially as alien and oppressive; the resulting sense of release, represented mythically through allusions to giantism, immediately takes the form of an imaginary act of cataclysmic violence against now-diminutive mankind. What is the source of this fantasy of unlimited power, and what is sentimental about it? To answer both questions in a word, regression. What Ellena and Clemens conspicuously do *not* do when 'surrounded' or 'enchained' is to stand upon their dignity, hurling Lear-like defiance at the mighty elements afflicting them; instead, through magnifying the 'stupendous,' 'prodigious' vastnesses that hem them in, they seem first to propitiate and then to merge with the very forces that had made them anxious. Here explication must be eked out with frank surmise. In passing from feelings of insufficiency and alarm to sensations of untrammeled giantism, Ellena's and Clemens' essential step appears to be the recovery of an infantile perspective from which everything looks huge; the path is regressive, leading back to a state of total vulnerability and dependence and arriving ultimately at an undifferentiated oneness with quasi-parental powers, no longer threats to but extensions of oneself. Whatever its adequacy as a model of the sublime experience, and whatever psychological idiom is used to describe it, this pattern characterizes the wishful thinking of various sentimental heroes, whether their fantasies stop at the point of dreaded but longed-for annihilation of the self, or culminate in the starkly aggressive giant-phase imagined by Radcliffe and Clemens.

II

The most recent editor of *Colonel Jack* calls it 'a sentimental novel in embryo,' and has 'counted thirty-three instances of weeping and at least two swoonings in the novel'; but 'Looked at in another light,' Professor Monk goes on to say, '*Colonel Jack* may be seen as an adumbration of the *Bildungsroman*.'[12] My own view is that the book is sentimental not because of the quantity of tears shed but because of the situations that give rise to its lachrymosity, and because of the structure of the novel, which negates the essential spirit and shape of a *Bildungsroman*. A *Bildungsroman* may be what we expect, what Colonel Jack wants his story to be, and what in his more sanguine moments he persuades himself it has become. But any such pattern is belied by the unfolding of the hero's experience, in which an Oedipal predicament is compulsively reenacted rather than resolved. The novel does trace a career from childhood through manhood, and by the end Jack has acquired wealth and some of the other accoutrements of gentility. But despite the social and geographic range of his adventures, they tend to reiterate a limited set of basic situations, and far from learning or growing through his experiences Jack seems condemned forever to the plight in which he first enters the world. He is an orphan, persuaded by what he calls 'oral tradition' that his 'Mother was a Gentlewoman, that [his] Father was a Man of Quality,' and thus that his forlorn circumstances belie his true nature and rightful place in the world. Here we have a standard *donnée* of romance, yet Defoe's hero does not pass through various ordeals which culminate in triumphant public recognition. Instead, the first half of the book consists of Colonel Jack demonstrating to a series of surrogate fathers that he is a worthy son; and his worthiness lies less in any mastery over adverse circumstances than in an immunity to the baseness of his surroundings, his associates, and even some of his own actions. The complete sentimental hero scarcely acts at all, but is acted upon and reacts; Colonel Jack undeniably does things, some of them not very savory, but responsibility for his actions is shifted elsewhere. Most sentimental novels contain plenty of aggression, but it is directed either against the hero himself by a hostile world, or against a series of victims with whom the hero commiserates. In this book the hero is permitted to exploit others by portraying himself as the passive, reluctant, and censorious witness of events initiated by ne'er-do-wells like his double, Captain Jack, which nevertheless have Colonel Jack himself as their beneficiary.

In the second half of the book, Colonel Jack demonstrates in his dealings with four successive wives that matrimony spells betrayal; he himself is always the injured party, whose devotion is no safeguard against female perfidy. This makes it sound, though, as if Colonel Jack becomes a misogynist, which is not the case, for once again he is incapable of learning from experience. The failure of one marriage does not teach him the secret of success in the next, let alone the lesson that he is not cut out for a husband: repeated failure merely underlines his incurable naivete as fated victim of feminine wile, greed, and lust. This cycle of defeat, which reinforces Colonel Jack's sense of aggrieved innocence at the expense of certain other marital gratifications, is broken only with the final marriage, to the original and most culpable of his wives, who turns up in his Virginia household as a transported criminal. The lowly servant is restored to eminence as mistress of the plantation, and since both parties are by now too old for sex to be an issue, the marriage proves a happy one. But it is impossible for Colonel Jack to sustain the role of dispenser of forgiveness and largesse. His posture toward the world remains through all his vicissitudes essentially infantile. The brief interludes in which he exercises patriarchal power, toward Mouchat the slave or his prodigal ex-wife, represent not the assumption of adult responsibilities but short lessons in how he himself, the most deserving child of all, ought to have been treated by his own parents – that is, with solicitous generosity rather than punitive neglect. Similarly, his effusive gratitude toward a series of forgiving father-figures seems designed to show how becoming the hero's response would have been had his own father treated him properly instead of abandoning him.

At all events, Colonel Jack's relationship with his final, ideal wife involves a rapid reversal of roles. The appearance in Virginia of some transported felons threatens Jack's liberty, for he too had taken part briefly in the Jacobite uprising and now fears 'being discover'd, betray'd, carried to *England*, hang'd, quarter'd, and all that was terrible, and my very Heart sunk within me' (p. 269). In his feckless anxiety he leaves everything to his wife, who confines him to his room, tells everyone he is suffering from gout, and then for three months keeps his legs wrapped in flannel. Jack reports that 'I gave my self chearfully up to her Management' (p. 271), and this is in fact the most cheerful portion of his narrative, for he has at last obtained the filial security hitherto denied him, down to the detail of being protected from the world by maternal swaddling. Behind his quest for riches and gentility, then, lies a deeper and more persistent longing for the imagined bliss of babyhood. A quest of the former kind may have affinities with the *Bildungsroman*, yet the quest that more decisively motivates Colonel Jack is basically at odds with the *Bildungsroman*, for it idealizes infancy rather than maturity, and stasis rather than growth or development. The object of the hero's nostalgic yearnings – a haven of undemanding and unvarying devotion – promises to materialize with each fresh human encounter, but on each occasion proves only partially, symbolically, or temporarily attainable; the sequence of his adventures is therefore largely cyclical, and in this respect too *Colonel Jack* differs fundamentally from the typical *Bildungsroman*, which is linear and progressive in structure.

Colonel Jack's craving for devotion calls for further comment, not only because Defoe's characters are usually seen as desiring more tangible goods, but because the attachment in question seems to me what sentimental heroes as a group are in search of. The absence of women scarcely seems to ruffle Crusoe on his island, and the equanimity of Moll Flanders and Roxana is undisturbed when husbands, lovers, and children disappear; yet these characters all dream of finding themselves in a relationship like Crusoe's with Friday – that is, as the adoptive parent of an absolutely dependent, docile, and grateful child. Roxana has no such good fortune – as punishment for a lifetime of mischief, she is pursued by a daughter with none of these engaging traits – and Moll's ultimate experience of this blessing in the shape of her long-lost son Humphry is so abrupt and undeserved as to strike most readers as grotesque rather than idyllic. Crusoe's attachment to Friday, however, is equally remote from the stark utilitarianism imputed to it by some critics and from the veiled homosexuality alleged by others; those who would characterize it as oedipal fantasy are perhaps equally reductive but nearer the truth. In *The Family Instructor*, Defoe had explored the tragic consequences of filial rebelliousness and paternal vengefulness, including the symbolic castration and literal death of a defiant son. Four years later, in *Robinson Crusoe*, he portrays a fantasy-resolution of tensions between parent and child, and in his novels of the next five years (the continuation of *Crusoe, Moll Flanders, Colonel Jack*, and *Roxana*), dealings between lovers or spouses are represented as mutually satisfying insofar as they approximate the ideal terms on which Crusoe and Friday stand with each other. Characters can be touchingly fond of one another in Defoe's fiction, but seldom as adult members of opposite sexes. The other works which I shall be considering resemble Defoe's in this respect: the establishment of emotional bonds between people is an insistent theme, but proves an impossibility unless the sentimental hero is in one way or another palpably dominant or submissive. He must be shielded by age, economic or social distance from the demands posed by sustained mutual dependence, and he finds such demands especially threatening in their emotional and sexual manifestations.

III

What I take to be the essential characteristics of the sentimental novel are found in fuller and purer form in *The Man of Feeling*.[13] As author, Mackenzie puts himself at three or four removes from his hero, Harley. There is first of all an editor who introduces the book, telling how he got the fragmentary manuscript from a country curate who was using it as gun-wadding on their hunting expeditions. The curate in turn had come upon it among the effects of its presumed author, a 'grave, oddish kind of man' who shunned adult company but was 'gentle as a lamb' and enjoyed 'playing at te-totum with the children.' This author-figure, finally, is a friend of Harley – but he is also an omniscient narrator, capable of recounting not only Harley's unexpressed thoughts and feelings, but his actions when alone. The supposititious author and editor are not only sympathetic toward Harley but in important respects just like him; at the same time, both are assigned a capacity for urbane irony which Harley does not share. Like most sentimental novelists and most sentimental readers, Mackenzie (or the ultimate 'implied author') takes a somewhat equivocal position toward his subject matter. In his horror at the brutality, the indifference, and the treachery of ordinary adult 'civilized' life, and in his sympathy for its victims, he is very close to his hero. But the very qualities that distinguish Harley as a sentimental hero tend to keep him from judging the world harshly or condescendingly: this would be to confer on him a power to retaliate which would belie his character as humble, charitable, downtrodden innocent. Mackenzie, however, wants to register not only Harley's helpless dismay but his own active indignation at the world's villainies, and it is through his editor, his narrator, and other spokesmen who turn up in the course of the story that Mackenzie can pass emphatic judgment on them. Moreover, there are some features of his hero with which he evidently does not wish to be identified: by making his subordinate narrators speak of Harley from time to time with gentle but wry amusement, the author can prevent our supposing that he is as naive or ineffectual as this 'child in the drama of the world.'[14] In short, Mackenzie seeks to present himself as a genuine man of feeling but also as something of a man of the world: framing devices permit him this necessary combination of oneness with the hero and distance from him.

The pattern I have just described holds true, moreover, of the hero's relation to other people within the book, and of the reader's relation to the hero. Like all sentimental heroes, Harley exercises great generosity and compassion – toward those less fortunate than he. The objects of his alms and tears sometimes reciprocate with tales of their own beneficence toward others still lower on the ladder of helplessness and woe. Whether or not one's feelings of pity necessarily imply a sense of superiority to their object, the sentimental novel suggests that for pity to be a pleasurable emotion some such comparison, favorable to oneself, must be drawn. Not that the principle is openly avowed in sentimental novels: to declare baldly, as Hume does in his *Treatise on Human Nature*, that 'The misery of another gives us a more lively idea of our happiness,' and 'therefore, produces delight,'[15] would be fatal to the entire enterprise. Within the novels, gestures of commiseration are portrayed as uplifting to both parties; that the bestower is in some sense gratified at the expense of the recipient, whom he has a certain interest in not raising to his own level, is unthinkable. Or at any rate the thought never seems to occur to the sentimental hero; nor can the thought occur to the reader without destroying the flattering illusion that his pleasure in witnessing so much distress does credit to the goodness of his heart. Both kinds of pleasure are accessible to the reader, of course, so long as the former sort remains unconscious: that is, he can think well of himself as a man of feeling in pitying the misfortunes of the sentimental hero, and at the same time think well of himself as the one giving rather than receiving pity.

However we choose to regard our benevolence toward a hero like Harley, this response does seem to involve a certain distance between us and him. Another kind of distancing results from the attitude of our culture toward sentimentality itself: we laugh uneasily at so-called heroes who cry so easily and so copiously, we find embarrassing and slightly ludicrous their tendency to exaggerate, we are disturbed yet contemptuous about what we take to be their self-pitying self-indulgence. This would be enough to account for the condescending tone in most modern criticism of sentimental fiction, even if there were no more legitimate aesthetic grounds for it. Yet distancing is not the whole story: the modern, 'cool' sensibility that recoils with amusement from the traits I have just mentioned nevertheless hankers on some level after the pastoral world that they all serve to create. Here men are still capable of intense emotions; here men still care about each other; here men do not disregard pain and suffering. The outer world which Harley encounters may be anything but pastoral, and is in fact more cruel, rapacious, and gross than our familiar one; yet his sheer responsiveness to it constitutes a kind of pastoral alternative to the cynical, 'adult' blunting of response that the world more commonly induces. Thus Harley's spontaneity, naivete, and innocence make him a pastoral figure with whom we in part wish to identify, despite (or perhaps because of) our own compromised, inhibited worldliness.

Moreover, he witnesses or is told about instances of such melodramatic wrongdoing that his reaction is one of pure revulsion. Villains and villainy are presented so starkly that neither he nor we are perplexed by difficulties of evaluation; we are spared the moral workout that life and much other literature demand of us, and invited instead to check the intensity of our response against the example set us by the hero. What matters is not the qualitative accuracy of moral judgment, but the quantitative adequacy of moral feeling – the goodness not of our heads but our hearts. The focus within the novel is not on actions, which involve choice and responsibility, but on reactions – particularly reactions so abrupt as to preclude deliberation. The very idea of pausing to weigh motives and circumstances is alien to the man of feeling; it smacks of the prudential, calculating, worldly wisdom that the sentimental novel sets out to discredit, and introduces an element of cold-blooded circumspection into a process which (in the sentimental view) ought to be instinctive and instantaneous. As has often been pointed out, this aspect of sentimentalism can be seen as part of a larger eighteenth-century debate between those who held that man is endowed with an innate, intuitive moral sense and those who based ethics on ordinary rationality. But for our purposes, what is most significant about the ethical allegiances of sentimentalism is that they too engage the reader through a kind of pastoralism, for they invite him to enter a world in which moral issues are simple and clear-cut. All that is required of him is that he react with an appropriate degree of sympathy to distressed innocence and of abhorrence to vice – not that he painstakingly make his way through the twilight zone between them.

One further source of appeal in books like *The Man of Feeling* should be mentioned in this connection. Within the story Harley is not exactly quiescent, since his feelings are in constant turmoil, but action is not something he initiates or performs but undergoes and responds to; his life touches him deeply, but he seems powerless to affect its shape or outcome. In all this his role resembles that of a reader more than that of a conventional hero, and the resulting emphasis on passive responsiveness relieves the reader of certain burdens just as it does Harley. We are not challenged to bestir ourselves, to gird up our loins, to sally forth as pilgrims or soldiers in one or another cause, as we are by much other literature. This is seen as a problem by Hugh Murray, author of *The Morality of Fiction* (1806), who remarks that 'There is perhaps only one point of view in which the tendency of [Mackenzie's] writings may perhaps be objected to. They seem to contain something peculiarly enervating and unfavourable to active exertion' (p. 145). Whatever the moral drawbacks of lotus-eating, there is no question that it has a certain psychological appeal, and Murray is right to imply that *The Man of Feeling* lulls us in this way – even if its outward effect on early readers looked more like that of onion-peeling than lotus-eating.

This can be seen particularly in Mackenzie's treatment of death. Throughout the book the orphan Harley is sentimentally in love with the unattainable Miss Walton. But sex is everywhere associated with betrayal, and is one of the chief sources of evil and misery: the Misanthropist is soured by a trusted friend eloping with his fiancée, the Prostitute is driven to the brink of the grave by the conventional consequences of a conventional seduction, and Signor Respino nearly ruins an entire family out of 'criminal passion' for the incorruptible wife. 'Passion' of the sexual variety is invariably 'criminal' – which puts Harley in an awkward position as a lover, just as it had Colonel Jack. When Miss Walton eventually reveals to Harley that she is not unattainable but had secretly loved him all along, there is only one way out of his impasse: 'He seized her hand – a languid colour reddened his cheek – a smile brightened faintly in his eye. As he gazed on her, it grew dim, it fixed, it closed. – He sighed, and fell back on his seat. – . . . His physician happened to call at this instant. – . . . But Harley was gone for ever!' (pp. 130–31).

Marriage represents the ultimate threat to the innocence of the sentimental hero: by 'making a man of him,' sexual consummation would be a betrayal of his essential childlikeness and an assumption of all the compromises, grossnesses, and responsibilities of adulthood in a fallen world. Colonel Jack solves this predicament in a typically Defoean way, by marrying repeatedly but insisting that the betrayals involved were all the women's doing. Harley's gentle retreat into death is not only more gallant (in its own perverse way) toward poor Miss Walton, but a more consistent and plausible finale to Harley's brief career than marriage would be. Death is alluded to throughout the novel, not as the steady goal of a unified plot, but as an object of wanly pleasurable contemplation for those condemned to a world they long to escape. The book begins as it ends with the author in a state of pleasing melancholy, discussing graves; as to Harley himself, the following lines from 'LAVINIA. A Pastoral' sum up his longings: 'Let me walk where the new-cover'd grave / Allows the pale lover to rest! / When shall I in its peaceable womb / Be laid with my sorrows asleep!' (p. 117). These lines suggest the way in which Mackenzie repeatedly sets up death as an alternative to sexual consummation, analogous to it but vastly more desirable – especially if as in Harley's case the hero can be 'buried in a certain spot near the grave of his mother' (p. 132). At the same time, by not actively pursuing death, Harley remains a 'purer' sentimental hero than someone like Werther, for the carrying out of such a project as Werther's suicide would mark a drastic departure from Harley's childlike unfitness for decisive action of any kind.

IV

The *Bildungsroman* does not ordinarily regard infants as trailing clouds of glory, and it attaches such importance to learning processes that the question of whether man is innately good or depraved is not crucial to it. The sentimental novel not only introduces actual infants in idealized roles, but finds in childhood generally the same virtues that were being imputed to the Noble Savage during the eighteenth century. Sentimentalism is akin to primitivism insofar as it looks upon social institutions as thwarting or perverting man's natural dignity. Normal education is thus a force for evil. In the *Bildungsroman*, satires on education aim at practical reform, and assume that one can and must learn to live in the world, whereas the sentimental novel challenges not only the methods but the goal of conventional education. Skepticism about formal education is only one expression, however, of the more general sentimental principle that the path from innocence to experience is a downhill one. A novelist like Fielding may attach positive value to a young man's acquisition of prudence, but for the sentimental novelist the wisdom of the serpent does not complement but contaminates the innocence of the dove. The sentimental version of the story of a good-natured young man who eventually learned prudence and took a responsible place in society would have to represent this process as degeneration rather than growth; yet in its very acknowledgement of process it would tend to become a rueful or ironic version of the *Bildungsroman*, and no longer a sentimental novel. In the sentimental novel, at any rate, the hero does not mature or degenerate, largely because the two processes are regarded as synonymous, and because process itself is a sentimental *bête noire*.

In such novels as *The Man of Feeling*, then, or *A Sentimental Journey*, the action may be as peripatetic as that of *Tom Jones*, and the hero may encounter as socially and morally varied a series of other characters, but the result tends to be a reiterated confirmation of attitudes he set out with, not a revision or revaluation of them. In Mackenzie's novel, particularly, the indictment of the world becomes more comprehensive with each episode, but not more complex or profound. Great stress is laid on openness to experience, but only in the sense that the hero must be prepared to have his susceptibilities set a-jangling in all sorts of odd moments and unlikely places; such openness does not extend to the point of allowing the hero to be transformed by his experience. Affected, yes – he must be; changed, no; he may become sadder, but he can scarcely grow wiser. Far from being embarked on a voyage of discovery, in search of something he doesn't already know or have, he is on a mission of recovery, trying to recapture a sense of fixity amidst distressing flux, or to regain a long-lost haven of secure devotion.

It might be objected, however, that the sentimental hero obeys yet another impulse, the urge to (as the epigraph of *Howard's End* puts it) 'only connect.' Is not the famous conclusion of *A Sentimental Journey* – 'So that when I stretch'd out my hand, I caught hold of the Fille de Chambre's / END OF VOL. II.' – a typically merry and equivocal version of what is after all a major preoccupation of the book, the collapsing of artificial distances between people?[16] Does not sentimentalism in general seek to demonstrate that men are not condemned by their egoism to mutual isolation, and that genuine communication and fellow-feeling are in fact possible through the agency of sympathy?

To this I would reply that sentimental authors and heroes alike yearn to reestablish a sense of lost human contact and community, but that their successes in this undertaking are at best qualified, fragmentary, and precarious. The problem is that the heroes themselves are extreme instances of the very condition they set out to overcome: unwilling or unable to emerge from their own self-protective cocoons, they can make contact only with those who lack the same defensive outworks, owing either to a disaster which has stripped them away, a social inferiority which has prevented their formation, or a youthfulness so tender that they have not yet had time to develop. Yorick, for example, enjoys more than one vision of idyllic community. There is not only the fragment about Abdera early in the book, but the chapters entitled 'The Supper' and 'The Grace' toward the end, in which a rustic patriarch and his 'joyous genealogy' perform first a 'feast of love' (p. 281) and then a dance that ritually signifies their harmony with each other and their creator. Yorick makes much of his rapid initiation into this pastoral paradise – of the 'honest welcome' he receives, and of his sitting down 'at once like a son of the family' – but along with the old man and his wife he can only watch the dance, not take part in it. Before the chapter ends he is referring to his host with kindly approval as 'an illiterate peasant,' and this distancing becomes even more pronounced a dozen lines later when he apostrophizes the Savoyards as 'Poor, patient, quiet, honest people!' (p. 285). His tone in speaking of The Folk is certainly more benign than that of the splenetic travelers he satirizes, yet it is a benignity that constantly implies apartness, not oneness with its object.

At the other social extreme from the scene just mentioned stands Yorick's equally hospitable reception by Parisian society, which is chronicled only four short chapters earlier. Here too Yorick is gratified by speedy acceptance, but here too he is not at home: 'the better the *Coterie* – the more children of Art – I languish'd for those of Nature' (p. 266). So he leaves Paris, regarding as a 'most vile prostitution' of himself the witty flattery that has enabled him to get on with these people. For Yorick, then, genuine assimilation is as impossible among the children of art as among those of nature. Both modes can be tasted and savored – he recounts the successes of his 'vile prostitution' with evident relish, just as he says that the sweet morsel and the delicious flagon he shared with the Lyonese peasants 'remain upon my palate to this hour' (p. 282) – but neither can engage him fully. He remains the guest, the voyager, the alien, set apart less by his Englishness, his class, or his calling, than by his absorption with the spectacle of himself dealing with other people. Within Yorick seems to lurk a self that observes his doings with charity, with amusement, but in any case with some detachment. This self-consciousness may itself be a means of partially deflecting or eluding the world, a barrier against those who reciprocate Yorick's wish 'to spy the *nakedness* of their hearts' (p. 217). Yorick's ideal is a kind of instant intimacy which leaves him free to post on to the next one. The abruptness with which chapters begin and end, the leaps signified by the long dash, the interjection of fragments labeled 'fragments,' all suggest stylistically and typographically an unwillingness to connect in any sustained way. And all the intense gazing and touching, which proves to be not foreplay but a sentimentally *ersatz* version of consummation itself, is a fair emblem of both how much and how little Yorick manages in the way of human contact and communication.

I have suggested that the sentimental novel holds up as ideals of adult behavior traits associated then as now with infancy. Chief among these is a capacity to feel and to express one's feelings with intensity, spontaneity, and directness; and these feelings run to extremes of elation and distress, not only because youthful susceptibility to both pleasure and pain is still undulled by worldly experience, but also because the child or childlike adult still possesses the power of sympathy in all its freshness, and can thus enter fully and immediately into the joys and sorrows of others. This feature of sentimentalism, already alluded to as a version of pastoralism, is evidently one source of its appeal: we may be unmoved by exhortations to return to our original innocence, but it is gratifying to be able to remain as we are yet recapture the keen sensations that go with innocence. Two weeks after he has met Charlotte and her six little siblings, Werther writes, 'Yes, dear Wilhelm, of all living things on earth, children are closest to my heart. . . . I repeat over and over again the golden words of the Teacher of men: "Except ye become as little children!"' (p. 42). The 'as' is crucial: heroes of sentimental novels may interpret this passage as a divine injunction to regress, but readers of sentimental novels can put a more figurative construction on Christ's words, and without giving up their flawed but comfortably familiar adult selves can momentarily reenter in imagination a world where everything is fresher and simpler and cleaner.

Here one might object that there is great freshness and even a certain kind of simplicity in the world as Yorick perceives it, but that all the *un*cleanness indicates that Sterne was mocking rather than celebrating sentimentalism. In my opinion Sterne does not mock sentimentalism, but adopts various retaliatory strategies against those of his readers who might be inclined to mock. One such strategy is to allow lewdness to enter the novel, but to see to it that the responsibility for putting it there lies with the reader. In the 'Case of Delicacy,' Yorick doesn't tell us what he 'caught hold of': the story breaks off with 'END OF VOL. II,' and any continuation is the work of our own gross minds or John Hall-Stevenson's, not Sterne's. True, Sterne can be said to have anticipated, and even to have deliberately induced this and other bawdy imaginings on the part of his readers; but if this is so, the object of irony is not Yorick's self-deception, as some critics have argued, but the reader's own pretensions to high-mindedness. Other passages might be brought forward, however, in which the 'knowingness' is not confined to author and reader, but shared by Yorick; and when we consider further that the historical Laurence Sterne was at no more pains to distinguish himself from Parson Yorick outside the narrative than he is as author inside the narrative, how much innocence can we persist in claiming for the hero of *A Sentimental Journey*?

Yorick's innocence need not be that of Maria, the 'shorn lamb' whose utter *tristesse de vivre* precludes any sense of taintedness; or that of La Fleur, the *un*shorn lamb whose utter *joie de vivre* has paradoxically the same immunizing effect; or even that of the Abderites, who are reclaimed from vileness and profligacy by the spell of art, and enjoy a return to the golden age marked by sheer obliviousness to their former depravity. Yorick's innocence is not like any of these; he can appreciate sad or cheerful or oblivious innocence, but does so from a perspective of awareness ordinarily found in the narrators and readers rather than the heroes of sentimental novels. One way of getting at what Yorick's innocence does consist of is to consider the motif of impotence.[17] The sentimental novel takes what are commonly looked upon as guilt-arousing, anxiety-producing incapacities and proclaims them special gifts: thus unaggressiveness, gullibility, impracticality, and so on are prized as signs that one remains close to God, one's neighbors, and one's own ideal childlike nature. Approached in this light, sexual impotence is a bold but apt emblem of being outside the compromising fray, of ultimate irreproachability. Like the more common sentimental device of swooning, it is a way of absenting oneself from threatening situations, or of admitting at most an altogether passive presence. Yorick's knight-errantry regularly ends in retreat, and although successive chapters may be entitled 'The Temptation' and 'The Conquest,' this is only because Yorick can proclaim as a 'decisive victory' what would ordinarily be thought of as a humiliating defeat. Yorick's continence is not achieved but thrust upon him, yet his knack of finding in failure itself occasion for triumph is crucial to the sentimental ethos, which puts a premium on a distinctly fugitive sort of virtue. Yorick may undergo chivalric ordeals, but the innocuous outcome of these so-called 'trials' owes less to moral choice or determination on Yorick's part than to physical disability, to the fact that Yorick is (as Sterne facetiously described himself as being) 'totally spiritualized out of all form for connubial purposes' (p. 243n.). This being the case, it seems less appropriate to speak of virtue than of a quixotic innocence, akin to that of God's other helpless 'naturals,' the very young, the very old, the victims of wounds in the groin, and the deranged. In the phrase 'virtue in distress,' then, neither term quite corresponds with my own sense of the predicament of the sentimental hero. Instead of wrestling with the trials and temptations of world, flesh and devil, as the epithet 'virtuous' implies, the sentimental hero seeks to recover a state in which all impulses are in some sense pure, an innocence prior to (rather than triumphant over) guilt and anxiety. For the sentimental heroine, the alternative to total purity is utter depravity; for most sentimental heroes the polarity is less melodramatic, but it nevertheless seems more appropriate to speak (even in Yorick's case) of their innocence than their virtue.

Moreover, for a tale to be sentimental, virtue (or innocence) need not be in distress but merely in jeopardy, and the protagonist may be quite unaware of his danger: the one party who must sense the presence of a threat is the reader. Nor is the reader's pleasure necessarily greater (or more distinctively sentimental) when threats materialize and protagonists actually suffer misfortune; there may be equal pleasure in a tale that transforms harsh settings into what Renato Poggioli calls 'pastoral oases,' and wolves into shepherds.[18] A narrative that challenges in this fashion ordinary sentimental assumptions about the world – that it is populated chiefly by wily predators, and that to remain unscathed one must retreat from it – may itself be thoroughly sentimental.[19]

V

I have maintained that sentimental novels usually involve the quest for a haven secure from the world, but that the very nature of this goal tends to prevent any but fleeting, partial, or symbolic attainments of it short of death; I have suggested that this helps to account for the failure of sentimental novels to achieve much in the way of genuine resolutions, let alone triumphant finales, except when death is the ultimate answer to the problems of hero and author; and I have noted in sentimental novels an absence of the kind of cumulative development that eventually transforms the hero of a *Bildungsroman* into an adult. But different social assumptions about masculinity and femininity make sentimental novels about young ladies significantly different, with respect to each of these contentions, from those about young men, so I should now like to consider briefly what becomes of the sentimental novel when its central figure is not male but female.

The first thing to note is that in the eighteenth century the idea of a woman of feeling was much less anomalous and paradoxical than that of a man of feeling, for it was a role that tended to reinforce rather than subvert common assumptions about femininity. Proneness to tears is weakness, weakness is effeminacy, and effeminacy is shameful – unless one is in fact a woman, in which case such traits are natural and becoming. The sentimental hero violates sexual stereotypes and is praised for doing so, but this calls for a great deal of authorial justification. The creator of a sentimental heroine is not only spared this kind of special pleading, but released from the necessity of portraying the sentimental figure as misunderstood, despised, and alienated from the bulk of society. Since she shares the dovelike innocence and diffidence of the sentimental hero, the sentimental heroine will be similarly vulnerable to the aggressions and duplicities of worldings; but since the qualities that make her vulnerable are those that the community values in young women, the fact that she has them may facilitate her integration into adult society. The sentimental hero is called upon by the world to renounce childlike virtues for manly ones, and chooses not to; the sentimental heroine faces no such impasse, since the virtues demanded of her as a woman remain those prized in her as a child. The transition from boy to man is seen from the sentimental perspective as a fall from grace, from the worldly perspective as a necessary and desirable shedding of puerility, but in either case as a drastic change; whereas all parties see fundamental continuity (not to say identity) between girl and woman. Since the sentimental view of women was not at odds, then, with the view of the world at large, the glorification of sentimental heroines posed no such artistic or ideological challenge as the idealization of sentimental heroes.

At any rate, the incompatibility I have spoken of between the sentimental novel and the *Bildungsroman* scarcely exists when the main character is female; and while the sentimental heroine is seen as a superior person, like her male counterpart, there is nothing eccentric in her position, in relation either to the rest of her own sex or to the opposite sex. Such merging of the sentimental novel with the *Bildungsroman* and of the sentimental heroine with her environment can be seen in a work like Fanny Burney's *Evelina,* which has as its subtitle *The History of a Young Lady's Entrance into the World.*[20] Many features of this world are perceived as alien and threatening – the rakish aggressiveness of Sir Clement Willoughby, the encroaching vulgarity of the Branghtons and Madame Duval, the heartless boisterousness of Captain Mirvan, the mindless arrogance of Mr. Lovel – but instead of driving Evelina out of 'the World,' they themselves are gradually pushed to the margins and Evelina can assume her rightful place at its center. Moreover, this happens without Evelina having to relinquish her feminine passivity. Evelina's worst tormentors, Madame Duval and Lovel, are both brutally scourged by Captain Mirvan, and although critics have been puzzled and disturbed by all the Punch-and-Judy style violence on the part of the Captain, its evident function in the book is to settle scores with Evelina's persecutors without imputing the least trace of vengefulness to the heroine herself.

Evelina is commonly regarded not as a sentimental novel but as a kind of *Bildungsroman* enlivened by social comedy, or as a social comedy given substance and continuity by the 'Entrance into the World' plot. I would not dispute such placings of the book, although some accounts of the heroine's learning and growth strike me as exaggerated; my point is rather that in a book about a young lady, such features can coexist with sentimental ones in a way hardly possible in books about young men. In what ways, then, is *Evelina* a sentimental novel? The work consists largely of Evelina's letters from London, Clifton, and the Bristol Hot-wells to the Reverend Arthur Villars, her adoptive father, at Berry Hill. In the course of the story, Evelina is courted by Lord Orville, no less a paragon in his way than she in hers, and acknowledged as a daughter by Sir John Belmont, who had abandoned Evelina's mother before the heroine's birth. The eighty-fourth and concluding letter from Evelina to Mr. Villars reads as follows: 'All is over, my dearest Sir, and the fate of your Evelina is decided! This morning, with fearful joy, and trembling gratitude, she united herself for ever with the object of her dearest, her eternal affection! I have time for no more; the chaise now waits which is to conduct me to dear Berry Hill, and to the arms of the best of men. EVELINA' (p. 406). Now the ever-considerate Lord Orville had arranged matters so that he and his bride, instead of proceeding directly to his seat in Lincolnshire, would first pass a month with Mr. Villars at Berry Hill; nevertheless there is a certain ambiguity in the final words of Evelina's final letter – 'to dear Berry Hill, and to the arms of the best of men.' It is her wedding day, after all, but the arms of the best of men, in which she and her story are to be wrapped up, appear to be those of her doting foster father.

Evelina is a sentimental novel, then, first of all in showing that you can go home again – and of course in assuming that you want to. But the fact that this family reunion can also accommodate a strange man, in no less a role than that of husband, marks a significant contrast between *Evelina* and sentimental novels with male central figures. Unlike the sentimental hero, the sentimental heroine can be married without forfeiting her title to that character. For Mackenzie's Harley, to marry would mean assuming the roles of dominance, aggressiveness, and general potency which he is intent on avoiding; for an Evelina, marriage involves not a betrayal but a public validation of her submissiveness and general dependence. For this to be so requires a playing down or suppression of any evidence that the young lady is physically attracted to the man, which would jeopardize the innocence indispensable to her character as sentimental heroine. On this matter Burney is very circumspect, not only in her presentation of Evelina herself but in the antithesis she sets up between the two chief young men in Evelina's life, Sir Clement Willoughby and Lord Orville. Burney's aim and method come out clearly in Evelina's saying, 'I could not but remark the striking difference of [Sir Clement's] attention, and that of Lord Orville: the latter has such gentleness of manners, such delicacy of conduct, and an air so respectful, that, when he flatters most, he never distresses, and when he most confers honour, appears to receive it! The former *obtrudes* his attention, and *forces* mine; it is so pointed, that it always confuses me, and so public, that it attracts general notice' (p. 330). The imagery of the second sentence suggests that more than mere 'attention' is at issue: Sir Clement's '*obtrudes*,' is 'pointed,' and is very conspicuous, so that Evelina feels violated and pained by it. However one chooses to interpret Evelina's language, it is clear here and elsewhere that Sir Clement is the embodiment of aggressive masculinity, which is treated as something unsettling not only to the heroine, but to the harmony of society at large. Lord Orville, on the other hand, is carefully desexualized – 'so *feminine* his delicacy,' Evelina exclaims at one point – without being altogether emasculated. He can act boldly, responsibly, and decisively among men, as when he flings out of the room the monkey that has attacked Mr. Lovel and terrified everyone else, yet he is all gentleness, modesty, and tact among women, and particularly with Evelina. This combination – the lion among men who is a lamb before women – marks Lord Orville as distinctly the hero of a female sentimental novel, since the hero of a male sentimental novel tends to be more uniformly lamblike.

The significance for our purposes of a book like *Evelina* can be summed up as follows. In a novel focusing on a young woman, the sentimental ethos can be reconciled with 'Entrance into the World,' since the sentimental heroine epitomizes the popular ideal of what a young woman should be; and such a book can have a coherently progressive plot culminating in marriage without ceasing to be a sentimental novel, since the traits that go to make up a sentimental daughter or sister are those that society continues to look for in wives and mothers. Where women are concerned sentimentalism can be a powerful agent of socialization, a process scarcely possible for the hero of a male sentimental novel. In the female sentimental novel, however, the sentimental male himself need no longer be at odds with society. Through the lion/lamb disjunction, a modicum of conventional masculinity is allowed him, but it is quarantined in clearly designated spheres of male activity, so that he is made amenable to the same kind of socialization and domestication as the heroine herself.

The fact that it could thus be enlisted in the service of social stability and integration helps to explain the long-lived popularity of the female sentimental novel, for it has held out to women the gratifying prospect that their psychological and moral ideals would not unfit them for the world but guarantee their admittance to it on the best possible terms. With the male sentimental novel this has never been the case: instead of mildly expiring, the latter-day sentimental hero may 'light out for the territory,' but there is no more place than ever for him in the world, and his appeal must always be to that side of the reader that similarly 'wants out,' and that responds to the world's challenges as Huck does to the Grangerfords', by saying 'I am only a boy.'

Notes

1. 'For 150 years villainy and articulateness have been confused in the American mind': see Irvin Ehrenpreis, 'The State of Poetry,' *NYRB*, 22 (Jan. 22, 1976), 3.
2. The difficulty faced by most of the characters in *Hard Times* – that to speak well is in a sense to speak badly, and vice versa – is resolved by a narrative voice capable of both urbane lucidity and humane sincerity. Dickens' ideal is

not the speech habits of a Blackpool or Sleary, but a cultivated idiom enlivened by an imaginativeness like Sleary's and an earnestness like Stephen's. Nor is this the only respect in which the narrative voice embraces the positive values yet transcends the 'muddled' limitations of each individual character, thus becoming more exemplary than any one of them.

3. Paul-Gabriel Boucé, *Les Romans de Smollett* (Paris, 1971), pp. 438–39.

4. The term is used by Robert L. Platzner in 'Mackenzie's Martyr: The Man of Feeling as Saintly Fool,' *Novel*, 10 (1976), 59–64.

5. The 'knowingness' that Coleridge speaks of may be peculiar to Yorick among sentimental heroes, but it is a common feature of the third-person narrative voice in sentimental novels. Even in its naive or clichéd forms, the sentimental novel brings together authors and readers significantly unlike its own heroes. The qualities that go to make up a sentimental hero are not those required to create or appreciate such a character, for much the same reason that pastorals are not written by or for the same sort of people they are about. Shepherds untainted by the world which authors and readers inhabit can express unreservedly, or embody with allegorical completeness, various ideals toward which the worldlings are at best ambivalent. The transaction between poet and reader must in some degree pass over the heads of the pastoral figures themselves. To endow them with knowingness would compromise their ability to hold, express, and act upon their views with utter singlemindedness. A penchant for unqualified commitment separates pastoral characters from their authors and readers as much as what they are committed to, and this tends to be true of sentimental heroes as well.

6. Ronald Paulson, *Satire and the Novel in Eighteenth-Century England* (New Haven, 1967), pp. 219–65; R. F. Brissenden, *Virtue in Distress: Studies in the Novel of Sentiment from Richardson to Sade* (New York, 1974), p. 271f.

7. On sentimental optimism vitiating or superseding satire, see Andrew M. Wilkinson, 'The Decline of English Verse Satire in the Middle Years of the Eighteenth Century,' *RES*, n.s. 3 (1952), 222–33, and Paul Fussell, *The Rhetorical World of Augustan Humanism* (Oxford, 1965), pp. 22–24, and *passim*. On sentimental pessimism, Brissenden is most illuminating.

8. One might suppose that a view of man as *not* innately depraved, yet thrust into an irredeemably corrupt and inevitably corrupting world, would inspire an even profounder, more incapacitating gloom than that of the Tory satirists. The sentimental hero often seems inhibited from satire by just such considerations – reinforced, to be sure, by his not wanting to defile himself with its pitch, and by his sense that satire, like most other strenuous, purposeful undertakings, would be an expense of spirit more vexatious to his own nerves than to its thick-skinned objects. But the author of a sentimental novel, whose sense of things is apt to be significantly different from his protagonist's, need not be disabled as a satirist on any of these grounds.

9. Ann Radcliffe, *The Italian* [1797], ed. Frederick Garber (London, 1971), pp. 90–91.

10. An ampler investigation of this topic would have to take into account the provocative central chapters of Thomas Weiskel's *The Romantic Sublime: Studies in the Structure and Psychology of Transcendence* (Baltimore, 1976).

11. Letter to Jane Clemens of October 25, 1861, quoted in Stephen Fender, '"The Prodigal in a Far Country Chawing of Husks": Mark Twain's Search for a Style in the West,' *MLR*, 71 (1976), 741.

12. Daniel Defoe, *Colonel Jack* [1722], ed. Samuel Holt Monk (London, 1965), Introduction, pp. xv–xvi.

13. Henry Mackenzie, *The Man of Feeling* [1771], ed. Brian Vickers (London, 1970).

14. *The Man of Feeling*, p. 17. The relation of Mackenzie to Harley is nearly reversed in the Alice books, where Lewis Carroll is much more sentimental than Alice herself. Mackenzie shares with his reader an amused, urbane superiority that qualifies Harley's infantile tendencies. The reader addressed in Carroll's prefatory poems is an idealized child and the poems themselves are escapist and regressive, yet these sentimental tendencies are somewhat belied by the common-sensical Alice, whose cat Dinah will 'eat a little bird as soon as look at it' without Alice thinking the worse of her for it. Thus Lewis Carroll can be described as sentimental although his heroine cannot, whereas both textual and biographical evidence suggest that the creator of the quintessentially sentimental Harley was a shrewd, genial, robust person. A totally, homogeneously sentimental novel could never get itself written, authorship itself being an unsentimental assumption of authority. On the sentimental pretence that 'no sophisticated "author" mediates between the reader and the work,' see the interesting remarks of Leo Braudy in 'The Form of the Sentimental Novel,' *Novel*, 7 (1973), 5–13, p. 6.

15. David Hume, *A Treatise of Human Nature* [1739], ed. L. A. Selby-Bigge (Oxford, 1896), p. 375.

16. Laurence Sterne, *A Sentimental Journey through France and Italy by Mr. Yorick* [1768], ed. Gardner D. Stout, Jr. (Berkeley and Los Angeles, 1967).

17. Sexual impotence – which 'hovers like a dubious halo over the head of every Shandy male, including the bull' (James A. Work, Introduction to *Tristram Shandy* [New York, 1940], p. ix) – has been variously interpreted by commentators on *A Sentimental Journey*: cf. John A. Dussinger, *The Discourse of the Mind in Eighteenth-Century Fiction* (The Hague, 1974), pp. 188 f., and (on the significance of 'a refusal of sexual consummation') Braudy, p. 12.

18. My notion of the pastoral-sentimental relationship owes much to Poggioli's two essays, 'The Oaten Flute,' *Harvard Library Bulletin*, 11 (1957), 147–84, and 'Naboth's Vineyard Or The Pastoral View of the Social Order,' *JHI*, 24 (1963), 3–24; cf. also William Empson on the Alice books in *Some Versions of Pastoral* (New York, 1950), pp. 253–94.

19. A good example – trifling artistically, but interesting thematically – is a short story by Elbert Hubbard called 'Five Babies' (*The Mintage* [East Aurora, 1910], pp. 9–15). On a midwestern railroad journey, the narrator encounters five children aged from three to ten travelling alone from Germany to Chicago, where their grandmother is to meet them. 'But to be alone in Chicago would be terrible! Would she come? . . . "Will she be there – will she be there?" I asked myself nervously' (pp. 11, 12). Grandmother *is* there, it turns out; meanwhile passengers and staff have vied in kindly solicitude toward 'the babies.' We glimpse a latter-day incarnation of the outwardly unsentimental benevolist, a 'big, bold, bluff, and bronzed' conductor, 'beneath his brass buttons a heart beating with a desire to bless and benefit.' Hubbard finds the spectacle 'something to renew one's faith in humanity,' eventually concluding from the episode that 'Even a great Railway System has a soul.'

    Few readers whose belief in the souls of corporations had been shaken by *The Jungle* could have had their faith restored by 'Five Babies.' My point is that this little essay in boosterism stands in a sentimental tradition, and appeals to a sentimental response, even though innocence is represented as communally cherished rather than distressed. Here on the Grand Trunk

Railway there are none of the Confidence Men of the steamboat *Fidele*. Hubbard does not deny that innocence may be persecuted, led astray, or neglected – indeed, the story owes its minimal suspense to our sense that evil *can* befall these lambs en route to Chicago – but he endorses the Dickensian principle that encountering true innocence is more likely to bring out the vestigial good even in the worst of us.

20. Fanny Burney, *Evelina* [1778], ed. Edward A. Bloom (London, 1968).

3 Deserts, Ruins and Troubled Waters: Female Dreams in Fiction and the Development of the Gothic Novel

MARGARET ANNE DOODY

Margaret Doody is one of the most versatile critics and scholars of eighteenth-century literature, with important books on Richardson, eighteenth-century poetry, Frances Burney, and the history of the novel to her name (see Introduction to *The English Novel Volume I: 1700 to Fielding*, pp. 11–12). She is also one of the most influential feminist critics in the Anglo-American mode. This essay represents two of her strengths as a feminist critic. In its descriptive dimension, it greatly expands the reader's knowledge of the range and kind of novels by women in the later eighteenth century (the thoroughness of the descriptions necessitates some editing of plot summary and quotations). For example, she claims that Sophia Lee's *The Recess* (1783–85) is the first fully developed English gothic novel and the first historical novel in English. In its critical dimension, Doody's essay shows how the improbable devices associated with sentimental and gothic fiction – dreams, nightmares, madness – serve as means for women to articulate their peculiar pain and anxiety within patriarchal society.

> My Harriet has been telling me how much she suffered lately from a dream, which she permitted to give strength and terror to her apprehensions from Mr. Greville. Guard, my dear Ladies, against these imbecillities of tender minds. In these instances, if no other, will you give a superiority to our Sex. . . .[1]

So says Richardson's Sir Charles Grandison, airily dismissing Harriet's disturbing sequence of nightmares. Sir Charles voices the accepted rational and masculine view. In eighteenth century English fiction, until the appearance of the Gothic novel, it is women, not men, who have dreams. Masculine characters rarely dream; those who do are usually simpletons whose dreams can be jocosely interpreted. Heroes are not dreamers.

This certainly marks a change from earlier literature. In Elizabethan and Jacobean drama, for instance, men have very vivid dreams. In the seventeenth century all sorts of men regarded dreams as significant, bearing a message from God. Men with diverse religious views, such as Laud and Bunyan, thought their dreams worth recording. The credit given to dreams became associated with religious wars, fanaticism, and all kinds of irrational and useless behavior. In the eyes of later generations, reality is the thing. Defoe alone among the novelists maintains an old tradition, believing in the spiritual import of dreams and prophetic apparitions. His central characters, male and female, have revelatory dreams. But Defoe was considered a writer for the low, the unenlightened. In polite eighteenth-century fiction, men – if they are admirable, if they are strong – must be shown to be in touch with reality; they exert rational control without idiosyncratic private assistance from the Voice of God and without any awkward manifestations of the unconscious self. Men belong to the scientific world rather than to that of superstition; hence, they do not have prophetic dreams or premonitions. They exercise masculine authority in a world whose ways, even if sometimes distasteful, are comprehensible. They are either essentially in control, or they are failures, deserving of pity or contempt. The strong man does not have the dreams or nightmares which reveal self-division or perturbation. The only real exception is Lovelace, whose remarkable dream is a sign of (deserved) disintegration and dereliction, and who appears in a novel which has its roots in seventeenth-century comprehension of experience. Even there, the dream is connected with, and serves as a punishment for, Lovelace's moral madness. As Michael DePorte has shown, eighteenth-century psychology saw dreaming and madness as closely connected, and was frightened of both.[2] [. . .]

Masculine novelists must show the world of men as objective, not subjective. The same considerations do not apply, or not quite in the same way, to the presentation of women. Richardson, whose guiding interest was in the subjective, necessarily wrote about women. Clarissa, in her dreams and madness, is not morally reprehensible. *Grandison*, more completely a novel of its time than *Clarissa*, has a hero who is supposed to epitomize all the current conceptions of good masculinity; it is the women around the hero who have weaknesses and perturbation. It is the women who have dreams. Sir Charles teases Harriet about having allowed herself to be affected by 'a dream, a resverie,' and the embarrassed heroine confesses apologetically, 'I own I should have made a very silly, a very pusilanimous [*sic*] man' (III, 248). Dreaming is feminine; men are not to be subjected to inner terrors.

Women, weaker than men, not in control of their environment, are permitted to have dreams. The censorship of dreaming doesn't quite apply to them. Officially, in the eighteenth century, women are thought of as weak and superstitious; they have something of an archaic consciousness, not enjoying the full benefits of masculine reason and masculine knowledge of reality. Their dreaming is not necessarily insanity, nor is it the sign of an unbecoming and ignoble weakness. A female character can be shown as dreaming – or having nightmares or delusions – without forfeiting the reader's respect. The 'imbecillities of tender minds' are not unattractive. A female dreamer does not seem comic, nor need the fact that she dreams be interpreted as a distasteful psychic dereliction. Women are often seen as living an inward life rather different from that of men, whose consciousness is more definitely related to the objective world and to action within it. Women, less able to plan and execute actions, are seen as living a life closer to the dream-like, and closer to the dream-life.

That this is so can be seen in Pope's presentations of both Belinda and Eloisa. The dreams of both are related to their sexual natures, and to disturbances about their sexual nature. It has often been pointed out that the imagery in *Eloisa to Abelard* prefigures the Gothic manner:

methinks we wandring go
Thro' dreary wastes, and weep each other's woe;
Where round some mould'ring tow'r pale ivy creeps,
And low-brow'd rocks hang nodding o'er the deeps.
(ll. 241–44)

This imagery – the imagery of the sublime – is certainly present in the national consciousness, but can be used freely here precisely because the poet is dealing with a woman's experience. When we read *The Dunciad* we may wonder if the sublime and the dreamlike are not both thought of as dangerously associated with the feminine; it is the 'mighty Mother' who threatens masculine rational objectivity. In *Eloisa* Pope treats his subject sympathetically. There is no need to ask about meaning or sense aside from the psychological. Eloisa need not be asked to do anything in the objective world because she cannot. There is no event in the poem; the poem is Eloisa, that passive victim and active dreamer whose sexual nature is inseparably associated with pain, dread and guilt. When the feminine is feminine, there is no need for hostility. We do not need to ask, while reading about Eloisa's dream, if the character is evincing the inferiority of her sex and the superiority of the other – ultimately, she is, perhaps, but we need take her only as she is, attending to her experience. The poem was popular with women, especially with the ladies of the town, who must have taken the work as a vindication of feminine passion.

When women writers themselves describe feminine dreams, the effects are both similar to and different from those in Pope's poems. In writing novels the women writers, although dealing with the objective everyday world, felt free to include dream experience as part of the heroine's life. Unlike Defoe, they do not follow the old tradition which relates the dream to the promptings of God or the Devil. Female novelists interest themselves in the psychology of the heroine; her subjective life has meaning, and her dreams cry out for interpretation, but not the old religious meaning or spiritual interpretation. The reader's sympathetic understanding of the dream rises from an understanding of the character in her situation. The dreams delineated by women writers are much lonelier and more complex than those which Pope describes. What gives rise to the dream may not be quite what we expect, and the dream-content is powerfully related to the sense of individuality under attack. Women's heroines usually are not as simply hopeful as Belinda or as simply grief-stricken as Eloisa. In an apparently placid situation the heroine's relationship to a lover or to marriage may be fraught with anxiety amounting to dread. The heroine has a strong but divided sense of self, and the self is usually suffering from something more complicated than simple desire or simple grief. Some sort of good self-realization is being thwarted, and tension and terror arise from a sense of incomplete and unsatisfactory alternatives. The pain is related to the woman's sexual nature; the sexual nature and the whole sense of identity do not coincide satisfactorily, and the individual is threatened with severe loss.

One of the most interesting examples of the disturbing feminine dream occurs in Jane Barker's *Love Intrigues: The History of the Amours of Bosvil and Galesia* (1713). The heroine is in a constant state of uneasy suspense about her relationship to Bosvil and his on-again-off-again courtship (if that is what it is). When Bosvil appears to have abandoned her, the heroine goes for solitary rambles and begins to write poetry. Deciding to dedicate herself to her work, she writes verses on an ash tree in a grove:

Methinks these Shades, strange Thoughts suggest,
Which heat my Head, and cool my Breast;
And mind me of a Laurel Crest.

Methinks I hear the Muses sing,
And see 'em all dance in a Ring;
And call upon me to take wing.

We will (say they) assist thy Flight,
Till thou reach fair ORINDA's Height,

If thou can'st this World's Follies slight.
. . .
Then gentle Maid cast off they Chain,
Which links thee to thy faithless Swain,
And vow a Virgin to remain.

After this self-dedication, Galesia devotes herself to poetry and study: 'Thus I thought to become *Apollo*'s Darling Daughter, and Maid of Honour to the Muses.'[3] Her activities become important in themselves, but when Bosvil returns and appears to be on the point of a declaration she drops her studies. Things are apparently going prosperously, but she is still in a state of suspense about herself and her future. While in this state of suspense, she has an important dream:

> I thought my self safe landed on Love's Shore, where no cross Wind, unseen Accident, cou'd oppose my Passage to *Hymen*'s Palace, or wrack me in this Harbour of true Satisfaction. . . . Now my Thoughts swam in a Sea of Joy, which meeting with the Torrent of the foresaid Vexations, made a kind of dangerous Rencounter, ready to overset my Reason. I pass'd some Nights without Sleep, and Days without Food, by reason of this secret Satisfaction. At last, being overcome with a little Drowsiness, I fell asleep in a Corner of our Garden, and dream'd, that on a suddain, an angry Power carried me away, and made me climb a high mountain: at last brought me to that Shade where I had heretofore writ those Verses on the Bark of an Ash, as I told you, in which I seem'd to prefer the Muses, and a studious Life, before that of Marriage, and Business. Whereupon,
>
> — *My uncouth Guardian said,*
> — *Unlucky Maid!*
> *Since, since thou has the Muses chose,*
> Hymen *and Fortune are thy Foes.*
>
> (pp. 32–33)

In a later edition of this novel (1719) the dream is more surprisingly revealing:

> . . . a mountain where I met *Bosvil*, who endeavour'd to tumble me down, but I thought the aforesaid Power snatch'd me away, and brought me to that Shade. . . .[4]

The dream is not related only to Galesia's lover, or even primarily to her repressed passion for him. The dream is related to her own sense of an enforced choice, and to a decision she must make about her own nature. If she is 'Apollo's Daughter,' she must give over the desire for marriage, for sexual fulfillment. She recognizes and fears the penalty of sexual frustration even while her own sense of herself makes her unhappily reject the man she loves. Her own will does not govern the nature of the alternatives. In the second (and unexpurgated?) version of the dream, the high mountain represents a freedom from anxiety, a sexual aspiration fulfilled – but it cannot be obtained after all; she is transported back to the 'Shade' of her intellect. In some fashion she knows that the affair with Bosvil will never mature (as it does not – the subtitle of the story is ironic). What makes the dream terrifying is the helplessness, the sense of being 'snatch'd away' from fulfillment and being compelled to confront the truth about herself. A modern psychological allegorist must inevitably see the 'power' as representing not just Fate (though external conditions make this division inevitable), nor the irresistible power of Apollo, but Galesia's inner nature which makes a bitter choice her will does not know how to make. She had made a life for herself without Bosvil, and this has been more than a substitute for him. She had decided on a single life (in which she could use her intellect) – although she didn't expect herself to take her at her word. Her dream-journey travels over the landscape of her divided self – and the dream vision powerfully intimates anxiety and loss.

[. . .]

There is an eighteenth-century heroine who is very firmly 'of *Don Quixote*'s Sentiments.' Arabella in *The Female Quixote* (1752) determinedly lives her life in a kind of dream reverie. By imagining that the real world is like that of her favorite romances, she interprets everything as she pleases, in the only manner which appears to allow importance to feminine nature. Unlike Don Quixote's illusions the attractive Arabella's much simpler ones are almost entirely related to her sexual nature. Her desire for and fear of men both have real meaning; men rule her world, and pay little attention to the female identity. The dream-life is also well-designed to protect her from her basic anxiety: that she is a woman and thus does not count for much, that all her actions will be controlled and that everything about her is to be made safe and dull.

As the Countess informs the heroine, good respectable women do not have adventures, and they have no histories.[5] That nothing should ever happen to one, that a strong consciousness should never be allowed to emerge – this is the most frightening anxiety of all. It is no wonder that the adolescent girl defers recognition of this for as long as possible, and that she does not care for images of safe plateaux. She makes a history for herself and reconstructs the landscape into the landscape of romance and dream. In the long conversation with the divine who ultimately helps to convert her to right-mindedness, Arabella gives up her imagery only under protest:

> What then should have hinder'd him from placing me in a Chariot? Driving it into the pathless Desart? And immuring me in a Castle, among Woods and Mountains? Or hiding me perhaps in the Caverns of a Rock? Or confining me in some Island of an immense Lake?
>
> From all this, Madam, interrupted the Clergyman, he is hinder'd by Impossibility.
>
> He cannot carry you to any of these dreadful Places, because there is no such Castle, Desart, Cavern, or Lake.
>
> You will pardon me, Sir, said *Arabella*, if I recur to your own Principles:
>
> . . .
>
> Universal Negatives are seldom safe, and are least to be allow'd where the Disputes are about Objects of Sense; where one Position cannot be inferr'd from another.
>
> That there is a Castle, any Man who has seen it may safely affirm. But you cannot with equal Reason, maintain that there is no Castle, because you have not seen it.
>
> . . .
>
> Castles indeed, are the Works of Art; and are therefore subject to Decay. But Lakes, and Caverns, and Desarts, must always remain.[6]

We rather agree with Arabella, that 'Lakes, and Caverns, and Desarts must always remain' – that they certainly remain as part of the landscape of the mind. This is strikingly borne out by a passage in a highly realistic novel which appeared about the same time. The heroine of Eliza Haywood's *The History of Miss Betsy Thoughtless* (1751) portrays an archetypal young coquette, but there is more to her than that; she has a strong personality, and the author represents her sympathetically, making the reader understand the causes of Betsy's 'thoughtlessness' and appreciate the mixed and often irrational and unconscious motives for her actions. After several false flirtations, and after losing Trueworth, the man she really loves, Betsy is in an emotional condition to accept the control of her guardians, who wish to settle her in marriage. A marriage is soon arranged between Betsy and the apparently pleasant and wealthy Mr. Munden – whom Betsy does not dislike, but whom she does not really know. The girl suddenly realizes that she is engaged [she goes to bed and has a dream]:

[. . .]

> In this humour she went to bed, nor did sleep present her with images more pleasing; – sometimes she imagined herself standing on the brink of muddy, troubled waters; – at others, that she was wandering through desarts, overgrown with thorns and briars, or seeking to find a passage through some ruin'd building, whose tottering roof seemed ready to fall upon her head, and crush her to pieces.
>
> These gloomy representations, amidst her broken slumbers, when vanished, left behind them an uncommon heaviness upon her waking mind: – she rose, – but it was only to throw herself into a chair, where she sat for a considerable time, like one quite stupid and dead to all sensations of every kind.[7]

Like Galesia's, this dream results from an apprehension of the self under attack, and from a sense of severe loss which cannot be exactly defined. The heroine has been disturbed by a sense that there are alternatives which her world does not acknowledge as real. Her questioning is accompanied by sharp resentment: 'they want to deprive us of all the pleasures of life, just when one begins to have a relish for them.' Her articulate resentment does not make her less helpless; the dream urges upon her the truth about her loneliness and danger, facts which are too large to be contained in (or dismissed by) her unhappy articulate ruminations. In Betsy's dream the images of Arabella's romance are present, but transformed and given new vividness by dread. The dreamer is trying to go somewhere – away from or towards something? – but her passage is slow and fearful. She is threatened by 'annihilation'; the world is terribly unsafe. The subjective consciousness tells her truths which her real everyday world will not acknowledge. In this novel the author has identified the heroine's condition and her dream with the difficulties attendant upon woman's role and woman's lot. The author, through her heroine, makes a generalization which the reader is intended to recognize. The dreamer does not merely present an idiosyncratic individual problem. Frightening images, 'gloomy representations' are the necessary and appropriate symbols of the consciousness of unhappy women – imprisoned by social conventions, threatened by slavery, and plagued by loneliness. Betsy's world cheerfully bears her off to the marriage with Munden, a union disastrous in all respects. Her intuitions were right, but there seemed to be no way for her to make her intuitions count in the real world.

Betsy's dream embodying her fear of marriage finds an interesting parallel in the experience of another and much more admirable heroine, the creation of a first-rate male novelist. Richardson's Harriet Byron dreams very vividly before her approaching marriage – a marriage not to a man she barely knows, but to the man she most desires. Richardson, never a simple novelist, does not imagine that an apparently idyllic prospect is a simple matter for the woman concerned.[8] Harriet is at the point of her life where she should be most happy; the man whom she feared she had lost to the beautiful Italian, Clementina, has been set free to return to her and express his love. Yet, now that she is faced with a reality instead of the unrequited love she has been nourishing for so long, her unconscious mind reveals that she is far from being totally at one with herself in her response to a new, unexpected and very demanding 'happiness.' It is she who has insisted on continuing in a state of suspense, telling Sir Charles that she wishes him to hear from Italy before she marries him, thus giving her rival time to change her mind; Sir Charles is sure all is settled.

In her shifting nightmare visions, objective fears (that her rejected suitor may attack Sir Charles) mingle with less exact and less obvious ones. Her resentment of Sir Charles for his love of Clementina, her guilt about taking him from somebody else, and her fear of the man himself, with his total righteousness and domineering masculinity – all these mingle in shifting visions which express a very tense (and intense) life going on beneath the surface of the happily engaged girl. Her earlier anxious puzzling over the case of Clementina (who, she has thought, 'deserved' Sir Charles more than she) is not at an end. The land she has never seen asserts itself in her dreams, as Italy and England (that is, Clementina and Harriet) exchange their natures. Everything is shifting, unstable, expressive of different kinds of loss. Harriet's series of dreams arises from a highly charged sexual state, and presents a panic about identity and about the future. She later tells Sir Charles about part of it (not the whole), and Grandison can dismiss it as 'a dream, a resverie' unworthy the attention of an intelligent being. That is not what Harriet or the reader feels – we, like the heroine, are compelled to experience something frightening and significant:

> . . . going immediately from my pen to my rest, I had it broken and disturbed by dreadful, shocking, wandering dreams. The terror they gave me, several times awakened me; but still, as I closed my eyes, I fell into them again. Whence, my dear, proceed these ideal vagaries, which for the time, realize pain or pleasure to us, according to their hue or complexion, or rather according to our own?
>
> But such *contradictory* vagaries never did I know in my slumbers. Incoherencies of incoherence! – For example – I was married to the best of men: I was *not* married: I was rejected with scorn, as a

presumptuous creature. I sought to hide myself in holes and corners. I was dragged out of a subterraneous cavern, which the sea had made when it once broke bounds, and seemed the dwelling of howling and conflicting winds; and when I expected to be punished for my audaciousness, and for repining at my lot, I was turned into an Angel of light; stars of diamonds, like a glory, encompassing my head: A dear little baby was put into my arms. Once it was Lucy's; another time it was Emily's; and at another time Lady Clementina's! – I was fond of it, beyond expression.

I again dreamed I was married: Sir Charles again was the man. He did not love me. My grandmamma and aunt, on their knees, and with tears, besought him to love their child; and pleaded to him my Love of him of long standing, begun in gratitude; and that he was the only man I ever loved. O how I wept in my dream! . . .

My sobs, and my distress and *theirs*, awakened me; but I dropt asleep, and fell into the very same resverie. He upbraided me with being the cause that he had not Lady Clementina. He said, and *so* sternly! I am sure he cannot look so sternly, that he thought me a much better creature than I proved to be: Yet methought, in my own heart, I was not altered. I fell down at his feet. I called it my misfortune, that he could not love me. . . . And then I said, Love and Hatred are not always in one's power. If you cannot love the poor creature who kneels before you, *that* shall be a cause sufficient with me for a divorce. . . . I will bind myself never, never to marry again; but you shall be free – And God bless you, and her you can love better than your poor Harriet. Fool! I weep as I write! . . .

In another part of my resverie he loved me dearly; but when he nearly approached me, or I him, he always became a ghost, and flitted from me. Scenes once changed from England to Italy, from Italy to England: Italy, I thought, was a dreary wild, covered with snow, and pinched with frost: England, on the contrary, was a country glorious to the eye; gilded with a sun not too fervid; the air perfumed with odours, wafted by the most balmy Zephyrs from orange-trees, citrons, myrtles, and jasmines. In Italy, at one time, Jeronymo's wounds were healed; at another, they were breaking out afresh. . . . There was a fourth brother, I thought; and he, taking part with the cruel Laurana, was killed by the General. . . .

But still, what was more shocking, and which so terrified me that I awoke in a horror which put an end to all my resveries (for I slept no more that night) – Sir Charles, I thought, was assassinated by Greville. Greville fled his country for it, and became a vagabond, a Cain, the Accursed, I thought, of God and Man – I, your poor Harriet, a widow. . . .

(*Grandison*, III, 148–49)

The reader is invited to unravel the dreams, to answer Harriet's question 'whence proceed these ideal vagaries?' They are all related to the heroine's experience, and make a good deal of sense. Harriet has long desired Sir Charles and has feared that he rightly judges her as inferior to her rival. The first part of her dreaming expresses fear of rejection, her sense of guilt and unworthiness. The sequence winds from the image-filled sets of strong sensational impressions (cavern, sea, winds, diamonds, baby) to a rationalized scenario in the terms of social realities (in the social world, the worst final rejection is to be divorced, and this Sir Charles could inflict upon her). That rationalized dream allows an imagined dialogue, but the images insisting on worth have been negated. The reassuring picture of herself crowned like the Virgin Mary, and blessed with a child which belongs to all the rejected women, gives way to a scene of humiliating feminine supplication. Then the dreaming plunges again into disintegrated and wild impressions and images which words cannot reach. Sir Charles is a ghost – or she is – so they cannot approach each other. Scenes change. Italy (which she has feared) is cold; England (herself) becomes warmly Mediterranean; this must be at least in part Harriet's assertion that she has as much warmth and passion as the Italian lady. The dreams become more violent. In real life, Clementina's brother Jeronymo (whom Harriet has never met) has been wounded in a manner that implies he has lost, if not his manhood, any future hope of exercising that manhood. This Italian Fisher-King, who has adopted Sir Charles as his brother, is in the dream evidently another manifestation of the unsatisfactory lover himself. Clementina's 'fourth brother' is actually Sir Charles, the adopted brother; here he is imagined as being cruel to Clementina, in company with Clementina's worst persecutor, her cousin Laurana. If the cruel cousin had made Clementina's insanity worse, it was Sir Charles, unsatisfactory suitor of the Italian girl, who caused her madness in the first place. Harriet is at once identifying herself with Clementina, tormented by Sir Charles, and also 'killing off' the Sir Charles who was once the lover of Clementina. But in killing the 'bad' Sir Charles who did what Harriet did not like, the dreamer is also killing the 'good' Sir Charles whom she loves – so there is a real connection between what precedes her last dream of horror and that dream itself. The last dream, which awoke her in 'horror,' is a more rational one. The anger, frustration, and vengefulness are projected entirely upon Greville – who in real life poses the only threat to Sir Charles's safety. In that last dream Harriet's suitor abandons her unwillingly, but the loss is more final, more certain, than the others.

In her dreaming the English girl who is engaged to the best of men has actually adapted a nightmare of her rival as described in a letter which Harriet has read. Clementina, who has gone mad from love for the man who is not a Catholic and whom her family will not, in effect, permit her to marry, also dreams out of a sense of loss. Her loss, one which is very real, is associated with severe doubt about her own identity, and with an anxious sense of guilt. At one important point, Sir Charles has said a final farewell to the family and left Bologna without Clementina's being allowed to know of his departure. When she does not see him, she imagines that her irascible brother, the General, has murdered their guest:

> She took Camilla under the arm – Don't you know, Camilla, said she, what you heard said of Somebody's threatening Somebody? – Don't let anybody hear us. . . . I want to take a walk with you into the garden, Camilla.
>
> It is a dark night, madam. . . . Be pleased to tell me, madam, what we are to walk in the garden for?
>
> Why, Camilla, I had a horrid dream last night; and I cannot be easy till I go into the garden.
>
> What, madam, was your dream?
>
> In the Orange-grove, I thought I stumbled over the body of a dead man!
>
> And who was it, madam?
>
> Don't you know who was threatened? And was not Somebody here tonight? And was not Somebody to sup here? And *is* he here?
>
> The General then went to her. My dearest Clementina; my beloved sister; set your heart at rest. Somebody is safe: Shall be safe.
>
> She took first one of his hands, then the other; and looking in the palms of them, They are not bloody, said she. – What have you done with him, then? Where is he?
>
> Where is who? –
>
> You know whom I ask after; but you want some-thing against me. (II, 241)

Neither Clementina's nor Harriet's dream is prophetic; although each is used to heighten suspense (about possible violence to Sir Charles), that is not the main function. Each of these dreams is most strongly related to the psychological state of the dreamer, accurately depicting the acute fears of her helpless condition. These dreams are true, not as prophecies of the future but as expressions of a subjective reality and of the imperfections in both subjective and objective worlds. We see in them what an outer, uncontrollable world has done to the inner life, and not a mere reprehensible derangement. It is noticeable that Clementina's dream is shorter than Harriet's, less complex, betraying no impulse to rationalize or re-arrange; in her dreams, as in everything else, Clementina tends to accept what is given her. In her dream she expresses her knowledge of the violence of the oppressive family which is trying to 'kill' what she desires. Confusing dream with reality, in the liberty of her madness, she can look for tokens of bloodshed on the hands of her family, thus accusing them as her unconscious mind accuses them; she does not feel *safe* with her family. With the foolish but not senseless cunning born of 'insane' secret insight, she refuses to utter the name of the man she loves, as her family are punishing her for loving him; she treats the family as a tribunal before which she must not commit herself: 'you want something against me.' She would prefer to go into the imprisoning and maze-like garden rather than to stay and talk. She would rather find the corpse than talk to the murderers.

Both dreams invite the reader to participate in the dreamer's vision; he must not accept either dream as presenting literal scientific truth of fact, but he must allow images and emotions to play on his sensibility. The combined imagery of 'garden,' 'dark night,' 'Orange-grove' and 'dead man' is powerful: darkness over Eden, life and fruitfulness giving way to death, fear, sexual loss. That potent image-cluster recurs, elaborated, in Harriet's dream with its magnificent sequence of images: 'subterraneous cavern,' 'howling winds,' 'diamonds,' 'baby,' 'tears,' 'ghost,' 'dreary wild,' 'snow,' 'frost,' 'sun,' 'orange trees, citrons, myrtles and jasmines' – all ending again with the corpse of Sir Charles. Clementina mad and miserable, Harriet sane and happily engaged, both inhabit a dream-world of loneliness, helplessness and dread which the reader is invited to share and understand. Dreams assist them in their struggle for self-knowledge, for fuller being. Dreams are not trifling or contemptible – if the dreamer is a woman. Even Richardson, with his strong respect for the value of subjectivity, could not show a good man having dreams or being affected by them. In a man such dreaming would be (as Harriet shamefacedly admits) 'pusillanimous.' But that is hardly a defect in a woman, and her dreams and fantasies can be fully expressed, because they pose no threat to the public rational order. If Sir Charles were to dream, the ranged arch of empire might fall.

Richardson's enquiring and sympathetic view of feminine dreaming extends to a view of madness – feminine madness – which is curiously out of keeping with the general notions of his time. DePorte quite truly says that the Augustan age distrusted a subjectivity of which madness was the final expression, and identified madness with egotism: 'The lunatic is typically represented as a person with no sense of limit.' This never quite applied, I think, to women; their breaking down is often seen more tenderly, as in the case of Belvidera in *Venice Preserved*. Fictional women often go mad because more is put upon them than they can bear; they are often fragile, deficient in egotism rather than guilty of an excessive sense of self. This tradition of feminine madness (especially in drama) permitted Richardson to draw the sympathetic and virtuous Clarissa and Clementina. There is an important difference between his presentation of female madness and that of the stage-plays. Richardson's heroines' madness does not mark the end of their lives. Madness is a phase through which the heroine lives and from which she learns; it arises from an insufficient and underdeveloped sense of self, and pushes the woman onward to a stronger and more integrated state of being. Derangement has its creative aspects, as Jung and R. D. Laing were later to point out. The intensity of the heroines' experience supplies something which commonplace life denies, and which social life tends (often wrongly) to deny to women. After Richardson, other eighteenth-century novelists of both sexes could feel safely justified in portraying the good heroine going mad and emerging from this experience with some access of strength.

Masculine madness is a much more tricky subject; indeed, in most eighteenth-century literature it could not be presented at all, save as a sign of consummate folly, or of vice reaping its reward. To say a *man* is mad is the perfect insult (see *The Dunciad*). Smollett met with failure in *Launcelot Greaves* because his hero – a young Quixote – could not be accommodated either by the novel form or by novel readers; the author eventually plays safe by indicating that the hero's derangement is just a game, a sham role he can drop at will. It is the heroine who has the more distressing experience of being shut away in a madhouse, and the hero who gallantly rescues her. Smollett's interests lay beyond, while including, the satiric, but he perpetually has to return to the acceptability of satire. His interest in pathological states is a remarkable feature of his works, although he never quite managed to give full embodiment to his perceptions.

Madness or derangement in a man is associated with the ideas of failure and ridicule; in orthodox eighteenth-century literature its point is satiric and not psychological. Launcelot Greaves moves through an outer world, not, like Arabella Stanley and Female Quixote, through inner regions. Geoffrey Wildgoose, the Spiritual Quixote, has no identity beyond being a satiric caricature of the absurdities of Methodism as his author sees them. It is no wonder that Mackenzie's *The Man of Feeling* (1771) seems such an odd novel, and has puzzled so many readers, some holding that it exalts sensibility while showing the cruelty of a world which denies it, others holding that it ridicules sensibility by showing the absurdity of its excess in relation to the real world. The novel does both, unevenly. Mackenzie, a good but not a great novelist, could not get out of the problem he had set himself, for he was too much a man of his age not to want to laugh at a man who can't manage the real world. There is no possible end except killing the hero off before he does anything of importance, like getting married. A man who is so pusillanimous is too mentally impotent to be fully sexual.[9] *Tristram Shandy* deals with a kind of madness by recreating Renaissance comedy about theories and the workings of the reason. In comically asserting the madness of us all, it gets away from madness as suffering, or madness as threat. The world is irrational (but entertaining) and we are absurd if we take ourselves too seriously. In that kind of festive madness born of science, women have no place. (The dull Mrs. Shandy has no hobby-horse.) The novel talks about suffering, while insulating us from it, just as all good surrealist farce does. We don't worry about the mental states of the Marx brothers in their films, or the Monty Python characters – neither do we feel grief or dread about Walter and Toby. *Tristram Shandy* is a brilliant manifestation of a comic art which makes masculine responsibility tolerable. It essentially affirms what it appears to deny. Sterne's way of dealing with masculine aberration is the only one that can work perfectly in mid-eighteenth-century literature.

The difference between concepts of men and women in the period can be seen in the simple and striking fact that feminine madness is not funny, whereas masculine madness is an almost irresistible source of jest. Female madness is not funny because women never have quite the sort of sanity that is demanded of men. They never have rational control of the world, so when they lose rational control of themselves they are not contradicting their essential nature. A woman may be deranged without losing credibility, sexual attractiveness, or value. The women novelists themselves become fond of presenting female characters who temporarily lose their reason and enter into a heightened state of morbid perceptiveness. In a realistic novel the heroine's venture into an hallucinatory state is perhaps the wildest 'adventure' she can be allowed (compare Arabella); the women novelists also found in the presentation of an extraordinarily irrational state a means of expressing the extreme of feminine pain, and of giving that full value as an experience without the encumbrance of sententious precepts about contentment, good conduct, and good sense. As in the cases of the dreaming heroines, we have the pattern of uneasy loss leading to a crisis which precipitates an anguished vision. The bounds of reality dissolve, and the heroine is left alone in delirious terror which is more insistent and prevalent than a dream – the nightmare terror takes control for a while of vision, actions, and speech.

The heroine of Fanny Burney's *Cecilia, or Memoirs of an Heiress* (1782), a woman of pleasant good sense in a society which is neither kind nor sensible, is subjected to increasing pressures by people who see her only as 'an Heiress.' Constantly robbed of value and always threatened by the loss of the man she loves, she undergoes an anxiety which even her secret marriage to her lover, Delvile, does not solve. Already suffering from guilt and from uncertainty about the future, she then hears that Delvile has been injured in a duel. She, like the dreamers but more violently, then loses self-control and acts out her worst fears as she rushes frantically about the London streets in search of her husband, obsessed by the idea that he is both injured and in danger from the law. [She finally falls breathless and panting on the floor of a pawnbroker's shop.] [. . .]

In the pawn-broker's shop Cecilia is given refuge, and treated as a madwoman; the woman of the house, having locked her in a chamber, brings her a quantity of straw, 'having heard that mad people were fond of it.' Cecilia can recognize no one; her maid is astonished and afflicted by what she finds:

> She wept bitterly while she enquired at the bed-side how her lady did, but wept still more, when, without answering, or seeming to know her, Cecilia started up, and called out, 'I must be removed this moment! I must go to St. James's-square, – if I stay an instant longer, the passing-bell will toll, and then how shall I be in time for the funeral?'[10]

Such scenes do not seem out of place in this comic narrative because the author's comedy throughout is closely related to frustration, and to irritation of the nerves. The comic figures are baleful; the suspense in scene after scene arises from the frustration of the heroine's wishes, or the relentless application of pressure to the heroine and her weak if well-meaning lover. Almost always surrounded by crowds, Cecilia has always been alone, and the scene in which, in her delirium, she rushes through the crowded streets is a repetition and culmination of many previous scenes involving desire thwarted, and anxious hurrying forward impeded. Most notably it reflects the long episode in which Cecilia tried to make her way secretly to London for a clandestine marriage, only to have her journey obstructed by the meeting with 'friends,' the comic figures who dog her steps and obstruct her purposes. At least in the delirious running she gains a kind of relief – a relief possible only once she forgot her situation, her intention, and herself; she acquires speed for the first time. She can run with the feeling of supernatural ease as one does in a nightmare, and goes hurrying towards what she desires and fears, the image of her husband bleeding and dying. Real London totally disappears and the nightmare takes over the vision of waking life.

Fanny Burney was evidently impressed and moved by her own scene here; her next heroine also falls victim to delirium, and the visions of Camilla's madness are set out at greater length and are much more complex and forceful, drawing the reader into the experience.

Camilla's dream-visions make sense and have their effect because of their context; panic and pain are heightened because of the heroine's growing and intolerable sense of loss, loneliness and guilt. Camilla, believing herself responsible for her father's having been imprisoned for debt, returns to her uncle's home, which has always sheltered her, to find it 'despoiled and forsaken'; her uncle has sold everything and moved away in his determination to help the Tyrold family repay their debts. Camilla, frightened to go home and now 'all at war with herself,' goes to the home of her unhappily married sister Eugenia, but Eugenia's brutal husband Bellamy turns her away. Camilla then reluctantly begins her journey towards her parents, but stops at a small inn, as she wants to write to her mother and be sure she is forgiven before she returns. There is no answer to the letter in which she explains her situation – without a home, without money. She begins to fall ill, and to hope for death. Then a murdered man is brought to the inn. Camilla passes the room in which the corpse lies, goes in and, moved by 'enthusiastic self-compulsion,' lifts up the cloth that covers the face, and sees it is Bellamy. She faints, and is taken to a room, there to lie neglected and deathly ill. She no longer desires death, but is profoundly frightened of it – she fears she has added suicide to her previous sins: 'self-murdered through wilful self-neglect.' After begging for a clergyman to be sent for, she tries in vain to compose herself[11] [. . .]

Camilla's [subsequent] vision (the chapter is called 'A Vision') is, despite some awkward phrasing, probably the most impressively horrifying of all the dreams I have cited. The author seems determined to deal with the very source of Burke's Sublime: the fear of death. The sensations of dying are acutely painful, with no control and no central identity; her consciousness is apparently broken up, scattered over her body and over the universe. Her whole being becomes a tribunal of voices. Camilla is being tried by an invisible Inquisition of her scattered self. The marble immobility is horrifying, but not as horrifying as the judgment which is condemning her, not to Hell but to 'annihilation,' the absolute loss. She grasps at an identity which will not stay. The image of writing with an iron pen and making no mark is a particularly striking emblem of waste, and of lack of personal significance – she has made no impression on life. The act of writing, itself so much an act of conscious intellect, seems to foreshadow a fate truly worse than death, a future of impotent consciousness which tries to communicate its worth and is condemned ever to fail. (It may be remarked that this seems particularly an author's image of hell.)

The author has drawn upon the older religious tradition of the inspired dream here, yet the whole is intimately related to Camilla's psychology and situation, and what emerges is not simply didactic. Ostensibly, the author is concerned with making the reader vividly aware of the heroine's fault, her sin of egotistical self-destructiveness, like that of the later Marianne Dashwood. Yet this does not explain what the dream-vision feels like in its context in the novel. Camilla's life has been one of perpetual frustration, which the reader has shared. The man whom she loves has fallen victim to his jealous mania and has rejected her. Camilla has made a few trifling errors, for the most part the result of unscrupulous other people misunderstanding or manipulating her. Her family's financial trouble has come largely from her scapegrace brother Lionel who has blackmailed Camilla into lending him money and shielding him. Nothing in her life has gone right, and the novel, while apparently pursuing the educational story of a young lady who, although led into a few indiscretions, was amiable and educable, has actually become a gigantic defence of the tormented Camilla against the rest of the unjust world. The abandonment into which she has been plunged is a form of suffering much worse than she can conceivably be said to merit: Fanny Burney's description of her torments is of a piece with that author's constant intuition (or suspicion) that it is a woman's lot to be thwarted, isolated, and unrecognized. Camilla's delirious dream-vision resembles the dreams of Charlotte Brontë's Lucy Snow when that heroine lies ill with fever in the pensionnat. Both heroines express an unmerited sense of total failure, a haunting sense of being unloved, unlovable, worthless and meaningless. Fanny Burney here differs from the other novelists of her century in not presenting her heroine's tormenting dream as arising from a primarily sexual problem; Camilla's dread is born of a half-acquiescent, half-rebellious judgment that her life has been meaningless. The dream is a frightening account of the greatest imaginable frustration and loss, and an expression of the total guilt which seems the feminine emotion appropriate to eternity.

I have perhaps cheated somewhat in discussing *Camilla* here, before the Gothic novels, for it is certainly true that the Gothic novel was under way before Fanny Burney's third work (1796), and it seems that she had begun to be influenced by Gothic devices here, as she certainly was in her last novel. It also seems evident that the women writers of Gothic novels were strongly affected by *Cecilia* (which contains, among other things, the scene of the secret wedding frighteningly interrupted, so like that in *The Italian*). But certainly

Cecilia and *Camilla* belong, with *Betsy Thoughtless* and *Grandison*, to the class of comic social novels. The heroine moves in the recognizable world of daily common life, and has to learn to cope with her own feelings and with society. It is true of *Camilla* as of all the other dream-containing novels I have mentioned that the heroine has to wake up (is allowed to wake up) from her dream – or nightmare – or vision. There is a real world to come back to, and the horrid landscapes and frightful, if exciting, images exist only momentarily. The authors who deal with dreams can do so only temporarily; not too much can be made of a heroine's dream, for after all it is only a dream. The passages I have quoted stand out a trifle oddly in the novels in which they occur, for they introduce suggestions which cannot be fully taken up by the author. Certain levels of consciousness don't repay investigation in a certain type of novel. Charlotte Lennox deals with the matter in an original way, and is the most consistent in presenting her heroine's whole career in terms of her wilful waking dream – but in her anti-romance (also a salute to the romance) Charlotte Lennox uses satiric control to keep the wholly disturbing at a distance. Satiric control works well in the novel she created, for she succeeds in making us forget alternatives, but there were other novelists who wanted to say that Arabella's contradictory fears, of being violently ravished or of being left hopelessly repressed and dull, were entirely relevant to what happens in the real world. Richardson certainly believed in the truthful intuitions of both kinds of fear. It was left to later (I certainly do not say superior) novelists to deal extensively with fear, desire and repression in terms of the nightmare images used by earlier novelists only occasionally to provide momentary glimpses into the perturbed depths of the feminine psyche. That is, the occasionally glimpsed landscape of feminine dream was to become the entire setting in another, non-realistic, type of novel.

That the first writers of the Gothic novel in English were women does not seem a mere coincidence. Clara Reeve, Sophia Lee, Charlotte Smith, Ann Radcliffe – with this last name we come to the point at which the Gothic novel is fully developed, however much later writers may have contributed to embellish and alter it in their own fashions. The only notable exception is of course Horace Walpole whose *Castle of Otranto* (1764) gives us the trappings of the Gothic story without its essence. He who can be stirred to fear by any page of that work must have a constitution more pusillanimous than most. As Clara Reeve noted with some puzzlement, the story is full of silly machinery and ridiculous images which produce a comic effect.[12] Walpole refuses to give way to any belief in the reality, at any level, of what he was writing; Reason was certainly on the throne. It isn't witty, it isn't gentlemanly, to be agitated. The source was a dream, and wit can conquer dreams. Walpole gave some of the old-time trappings a literary respectability which was to become useful later; he could not use them. Clara Reeve, without a quarter of Walpole's talent, and suffering the additional disadvantage of a heavily conscious adherence to propriety, wrote a dull novel which is almost redeemed by some vivid passages in which fear is handled and not fobbed off. Our eyes are not upon a heroine who has to learn, but upon a strange older world not subject to modern rationality.

The writers of the Gothic novel could give their full attention to the world of dream and nightmare – indeed, the 'real world' for characters in a Gothic novel is one of nightmare. There is no longer a common-sense order against which the dream briefly flickers; rather, the world of rational order briefly flickers in and out of the dreamlike. There is no ordinary world to wake up in. The extraordinary world of Gothic romances differs markedly from the realms of the old seventeenth-century productions. What strikes the reader who moves from the eighteenth-century Gothic works to the romances of, for instance, Madeleine de Scudéry is the great *calm* of the older works. Everything is spacious, everything is leisurely. The sublime exists to be contemplated, not to horrify. The description of the burning city at the beginning of *Le Grand Cyrus* (1653–55) is an impressive version of an awe-ful sight, but it is not intended to send a thrill of dread along the nerves. It is not seen as threat, but as stupendous spectacle – which the hero himself has caused. There is in the old romances a great deal of battle and bloodshed, but little sense of violence. Throughout, a beautiful grandeur saves us from a sense of oppression. These works are as much tributes to the beauty of reason as, say, the work of Bernini. One is not helpless because everything is explicable and harmonious. The power of the characters to expound and define (they are among the most articulate characters known to fiction) is just as heroically impressive as the heroines' beauty or the heroes' prowess. Experience is wonderful, not tormenting. We feast on grandeur, and do not shrink before the mysterious. Emotions are intense but not perturbing.

The feelings which the new form, the Gothic romance, deals with constantly – feelings which sharply set it off from the older sort of romance – are inner rage and unspecified (and unspecifiable) guilt. These passions are essentially related to all sorts of other emotions – fear, anxiety, loneliness – which are unstable, powerful, and unpleasantly associated with helplessness and with some kind of sense of inferiority. It will, I think, be acknowledged that all the dreams of heroines to which I have referred bear a weight or inner rage and/or guilt in each case. The one instance that looks like an exception, Arabella's fantasy, is certainly not an exception; the heroine adopts the manners of her favorite heroines in order to justify her expressions of anger and disdain. Her fantasy is a feeble (and unreasonable) rebellion. Inner rage and overwhelming guilt are, in eighteenth-century circumstances, very feminine emotions – women have to suppress rage because they cannot control things; women feel guilty because they continually fail to live up to expectations. If they are to be judged by anybody (Apollo, Mrs. Tyrold, Sir Charles) they will be found wanting. The Gothic romances find an embodiment for these feelings, and work them out using the dream-language to new purposes.

All the imagery we have met in these fictional dreams of women is to be found in the Gothic novel: mountain, forest, ghost, desert, cavern, lake, troubled waters, ruined building with tottering roof, subterraneous cavern, sea, 'howling and conflicting winds,' snowy wastes, the bleeding lover, orange groves, corpse, iron instruments, invisible voices and dread tribunals – and, with these, sudden changes of place, preternatural speed, irresistible forces. In the Gothic novel these things are not the illusions which result from momentary feminine weakness – they constitute objects and facts in the 'real' outer world, whose nature it is to create dread.

The first English novel in which the dream-world expands to take on the contours of the whole world is not the witty *Otranto* nor the cautious *Old English Baron* but that wild tale by Sophia Lee, *The Recess* (1783–85). This work, one of the first English historical novels,[13] tells the story of two women, the legitimate but concealed daughters of Mary Queen of Scots; the historical unreality of these beings, whose lives are not to be found recorded on any page of history, works, oddly, in the novel as a kind of substantiation of these buried lives. Matilda and Ellinor are brought up in a subterraneous cavern, their identity a danger to their mother, to themselves, and to all who come into contact with them. They live secluded in this Recess, a place beautiful but claustrophobic, a combined palace and prison, womb and grave. St. Vincent's Abbey was destroyed in the Reformation; part of the Abbey has been rebuilt as a palatial residence, but the secret refuge is buried under ruins. In their furnished cavern, the children see the very beams of the sun only dimly, as it is filtered through 'casements of painted glass' (I, 3). Their adult ventures into the world above their subliminal shelter lead both to release and disaster. Leicester comes upon the girls on one of their rare excursions above ground; he falls in love with Matilda (and she, most ardently, with him). He contrives to marry her secretly, and takes her and her sister about with him in disguise. The unacknowledged wife and her sister even serve in the court of their greatest enemy, Queen Elizabeth, who of course does not know who they are. As Ellinor says later of this life, 'we were all an illusion' (II, 165).

Part of the fascination of the novel is that the girls, the story's centers of consciousness, lead in a sense the life of phantoms – they cannot be real, they must not be known. They are the mystery of this Gothic novel; it is the villains who endeavor to discover them. Their lives are a perpetual image of guilt; their existence is not only a threat to themselves and their lovers but a Damocles' sword hanging over the life of their mother, the imprisoned Queen. Mary's daughters see her only once, through a grated window; they thrust their hands through the bars, but cannot touch their mother or talk with her.

Every action is doomed to loss – and dread; every relationship is fated to be fractured by history. When Queen Elizabeth discovers Matilda's identity and her marriage, Leicester flies with her to the Continent – where they are betrayed by Matilda's own relative, who allows the Queen's agents to come upon them at dead of night; Matilda's husband is murdered before her eyes. There is no happy mistake, or restoration, or awakening; Matilda's only consolation is in watching by the coffin of her dead love. Her pretended friend, Mortimer, offers to rescue her; Matilda awaits him in the convent chapel at midnight, listening to the bell strike through the cold air while she rests her head upon Leicester's coffin, from which she refuses to be parted, much to Mortimer's chagrin. As the reader expects, the rescuer has his own designs upon Matilda, and she is a prisoner in the ship which carries her to Jamaica. The novel is full of rapid movement, of dream-like wandering from scene to scene; apparent release from one frightening situation proves only an introduction to another, although the images change with dreamlike completeness which yet is continuity.

Matilda, pregnant with Leicester's child, is comforted by the presence of the faithful Rose Cecil, who has been herself in love with Leicester and has followed him through the world. Like the dreaming Harriet Byron, Matilda is rescued from the fear of sea and wind by being presented with a baby, the child which her rival could not have. After Matilda has given birth, Rose's mind begins to give way to increasing melancholy which leads to an unexpected and rapid climax:

> One evening . . . I perceived her more than usually disturbed. Neither my prayers, nor the pouring rain could bring her from the balcony, where for hours she told her weary steps. I started at last from a momentary slumber on her re-entering the cabin. The dim lamp burning in it, shewed her with a slow and tottering pace approaching the last asylum of Lord Leicester; sinking by this

> repository of her breaking heart, she clasped her hands upon her bosom with a most speaking sense of woe; while over it her fair locks fell wild and dishevelled, heavy with the midnight rain, and shivering to its beatings. The wet drapery of her white garments spread far over the floor, and combined to form so perfect an image of desolation, as froze up all my faculties. I struggled for articulation. A feeble cry alone escaped me. She started at the sound from her icy stupor, and glanced her eyes every where, with that acuteness of perception which marks a disturbed imagination. . . . Springing up with etherial lightness, even while her feeble frame shivered with agony and affection, she fixed on my convulsed features a long, long look, then waving majestically a last adieu, rushed again into the balcony. Unable to move a limb, my harrowed soul seemed, through the jar of the elements, to distinguish her dreadful plunge into the world of waters.
>
> (II, 100–01)

This striking scene is an embodiment of feminine pain. The heroine, like the female dreamers, is conscious of danger but is unable to move or speak. Matilda shares the consciousness of her admirable rival, who seems like a dreamer's other self; Rose seems rather like Harriet in the earlier parts of her nightmare. At the end of the scene Rose dissolves into the elements; the plunge into the depths offers the final release from the sense of woe. The central characters, the two sisters, are perpetually hovering above depths into which they fear or desire to descend.

Ellinor's account of her life is even more violent than Matilda's, with more inner loss involved. One of the novel's points is that the two sisters in their adult life are separate in views and circumstances. When we read Ellinor's narrative we find with surprise that the sisters have always been different, and Matilda's views of events can no longer be seen as the only ones. It is an interesting shock to discover that Ellinor, while always loving her sister, never trusted Leicester. Ellinor herself is in love with Essex – another love which is doomed to disaster – and cannot see his faults of weakness which accompany the charm. Ellinor has more to bear than her sister. After Matilda's flight, she is left to bear the brunt of the anger of Elizabeth and Burleigh. Ellinor is imprisoned – in St. Vincent's Abbey:

> [H]e ordered his servants to bear me into the grated room at the end of the eastern cloister. You cannot but remember the dismal place. Half sunk in ruin, and overhung with ivy, and trees of growth almost immemorial, it appeared the very cell of melancholy. . . . The pale gleams of the moon seemed every moment to people

> the dungeon they glanced through – my pulse beat with redoubled strength and quickness – the whole cloister resounded the long night with distant feet, but they came not to me – fearfully I often started when sinking into a lethargy, rather than slumber, by the echo of some remote voice, which fancy continually told me I knew, but it died away ere memory could assign it an owner. . . .
> (II, 214–15)

Ellinor's reason slowly starts to give way under this treatment, and her tortured experience is closely associated with fear of a most undesired marriage, and with guilty responsibility. Burleigh forces her into marriage with the unloveable Lord Arlington, after making her sign a dishonest document swearing that neither she nor Matilda is the child of Queen Mary. Ellinor signs – with the death warrant for her mother before her eyes; she does not know that 'our sainted mother was led to execution, almost at the very moment I was defaming you and myself to save her' (II, 236). Ellinor's fearful midnight marriage increases her despair: 'Wedded – lost – annihilated' (II, 235). The news of her mother's execution overthrows a reason which she never quite recovers:

> Severed at once from every tie both of nature and of choice, dead while yet breathing, the deep melancholy which seized upon my brain soon tinctured my whole mass of blood – my intellects strangely blackened and confused, frequently realized scenes and objects that ever existed, annihilating many which daily passed before my eyes. . . . There were moments when I started as from a deep sleep, (and oh, how deep a sleep is that of the soul!) – turned my dubious eyes around with vague remembrance – touched my own hand, to be convinced I yet existed – trembled at the sound of my own voice, or raising my uncertain eye toward the blue vault of Heaven, found in the all-chearing sun a stranger. – Alas! my sister, look no more in this sad recital for the equal-minded rational Ellinor you once saw me; sensations too acute for either endurance or expression, from this fatal period blotted every noble faculty, often substituting impulse for judgment. Always sensible of my wandering the moment it was past, shame continually succeeded, and united every misery of madness and reason.
> (II, 237–38)

Ellinor's narrative, which often does break into rambling, provides a contrast to Matilda's more straightforward account. Ellinor's life is a nightmare within the nightmare, and she subsides into dreaming:

> I dreamt of Essex – Ah, what did I say? I dreamt of Essex – Alas, I have dreamt of him my whole life long! – Something strangely intervenes between myself and my meaning.
>
> (II, 243)

Life is a painful dream, with fits of hectic joy. Ellinor recovers after Arlington's death, escapes to Ireland and Essex, but these lovers are soon separated again. Essex, who matches Ellinor in 'substituting impulse for judgment,' is led to his foolish return to the Queen and his mad rush upon London – and to the Tower and the block. Ellinor is brought to see him the night before his execution, but merciful insanity intervenes and she does not know him, or realize what is happening. After his death she is doomed to repeat the experience of his execution over and over again, going through the Tower and even the Queen's palace, looking for her lover [. . .]

The Queen takes Ellinor, in this mad visitation, for a supernatural accuser. But Ellinor herself suffers from guilt, because she feels she has failed in her responsibility to her mother and to Essex. The fulfillment of any desire is colored with guilt:

> 'Me married to him! resumed our friend, replying to some imaginary speech, – oh, no, I took warning by my sister – I will have no more bloody marriages: you see I have no ring, wildly displaying her hands, except a black one; a *black* one indeed, if you knew all – but I need not tell *you* that – have I, my Lord?'
>
> (III, 184)

Pitiless Fate impels the tale to its inevitable end, the obliteration of Mary's unacknowledged descendants. What is feared is not worse than what happens. The aberrations of Ellinor's mind are merciful in comparison to the reality. Unlike Clementina, or Cecilia, Ellinor cannot be brought back to the comfort of the real world, because there is no comfort in her real world, and her madness is a simple reflection of what exists outside herself. It is true that Ellinor is self-divided; indeed, she keeps slipping into the identities of her mother and her lover: 'I fear I begin again to wander, for my hand writing appears to my own eyes that of Essex' (II, 275). But Ellinor's self-division is not the expression of a merely individual psychological difficulty. Her varying identities have a common substance: her mother, her lover, herself, Matilda, Leicester all suffer under a common tyranny. The only way of escaping this tyranny in the real world is by concealment of oneself (in the subterranean life) or by annihilation in death (courted in different ways by Rose Cecil and Essex). The buried life (as symbolized by the life of the Recess itself) is confining, dim, unsatisfactory: 'how deep a sleep is that of the soul!' But life in the world is irrational and brutal; consciousness is punished rather than rewarded. The only choice seems to be between two dreams – lethargic reverie, or nightmare.

This novel, which is, with all its defects, often interesting and even striking, can claim the distinction of being a pioneer work in two literary kinds. It is the first fully developed English Gothic novel, and it is also one of the first recognizable historical novels in English. The two facts seem connected. This Gothic story about sixteenth-century characters is a judgment of the real world; history is a chronicle of pain and sorrow. Institutions, power, political activities are the nightmarish cruel realities from which no one can escape. All the characters are trapped in their own historical situation; what we have here may not be exactly the history of the textbooks, but we are presented with an historical situation. The past affects the present. The past (Henry's dissolution of the monasteries, the suppression of Catholicism, Mary's flight) really has happened. The actions, loyalties, motives of all the characters are affected by what has happened before they come upon the scene, and by contemporary realities over which the individual rarely has control. The world functions on power which is both necessary and deeply destructive. The woman who is powerful (Elizabeth) perverts her nature in exercising power; the men who wish to use power drive themselves on to feverish activity and are ultimately ridden over by history. The women whom the author sees as good (Mary of Scotland, Matilda, Ellinor, Rose, young Mary) are more passive (not entirely passive), but they are inevitably implicated in events which they affect but cannot control. Like the heroines of Jane Barker, Richardson, and Fanny Burney, the heroines are moved by guilt and fear – but in this case guilt and fear are not just the property of dreaming young ladies, although it is the female characters who give expression to these emotions. The men are un-Grandisonian; they rage, and are helpless, and fail in their grand designs. Guilt and fear are diffused throughout the whole historical dream and all of it – ruined monastery, pomp and pageantry at Kenilworth, axe and Tower and palace – is at once both real and nightmarish, both inescapable and absurd. It is in the Gothic novel that women writers could first accuse the 'real world' of falsehood and deep disorder. Or perhaps, they rather asked whether masculine control is not just another delusion in the nightmare of absurd historical reality in which we are all involved. The visions of horror are not private – they have become public.

The visions of horror are certainly related to public issues rather than to purely private life in the works of Charlotte Smith. It is evident in her first novel, *Emmeline* (1788) that the writer has recognized in the development of Gothic effects a feminine tradition particularly suited to the discussion of women's difficulties and their social causes. In this she anticipates Mary Wollstonecraft's achievement in *The Wrongs of Woman*. (Mary Wollstonecraft herself, in a less advanced stage of her feminist career, reviewed *Emmeline* rather severely, seeing in it too much sympathy with certain kinds of female dreams and desires. Such reading encourages the search for *'adventures'* at the expense of duty and contentment; one remembers Mrs. Lennox's Arabella.)[14]

The Gothic elements in *Emmeline* appear only sporadically; the author is primarily interested in contemporary social problems, and uses all the elements of fiction which will serve her turn, without fully developing any. As some early readers noticed, she is indebted to Fanny Burney's earlier novels for social comedy and for plot complication. Mrs. Smith in her first work stands uneasily between old and new. Her heroine has nightmares rather than living in nightmare, but at one point the author does made an interesting transition between dream and reality, in which the reality seems a continuation of the dream. This is the scene in which Emmeline, aroused from bad dreams ('horrid visions' rather like Harriet Byron's concerning Greville's attack on Sir Charles), waits by the window for the dawn. The atmosphere, with the starlight, the dimly seen garden and the 'low, hollow murmur of the sea' is well created. In the faint and uncertain light the heroine sees the figure of a man who moves like a phantom over the lawn; 'on perceiving the first rays of the morning, he "started like a guilty thing," and swiftly stepped away to his concealment' (*Emmeline*, pp. 465–66).

There is no prolonged mystery; the mysterious stranger is soon identified as the man with whom Emmeline's friend, the unhappy Adelina, committed adultery; Fitz-Edward has come to watch the house of the woman he loves but dares not approach. His Hamlet's-ghost appearance is an emblem of his forlorn, penitential and helpless condition, for both he and Adelina are in a shadowy social and emotional limbo. Emmeline's own case, the unwilling engagement to a man she does not wish to marry, is thematically related to that of the unhappily married Adelina. The self-division, uncertainty and even horror inspired by the prospect of marriage as seen in the dreams of earlier heroines are, in this novel, projected upon outward circumstances.

The atmosphere surrounding Fitz-Edward's appearance suggests the unhappiness caused by oppressive reality – marriage laws, position of women, bonds of custom. Truth cannot come by daylight; the world pushes some emotional realities into shadows. The novel patently argues about these things; the miseries of bad marriages are forcefully described, and the novelist depicts both the adulteress and her lover with a good deal of sympathy. By the end of the novel the virtuous heroine has broken her engagement, and it is indicated that Adelina, now a widow, will marry her lover with her family's eventual approval. The author certainly tells us what she wants to see changed. She is always interested in the objective world, the political world.

In this novel she is not sure of all her effects; she wants to be both realistic and Gothic, and the Gothic moments tend to be spasmodic and self-contained. It was not until after the advent of Mrs. Radcliffe's works that Charlotte Smith discovered how to make the elements of Gothic romance work in harmony with her radical themes. Mrs. Radcliffe is of course not consciously 'a radical' at all, but in her works that which inspires horror is given a pure and consistent objective reality; it is not dropped in for merely perfunctory effect, and it has a significance which is always in some sense a historical significance. Charlotte Smith took, I think, what she needed from Mrs. Radcliffe, which was not what she could take from Sophia Lee's inward-turning passionate wraiths. Charlotte Smith is not extremely interested in the inner life of characters; her interests lie outward, and she wants to change the world, to make it less painful rather than to analyze pain as Sophia Lee does. She needed a more objective means of sanctifying anger and purging guilt in the presentation of her well-intentioned heroes and heroines caught in the turbulence of contemporary history. Her best Gothic effects are to be found in *Desmond* (1792), especially in the sequence in which the hero and heroine plunge about the fortified manor of one of the last die-hard aristocrats of revolutionary France. There, historical reality provides appropriate Gothic imagery for all oppression and greed, an objective correlative for what men in power have done to other men and to women in the true nightmare which is history. The intuitions of Mrs. Haywood's splenetic Betsy are vindicated indeed. The private protests of feminine dreams have become public, rational, schematic objections to institutions and traditions clearly seen and defined. It is not surprising that the English Gothic novel, with its roots in the dreams of women, should become, along one line of its evolution, the novel of feminine radical protest.

The achievement of Mrs. Smith in her major works was to be of importance for later writers. In a highly original manner she relates individual difficulties, states of mind, and views to larger cultural conditions. Her insight into the significance of the Gothic is a result of this desire to connect. Scott is indebted to her, and so too, although less directly, is George Eliot. Yet, with all her originality and even brilliance, Mrs. Smith is merely a writer of great talent, not a genius.

She possesses the limitations of her qualities which are intellectual rather than powerfully imaginative. The melancholy which Scott noted as one of her most marked characteristics is subtly at odds with her urge to put things right. In defining matters clearly and programatically, she tidies away the nightmare. Once the cause of nightmare is rationally defined as social oppression, then the visions of terror are merely symptoms of a wrong that can be put right. The sublime, the horrifying, lose their mysterious hold on us; the force of imagination, the power of the inner life, are rendered negligible. In the development of the Gothic novel it is Ann Radcliffe who is the major innovator, in subtle ways as well as obvious ones. She has been accused of disappointing readers with too-careful explanations of her mysteries, but of course she never really tidies up the suggestive horror at all, any more than she removes Vesuvius from the landscape of Vivaldi's Naples.

In Mrs. Radcliffe's novels we find the world of nightmare made into an objective art which is neither self-indulgent nor dogmatic. She uses the objective third-person narrator to convey the impression of truth; we are not, as in *The Recess*, locked into the subjectivity of a female victim. The Gothic atmosphere is all-pervasive, not residing in occasional pieces of machinery as in the tricksy *Otranto* or the sedate *Old English Baron*. Her novel represents an expansion and clarification of the motifs of fear and anxiety, and the imagery acquires a new conviction from careful and consistent use. In her first novel, *The Castles of Athlin and Dunbayne* (1789), there is a deliberate economy of effect, as if she were dubious about cheapening her resources. The action is simpler than that in any of her other novels, and the major setting, the castle of Dunbayne, is a stark place in barren surroundings; the author is trying to capture the bare grandeur of her idea of ancient Scotland, with its clan warfare, clan loyalties and primitive way of life.

The hero, Osbert, is at the novel's outset a victim of history; his father, the chief of Athlin, has been killed by the haughty Malcolm of Dunbayne, and the clan hopes for revenge when the young Earl is of an age to lead his clan 'to conquest and revenge.'[15] This rather lonely young man is both martial and imaginative:

> He delighted in the terrible and in the grand, more than in the softer landscape; and wrapt in the bright visions of fancy, would often lose himself in awful solitudes.
>
> It was in one of these rambles, that having strayed for some miles over hills covered with heath, from whence the eye was presented with only the bold outlines of uncultivated nature, rocks piled on rocks, cataracts and vast moors unmarked by the foot of traveller,

> he lost the path which he had himself made; he looked in vain for the objects which had directed him; and his heart, for the first time, felt the repulse of fear. No vestige of a human being was to be seen; and the dreadful silence of the place was interrupted only by the roar of distant torrents, and by the screams of the birds which flew over his head. He shouted, and his voice was answered only by deep echoes from the mountains. He remained for some time in a silent dread not wholly unpleasing, but which was soon heightened to a degree of terror not to be endured; and he turned his steps backward, forlorn, and almost without hope. His memory gave him back no image of the past; and having wandered some time, he came to a narrow past, which he entered, overcome with fatigue and fruitless search. . . .
>
> (pp. 9–10)

We have here the desert, the silent anxiety-filled wilderness which is the landscape of nightmare. The phrase 'His memory gave him back no image of the past' is more than an elegant periphrasis for 'he could not remember having seen any of this landscape before'; the phrase itself suggests the horrors of a mind without recollection, with no recallable past, finding itself arbitrarily placed in a scene utterly alien – the condition of dream. But the dream is reality, and the figure who stands in the place of the dreamer is masculine. At last an eighteenth-century hero experiences real terror.

When Osbert leads the expected attack on the castle of Dunbayne, himself fired with ardent belief in his cause, his clansmen are surprised by the enemy. The attack is a failure, and Osbert and his friend, the valiant young Alleyn, are imprisoned, separately, in the dungeons of the castle. Here, both young men experience fear – and helplessness:

> Reflection, at length, afforded him time to examine his prison: it was a square room, which formed the summit of a tower built on the east side of the castle, round which the bleak winds howled mournfully; the inside of the apartment was old, and falling to decay: a small mattress, which lay in one corner of the room, a broken matted chair, and a tottering table, composed its furniture; two small and strongly grated windows, which admitted a sufficient degree of light and air, afforded him on one side a view into an inner court, and on the other a dreary prospect of the wild and barren Highlands.
>
> Alleyn was conveyed through dark and winding passages to a distant part of the castle, where at length a small door, barred with iron, opened and disclosed to him an abode, whence light and hope

> were equally excluded. He shuddered as he entered, and the door was closed upon him.
>
> (pp. 35–36)

After an interview with the cruelly vengeful Baron, Osbert feels 'perfect misery' and even thinks of suicide:

> the cool fortitude in which he had so lately gloried, disappeared; and he was on the point of resigning his virtue and his life by means of a short dagger, which he wore concealed under his vest. . . .
>
> (p. 39)

The perturbation of this novel's heroes is in marked contrast to the sedate emotions of Mrs. Reeve's Edmund, who, in the haunted room, is *almost* allowed to feel fear:

> He recollected the other door, and resolved to see where it led to; the key was rusted into the lock, and resisted his attempts; he set the lamp on the ground, and exerting all his strength opened the door, and at the same instant the wind of it blew out the lamp, and left him in utter darkness. At the same moment he heard a hollow rustling noise like that of a person coming through a narrow passage. Till this moment not one idea of fear had approached the mind of Edmund; but just then, all the concurrent circumstances of this situation struck upon his heart, and gave him a new and disagreeable sensation. He paused a while; and, recollecting himself, cried out aloud – What should I fear? I have not wilfully offended God, or man; why, then, should I doubt protection? But I have not yet implored the divine assistance; how than can I expect it! Upon this, he kneeled down and prayed earnestly, resigning himself wholly to the will of Heaven; while he was yet speaking, his courage returned, and he resumed his usual confidence. . . .[16]

It is the *reader's* fear with which the author plays briefly, while not quite allowing her *hero* to be fully afraid. His usual confidence governs Edmund through the rest of the action – even in the long sequence of dreams he is touched not by horror but by blessings. 'Every succeeding idea was happiness without allay; and his mind was not idle a moment till the morning sun awakened him.' The dream-sequence is not fearful, but assures him of his true identity and inheritance. Edmund has no reason to fear – he is good old English manliness (with suitable if anachronistic Protestant rational piety). He waits for his appropriate reward. But Osbert, although courageous, is really afraid. His cool fortitude can disappear. Here is a man who is subject to failure, distress, captivity – just like the heroine (whom he will eventually meet, a fellow-prisoner in this castle). These moments in which the hero experiences terror seem so natural in Mrs. Radcliffe's novel that no one is likely to remark them as offering anything startlingly new. The author makes no pother about it – she certainly is not making any dogmatic statement, feminist or otherwise. She serenely takes it for granted that terror is so important an experience that all human beings can have it – that the nightmare apprehensions are universally true, and related to real life. Inner rage, guilt, anxiety and dread are not the exclusive property of women. In showing this, in making this truth objective, she brings the Gothic novel to maturity as a genre with something important to say about the unknown darkness which shadows all our lives. Her characterization is simple and conventional (necessarily, for her purpose); her notion of what can be felt by human beings (for which the characters act as signals) is unconventional and profound.

In her next novel, *A Sicilian Romance* (1790), Mrs. Radcliffe is confident enough to attempt more elaborate effects. Lovers are rapt from each other with the speed of nightmare; we move from landscape to landscape, from warm to cold, from height to depth, from brilliant light to eerie dark, whirling about a wild exotic world as Harriet Byron did in her dreams. There is a luxuriance of striking images: the ancient castle of Mazzini; the sea; the 'dark rocky coast of Calabria'; 'Mount Etna, crowned with eternal snows, and shooting from among the clouds'; the festivity of the ball with the illuminated forest in the background: 'long vistas . . . terminated by pyramids of lamps that presented to the eye one bright column of flame.' We have the wicked marchioness's pavilion by the sea-shore, 'hung with white silk . . . richly fringed with gold' where 'alternate wreaths of lamps and of roses entwined the columns' in contrast to the bleak haunted gallery, the piles of fallen stone and the dark dungeons. We move from the haunted castle to the Abbey of St. Augustine, where to the sound of the organ's 'high and solemn peal' the dying nun 'covered with a white veil' is borne to the altar by white-robed nuns 'each carrying in her hand a lighted taper.' There is the tempest at sea, the shipwreck, the bandits' cavern filled with the bodies of their victims, the living tomb of the real marchioness. And at the end there is the impressive setting where Ferdinand at last finds the members of his real family gathered together, an image which combines flame and darkness, sea and rock, stronghold and tempest:

> At length he discerned, amid the darkness from afar, a red light waving in the wind: it varied with the blast, but never totally

> disappeared. He pushed his horse into a gallop, and made towards it.
>
> The flame continued to direct his course; and on a nearer approach, he perceived, by the red reflection of its fires, streaming a long radiance upon the waters beneath – a light-house situated upon a point of rock which overhung the sea.[17]

(Virginia Woolf is not the first female novelist to direct us to the Lighthouse.) In *A Sicilian Romance* there is a variety of impressively intense dream-like sensations – dream-like in their intensity, in their unquestionable reality. Guilt and sorrow are the substance of the tale, and the innocent characters, Ferdinand, Julia and Emilia, children of the wicked father and his ill-used first wife, bear the burden of the mystery of ancient unknown evil. Julia and Ferdinand, troubled by the strange lights and sounds which appear to emanate from the disused wing of the castle, determine to discover what lies behind the deserted gallery. Ferdinand breaks the lock and they enter: 'The gallery was in many parts falling to decay, the ceiling was broke, and the window-shutters shattered, which, together with the dampness of the walls, gave the place an air of wild desolation' (I, 90). In this novel it is *home* – that home which young ladies are supposed to love and cherish – which is wild and unsafe.

When they see a light passing by a large staircase at the end of the gallery, Ferdinand determines to follow it; he goes down, and through a passage which grows narrower and less passable: 'fragments of loose stone made it now difficult to proceed.' He finds a door, and on the other side of it a staircase leading up to the south tower:

> After a momentary hesitation, he determined to ascend the staircase, but its ruinous condition made this an adventure of some difficulty. The steps were decayed and broken, and the looseness of the stones rendered a footing very insecure. Impelled by an irresistible curiosity, he was undismayed, and began the ascent. He had not proceeded very far, when the stones of a step which his foot had just quitted, loosened by his weight, gave way; and dragging with them those adjoining, formed a chasm in the staircase that terrified even Ferdinand, who was left tottering on the suspended half of the steps, in momentary expectation of falling to the bottom with the stone on which he rested. In the terror which this occasioned, he attempted to save himself by catching at a kind of beam which projected over the stairs, when the lamp dropped from his hand, and he was left in total darkness. Terror now usurped the place of every other interest. . . .
>
> (I, 92–93)

What was once the dream-experience of a terrified woman like Betsy Thoughtless, 'seeking to find a passage through some ruin'd building,' is now the experience of a hero, and equally terrifying. The effect is even more remarkable in the context of the whole novel. This dilapidated and threatening region of the castle contains the heart of the mystery, the mother, imprisoned by her cruel husband and condemned to a perpetual living death beneath these ruins. The children circle around and about their mother, like creatures perplexed in a maze, but they do not know what is at the heart of the maze – their ignorance condemns her to continued burial. Later, when Ferdinand is, at his father's command, cast into a dungeon, he hears a sound which frightens him, changing dejection to horror:

> It returned at intervals in hollow sighings, and seemed to come from some person in deep distress. So much did fear operate upon his mind, that he was uncertain whether it arose from within or from without. He looked around his dungeon, but could distinguish no object through the impenetrable darkness. As he listened in deep amazement, the sound was repeated in moans more hollow. Terror now occupied his mind, and disturbed his reason; he started from his posture, and, determined to be satisfied whether any person beside himself was in the dungeon, groped, with arms extended, along the walls. The place was empty; but coming to a particular spot, the sound suddenly arose more distinctly to his ear. (I, 223)

Ferdinand comes to believe that his dungeon is haunted by some malign spirit, and thinks it must be the spirit of a man his father had murdered, come for purposes of vengeance upon the whole family: 'At this conviction, horror thrilled his nerves' (I, 224). Much later, we find out that the mother had heard someone in a dungeon nearby, and had tried to call out to her fellow-prisoner, not knowing he was her son.

The macabre theme has a psychological resonance as, in different ways at different times, Ferdinand and Julia both pursue and unwittingly reject the buried mother. The theme culminates in the most powerful and surprising scene in the novel, when Julia, after making her way through the robbers' cavern, forces her way along narrow tortuous passages, without an object save escape:

> She groped along the winding walls for some time, when she perceived the way was obstructed. She now discovered that another door interrupted her progress, and sought for the bolts which might fasten it. These she found; and strengthened by desperation

> forced them back. The door opened, and she beheld in a small room, which received its feeble light from a window above, the pale and emaciated figure of a woman, seated, with half-closed eyes, in a kind of elbow-chair.
>
> (II, 158)

Themselves prisoners and victims, Ferdinand and Julia are also ignorant accomplices in the crime against their mother, that unsuspected living ghost. They feel guilty. Julia feels that sharing her mother's prison for life would not be too small a compensation, while Ferdinand, mistaking his mother's voice for that of a vengeful spirit threatening father and children, has felt a horror which threatened to overturn his reason. The irony of the tale is that the children are guilty while innocent: they have not rescued their mother; they have feared what they would love. The novel's fable is a large image of guilt – guilt and fear are in the children's case undeserved and inescapable. The whole story makes the nightmare realm of guilt, rage and loss an appropriate environment for both sexes.

Of Mrs. Radcliffe's later novels it is scarcely necessary to treat, for they are better known. In what is probably her best work, *The Italian* (1797), the reader shares the separate experience of both Ellena and Vivaldi, and the hero's experience is even more frightening than the heroine's. Everyone remembers Vivaldi's being brought into the fortress of the Inquisition, and the scenes of his interrogation before mysterious tribunals, in the depths of the labyrinth behind iron doors. These scenes touch on our terror of being tried, of facing accusation without defence, of being tainted with unspecified guilt while innocent of crime. In these scenes before the tribunal, with unseen speakers and strange instruments of torture, the iron implements and accusing voices of Camilla's dream are represented in a new guise; the tribunal is full of father figures, masculine justice is presented as it appears in the historical institution whose nature is to create guilt – and the reader is at full liberty to shout 'No!' instead of acquiescing in the judgment. The Inquisition is given the fearful reality of the local habitation and the earthly name. It is capable of shocking the mind with the dread of what is fearfully unreasonable and painful in consciousness, from which one cannot be dismissed by awakening, while at the same time conveying the fact that the public world is inescapably harsh, crushing the individual in the name of order and reason, attempting to make both masculine and feminine sexual identity and inner existence into guilt. The hero is really afraid, and, when he 'at length found a respite from thought and from suffering in sleep,'[18] he has a frightening dream in which the unknown monk appears, holding a bloodstained poniard. When he awakens he finds 'the same figure standing before him' although in this reality into which the dream has melted, the monk does not at first seem to be holding a dagger. It is only after the strange conversation with Vivaldi that the intruder shows him a poniard and asks him to look at the blood upon it: 'Mark those spots . . . Here is some print of truth! To-morrow night you will meet me in the chambers of death!' (p. 323). Clementina had looked for marks of blood that were not there: reality and dreaming melancholy were separate. Now within the environment of nightmare man as well as woman is the victim, and dream and reality are indistinguishable.

The Gothic novel as Mrs. Radcliffe developed it takes the images of nightmare and gives them a strong embodiment; they are the framework of life, they are reality. The images and their concomitant emotions are no longer the figments of a particular feminine consciousness within the novel, nor do they, as in *The Recess*, provide an environment for feminine consciousness alone. They cannot be dismissed as symptoms of a peculiar psychological state. This is not to deny the value of the more realistic novel dealing with fully developed psychological characters in a social world – I certainly do not hold that Mrs. Radcliffe is superior to Richardson. But the eighteenth-century novel could not go beyond a certain point in developing the consciousness of human beings as long as it maintained very rigid notions of the strength of the male sex and subscribed to very limiting beliefs about superior rational consciousness and about the orderliness of the real world – notions and beliefs which inhibited any apprehension of deep disorders and fears. The Gothic novel has a value in this alone in making accessible what was strange and elusive, and so paying full attention to what had been underdeveloped in the work of earlier novelists. The dream scenes I have cited – especially those from *Grandison* and *Camilla* – are unsatisfactory, not because they are bad (on the contrary) but because they are so powerful that they threaten the stability of the world which the novelist would like us to inhabit; we cannot shrug these things off so easily once they have passed.

Mrs. Radcliffe admits that the world of Nature and of Man is dangerous, and that danger is in the nature of things. She admits dread as a natural experience – and the readers themselves take their part in it, for we need, like the boy in the old tale, to learn what fear is, 'to shiver and to shake.' Adolescent heroines had previously been shown as troubled by dubious fears and mysterious dreads upon their coming to maturity. Mrs. Radcliffe also associates fear with maturing, and assumes, quite calmly, that men can be afraid. A whole tradition of intrepid heroes bites the dust as soon as Osbert (uninteresting in himself, but interesting for his experience) undergoes helplessness and terror, even (at one juncture) to the point of fainting. The late-Renaissance conventions of masculine control in an orderly universe within which men regulate events – these are swept aside. It was good that this should be so, not because previous fictional conventions had produced works untrue or bad in themselves, but because at this point they could yield nothing new. The novel had been too much affected by certain beliefs, hemming itself into a tight corner with too little room for truth. Masculinity was to be found only in virtuous assurance or amiable eccentricity. We could have been stuck with the tiresome procession, emerging from the works of poorer novelists, of good untroubled heroes and virtuous heroines.

In the Gothic novels, heroes and heroines share the nightmare – and the nightmare is real. At least, that is what they can share as soon as Mrs. Radcliffe's first work had appeared in 1789. It has not, I think, been sufficiently recognized what a liberating effect this was to have on subsequent novelists and subsequent heroes – whether or not the novels deal in the Gothic. Charlotte Smith in *Desmond* plucked up the courage to present a hero who is anxious and self-divided, impressed by dream, reverie and recollection; at the same time he is a hero confronting the outrageous ghastliness of history, past and present. He, like the later Vivaldi, and so many heroes after them, tries to make sense of a world which is (unlike the worlds of Tom Jones and Grandison) not readily amenable to good sense. After Mrs. Radcliffe, there need be no more condescension about 'the imbecillities of tender minds'; it is not stupid or feeble or criminal to recognize that the outer world and the world within are mysterious and perturbing. Without Mrs. Radcliffe's novels, Scott could not have written as he did; his heroes explore the unknown, and experience that fear of present and future which allows the author to give every place and event its full meaning. That some of his heroes are unusually passive the author himself remarked (in his jovial review of his own works); they are thus because thus the author can tell the truth about human life in the onrush of history, which expresses man's needs and desires but over which no man or woman has very much control.

Scott's most exotic hero, Ravenswood in *The Bride of Lammermoor* (1819), is a tormented and divided man, both strong and weak, no mere flaccid victim but ultimately a victim indeed. This good young man, the sexually exciting lover so fascinating and disturbing to Lucy, has his own weaknesses, unfulfilled desires and fear of loss – he is no Lovelace, for not only does he mean well but in himself he has scarcely the illusion of control, still less of the power to manipulate men and women. In his forlorn castle at Wolf's Crag, the remnant of a dead ancestral power, he is one of the victims in the dungeons of history.

The later novelists of the nineteenth century did not need to flinch in presenting their heroes as wanderers through a strange and puzzling world, men who feel guilt without being villainous, men who know weakness, self-division, terror and failure. One could make a long list of names culled from the Victorian novel of heroes who know weakness and fear: Henry Esmond, Arthor Clennam, Pip, Paul Emanuel, Lydgate, Clym Yeobright. These men are interesting. Men could not be fully present in the novel until they could be shown as self-divided, wary, torn by their own unconscious and divided motives, even weak, erring and guilty – and shown thus without being exhibited as villains or failures. It was the Gothic novel, in all its implication, that saved men from being seen as the sex without a full consciousness. The Gothic novel gave them the freedom to have – and to live in – nightmares.

Notes

1. Samuel Richardson, *Sir Charles Grandison* (Oxford English Novels Edition, London, 1972), Part III, p. 242.
2. Michael V. DePorte, *Nightmares and Hobbyhorses: Swift, Sterne, and Augustan Ideas of Madness* (San Marino: The Huntington Library, 1974).
3. Jane Barker, *Love Intrigues* (New York: Garland Press Reprint, Foundation of the Novel series), pp. 14–15.
4. Barker, *The Entertaining Novels of Mrs. Jane Barker* (2 vols., London: 1719), II, 29.
5. See ch. vii, Book VIII of *The Female Quixote.*
6. Charlotte Lennox, *The Female Quixote* (Oxford English Novels Edition, London, 1970), pp. 372–73. Some critics have suggested that the chapter from which this passage comes (Book IX, ch. xi) was written wholly or in part by Dr. Johnson; Duncan Isles considers the claim 'by no means adequately supported' although admitting the influence of Johnson's 'ideas and phraseology' in the chapter. See Isles's Appendix to the above edition, p. 421.
7. Eliza Haywood, *The History of Miss Betsy Thoughtless* (4 vols., London: 3rd edition, 1752), IV, 22–25.
8. Conversations with women of various ages have led me to believe that dreams of fear are extremely common before marriage, and are quite separate from fear (if any) of sex. Young women who have had pre-marital sex, often for some years, with the man they intend to marry, seem to be just as much afflicted with nightmare prior to marriage as were women of a previous generation who went virgin to the bridal, and their fear-dreams embody the same images.
9. I am indebted to George Starr's discussion of *The Man of Feeling*; see above, pp. 39–43.
10. Frances Burney, *Cecilia, or Memoirs of an Heiress* (5 vols., London: 1782), V, 333.
11. Frances Burney (D'Arblay), *Camilla, or A Picture of Youth* (Oxford English Novels Edition, London, 1972), pp. 874–76.

12. See Clara Reeve's Preface to the Second Edition of her novel, in *The Old English Baron* (Oxford English Novels Edition, London, 1967), pp. 4–5.

13. Sophia Lee was indebted to the Continental novel, especially to Prévost. *The Recess* caused some stir; it went through a good number of editions and appeared in several translations. Despite its anachronisms and its juggling of facts, it was hailed by some English reviews for its historicity in introducing credible characterizations of Queen Elizabeth, Leicester, *et al*. See Devendra P. Varma's Introduction to the Arno Reprint edition of *The Recess, or A Tale of Other Times* (3 vols., New York: Arno Press, 1972).

14. See Ann Henry Ehrenpreis' Introduction to *Emmeline, The Orphan of the Castle* (Oxford English Novels Edition, London, 1971), pp. viii–ix.

15. Ann Radcliffe, *The Castles of Athlin and Dunbayne: A Highland Story* (1821 edition, as reprinted, New York: Arno Press, 1972), p. 7.

16. Reeve, *Old English Baron*, pp. 42–45.

17. Radcliffe, *A Sicilian Romance* (1821 edition, as reprinted in 2 vols., New York: Arno Press, 1971), II, 209–10.

18. Radcliffe, *The Italian, or The Confessional of the Black Penitents* (Oxford English Novels Edition, London, 1968), p. 318.

Part II

Smollett

4 A Diffused Picture, an Uniform Plan: Roderick Random in the Labyrinth of Britain

JOHN BARRELL

John Barrell is a Marxist critic with well-developed interests in landscape poetry and the visual arts. He combines social criticism with an acute sense of how it can derive from an attention to literary forms and conventions. An issue which unites much of his criticism, including the essay below, is the problem of perspective. That is, a writer's conviction that society is coherent, is itself a fiction, a product of a specific ideology, since it is actually a conglomerate of competing interests. The fantasy of coherence in the mid eighteenth century is made possible by two devices: the idea that the gentleman, or some such disinterested figure, can step back to frame a picture of society from a convenient distance; and the idea of a 'common language' which resists the localism and particularity of regional dialects. *Roderick Random* exemplifies these principles. The book describes an enormous range of callings and languages, all of which are represented almost pictorially or statically. Roderick's vigorous mobility (by contrast) is one feature of the plot allowing Smollett to create the illusion that his hero is a gentleman who can comprehend British society as a unified and organic whole.

A diffused picture: the variety of languages and occupations

The language of *Roderick Random* is remarkable for a diversity which is, however (though to a lesser degree), a feature of Smollett's other novels and of Fielding's as well. Roderick himself is born and brought up in Scotland, and in the early part of the book we are told on a number of occasions that his accent betrays his place of origin. When he and his valet Strap set out from Newcastle on the road to London, they are picked up by a waggon driver in whose speech is phonetically represented the accent of the north-eastern counties. The first word they hear in London, 'Anan', is at once a representation of the vulgar pronunciation of London, and an indication that as Scots they are 'unintelligible' to Londoners – the word translates as 'Eh?

What did you say?'[1] When Roderick is applying for a position as surgeon's mate, he is told how to make his application by a fellow applicant who speaks in 'broad Scotch'. The surgeon's mate aboard his ship speaks with the thick Welsh accent of Fluellen, and sings in the Welsh language. An irascible Irishman speaks in the 'true Tipperary cadence', and expresses himself with what Roderick regards as equally typical Irish illogicality; other Irishmen on board Roderick's ship address each other in Erse.[2] When Roderick returns to England after a voyage to the West Indies, the first people he meets are a pair of agricultural labourers, whose Sussex accent is phonetically represented; and their squire speaks an only slightly less broad version of the same accent.[3] A short section of the novel takes place in France, where Roderick hears Dutch spoken as well as French and English; but even in England itself we hear Latin, Italian, and various versions of French – a sort of *franglais* and the dialect of Gascony.[4] The occupational dialect of various members of the professions is fully represented: the naval language of Roderick's uncle, Tom Bowling, and of the ratings on board the *Thunder*; the terms of law and physic in the mouths of their practitioners; the sermon-like cadences of a parson; the irascible language of junior army officers, and the terms of fortification in the mouth of a general;[5] and the unintelligible accent of a Scottish schoolmaster who offers to teach the 'pronunciation of the English tongue, after a method more speedy and uncommon than any practised heretofore', of whom Roderick remarks, 'three parts in four of his dialect were as unintelligible to me, as if he had spoke in Arabick or Irish'.[6]

In addition to the foreign languages, the regional dialects, and the occupational habits of expression represented or referred to in the narrative, there is a multiplicity of versions of English in one or another way 'uncommon': a vulgar attempt at a genteel love letter, reminiscent of a similar effort in *Jonathan Wild*, and phonetically spelt; the pedantic fustian of the Scottish schoolmaster; the over-refined English of a homosexual naval captain; 'Billingsgate', a generic name for utterances richly profane and obscene; the vulgarly practical language of an over-thrifty apothecary and his wife; and various others.[7] These languages might be imagined to represent Britain as that anarchy of tongues, that Babel, which was the nightmare of the grammarians and the horror, also, of one of the characters in the novel, who fears that 'our language' may become 'a dissonant jargon without standard or propriety'.[8] It would require, it seems, the gift of tongues to understand, let alone to speak all the languages in the novel; for one of the arguments advanced in the century in favour of the need for a 'national' language was that northcountrymen, for example (as Roderick was), could not understand westcountrymen, and that 'even in Kent, and Berkshire, we hear words and sounds, that are not known in Middlesex';[9] whereas the language of the polite was universally understood.

I make no apology for following that list of languages with another [list], the longest and not the last, by which something of this book's extraordinary determination to represent the diversity of British society can be exemplified; for still more remarkable than the number of languages imitated or referred to in *Roderick Random* is the number of occupations followed by the characters in the book, or mentioned in the course of the narrative. There can be few works in any period of English literature since the fourteenth century which offer an account of English society as marked as is that of the eighteenth-century episodic novel by what Ferguson was to term 'the separation of arts and professions'.

Of characters, then, with some pretensions to politeness, learning, or skill in the arts, Smollett represents or mentions schoolmasters, a school usher and a teacher of languages, various members of the clergy – rector, vicar, curate, catholic priest; actors, a theatre proprietor and a theatre manager, a musician, a painter, an ambassador and his secretary, a member of parliament, various surgeons and physicians, clerks, a barrister, and various authors – a poet, a historian, and a journalist. Among tradesmen of various ranks we meet, or hear of, barbers, apothecaries, a pedlar, innkeepers, pawnbrokers, a money-lender, a snuff-seller, tailors, a periwig-maker, a wine merchant, a blacksmith, a chandler and a ship's chandler, a jeweller, merchants and merchant adventurers, a used-clothes salesman, a shoemaker, milliner, weaver, butcher, baker, cheese monger, waggon-master, printer, chemist, carpenter, glass-blower, watchmaker, bookseller and ballad-hawker. In addition to merchant seamen, the navy is represented by the ranks and occupations of admiral, captain, lieutenant, chaplain, surgeon, surgeon's mates, midshipman, clerk, boatswain and boatswain's mate, purser, steward, quartermaster, steersman, gunner, foremast man, and cabin boy; together with an officer, sergeant, corporal and drummer of the marines, and at the Admiralty, first-secretary and under-secretary, upper-clerk, under-clerk and beadle. The army is represented by the ranks of general, colonel, lieutenant, ensign, cornet, recruiting sergeant, private soldier and drummer.

Among the occupations of women can be listed bawd, kept woman, prostitute, sweeper, barmaid, chambermaid, dairymaid, cookmaid and cook, housekeeper, governess, midwife, cinder-wench, waiting-woman, milk-woman, oyster-woman, fish-woman, bum-boat woman, and bunter (these last two, respectively, a woman who from a small boat supplies provisions to ships in port, and a woman who lives by picking up rags in the street). In agriculture we meet farmers, labourers, overseers of estates and 'peasants' of unspecified condition. Apart from the farm labourers, others with menial employments include footmen and *valets de chambre*, a drawer, waiters, a tavern porter, street porter and janitor; a coachman to a private family, a stage-coachman, hackney-coachman, carman, draymen, chairmen and a waggon driver; a gardener, ostler, cook, bargees, chimney-sweepers and dustmen; and among those whose profession is to enforce the law or to break it, we can list an exciseman, constables, watchmen, bailiffs, turnkeys, a judge, justices of the peace, highwaymen, a confidence-trickster, card-sharpers, smugglers and foot-pads. This inventory is probably not exhaustive.

At the time that Smollett was writing *Roderick Random*, he was also engaged in the translation from the French of *Gil Blas*, Le Sage's episodic novel of seventeenth-century Spain.[10] Among the various aspects of the influence of *Gil Blas* on *Roderick Random*, the preoccupation with naming and representing the vast variety of occupations in society is one of the most striking. But in Le Sage's novel, though it is over half as long again as Smollett's, this occupational variety is less than in *Roderick Random*; and the practitioners of occupations are far more often merely *named* or referred to, less often represented in the action of the novel, by Le Sage than by Smollett. Nor are they usually so precisely specified – apart from an 'under-candle-snuffer' in a theatre (Smollett's translation), few if any have the richness of definition we find, for example, among Smollett's occupations of women or tradesmen.

What is more, in *Roderick Random* people *are* what they do: the minute differentiation of occupations is reinforced by representing each practitioner to whom Smollett assigns a name as the stereotype of, and so as entirely defined by, their occupations. Tom Bowling is repeatedly referred to, and refers to himself, as a 'tar'; a soldier is a 'son of Mars', 'a gentleman of the Sword'; schoolmasters are 'pedants'; a physician is a 'quack';[11] a squire who 'minded nothing but fox-hunting, and indeed was qualified for nothing else', becomes simply a 'fox-hunter', a 'spark', 'this young Acteon'; painters and actors are monkeys and apes, on account of the imitative nature of their arts.[12] The stereotypes are reinforced by description: the 'whole figure' of a usurer is 'a just emblem of winter, famine, and avarice'; and Bowling is appropriately bandy-legged, weather-beaten, his identity as 'tar' marked by the pitch which stains his breeches.[13]

Those characters who are named are named largely according to the occupations they profess: thus, for example, Potion is an apothecary, Rifle a highwayman, the name drawing attention both to his being armed, and to his practice of 'rifling' the possessions of his victims; Rapine is a usurer, Strap a barber from a family of shoemakers, Rinser a footman, Cringer a Member of Parliament, Staytape a tailor, Vulture a bailiff, Whipcord a ship's chandler and Gripewell a pawnbroker; Syntax and Concordance are schoolmasters, Bellower and Marmozet are actors. Sailors have such names as Oakhum, Marlinspike, Bowling ('bowline') and Rattlin ('ratline').[14] Scots are given recognizably Scottish names, with the exception of Random himself, whose Christian name however establishes his national identity; a Welshman is Morgan; Irishmen are called Odonnell, Oregan, and so on.

The characters in the novel are thus not only described primarily in terms of their occupational or national identities, they are named after them, so that those identities become the more fixed and all-determining; and those who have no occupations – aristocrats, squires, metropolitan men of fashion – are still named in such a way as to fix them in a character appropriate to their situation. We find squires called Bumpkin, Gawky, Gobble, Thicket and Top[e]hall; men and women of fashion are named after their habits of speaking, for theirs is a life not of action but of talk: Rattle, Chatter, Bragwell, Banter, Snapper; and Lords who imagine themselves to be on permanent exhibition, who move through the world conscious of their power and superiority, include Frizzle, Trippett, Stately, Shrug and Strutwell. The practice of naming characters in such a way as to confirm them in their occupational, social, or national identities is almost as old as comedy; what is unusual about *Roderick Random* is the profusion of such names implying the fixity of the characters in those identities: there are at least eighty such names, and every character represented or mentioned in the book who is named, is named after this fashion, with the single and significant exception of Random himself, whose name implies that only he eludes stereotypical definition.

We have seen that to be thus fixed in an occupational or other determining identity was understood in the writing of the mid eighteenth century to be a disability: the habit of concentration on one particular activity is inimical to the acquisition of that comprehensive view, to the attainment of that elevated viewpoint, from which society can be grasped in terms of relation, and not simply of difference; and the point is continually confirmed in this novel. Many of the characters in the book are represented as being entirely limited in their view of the world by the positions they occupy within it. The most notable of these is Roderick's uncle, Tom Bowling, the first of a sequence of sailors in Smollett's novels who understand the land as an extension, sometimes a puzzling one, of life at sea. It is not simply that he speaks always in naval terms; he is 'so much a seaman' that he applies those terms to everything he speaks of. On his first introduction, for example, he is attacked by some hounds and kills them, provoking the fury of their owner, Roderick's cousin 'the foxhunter':

> Upon which my uncle stepped forwards with an undaunted air, at the sight of whose bloody weapon, his antagonists fell back with precipitation; when he accosted their leader thus: – 'Lookée, brother, your dogs having boarded me without provocation, what I did was in my own defence. – So you had best be civil, and let us shoot a-head, clear of you.' Whether the young 'squire misinterpreted my uncle's desire of peace, or was enraged at the fate of his hounds beyond his usual pitch of resolution, I know not; but he snatched a flail from one of his followers, and came up with a shew of assaulting the lieutenant, who putting himself into a posture of defence, proceeded thus: – 'Lookée, you lubberly son of a w____e, if you come athwart me, 'ware your gingerbread-work. – I'll be foul of your quarter, d__n me.'[15]

So he continues throughout the book, as much liable to be misinterpreted by those who do not understand his terms as they are by him; for he is, according to Roderick, 'unacquainted with the ways of men in general, to which his education on board had kept him an utter stranger'.[16] A few other examples (for perhaps now we can dispense with lists) will perhaps do to confirm the degree to which so many of Smollett's characters are similarly strangers to the ways of men in general, on account of their 'faculty habits': the recruiting sergeant who talks military terms in his sleep; the barrister Roderick meets on the stage to Bath, who discusses warfare, and an *amour de voyage* between two fellow passengers, 'in terms': 'although the English had drawn themselves into a premunire at first, the French had managed their cause so lamely in the course of the dispute, that they would have been utterly nonsuited, had they not obtained a noli-prosequi'; the physician with an interest in etymology who had convinced himself that *bibere* means to drink, not largely but moderately; 'this was only a conjecture of his own, which, however, seemed to be supported by the word *bibulous*, which is particularly applied to the pores of the skin, that can only drink a very small quantity of the circumambient moisture, by reason of the smallness of their diameters'.[17]

An uniform plan

I have said more than enough to establish that the social world of *Roderick Random* is one of extreme differentiation and fragmentation; I now want to discuss how it is that the novel, and the society it creates, could nevertheless be understood by Smollett as coherent. For [the idea] that a novel which does not 'deviate from nature' in its depiction of the variety of the social world as Smollett understood it, and [the idea] that in achieving unity as a novel it could thereby reveal the usually invisible unity of the society it represented, were themes that engaged Smollett in two important theoretical comments on the form. In the dedication to his third novel, *Ferdinand Count Fathom* (1753), he writes:

> A Novel is a large diffused picture, comprehending the characters of life, disposed in different groupes, and exhibited in various attitudes, for the purpose of an uniform plan, and general occurrence, to which every individual figure is subservient. But this plan cannot be executed with propriety, probability or success, without a principal personage to attract the attention, unite the incidents, unwind the clue of the labyrinth and at last close the scene by virtue of his own importance.[18]

The 'picture', then, which is the novel, is 'diffused'; in a review of 1763, attributed to Smollett, he uses the word again – the novel is 'a diffused comedy unrestrained by the rules of the drama, comprehending a great variety of incident and character'.[19] It exhibits the variety of society, and of a differentiated, fragmented society imagined as scattered across the picture surface; but the insistence on diffusion, on difference, is contained by an equal concern with uniformity, with 'general occurrence' (or 'coming-together'), 'to which every individual figure is subservient'. Indeed, when Smollett writes that the characters are disposed in groups 'for the purposes of an uniform plan', he seems to be flirting with the language of natural theology, as if 'order in variety' is the novelist's plan and purpose for the world of the novel as it is God's for the world he has created; for like the universe described in the *Essay on Man*, the picture is at once diffused and *composed*, and its diffusion, like that of the divinely ordered economic society sketched out in Pope's poem, is not the enemy but the basis of its composition. It is from the position of the observer, outside the picture, that the scattered groups form some sort of coherent pattern, but, in the novel at least, that pattern is by itself only rudimentary, and needs to be confirmed by the activity of the principal personage, who attracts our attention, so that we follow his movement, as it were, from group to group; and in that way he ensures that we grasp the picture as an orderly arrangement of different 'passages', and thus he 'unites' the incidents that the picture displays.

The metaphor of the picture is important not only in the notion it offers of composition, of an order visible to those who stand outside it, but in the tensions it creates – and has already created in my account of Smollett's theory – by presenting the novel as a static composition through which the principal character moves in time. It is in the eighteenth century that criticism in England begins to differentiate between the visual and the literary arts particularly in terms of an opposition between the possibilities available to synchronic and diachronic narrative; and this passage seems not only aware of that critical opposition, but to exploit it. The discussion of all characters but the principal is concerned to emphasize their immobility in a manner we can relate directly to the fixed quality of characterization we have already noticed. They are passive beneath the hand of the artist: they are 'disposed', and 'exhibited' – in the review already referred to, the argument again makes use of a pictorial metaphor, and the point that the lesser characters should be subservient to the principal is again reinforced by a passive verb: they should be 'kept from advancing forwards'. The whole sentence from this review is worth quoting, to reinforce the tension that arises from an attempt to describe the *process* of a novel in terms of the static *product* which a picture may in some sense be regarded as. Writing of the principal character, Smollett says:

> He must still maintain his dignity, like the chief figure in the foreground in a picture; and the author, as the painter, must take care to preserve a 'keeping' in his performance; that is, all the other characters shall be in some measure, subservient to the principal, and kept from advancing forwards so far as to rival the chief of the drama, in the attention of the reader.

The movement from picture, through drama, to a work *read*, may be confused and yet is in another light entirely appropriate; for the lesser characters, 'exhibited in . . . *attitudes*' – the word calling attention to the fixed identities and positions attributed to characters defined by occupational or regional peculiarities – are discussed in terms of a picture, but the principal is referred to as the hero of a play, in which we can more plausibly imagine him moving around among various groups to whom fixed positions in the scene have been assigned. The whole work however, is a novel, which we encounter as 'readers', and create a visual equivalent of the characters described on the page according as we are encouraged to do so by the representational skill of the novelist.

The 'principal personage' is, then, mobile; he operates with active infinitives: 'to attract . . . unite . . . unwind . . . close'; and as important as the word 'unite' is 'unwind' for it seems he unwinds the 'clue' to the labyrinth of a society made up of different 'groupes', not only for the benefit of the spectator, but as a process from which he also learns. The discovery that the society of the novel is at once diffused and composed is made by that character in his own progress through it; at the end, when he 'closes the scene' – when he has threaded his way through to the far distance – he must occupy, as he looks back to the groups disposed between his position and the spectator's, a similarly comprehensive viewpoint as the spectator occupies, so that both are enabled to grasp that the people they observe are disposed not simply in groups but in comprehensible relations. The novel thus 'comprehends' the characters of life in two senses of the word: it includes them, and it is a means of understanding them; in a review of *Peregrine Pickle*, John Cleland put particular stress on this function of contemporary 'realistic' novels, that 'they may serve as pilot's charts, or maps of those parts of the world, which every one may chance to travel through; and in this light they are public benefits'.[20] The novel offers us an image of society as a labyrinth, as uncharted country, and also the understanding to find our way through it, and so to grasp how it is constructed.

Roderick's education

The lesser characters, then, as Smollet explains in the dedication to *Ferdinand Count Fathom* and in the review I have referred to, wait motionlessly to be brought into relation and connection by the mobility of the principal personage; and nothing makes that opposition clearer than the contrast between the names of those lesser characters, on the one hand, which fix them in their (mainly occupational) identities, and on the other the name of the hero himself, Roderick Random. In the first place, no doubt, the name is intended to draw attention simply to the fact that as Smollett says Roderick shares 'the disposition of the Scots', who are 'addicted to travelling';[21] for in the course of the novel Roderick moves from his family estate somewhere in Scotland, to Glasgow, to Newcastle, to London, to the West Indies, to Sussex, to the continent, to London, to Bath, to London again, back to Sussex, to South America, back to the West Indies, to London again, and eventually, of course, back to the family estate. But the emphasis Smollett puts on the necessary mobility of the hero in those critical remarks we have just examined invites us to see the name Random as drawing attention equally to the fluid identity of Roderick, which cannot be contained by or fixed in the frozen 'attitudes' of the characters 'subservient' to him. I have said that in *Roderick Random* people are what they do; but Roderick himself is the exception that proves the rule, for he changes his occupation continually, without ever taking on the stereotypical characteristics of the 'normal' practitioners of the various occupations he enters.

On leaving school, he becomes a university student with a bent towards 'the *Belle Lettre*'; and when his uncle is no longer able to support him in that condition, he takes a post as assistant to a surgeon. He is soon obliged by circumstances to leave that employment and Scotland as well, and on coming to London he attempts to qualify as a surgeon's mate in the Navy; and though eventually he succeeds in this, no vacancy can be found for him, and he becomes instead assistant to an apothecary. He is dismissed by his master on being falsely suspected of theft, and is pressed on board a man-of-war as a common sailor; but his qualities and qualifications being recognized he achieves the rank of surgeon's mate. On returning to England, he is shipwrecked on the Sussex coast, and is found employment as a footman to a gentlewoman, whose niece Narcissa he will eventually marry. In this condition he rescues Narcissa from an attempted rape by a neighbouring squire who is also, unfortunately, a justice of the peace; so that he is forced to leave this employment too. He is carried to France by some smugglers, and enlists as a private soldier in the French army; but meeting again his former valet, Strap, who has found means to make himself comfortably off, the two of them return to London with the idea that Roderick can be fitted out as a gentleman; and he duly becomes a fortune-hunter. He is not successful in finding a rich heiress to marry, and becomes briefly a place-seeker, attaching himself to an Earl who happens to be a homosexual, and who uses his apparent interest at court (for in reality he has none) to attract potential lovers; and so Roderick turns to fortune-hunting again, but quickly exhausts his funds and Strap's, falls into debt, and is carried to the Marshalsea. His debts are eventually paid by his uncle, who has made himself rich as a merchant adventurer, and who, about to set out on another voyage, employs Roderick as ship's surgeon, and lends him money to 'purchase an adventure' – goods for sale overseas – and thus to set up as a merchant adventurer himself. They carry a cargo of slaves to South America, where Roderick rediscovers his long-lost father, who had 'disappeared' when Roderick was still a baby. His father has also become rich by trade, and returns to Britain with his son, where he buys the family estate, and thereby Roderick becomes, finally, the gentleman he had always imagined himself to be.

The habit or necessity of moving from one position to another is of course a traditional feature of the picaresque novel: but it is treated quite differently by Smollett than it is by his available models in the genre. Thus Gil Blas, typically, changes masters on numerous occasions, but, typically again, he does not thereby change his *occupation* nearly as often; and though, like Roderick, he too becomes, briefly, a physician and a fortune-hunter, he usually appears as a footman, *valet de chambre* and (as his fortunes look up) as a steward or secretary of increasing but fluctuating influence, before becoming, like Roderick, a gentleman farmer. Until he achieves that position of independence, however, he is almost always more or less of a servant in some quality or another, as is usually the case with the heroes of such novels. It is the greater openness, the greater occupational diversity, of Smollett's eighteenth-century Britain as against Le Sage's seventeenth-century Spain, that enables and obliges Roderick to be represented as repeatedly changing his *occupation* rather than, simply, his *master*, as he proceeds through the novel; as it also enables and obliges Smollett to specify much more precisely the general variety of occupations in society than Le Sage does.

Roderick's claim to be a gentleman is not, indeed, very well founded, though Roderick – for the narrative is in the first person throughout – does not draw attention to the fact: he is the only son of the youngest son of a 'gentleman of considerable fortune and influence' though his father has evidently been brought up to expect to be able to maintain his condition as a gentleman – he has 'made the grand tour', and at the start of the novel does not seem destined to the fate of many youngest sons, to put his status at risk in becoming, say, a merchant, or an impecunious army officer, until he marries against his own father's wishes and is disinherited.[22] But it is Roderick's belief in his own gentility that enables him to accept the various 'low' employments he is forced into, without ever feeling himself to be what he does. Between quitting his post as an apothecary's assistant in London, and being impressed into the Navy, he lives briefly with a prostitute. She tells him the story of her life, and he reflects upon the greater wretchedness of her situation; for

> If one scheme of life should not succeed, I could have recourse to another, and so to a third, veering about to a thousand different shifts, according to the emergencies of my fate, without forfeiting the dignity of my character, beyond a power of retrieving it, or subjecting myself wholly to the caprice and barbarity of the world.[23]

'Without forfeiting the dignity of my character, beyond a power of retrieving it': Roderick is a 'gentleman-born'; whatever else he might have to become, as he veers about 'to a thousand different shifts', he is always that – the 'dignity of his character's is the dignity of his character as a *gentleman*, a character he wants only funds to support; so that whatever apparent occupational identity he may casually take on, whatever he may be forced to *do*, his true character is to do nothing, to be disengaged from the fixed identities assigned to those whose destiny it is to work for a living.

Throughout the novel he asserts his quality as a gentleman, even as it is questioned by other characters, and even though it is threatened continually by his need to earn his own bread. His uncle, who at first contemplated sending him to sea when he found himself charged with the responsibility of overseeing Roderick's future, agrees to send him to university only when he is persuaded by Syntax, the school usher, that Roderick's 'genius' would one day make his fortune on shore. It might then have followed that Roderick would have regarded his university education as a means of equipping himself to enter one of the learned professions; but though he has some interest in mathematics, natural and moral philosophy, and comes to understand Greek 'very well', 'above all things, I valued myself on my taste in *Belle Lettre*, and a talent for poetry, which had already produced some morceaus, that brought me a great deal of reputation'. Roderick uses his time at university, in fact, to become generally literate and polite, rather than to fit himself for any particular future occupation. On two occasions, the wisdom of a young man with his diminished prospects receiving an education at university at all is questioned: first by Mrs Potion, an apothecary's wife, who 'wished I had been bound to some substantial handicraft, such as a weaver or shoemaker, rather than loiter away my time in learning foolish nonsense that would never bring me in a penny'; and, second, by one of his examiners at Surgeon's Hall; 'my friends had done better if they had made me a weaver or shoemaker, but their pride would have me a gentleman (he supposed) at any rate'.[24]

Little as Roderick is able to 'support the character of a gentleman', this is his main concern throughout the novel: he asserts his gentility whenever it is questioned, and often when it is not. In a quarrel with his first employer, the surgeon Crab, he retorts that he is 'descended from a better family than any he could boast an alliance with'; challenged to a boxing match by a coachman, he replies that he 'would not descend so far below the dignity of a gentleman, as to fight like a porter' – and this when he is employed as a footman. Accused by a gascon soldier of having affronted, by his criticism of the ancien régime, the King of France, Roderick fights and loses a duel, but refuses to ask pardon, 'a mean condescension' which 'no gentleman . . . in my situation' should perform; and when confronted by the mother of Melinda Goosetrap, his first intended victim when he sets up as a fortune-hunter, he tries to compensate for having to acknowledge the smallness of his fortune, by pointing out that he is 'a gentleman by birth and education'.[25]

At every point in the novel when, for however brief a space, he appears to be comfortably settled and is not uncomfortably off, he makes a point of reassuming in public his true condition or something like it. Irritated that in the house of the London apothecary, Lavement, he is treated as 'a menial servant', he dresses himself in his best clothes, in which 'vanity apart', he made 'no contemptible figure', and manages to be mistaken by the daughter of the house for a man of far greater quality than his situation in the house suggests. He soon acquires the character of 'a polite journeyman apothecary' – the oxymoron directed ironically at his own vanity by the secure gentleman Roderick who, having recovered his father and estate at the end of the book, then sets out to write it, secure that his status will never again be called into question. Indeed, he soon comes to look upon himself as 'a gentleman in reality', and

> learned to dance of a Frenchman whom I had cured of a fashionable distemper; frequented plays during the holidays; became the oracle of an ale-house, where every dispute was referred to my decision; and at length contracted an acquaintance with a young lady, who found means to make a conquest of my heart, and upon whom I prevailed, after much attendance and solicitation, to give me a promise of marriage.[26]

That at this stage Roderick is far from being the 'gentleman in reality' he believes himself to be – one who not only is, but can support the condition of, a gentleman, is again clear to Roderick, the gentleman narrator: for gentlemen do not have to wait for holidays to go to the theatre, nor pride themselves on being deferred to in ale-houses, nor (it is to be hoped) mistake needy prostitutes, for that is what the young lady is, for rich heiresses, which is what she claims to be. But the point remains, that on all occasions Roderick is determined to cut the best figure he can and so at once to appear to be as much of a gentleman as his means will allow, and as little attached as possible to the occupation he happens at one time or another to be following.

In the same spirit of naive vanity which his later self can afford to record with playful irony, when he happens to get hold of some money in the West Indies, he begins to look upon himself 'as a gentleman of some consequence', buys himself a laced waistcoat, and makes 'a swaggering figure for some days, among the taverns'. Employed as a footman by Narcissa's aunt, he cannot resist revealing to aunt and niece that he is a master of Italian, French, and the learned languages, as well as that he has a talent for making elegant verses – for which admission he is rewarded by being treated by them rather with more reserve, than with more respect. When he re-encounters Strap in France, who has been left a considerable wardrobe by his deceased employer, a nobleman, Roderick gives a loving and long inventory of his clothes and trinkets (for Strap gives them all to him), and is delighted to be able to 'put on the gentleman of figure'. On his release from the Marshalsea and before he leaves with his uncle for South America, he finds time to appear in his 'gayest suit' at a coffee-house, to 'confound' a former friend with the magnificence of his dress; and when finally he is able to make an unquestionable assertion of his gentility, at the end of the novel, he is still vain enough to record that

> a certain set of persons, fond of scandal, began to enquire into the particulars of my fortune, which they no sooner understood to be independent, than the tables were turned, and our acquaintance was courted. . . .[27]

It is important that throughout these continual assertions that he is of gentle birth, and these continual attempts to appear as the gentleman he believes himself to be, Roderick does not really know how a gentleman should behave, and how he should appear; and this is true in spite of the fact that a number of the 'good' characters in the book acknowledge his 'true' status often enough. His schoolfriend Strap accompanies him everywhere as his humble valet, and does his best to keep him supplied with funds – and this in spite of Roderick's attempt to drop his acquaintance as an embarrassment, when he first believes himself to be 'a gentleman in reality', and in spite of his angrily describing his own extravagance as gentlemanly, and Strap's thrift as 'vulgar'; for Strap is Scotsman enough to accept his duty to serve a gentleman of his own locality, as unquestionably as ever an eighteenth-century highlander accepted the authority of his clan chief. Mrs Sagely, who first befriends him when he is shipwrecked in Sussex, immediately accepts Roderick as the gentleman he claims to be, in spite of his appearing at her house in nothing but 'a seaman's old jacket'; Narcissa, even before he has demonstrated to her his polite accomplishments, regards him as one 'who had so much of the gentleman in my appearance and discourse, that she could not for her soul treat me as a common lacquey' – and even her domestics come to refer to him as 'Gentleman John'.[28] Such people are ready enough to acknowledge that Roderick escapes being defined by the apparent identities – as vagrant, seaman, footman – that he is obliged to affect; but it is one thing for him to be recognized as being 'better' than what he appears to be, and another to be accepted as a gentleman when it is as a gentleman that he is trying to appear.

Thus, when he is able, after his period in France, to dress as a gentleman and to go to work, so to speak, as a fortune-hunter, he finds his gentility questioned as it never had been before. The fashionable physician Dr Wagtail introduces him to a group of gentlemen in London, as 'a mighty pretty sort of gentleman' who has 'made the grand tour – and seen the best company in Europe'; to which one of the group, Banter, replies that he takes Roderick to be 'neither more nor less than a French *valet de chambre*'; and though he later explains that this was a joke at Wagtail's expense, Roderick is 'extremely nettled' at the remark. As Roderick becomes known in London, Banter informs him that the 'town' has no high opinion of his pretensions to be a gentleman, and believes him to be nothing more than 'an Irish fortune-hunter' – a guess sufficiently close to the truth to discompose Roderick still more. Melinda Goosetrap circulates a rumour, again not far from the truth, that he is a fortune-hunter 'who supported himself in the character of a gentleman by sharping'; and Lord Quiverwit, a rival suitor to Narcissa, challenges Roderick to a duel, but questions whether he has 'spirit enough to support the character' he 'assumes'.[29] The opinions are largely the product of malice, but still serve to make us wary of accepting Roderick's status at his own estimate: for to achieve the character of a gentleman that Smollett finally establishes for Roderick at the end of the book, it is not enough to be of gentle birth; nor is it enough (though it is indispensable) to have the means to support oneself without any need to follow an employment; it is also necessary to behave, and to think like a gentleman, and this is something Roderick has to learn.

On his first appearance in London, dressed in the finery that Strap has made over to him, he goes to the theatre, and, to show himself off to proper effect, he sits in a front box.

> where I saw a good deal of company, and had vanity enough to make me believe, that I was observed with an uncommon degree of attention and applause. This silly conceit intoxicated me so much, that I was guilty of a thousand silly coquetries; and I dare say, how favourable soever the thoughts of the company might be at my first appearance, they were soon changed by my absurd behaviour, into pity or contempt.[30]

It is the very vanity that forces Roderick to claim to be, and to try to appear as, a gentleman on every occasion, that prevents him from behaving as the gentleman he is nevertheless always conscious of being. One obligation the plot must necessarily fulfil, if Roderick is to be established as a 'gentleman in reality', is of course to provide him with a fortune, not only that he may support himself in the condition to which he believes himself entitled, but so that he can put aside the lack of gentlemanly candour, of openness and frankness of dealing, involved in the attempt to support himself in that condition without the funds necessary to do so; but another and equally important obligation, though it is fulfilled rather perfunctorily, is to establish that by the end of the book Roderick has learned to be the gentleman that he will be accepted as without question in his future life. To some extent, of course, these obligations are one and the same, for his vanity and lack of candour were forced upon him by his poverty, and when that disappears, so, we may expect, will they. But as the various portraits of proud noblemen and fox-hunting squires make clear, there is more to being a gentleman than birth, money or even good manners: one must acquire that comprehensive view of society which is an exclusive but not invariable attribute of the true gentleman, and which brings with it that sureness and correctness of judgement in the affairs of society, so evident in the ironic tone of Roderick's narrative, and so lacking in his earlier behaviour which that irony is concerned to satirize.

Whatever vices have been cultivated in Roderick by the contrast between his birth and his fortune, it is pointed out by two characters, whose opinions we have every reason to trust, that his indigence and his sufferings have qualified him better to be a gentleman, than a youth and early manhood spent in affluence would have done. Miss Williams, the prostitute whom Roderick had earlier intended to marry, and who turns up towards the end of the novel as Narcissa's loyal maid and confidante, reassures him that

> altho' some situations of my life had been low, yet none of them had been infamous; that my indigence had been the crime not of me, but of fortune; and that the miseries I had undergone, by improving the faculties both of mind and body, qualified me the more for any dignified station.

The same point is made by Roderick's father, when he has heard the story of Roderick's life; he

> blessed God for the adversity I had undergone, which, he said, enlarged the understanding, improved the heart, steeled the constitution, and qualified a young man for all the duties and

> enjoyments of life, much better than any education which affluence could bestow.

That the life Roderick has led has 'improved' the 'faculties' of his body, has 'steeled' his 'constitution' as to have lived the life of such a squire as, for example, Narcissa's brother, hunting by day and drinking port by the bumper at night, would not have done, may be acknowledged without further comment. And that his sufferings have 'improved' his heart does not require much more: an essential qualification for being a gentleman as Smollett envisages the condition, is to be benevolent; benevolence is a quality notably lacking in the noblemen and gentlemen whom Roderick encounters in the book, from his grandfather who is described in the first paragraph of the novel as having a 'singular aversion' for beggars, to Narcissa's brother, again, who in the last paragraph of the book is still trying to appropriate her fortune by fraud. As is clear, for example, by his reaction on hearing Miss Williams's account of her life, and particularly by his treatment of the sick and the impoverished on board ship and in the Marshalsea, Roderick's own experience of hardship has taught him to do his best to alleviate the hardship of others; so that just as his father, before he disappeared, had been 'the darling of the tenants' on the family estate, so Roderick, on his return there, promises to be the same.[31]

What is for our purposes more in need of comment, is that Roderick's experiences have improved the faculties of his mind, have 'enlarged the understanding'; for if this argument of Miss Williams and Roderick's father can be made good, it must be by showing that his experiences, and particularly his experience of the numerous occupations he enters, has given him a more comprehensive grasp of the society he lives in, than a gentleman brought up in more fortunate circumstances could have acquired; and this is, perhaps, the crucial theme of the book. For in the course of Roderick's 'thousand shifts' – his employment for example in the various branches of medicine, on board ship, and as a soldier in the French army – he adds to the polite education he had attained at university, a practical knowledge of the procedures, and the language, of various professions and occupations, which is represented as being often more accurate than the knowledge which the various practitioners of those individual occupations have acquired. When he first goes to the surgeon Crab for employment, he reveals that in addition to having cultivated his interest in *belles-lettres*, he understands

> a little pharmacy, having employed some of my leisure hours in the practice of that art, while I lived with Mr. Potion: neither am I

> altogether ignorant of surgery, which I have studied with great pleasure and application.

The knowledge Roderick has acquired, he has acquired as a gentleman amateur, in his 'leisure hours', with application, but also with pleasure; and he adds to this knowledge during the period of his employment with Crab, to a point where he is evidently more qualified in the various branches of medicine than anyone in the novel who has received a professional training in the art, with the possible exception of Morgan, who also has a claim to be a gentleman. On a number of occasions he reveals a wide knowledge of the 'dialect', as Johnson calls it, 'of navigation': and in his discussion of the conduct of the seige of Cartagena, and of the battle of Dettingen, he reveals a full knowledge of the language of military strategy and fortification, a knowledge fuller, indeed, than that of an old general whom he meets, and who shows himself ignorant of what Roderick describes as 'one of the most simple terms of fortification'.[32] As we have seen, he also understands, and as narrator can represent phonetically, a number of regional pronunciations of English and the dialect words associated with them; and has a full knowledge of two modern and two ancient languages.

We can see, of course, Roderick's ability to reproduce this variety of languages simply as an exigency of the first-person narrative, which if it is to include such a variety, has to attribute a knowledge of them to the teller of the tale; but that is certainly to miss the point, that Roderick acquires that knowledge in the course of his life, and that it is in large measure his acquisition of them which enables him to appear at the end of the book as a complete gentleman of 'enlarged understanding' who is qualified therefore to write the account of British society that he is writing, and to 'unite the incidents' of the novel, and to 'unwind the clue of the labyrinth' made by the apparently 'diffused' panorama of characters 'disposed in different groupes, and exhibited in various attitudes'. The act of writing the book is, as we have seen, an act of looking back on that panorama from a viewpoint in the background of the picture which 'closes the scene', a viewpoint made as comprehensive as the reader's by virtue of the knowledge Roderick has acquired in threading his way among the various characters, and learning the procedures and languages of their various occupations, without, however, ever making the mistake of imagining that any one of those languages is in itself adequate to making a comprehensive description of the contents of the picture.

To show himself qualified to write the novel, therefore, Roderick must understand all the languages it must include, and must use them, also, only as each is appropriate, and not as, according to

Johnson, the members of occupational fraternities do, who make their knowledge 'ridiculous' by the 'injudicious obtrusion' of terms into conversations on general topics.[33] Thus, he does not, as Bowling does, apply the language of the sea to anything but the sea; or the language of law to warfare, as the barrister does; or the language of warfare to anything but its proper object, as does the soldier; nor must he allow his knowledge of words used in a technical sense in medicine to obliterate his knowledge of their use in common conversation, which is the offence of the physician Dr Wagtail. To use the terms of an art as if they can describe anything other than the objects of that art, is to show oneself lacking in that comprehensive knowledge, that enlarged understanding, which must grasp the diversity of the world if it is also to grasp its unity.

But to describe that unity, another language is required, a language poised impartially between all the occupational and regional dialects the novel exhibits; and this must be, of course, that 'common' language 'without which', according to Dr Concordance, Roderick will be 'unfit for business' in England,[34] and which is common only in the sense that it is free equally of all the vices of idiosyncrasy that characterize the other languages in the novel. This is the language of the narrative itself, which acts as a permanent and continual corrective on the various different dialects it encloses, so that each time that it appears, after a passage of occupational or regional dialect, it pulls us back to the central position that we must occupy, as we inspect the picture, if we are to understand the 'uniformity' it is concerned to elicit out of apparent diffusion. And this is also a language which Roderick, it seems, must learn; his education at a village school in Scotland left him speaking in a Scottish accent which identifies him as a Scot on a number of occasions in the early part of the novel – by Strap in Newcastle, by a confidence-trickster and by a justice of the peace in London. It seems to be only by about the time that he believes himself (however erroneously) to be a 'gentleman in reality' that he ceases to be identifiable by his accent; and it is only from about then – though Smollett's practice is not entirely consistent – that his own voice can enter the passages of dialogue in the novel; for had it done so earlier, Roderick the narrator would perhaps have had to record himself speaking a dialect which could be represented phonetically, as only the language of the centre, of the gentleman of metropolitan experience, whose language cannot be identified as 'a' language, cannot be. Roderick does of course speak, in some sense, before this point; but his early speeches are in various ways contained as a part of the narrative, and therefore appear as spoken in the language of the gentleman that he acquires only later. His speech may be marked by inverted commas, but in that case it will take the forms and tenses of reported speech; or it may take the form of direct speech, but without inverted commas, and this when the utterances of other characters are being framed and marked according to the usual practice of representing dialogue.

Roderick then must learn the language of the centre as he must learn the language of the circumference; and that he has acquired it with success is first evident when in the final paragraph of the final chapter, the tense changes to the present, and Roderick, at last in a position to offer a comprehensive account of his progress through the society of the novel, writes the first paragraph of Chapter I:

> I was born in the northern part of this united kingdom in the house of my grandfather, a gentleman of considerable fortune and influence, who had on many occasions signalized himself in behalf of his country; and was remarkable for his abilities in the law, which he exercised with great success, in quality of a judge, particularly against beggars, for whom he had a singular aversion.

This paragraph tells us almost as clearly as anything could of Roderick's success in supporting, now, the character of a gentleman, in that he has acquired the tone and the attitude appropriate to one. There is the 'genteel irony'[35] directed either against the judge's own opinion of himself, or against his reputation among those who, with equal lack of benevolence, unquestioningly believe that the interests of one's country are automatically served by an aversion for the indigent. There is Roderick's own implied benevolence, not only towards the beggars themselves, but towards his grandfather, whose 'aversion' he is content to criticize by that irony. And there is a confident, gentlemanly comprehensiveness of vision, evident in the word 'singular' – for a gentleman avoids singularity in language and behaviour, which (as Chesterfield warns) may 'give a handle to ridicule'[36] – and in his describing the place of his birth not as 'Scotland', as if it is disjoined from England, but as the 'northern part' of this 'united kingdom', as one portion of what he has come to understand as one unified society – and this less than two years after Culloden, for the victims of which Smollett had written an elegy, 'The Tears of Scotland' (1746), which expressed a courageous degree of resentment at the cruelty of the English.

Smollett and Chesterfield

Of Smollett's later novels, all but one describe the education of a gentleman who becomes eventually worthy of the station assigned to him. The exception is *Ferdinand Count Fathom* (1753), a novel whose name suggests that it should be regarded, in Cleland's terms, as a 'pilot's chart' of the progress through the 'ocean of life' of that other principal character in fiction who can be at once everything and nothing, the confidence-man. Of the others, *The Adventures of Peregrine Pickle* (1751) is probably the least interesting, and describes the youth and early manhood of a wandering hero, and the extremely lengthy process by which he learns the behaviour appropriate to a member of the substantial country gentry. *The Adventures of Sir Launcelot Greaves* (1760–1), a novel in the manner of *Don Quixote*, has as its central character a baronet who, before the opening of the novel, had been the ideal of the benevolent paternalist landowner but who, apparently unhinged by love, has taken to wearing armour and travelling the country 'to act as coadjutator to the law, and even to remedy evils which the law cannot reach'. The problem of the novel is whether Greaves is to be regarded by us, as he is by almost all the characters he meets, as a 'lunatic knight-errant';[37] for it is clear that he has a more complete grasp of the condition of England and of the virtues necessary to its government that anyone else in the book.

This is how Greaves describes the qualities necessary to a knight-errant:

> . . . towards the practice of chivalry, there is something more required than the virtues of courage and generosity. A knight-errant ought to understand the sciences, to be master of ethics or morality, to be well versed in theology, a complete casuist, and minutely acquainted with the laws of his country. He should not only be patient of cold, hunger, and fatigue, righteous, just, and valiant, but also chaste, religious, temperate, polite, and conversable, and have all the passions under the rein, except love, whose empire he should submissively acknowledge.

There is not much here, except that the knight be patient of cold and hunger, and that he submit to the empire of love, which we have not seen attributed throughout this book to the ideal of the eighteenth-century gentleman, who is certainly better described by this account than is the knight of romance; so that a part of the problem of determining whether Greaves is mad or not, is the question of whether anyone who seriously attempted, not simply to exhibit, but to employ the virtues of the gentleman in a society as corrupt as that described in the novel, would not appear to be an anachronism as ludicrous as Sir Launcelot, 'armed cap-à-pie'.[38] At the end of the novel, Greaves lays aside his armour and, if he had lost his senses earlier, may now be assumed to have recovered them; he marries and settles down again to the benevolent management of his estate. But the change seems to be handled more as a necessity for the conclusion of the novel than as an indication that earlier it had been Greaves himself, and not the other characters, whose understanding of virtue and corruption had been impaired.

Smollett's only epistolary novel, *The Expedition of Humphry Clinker* (1771) is also his last. The epistolary form is one which, from the point of view of one of the questions considered [here] – whether it was still possible in the mid eighteenth century to have a comprehensive view of society – must appear to propose a reply in the negative; for the form will normally attribute only a small portion of knowledge to each of the correspondents, and, in leaving the possibility of a complete knowledge only to the author and reader, implies that this completeness is available to them only *as* author and reader, who will have as fragmented a perception of the world they live in as do the correspondents of theirs. The novel describes a journey undertaken by a valetudinarian, a prickly Welsh gentleman called Matthew Bramble, who is seeking to recover his health. Accompanied by his sister, nephew, niece, a maid, and by Humphry Clinker whom he engages on the road as a manservant, Bramble goes to various spas, to London, Edinburgh, Glasgow and thus down the western side of England until, at the end of the novel, he is about to return to his estate. The chief symptom of Bramble's illness, or hypochondria, is a testy impatience with everything he encounters until, in the course of his travels, and by the education they provide, he 'has laid in a considerable stock of health', and has recovered the balanced and tolerant view of the world as it should be seen from the secluded, independent estate of a country landowner.[39] In recovering that view, he recovers the form also from the diffusion and fragmentation it threatens, and at the end of the book is in a position to offer apparently authoritative judgments on the action of the novel and the society it represents.

But of all the gentlemen whom Smollett thus brings to a clearer understanding of the world, it is Roderick whose experience is the most comprehensive, and whose education is the most remarkably unlike what [might seem] appropriate to a man of his position. Indeed, if we compare Roderick with the 'fine gentleman' defined by Steele,[40] he will seem almost a parody of that universal man. The gentleman, according to Steele, must have been 'led through the whole Course of the polite Arts and Sciences': well, Roderick had done his best to study the polite arts as an impecunious student at a Scottish university; as for the polite sciences, he can offer at least a competent knowledge of pharmacy and physic. 'He should be no Stranger to Courts and Camps' – Roderick has enlisted as the client of a nobleman without influence, has had some acquaintance with the less polite end of polite society in Bath and London, and has served as a private soldier in a foreign army. 'He must travel to open his Mind, and enlarge his Views' – Roderick has managed, as a mercenary, some sort of tour of Europe, and as a surgeon's assistant and merchant-adventurer has even been to the new world. 'He must not forget to add . . . the Languages and bodily Exercises most in vogue' – Roderick does well here, for in addition to the classical languages and French and Italian, he has acquired an understanding of a host of regional and faculty dialects, and as for bodily exercises, he has a great propensity to get into fights, and knows the jargon of pugilism.[41]

The gentleman that Smollett has defined, in Roderick and in his father, whose life has also not been without its vicissitudes of fortune, is strikingly unlike the gentleman Steele describes, or the one whom Chesterfield attempts to define in his letters to Philip Stanhope; or whom Dyer or Thomson had imagined surveying the varied landscape of English society, or whose language was being determined by eighteenth-century writers of grammars. For Smollett, it seems, birth, affluence, polite learning, and a freedom from occupational determination, are necessary but are not sufficient conditions for the nurture of a gentleman whose 'enlarged understanding' can grasp the pattern of connection and relation in the society he observes. As I have said, the notions and the language of the gentleman as they have been defined earlier in this book have been defined primarily by negation: they are not the notions and the languages of anyone whose occupational or regional affiliations we can recognize, and in this view a gentleman is in, so to speak, a condition of empty potential, one who is imagined as being able to comprehend everything, and yet who may give no evidence of having comprehended anything. The other gentlemen or aristocrats who appear in *Roderick Random* clearly fail to measure up to his ideal: the squires are certainly without the politeness that comes with education, or the benevolence that comes with understanding, and the noblemen are so locked within a world of courtly intrigue, patronage, and interest, that they have lost any sight of the true interests of the society they pretend to serve: both are without the benevolence, the sympathy, so important to Shaftesbury's notion of the gentleman: the ability to know how you would feel in someone else's shoes, and that Roderick has it is due to the fact that he has been in almost everyone else's shoes. Smollett's gentleman looks, by contrast with squire or nobleman, to be a very bourgeois ideal: though he must be well born, well off and well educated, he acquires his understanding, he earns it, by a practical acquaintance with the vicissitudes and varieties of social life, and comes to understand society as a whole because he comes to understand its parts, and not simply because, understanding nothing in particular, he is assumed therefore to understand everything in general.

From 1739 to the early 1750s Chesterfield was writing a long series of letters to Philip Stanhope, his illegitimate son, advising him on how to acquire a 'gentlemanlike manner', that 'je ne sçais quoi qui plait';[42] and though Chesterfield, of whose gentlemanly civility Smollett had no high opinion, has a good deal in common with Smollett in his estimation of the character and function of a gentleman, he differs from him on that subject in ways which point not only to what we could think of as the difference between an aristocratic, and Smollett's more bourgeois ideal of gentility, but also to what was becoming a new sense, in the middle and second half of the eighteenth century, of who it was who could understand the social and economic relations by which society coheres. Chesterfield is as certain as Roderick that 'sottish drinking' and 'rustic sports' will 'degrade' a gentleman; as convinced, if not more so, of the need for a gentleman to speak the language of 'good company', which is usually to be learned only from those 'of considerable birth, rank and character';[43] and he is equally concerned to establish that a gentleman has to acquire a knowledge of the world which cannot be acquired by, for example, the 'learned parson, rusting in his cell at Oxford or Cambridge', who

> knows nothing of man, for he has not lived with him, and is ignorant of all the various modes, habits, prejudices and tastes, that always influence and often determine him.

For Chesterfield no less than for Smollett, the knowledge of the world which is to be acquired by, and which distinguishes, a gentleman, is to be learned not only from books but practically, by intercourse with 'the world'. It is inimical to any singularity whether of character or occupation; for just as 'Whoever *is had* (as it is called) in company for the sake of any one thing singly, is singly that thing,' so to be a 'gentleman in reality' one must be as near as possible 'the *omnis homo, l'homme universel*',[44] whose faculties are developed in harmonious balance with one another, so that one is, ideally, no one thing in particular, but an epitome of all men in general.

But on what precisely constitutes the knowledge of '*l'homme universel*', and on how he acquires it, Chesterfield and Smollett are far apart. For example, one of Chesterfield's most repeated and most urgent injunctions to Stanhope is that he should at all costs avoid 'low company': 'people of very low condition, whatever their parts or merits may be', and especially that which 'in every sense of the word, is low indeed – low in rank, low in parts, low in manners, and low in merit'. Such company will communicate to Stanhope, however careful he is to avoid the taint, 'a vulgar, ordinary way of thinking, acting, or speaking', which 'young people contract' among servants; and for Chesterfield the keeping of low company is not to be justified, as it certainly is in the case of Roderick, on the grounds that it helps develop a full knowledge of the world. The 'world' is, in fact, a quite different place, a quite different notion, for Chesterfield and for Smollett: for Chesterfield, it is often best rendered as *'le monde'*; a gentleman is one *'qui a du monde'*;[45] and a knowledge of the world, though it is not, as the habit of referring to it in French suggests, exclusively a knowledge of the fashionable world, is largely that, and when it is more than that, can still to a surprising extent be learned in the fashionable world. Chesterfield intended Stanhope for a career in diplomacy and statesmanship, and is continually urging him to acquire, as he makes the grand tour, a knowledge of the laws, constitutions, customs, even the commerce of the countries he visits, as well as their languages; such knowledge is to be found, where not in books, by enquiry among the polite.[46] To it is to be added a diligent attention not only to the manners and address, but also to the weaknesses, of men of fashion, of the *'monde'*. It is such people that govern the world, and so who are, in a sense, the 'world' that Stanhope must learn to understand and manipulate.[47]

The knowledge of the world which Chesterfield, the Whig magnate, is trying to define is the knowledge appropriate to a far more considerable gentleman than Roderick would ever become or would ever wish to be: one who will 'contribute to the good of the society in which he lives' in a more dazzling manner than the retired country landowner. It is certainly not that minute knowledge that Roderick acquires, and could only acquire, from those who know their own business well, and nothing much besides. Thus Stanhope has no need to know anything of 'algebra, chymistry, or anatomy', which 'are never, that I have heard of, the objects of eloquence', and which, if introduced into private conversation, would indicate a man anxious to make an undignified display of his learning. Stanhope should learn perhaps 'a little geometry and astronomy; not enough to absorb your attention, and puzzle your intellects, but only enough, not to be grossly ignorant of either'. In general, 'those arts or sciences, which are peculiar to certain professions, need not be deeply known by those who are not intended for those professions',

> as for instance; fortification and navigation; of both which, a superficial and general knowledge, such as the common course of conversation, with a very little enquiry on your part, will give you, is sufficient.[48]

To become *'l'homme universel'* Roderick entered a series of different occupations or professions, and learned the arts, the sciences, the terms 'peculiar' to each – which, if they come to be satirized when used inappropriately, were still to be *understood* – so that his understanding of the world in general was based on his knowledge in detail of its component elements. To become the universal man as Chesterfield understands him to be, Stanhope need become only learned and polite: 'if you will but . . . exert your whole attention to your studies in the morning, and to your address, manners, air and *tournure* in the evenings, you will be the man I wish you'.[49] The theoretical knowledge of the world he requires will come to him from books; the practical knowledge will come to him in the assemblies of those *'qui ont du monde'*, from studying to imitate their manners, and to understand their characters.

The comparison of the gentleman as represented by *Roderick Random* and by Chesterfield provokes two related observations. The first is that however successful the novel may be in persuading us that only a gentleman like Roderick can seriously be imagined as able to perform the task of comprehensive observation, a gentleman like Roderick cannot seriously be imagined at all. 'Princes', writes *The Rambler*, 'when they would know the opinions or grievances of their subjects, find it necessary to steal away from guards and attendants, and mingle on equal terms among the people'.[50] But that dream of a temporary an informative descent, of a Prince Hal or a Peter the Great, is a dream of the folk-tale or the novel, and *Roderick Random* is a fiction of the comprehensive vision which announces that vision as capable now of being acquired only by the jack-of-all-trades, servant of none, that Thomson had been obliged to represent in the mythical exploits of Peter or the allegorical figure of the Knight of Industry, and that Smollett represents in a hero whose 'adventures', however much verisimilitude may attach to each of them individually, cannot possibly be imagined as occurring to any individual except in a work of fiction. We may read the novel either as a criticism, a parody even, of the idea of the gentleman and his ability to see and understand the variety of social identities and the relations between them, or we may read it as an extreme, a rather desperate attempt to vindicate them; but it does not matter much which reading we choose, for in either case the novel suggests only the impossibility of the gentleman in the real world doing what Roderick does, or what Thomson claimed Talbot or Lyttelton could do.

We are left, however, with another possible observation, as we are by Johnson, by Dyer, by Ferguson, by Smith: that the claim to a comprehensive knowledge may now be made instead by the writer –

for of course Smollett, to write the novel, must know all that Roderick knows. And such a knowledge may plausibly be thought to have been the possession of a writer such as Smollett was, or was to become, who published, in addition to his novels, poems, plays and polite essays, a medical treatise, a volume of travels, a *Complete History of England*, and an eight volume work entitled (if you please) *The Present State of All Nations*, as well as editing the *Critical Review*, a periodical concerned to digest and criticize the current state of knowledge across as many arts, professions, and sciences as possible. It is the knowledge such writers as Hume, or Goldsmith, or Johnson or Smith strove to acquire; which aimed to grasp the relations of a multitude of social activities and practices by paying a detailed attention to as many of them as possible; so that a comprehensive knowledge of society may certainly, by the third quarter of the century, be more easily imagined in the man of letters than in the gentleman of fashion.

This certainly seems to be the claim made by Fielding in *Tom Jones*, a novel not much less remarkable than *Roderick Random* for the variety of occupations and faculty languages included in its representation of 'the mazes, the winding labyrinths' of human nature and society. To these mazes, it seems, the gentleman, one who has set himself up in 'the business that requires no apprenticeship', is a far less sure guide than the author. Squire Allworthy is apparently the paragon of the retired and independent country gentleman: a man of 'solid understanding', 'a benevolent heart', 'vast natural abilities', a considerable share of learning, and a large estate;[51] and yet the plot of the novel is dependent upon his making, in its first seven books, a catastrophic series of misjudgements on the characters and actions of those over whom he exerts authority as relative, employer, benefactor or magistrate: misjudgements which are represented by Fielding as arising not only from the determination of others to deceive him, but from his own detachment from the society over which he presides, and with which – the term will be defined in a moment – he has no 'conversation'. The narrator, however, is careful to excuse rather than condemn Allworthy for these failures of judgement, for to do so is an opportunity for him to display an insight into Allworthy's character as well as into the characters of whom Allworthy, by virtue of his position and responsibilities, might have been expected to judge more competently.

That the writer of such histories as *Tom Jones* is, or should be, more knowing than the 'gentleman' is a point which Fielding does not leave to rest upon the mere fact of his being the *author* of the characters, the society, and the plot he creates: the author of such books requires qualifications not to be looked for in 'gentlemen' authors, however 'considerable' a figure they may make 'in the republic of letters'. For a historian, even in the sense of a novelist, in addition to learning and 'humanity', requires, according to Fielding, two qualifications without which a comprehensive view of the society he recreates in his writings is impossible: 'genius', and a 'conversation' which is 'universal'.[52]

'Genius' he defines as 'that power or rather those powers of the mind which are capable of penetrating into all things within our reach and knowledge, and of distinguishing their essential differences'; one aspect of genius is 'invention', by which 'is really meant no more (and so the word signifies) than discovery, or finding out; or to explain it at large, a quick and sagacious penetration into the true essence of all the objects of our contemplation'. It is genius that teaches an author 'to know mankind better than they know themselves', and can guide him through the 'labyrinths' of the world. A universal conversation – Fielding uses the term in the sense given by Johnson, of 'commerce', 'intercourse' or 'familiarity' – is one which involves a knowledge of 'all ranks and degrees of men';

> for the knowledge of what is called high life will not instruct him in low; nor, *è converso*, will his being acquainted with the inferior part of mankind teach him the manners of the superior.[53]

'A true knowledge of the world', he insists, 'is gained only by conversation, and the manners of every rank must be seen in order to be known'; only thus can an author discover those 'certain characteristics in which individuals of every profession and occupation agree', and 'one talent of a good writer' is 'to be able to preserve these characteristics, and at the same time to diversify their operations', which he is able to do only if conversant with, not only the 'wise, the learned, the good, and the polite', but with 'every kind of character from the minister at his levee, to the bailiff in his spunging-house; from the dutchess at her drum, to the landlady behind her bar'.[54]

But evidently the kind of knowledge acquired by such a writer as Smollett, Fielding, or Johnson, as much obliged by the exigencies of his trade to develop a wide understanding of society as stimulated thereto by a disinterested curiosity, is not the knowledge of Roderick. The range of Fielding's writing is no less wide than Smollett's, and includes numerous plays and periodical essays, some verse, a history, a journal, political and legal pamphlets, and essays on practical social administration; and no doubt he based much of his claim to a 'universal conversation' on his experience as a magistrate in London. Smollett's experience of other occupations than writing was unusually wide: he was a physician, and sometime a ship's surgeon; he had some specialist knowledge of pharmacy, and arguably of warfare; but much else of what he represents Roderick as discovering by practice, he had discovered himself in the course of his career as an author, whose trade is to find out by inquiry what others learn by experience; and the same of course was true of Fielding. It is the knowledge of men who, as novelists, can without undue difficulty display a knowledge adequate to the comprehension of the world they have constructed, because they have constructed it; and the condition of its construction was of course precisely that they could show it to be comprehensible. Writers such as Johnson or Ferguson, attempting to describe a world they thought of themselves as observing, not as inventing, were not over-convinced that the professional writer was much more adequate to that task than the detached and independent gentleman had been: and as much as anything else it was this crisis of social knowledge that [such] writers bequeathed to the Romantics.

Notes

1. Smollett, *The Adventures of Roderick Random* (London 1748); edited with an introduction by Paul-Gabriel Boucé (Oxford 1979; hereafter *RR*), p. 62. Among critical studies of Smollett, I have found these the most useful: Ronald Paulson, *Satire and the Novel in Eighteenth-Century England* (New Haven, Conn. 1967), ch. v; P. G. Boucé, *The Novels of Tobias Smollett* (London 1976); Damian Grant, *Tobias Smollett: A Study in Style* (Manchester 1977); John Sekora, *Luxury: The Concept in Western Thought, Eden to Smollett* (Baltimore, Md 1977); and G. S. Rousseau, *Tobias Smollett, Essays of Two Decades* (Edinburgh 1982).
2. *RR*, pp. 78, 176, 291.
3. *RR*, pp. 212, 343, 348.
4. *RR*, pp. 233, 223, 317.
5. *RR*, pp. 325, 332, 147, 267, 273, 22–3, 14, 43, 263.
6. *RR*, pp. 66–7.
7. *RR*, pp. 81, 96, 196, 259–60, 313, 22–3.
8. *RR*, p. 286.
9. James Beattie, *The Theory of Language* (1788); reprinted with an introduction by Kenneth Morris (New York 1974), p. 93; see also Hugh Jones, *An Accidence to the English Tongue* (London 1724); reprinted (Menston 1967), pp. 11–13. Jones makes similar points about the mutual unintelligibility of speakers from different regions of England, 'so would it be a good Diversion to a polite *Londoner* to hear a *Dialogue*' between 'a *Yorkshire* and a *Somersetshire* downright *Countryman*
10. The translation appeared several months after the publication of *RR*, also in 1748.
11. *RR*, pp. 10, 11, 22, 323, 5, 47, 116.
12. *RR*, pp. 7, 9, 10, xlvii, 277, 391.
13. *RR*, pp. 50, 8.

14. Changes in pronunciation since the mid eighteenth century have concealed the relation of these nautical terms and the names derived from them. 'Bowline' would have been pronounced 'bowlin', and 'Bowling', also 'Bowlin'; 'ratline' and 'Rattlin' would similarly have been homophones.
15. *RR*, pp. 15, 9.
16. *RR*, p. 8.
17. *RR*, pp. 43, 327, 325, 268.
18. Smollett, *The Adventures of Ferdinand Count Fathom* (1753); edited with an introduction by Damian Grant (Oxford 1978), pp. 2–3.
19. *Critical Review*, XV (1763), p. 532. This review is attributed to Smollett by P. J. Klukoff, *Notes and Queries* (December 1966), p. 466; see also Klukoff's essay, 'Smollett and the *Critical Review*: criticism of the novel 1756–63', *Studies in Scottish Literature*, vol. iv, no. 2 (1966).
20. *Monthly Review*, IV (1751), p. 356.
21. *RR*, p. xlv.
22. *RR*, pp. 1–2.
23. *RR*, p. 136.
24. *RR*, pp. 15, 20, 22, 86.
25. *RR*, pp. 28, 227, 247, 295.
26. *RR*, pp. 99, 104, 108.
27. *RR*, pp. 206, 224, 256, 401, 431.
28. *RR*, pp. 315, 216, 223, 227.
29. *RR*, pp. 270, 278, 284, 359, 364.
30. *RR*, p. 257.
31. *RR*, pp. 342, 415, 5.
32. *RR*, pp. 27, 264; for the quotation from Johnson, see *Dictionary*, 'Preface', p. 8.
33. See John Barrell, *English Literature in History, 1730–1780: An Equal, Wide Survey* (London 1983), p. 134.
34. *RR*, p. 96.
35. Lord Chesterfield, *Letters to his Son and Others*, Everyman edn (London 1929; hereafter Chesterfield); letter of 26 July 1748. Except where noted, all letters cited are to Philip Stanhope, Chesterfield's illegitimate son, and all dates of letters are old style.
36. Chesterfield, letter to Philip Stanhope (his godson), 31 October NS (1765).
37. Smollett, *The Adventures of Sir Launcelot Greaves* (London 1760–1), chs. ii, xix.
38. Smollett, *Greaves*, chs. vii, ii.
39. Smollett, *The Expedition of Humphry Clinker* (London 1771), Bramble to Dr Lewis, 20 November.
40. See Barrell, *English Literature in History*, p. 37.
41. *RR*, p. 155.
42. Chesterfield, 22 October 1750; 1 November 1750; 12 November 1750.
43. Chesterfield, 4 October 1746; 19 April 1749; 12 October 1748.

44. Chesterfield, 30 April 1752; 5 September 1748; 22 September 1749.
45. Chesterfield, 12 October 1748; 27 September 1749; 30 April 1752.
46. Chesterfield, 9 December 1746; 30 June 1747; 15 January 1748; 16 February 1748; 9 March 1748; 26 July 1748; 5 September 1748; 29 March 1750; 19 November 1750; 3 January 1751; 18 March 1751.
47. Chesterfield, 4 October 1746.
48. Chesterfield, 16 August 1741; 9 December 1749; 28 February 1751; 26 July 1748.
49. Chesterfield, 22 September 1749.
50. *The Rambler*, no. 150, 24 August 1751.
51. Fielding, *The History of Tom Jones* (London 1749), Book XIII, ch. i; Book X, ch. vii; Book I, ch. ii; Book I, ch. x.
52. Fielding, *Tom Jones*, Book XIV, ch. i; Book XIII, ch. i.
53. Fielding, *Tom Jones*, Book IX, ch. i; Book XIII, ch. ix.
54. Fielding, *Tom Jones*, Book XIV, ch. i; Book X, ch. i; Book XIII, ch. i.

5 Self and Society: Comic Union in *Humphry Clinker*

Robert Folkenflik

Robert Folkenflik has written extensively on the eighteenth-century novel, especially on *Pamela*. In this essay – primarily a formalist reading of *The Expedition of Humphry Clinker* – he develops a theme that also concerns John Barrell. Smollett's epistolary technique serves to emphasize the plurality and partiality of the different characters' perspectives on their experiences. Whereas Barrell argues that the fiction of the gentleman provides the unifying vision which harmonizes the variety of classes and regions Smollett describes, Folkenflik argues that a similar purpose is served, in Smollett's last novel, by the reader. And that harmony-in-variety, he suggests, is the novelistic equivalent to the union that, after 1707, created the idea of Great Britain.

The Expedition of Humphry Clinker was a new departure not only for Tobias Smollett, but for the eighteenth-century novel as well. Unlike the nearly monolithic *Pamela*, this epistolary novel never lets any view dominate to the exclusion of other perspectives. The letters, separate but read in a series, are the perfect medium for Smollett's central theme. *The Expedition of Humphry Clinker* is a novel about the necessity of human relationships presented through the medium of individual voices, and therefore any one perspective is partial, inherently at the mercy of the ironies of a larger view.[1]

The larger view is ours as readers. From the first Smollett forces us to move out of a particular consciousness and into another. In the Richardsonian novel one usually identifies with or sympathizes with the chief letter-writer. In a sense we are made the confidant whoever the actual recipients of the letters are, as any reader of *Pamela* or *Clarissa* can attest. Yet, though we sympathize with Matt Bramble, Smollett, by his presentation of all five letter-writers in a row, does more than make an ensemble introduction of his characters. Our movement in and out of their consciousnesses enables us to see their selfhood as comically limited, and leads us to encompass all their views in a tolerant and embracing vision which prepares us for the accommodation of their various views in one social vision of the good life at the novel's end. This interplay of perspectives within the framework of a broader vision, over and above some of the greatest characters in literature, gives the novel its comic vitality. It is as though Smollett, having explored the uses of first-person narration in *Roderick Random* and focused mainly on the hero in most of his other novels, had come to see the limitations as well as the value of his technique. *Humphry Clinker* is not a farewell to the picaresque, but a transcendence of it. It is a work of full maturity.

In the first letter of *Humphry Clinker*, Matt Bramble, vexed and litigious, complains of the inability of Dr. Lewis's medicine to help him move his bowels, but one may fairly say, as Win comically does later, that 'the whole family have been in such a constipation' (p. 155).[2] The action of the novel may be described as a purging through activity, preeminently travel, and the recognition of the importance of human relationships.

In his first letter we also find a significant connection between his familial relationships and his medical complaints: 'As if I had not plagues enough of my own, those children of my sister are left me for a perpetual source of vexation – what business have people to get children to plague their neighbours?' (p. 5). This is not only a denial of the relationship of Liddy and Jery to him but an unwitting disregard of his own begetting of a bastard. As for Tabby, 'I almost think she's the devil incarnate come to torment me for my sins; and yet I am conscious of no sins that ought to entail such family-plagues upon me – why the devil should not I shake off these torments at once? I an't married to Tabby, thank Heaven! nor did I beget the other two: let them choose another guardian: for my part I an't in condition to take care of myself; much less to superintend the conduct of giddy-headed boys and girls' (p. 12). Though the novel does not make the point didactically, Matt has indeed sinned in a way that makes 'family-plagues' an appropriate punishment. And his physical illness is linked directly to his faulty relationship to others, especially the members of his own family.

Recent critics have pointed out that Matt's problems are clearly psychosomatic, and that Dr. Smollett was undoubtedly following the best eighteenth-century medical theory when he has Matt say

> I find my spirits and my health affect each other reciprocally – that is to say, every thing that discomposes my mind produces a correspondent disorder in my body; and my bodily complaints are remarkably mitigated by those considerations that dissipate the clouds of mental chagrin.[3]
>
> (p. 154)

There is, however, a more primitive and mythic side to Matt's complaint. The bowels, as frequent Biblical passages make clear, are the seat of human compassion. At the time of Humphry Clinker's first appearance as bastard and orphan, dismissed by an ostler without aid because he was too sick to work, Matt says to Jery, '"You perceive . . . our landlord is a Christian of bowels"' (p. 82). Yet Matt seems all the more bound because he cannot reconcile his genuine humanitarian feelings with his relationship to other human beings.

Matt, as we recognize from the beginning of the novel, is a benevolent misanthrope, and his disposition leads to his doing good by stealth, to an unwillingness to acknowledge openly his social conscience. In his first letter he tells Dr. Lewis, 'Let Morgan's widow have the Alderney cow, and forty shillings to clothe her children: but don't say a syllable of the matter to any living soul. . . .' He then requests that Lewis lock his drawers and keep the keys. This is a necessary precaution, but the images of secrecy combine to give us a sense (despite Matt's generosity) of confinement, closure, of a hiding within.

Many of the problems Matt encounters (and not only his constipation) have to do with the proper relationship between interior and exterior. When he reaches Scotland, a place which he comes to like and admire, he says:

> The first impressions which an Englishman receives in this country, will not contribute to the removal of his prejudices; because he refers everything he sees to a comparison with the same articles in his own country; and this comparison is unfavorable to Scotland in all its exteriors, such as the face of the country in respect to cultivation, the appearance of the bulk of the people, and the language of conversation in general.
>
> (p. 231)

He is Matt Bramble, and his name suggests that his own exterior puts difficulties in the way of those who would perceive his goodness. His relation to others seems to be the complement of theirs to him. He at times describes himself as 'nettled' by Lismahago's behavior, and from the outset he considers Tabby a 'thorn in the side.'

Here, too, we ought to recognize the importance of Smollett's choice of the epistolary novel. The letters are a perfect means of dramatizing at once Matt's human feelings and his inability to relate directly to people. Even Matt's most splenetic outbursts are socialized and shared with a sympathetic epistolary audience, and his unquestionably warm friendship with Lewis is mediated by distance rather than being given as a face-to-face confrontation of the sort that so often proves difficult for Matt.

Humphry Clinker, the non-letter-writing eponym of the novel is the center around which the family forms. Commenting on Win's 'metamurphysis,' Tabby says it is due to 'our new footman, a pious young man, who has laboured exceedingly, that she may bring forth fruits of repentence. I make no doubt but he will take the same pains with that pert hussey Mary Jones, and all of you; and that he may have power given to penetrate and instill his goodness, even into your most inward parts, is the fervent prayer of your friend in the spirit, Tab. Bramble' (p. 275). We should not allow the unconscious *double entendre* to distract us from the accuracy of Tabby's remark. Humphry's goodness has indeed penetrated the characters. And though his Methodism is satirized, he is able to turn his inner light outward. Critics have puzzled over the fact that Humphry writes no letters, despite his position as the titular character. Yet given what I have been saying about the epistemological nature of epistolary fiction, we may see in Humphry the character whose importance consists in part of the fact that we have no privileged view of him. We must perceive him, as Matt does, entirely from the outside and must recognize that despite his shabby exterior and ludicrous religion, he is deserving of human love and communal acceptance.

At Scarborough, thinking that Matt's howls at the coldness of the water are cries for help, Clinker rushes fully clothed into the sea and 'saves' Matt, dragging him ashore by the ear. In a fit of pain and embarrassment Matt strikes him down and swims back out to the privacy of the bathing machine; but on thinking of Humphry's motives, he relents, opens the door of the machine and, in effect, apologizes. This is one step for Matt towards openness. Near the end of the novel the scene is replayed more seriously. True, we hear about it after the danger is past, and the description of Lismahago and Tabby, Humphry and Win is as farcical as ever, but Jery's reportage includes the dangers and the sentiment. Jery usually is the bemused spectator who looks at life as a farce or some other form of theatrical entertainment – in his own way as unwilling to go outside of self as Matt – but he begins this letter by saying '. . . I now sit down with a heart so full that it cannot contain itself; though I am under such agitation of spirits, that you are to expect neither method nor connexion in this address – We have been this day within a hair's breadth of losing honest Matthew Bramble . . .' (p. 311). After describing the flooding of the coach in midstream, and some of the antic rescues, he focuses on Humphry, who rushed to the submerged coach,

> and, diving into it, brought up the poor 'squire, to all appearance, deprived of life – it is not in my power to describe what I felt at this melancholy spectacle – it was such an agony as baffles all description! The faithful Clinker, taking him up in his arms, as if he had been an infant of six months, carried him ashore, howling most piteously all the way, and I followed him in a transport of grief and consternation. . . .
>
> (p. 313)

When Matt revives, Liddy, in a scene which may owe something to *King Lear* – Tate's *King Lear* – 'sprung forwards, and, throwing her arms about his neck, exclaimed in a most pathetic tone, "Are you – Are you indeed my uncle – My dear uncle! – My best friend! My father! – Are you really living? or is it an illusion of my poor brain!"' (p. 314). The progression of relationship in Liddy's exclamations dramatizes the recognition of their closeness (as does for that matter the reversal of Humphry's actual relationship – he carries Matt as though Matt were his child). In the same letter Jery describes what immediately follows this scene, the discovery that Matt is the actual father of Humphry Clinker. As all the characters are in the water together and rushing about to save each other from drowning, their essential kinship is symbolized.

Matt Bramble's travels reverse Gulliver's. He begins as someone who hates that animal, man (though like Gulliver's creator he is benevolent to individual members of the species). Matt feels himself to be old, a *laudator temporis acti* (this is one source of his satiric disposition), but instead of meeting a struldbrugg at the work's center, he meets a healthy and happy old man in a glen which is almost a 'perfect paradise.' This scene of near-paradisal health and comfort is in the tradition of rural retirement, but we should notice that here, as so frequently in this novel, the modality is not simply pastoral but georgic, the emphasis is not on rest but work. The 'Ode to Leven-Water' which immediately precedes this scene, written we are told by 'Dr. Smollett' – clearly the *genius loci* – depicts not only the singing of girls and the piping of shepherds but 'industry imbrown'd with toil' as well:

> Here are a great many living monuments of longaevity; and among the rest a person, whom I treat with singular respect, as a venerable druid, who has lived near ninety years, without pain or sickness, among oaks of his own planting. . . . He has a sufficiency to procure the necessaries of life; and he and his old woman resided in a small convenient farm-house, having a little garden which he cultivates with his own hands. This ancient couple live in great health, peace, and harmony, and, knowing no wants, enjoy the perfection of

> content. . . . I asked him the other day, if he was never sick, and he answered, Yes; he had a slight fever the year before the union. (p. 251)

'Before the union.' The phrase though comic is suggestive, for it points to, and associates health with, the interrelationship of the countries which compose Great Britain in this story of a Welshman's travels through England and Scotland. The movement towards union, in several senses of the word, is at the heart of the novel. We have the reunion of father and son when Bramble recognizes Humphry as his illegitimate child, and we have the traditional marital unions that conclude the comedy: Lydia and George, Tabby and Lismahago, Win and Humphry.

The novel has a logic and a tightness (despite its diversity) which may easily be overlooked. Travel and activity move one from internal to external concerns in a way which makes encounters with others inescapable and may lead to a recognition of the necessity of human relationships, of the significance of others. The Union of Great Britain is composed of disparate countries which come together to make one great nation. If the protagonist is Welsh and the country most praised is Scotland, we should also note that the solution to Matt's problems and the ideal of human harmony are to be found at Dennison's estate in England.[4] Despite Matt's idyllic description of Brambleton Hall when he reaches England, something has been wrong. At Dennison's where an image of social and spiritual relationships – wife, friend, curate – is part of the reclamation of a ruined estate (directly contrasted with the nearly disastrous consequences of Baynard's unharmonious marriage: his estate is saved only through the help of his friends following the providential death of his wife), Matt says that his old friend 'has really attained to that pitch of rural felicity, at which I have been aspiring these twenty years in vain' (p. 320). Is it a mere coincidence that Matt had abandoned Humphry's pregnant mother twenty years earlier?

The idea of the Union, which plays such a strong part in this novel, may have been in Smollett's consciousness at this time. Interestingly, two poems of Smollett's appear in Thomas Warton's anthology *The Union* (1753), which had gone through three editions by the time Smollett wrote *Humphry Clinker*, and more importantly in the early sixties, as the chief writer of *The Briton*, Smollett found himself in the position of defending at once Scotland and the government (mainly in the person of the Earl of Bute) by appealing to the ideal of Great Britain which, even for Scots, is 'incorporated by a solemn and constitutional treaty of union, intitling them to every right and privilege which any other Briton enjoys. . . .'[5]

Smollett may also have been stung by Sterne's depiction of him as Smelfungus in *A Sentimental Journey*, a travel writer whose absorption in selfhood keeps him moving, like Mundungus, in the relentlessly unappreciative straight road of his intinerary. In *The Expedition* Matt begins like the Smollett of the *Travels*, but he ends closer to Sterne, for whom a foreign country is a metaphor of the otherness of others which must (however precariously) be overcome if there is to be any human communication. When *Humphry Clinker* appeared, Horace Walpole called it a 'party novel' written 'to vindicate the Scots,' but the book is really written for the party of humanity and the defense of Scotland (unquestionably an important part of the novel) is subsumed in the larger issue of human and national union.[6]

The novel dramatizes the way in which we misjudge others or shift our opinions of them as we come to know them (and ourselves) better. In his first letter Jery describes his uncle as 'an odd kind of humorist, always on the fret, and so unpleasant in his manner, that rather than be obliged to keep him company, I'd resign all claim to the inheritance of his estate . . .' (p. 8). But in his next letter Jery admits that 'his disposition and mine, which, like oil and vinegar, repelled one another at first, have now begun to mix by dint of being beat up together' (p. 17). The culinary metaphor with picaresque overtones suggests the importance of travel. Much later the argument between Matt and the grotesque Lismahago, significantly over the value of the union to Scotland, draws them together rather than separating them:

> I must own [Matt writes to Dr. Lewis], I was at first a little nettled to find myself schooled in so many particulars. – Though I did not receive all his assertions as gospel, I was not prepared to refute them; and I cannot help now acquiescing in his remarks so far as to think, that the contempt for Scotland, which prevails too much on this side of the Tweed, is founded on prejudice and error.
> (p. 279)

The most extreme example of such a shift in attitude (excepting perhaps Matt's recognition of his own son in the person of Humphry Clinker, barebottomed Methodist) is Jery's change towards Wilson, Liddy's lover:

> Had you asked me a few days ago, the picture of Wilson the player, I should have drawn a portrait very unlike the real person and character of George Dennison – Without all doubt, the greatest advantage acquired in travelling and perusing mankind in the original, is that of dispelling those shameful clouds that darken the

faculties of the mind, preventing it from judging with candour and precision.

(p. 332)

Indeed, the young nobleman disguised as a strolling player is a hoary convention, but most of the elements of this novel, such as the benevolent misanthrope, the bastard who turns out to be an heir and the wholesale marriages at the end, are thoroughly conventional. Smollett has learned how to make such conventions, which are simply part of tying up his earlier fictions, fully meaningful. *Humphry Clinker* is *about* the establishment of relationships; the establishment of relationships simply brings *Roderick Random* to an acceptable end. As in the case of Matt, Jery's conception is changed by travel which leads to enlightenment. Jery does not blame Dennison's disguise but his own lack of discernment. All the same, the novel through its frequent use of the word 'metamorphosis' – itself metamorphosed into 'metamurphysis' (Tabby of Win), and 'matthewmurphy'd' (Win of Dennison) – insists upon the reality of the changes in people, changes which overcome differences in class, religion and nationality.

The events at the end of the novel give us, almost in the manner of Sterne, relationships which occur instantaneously but seem as though they had been of long endurance. Having expressed the wish to 'unite our families,' Dennison presents his son George, the quondam Wilson, and when Jery rushes to him with 'open arms,' 'they hugged one another as if they had been intimate friends from their infancy' (p. 330). Immediately thereafter Matt meets Dennison's friend Jack Wilson and 'receive[s] him like a dear friend after a long separation. . . .'

Though Smollett knows there are worlds elsewhere – his *Travels through France and Italy* prove as much – the sheer variety of the encounters he presents, and the fact that the travels and travellers give us a sense of the total Union (England, Scotland and Wales) makes us experience the book as an anatomy in Northrop Frye's sense, an exhaustive attempt to consider the whole of something in an intellectual and often satiric way (it is also to the point that the major recipient of the letters is a doctor and a dominant theme is the health of the protagonist and the body politic).

Matt's letters to Dr. Lewis form a prose epistle to Dr. Arbuthnot, the letters of a sick and splenetic man seeking his own health and anatomizing that of his society. Smollett seems to admit the kinship when he has Matt explicitly compare his friend to Pope's near the end of the novel: 'You are an excellent genuis at hints. – Dr. Arbuthnot was but a type of Dr. Lewis in that respect' (p. 350). Purged of his humors and his constipation, Matt stops writing letters. When his bowels refused to move, his letters overflowed with excremental imagery; but his experiences have been cathartic in more ways than one.

In his penultimate letter Matt, having found health and at his ease, sums up the wisdom of the novel:

> I am persuaded that all valetudinarians are too sedentary, too regular and too cautious – We should sometimes increase the motion of the machine, to *unclog the wheels of life*; and now and then take a plunge amidst the waves of excess, in order to case-harden the constitution. I have even found a change of company as necessary as a change of air, to promote a vigorous circulation of the spirits, which is the very essence and criterion of good health.
>
> (p. 339)

The whole passage is important for an understanding of the novel. The italicized phrase, adapted from John Armstrong's 'unload the wheels of life' in *The Art of Preserving Health*, is the action of the novel, as pertinent to Matt's attempt to get rid of his constipation as to his getting out of the self and coming to know others through his travels.[7] The waters of Bath failed, but he has indeed discovered the necessary relationship of human beings amidst the 'waves of excess,' the waters that nearly drown him but discover his son.

The quest after health and the way to live lead back to an ideal of active rural retirement, the very thing Matt had left. Yet it is a retirement with a difference. Matt has expiated his sins against human relationship and no longer suffers from 'family plagues.' Indeed, they are, as Win describes them, a 'family of love, where every sole is so kind and so courteous, that wan would think they are so many saints in haven' (pp. 338–39).[8]

The variousness of the episodes has led some critics to see *The Expedition of Humphry Clinker* as merely a high-spirited hodgepodge, very good of its kind but hardly united in any significant way. What they miss is the sense of unity in variety, of abundance and excess as the very stuff of life, a *discordia concors* in which distinct individuals, like the nations England, Scotland and Wales, come together in a union which gives health to all.

Notes

1. Critics of *Humphry Clinker* have recently been divided into two camps: those who see the work as unified in some distinctive way, and those who see it as slices of English life in the eighteenth century served up with a thin covering

of plot. Those writers who have been arguing for unity strike me as saying the most valuable things about the book. I have in mind, among others, Sheridan Baker, '*Humphry Clinker* as Comic Romance,' *Papers of the Michigan Academy of Science, Arts, and Letters*, 46 (1961), 645–54; B. L. Reid, 'Smollett's Healing Journey,' *Virginia Quarterly Review*, 41 (1965), 549–70; William Park, 'Fathers and Sons – *Humphry Clinker*,' *Literature and Psychology*, 16 (1966), 166–74; David L. Evans, '*Humphry Clinker*: Smollett's Tempered Augustanism,' *Criticism*, 9 (1967), 257–74; John M. Warner, 'Smollett's Development as a Novelist,' *Novel*, 5 (1972), 148–61. Monroe Engel's foreword to the Signet edition of *Humphry Clinker* (New York: New American Library, 1960) also belongs here.

2. All page references in the text refer to Lewis M. Knapp's Oxford English Novels edition of *The Expedition of Humphry Clinker* (Oxford University Press, 1966).
3. See, for example, William A. West, 'Matt Bramble's Journey to Health,' *TSLL*, 11 (1969), 1197–1208.
4. George Kahrl's emphasis in *Tobias Smollett: Traveller-Novelist* (University of Chicago Press, 1945), p. 130, on the strangeness of these Welsh visitors is only valid if it is seen with the knowledge that they are viewing countries to which they are nonetheless united.
5. *The Briton* (London, 1763), No. 4, 19 June 1762, p. 21. In 'The *Briton* and *Humphry Clinker*,' *SEL*, 3 (1963), 397–414, Byron Gassman considers the continuity of Smollett's political ideas.
6. For the relationship of Sterne to Smollett, see Gardner C. Stout, Jr.'s edition of *A Sentimental Journey* (University of California Press, 1967), passim, and Robert W. Uphaus, 'Sentiment and Spleen: Travels with Sterne and Smollett,' *Centennial Review*, 15 (1971), 406–21. Walpole's remark is quoted by Kahrl, p. 147, from *Memoirs of the Reign of King George the Third* (London, 1894), IV, 218.
7. John Armstrong, *The Art of Preserving Health*, Book II, in *The Poetical Works of J. Armstrong, M. D.* (Edinburgh, 1781). The relation of Armstrong's versified treatise on health to his friend Smollett's ideas in *Humphry Clinker* would repay closer investigation. The phrase may also owe something to Tristram's claim that Shandeism 'opens the heart and lungs, and like all those affections which partake of its nature, it forces the blood and other vital fluids of the body to run freely thro' its channels, and makes the wheel of life run long and cheerfully round' (Book IV, chapter 32). I quote the edition of James A. Work (New York: Odyssey, 1940), p. 338. Sheridan Baker, perhaps the earliest of a host of critics to comment on this parallel, ascribes it to his student Charles L. Terry, 'Comic Romance,' n. 15.
8. Ronald Paulson's notion of the 'family pilgrimage' is pertinent here. See his 'The Pilgrimage and the Family: Structures in the Novels of Fielding and Smollett,' in *Tobias Smollett: Bicentennial Essays Presented to Lewis M. Knapp*, ed. G. S. Rousseau and P. G. Boucé (Oxford University Press, 1971), pp. 57–78.

Part III

Sterne

6 The Comic Sublime and Sterne's Fiction

JONATHAN LAMB

In his work on Sterne, Jonathan Lamb has reclaimed an interest in theories of the sublime that have, in the last academic generation, been more or less the prerogative of critics of romantic and pre-romantic literature. Lamb quite firmly assumes what is a fact, namely that Longinus's theories of the sublime have a distinct history in the eighteenth century, and are not necessarily anticipations of the romantic period to come. Combining intellectual or cultural history with formal reading, Lamb argues that the sublime is a figural way of marking eccentricity, a feature associated in the eighteenth century (and after) with the English. Because the sublime is a device for marking individuality, it is also a way to think about the individual's opposition to social norms, of the kind described by George Starr's general essay on the novel of sentiment (see Chapter 2 above). Thus Sterne's endemic figural playfulness is justified at almost every turn by Longinus's theories.

The best writers of the early eighteenth century possessed a body of critical theory concerning epic and tragedy which they carefully elaborated, fiercely defended, and hardly ever put into practice. Pope saved bits of his burnt epic *Alcander* to insert as samples of bombast in his *Peri Bathous*, while Johnson was forced to accept the public's judgment against his *Irene*. Historical, political and social developments sapped the confidence and removed the subject matter necessary for the production of epic or tragic works and presented instead scenes of complicated insincerity to which the appropriate literary response was, ironically, the calculated improprieties of mock-epic and burlesque. The deliberate mismatching of style and subject mimicked and mocked the two-facedness of society, and only on these rather self-destructive terms were authors allowed access to the high styles and noble forms they had been reared to admire above all others. It is an extra irony that the age which was proving to itself so decisively the impossibility of ever writing truly great literature should have become fascinated by another contribution to the critical theory of literary grandeur, Longinus's *On the Sublime*. This treatise impelled Pope to write the finest parts of his *Essay on Criticism*; typically, it also provided a format he could travesty in the *Peri Bathous* or *Art of Sinking in Poetry*. Longinus, like the classical critics, seems to have supplied merely the high standards by which low scribbling could be judged, a clue for descending 'to the very *bottom* of all the *Sublime*' as Swift called it, and not a model for the true sublime. There is no doubt that the double vision of the satirists, the result of pursuing what was ridiculous in art so as to expose what was vicious in public morality, bred a sort of hopeless idealism, expressed as habitual unions of the highest styles with the lowest subjects, or vice versa, that is detectable in the humblest form of polemic, the threatening letter.[1] But with the possible exception of Horace, Longinus is the critic most congenial to irregular experiments in literature; and certainly as the century advanced he influenced and authorized radical departures in attitudes to epic, as well as to the Bible, metaphor and primitive language, which Northrop Frye has defined as Pre-Romantic 'process-writing.'[2] In this essay I want to trace a line of development from mock-epic theory and practice to the 'process-writing' of Laurence Sterne, not with the intention of contradicting Northrop Frye's conclusions but in an effort to give Sterne's innovations the Augustan context they deserve and a name – the comic sublime.

First of all I want to consider two related aspects of Augustan irregularity – that of forms and that of manners – in order to determine what elements in them were or might be construed as sublime. To begin with manners: by the early eighteenth century the English were strongly aware of peculiarities in their temper which served to distinguish them from the French and which went by the names of singularity and irregularity and later by the more familiar titles of originality and humorism. Nowhere is the expression of this island individuality better known than in the fields of criticism and medicine. Dryden, Pope and Johnson generously season the rules of neo-classical criticism with the exceptions of the wild beauties of English verse by opening appeals, as Johnson puts it, from criticism to nature. Meanwhile an unsteadiness of temperament, induced or aggravated by the weather, exhibits itself as 'the English malady,' whose 'atrocious and frightful Symptoms' are sung in poetry and detailed in medical works. Between the poles of nature and madness, various attempts at eccentric or random writing are made, from the obsessive oddity of John Dunton's semi-autobiographical *Voyage Round the World* to the casual elegance of Shaftesbury's *Miscellaneous Reflections*. Whether the author is a dunce or a man of learning and parts, this irregular method of opening his mind to the world is undertaken as the most honest because the least artificial: he draws his justification from the necessity and the integrity of the national temperament. Even 'Mr. Spectator' has the character of 'an odd unaccountable Fellow' which is reflected in the loose form of his periodical journalism and which is his warrant for observing society so acutely. It is this sort of unaccountable oddity that eventually characterizes the hero of the comic novel. Adams, Toby and Lismahago have thrived in spite or independent of common forms to become individuals whose minds are open but sometimes unintelligible books; and so they present a double aspect to the social world they have never joined, being both simple and yet honest, eccentric yet virtuous, foolish and yet somehow wise. From the start the odd writer or odd hero represents an equation between social folly and moral worthiness and between irregularity and integrity so tight that to note the one is to note the other. Toby's goodness is inseparable from his being a 'confused, pudding-headed, muddle-headed fellow,' while Parson Adams' character of perfect simplicity is illustrated by acts of folly and naivety that Fielding concedes from the outset are 'glaring.'[3]

The *locus classicus* for the discussion of the isolated, non-social and therefore original or humorous nature of moral integrity is Tillotson's sermon 'Of Sincerity towards God and Man' and the commentaries offered on it in *The Spectator*. This sermon is a favorite of Addison's and Steele's because it is quoted at length in three *Spectators* (Nos. 103, 352 and 557), and each time it provides a basis for the distinction between the odd value of the private individual and the vicious tendency of public manners. For his part Tillotson mourns the departure of 'The old English Plainness and Sincerity, that generous Integrity of Nature and Honesty of Disposition, which always argues true Greatness of Mind, and is usually accompanied with undaunted Courage and Resolution.'[4] It has been supplanted by empty terms of art and false offers of service and esteem, the debased currency of 'a Trade of Dissimulation.' In *Spectator* No. 103 the sermon enforces a compliment just made to the club by its reverend member, namely, 'that he had not heard one Compliment made in our Society since its Commencement.' Steele takes the opportunity to praise Tillotson for a style free from all 'Pomp of Rhetoric' and therefore utterly appropriate to the subject: he discourses as sincerely on sincerity, he declares, as Longinus discourses sublimely on the sublime. In number 352 the sermon offers a text for Will Honeycomb's complaint against the times, far from original, that youth is learning the vices of age and that everything 'candid, simple, and worthy of true Esteem' has been sacrificed to fashion and ambition. Addison quotes the sermon in number 557 to make his point that 'there is no

Conversation so agreeable as that of the Man of Integrity, who hears without any Intention to betray, and speaks without any Intention to deceive'; and he concludes his paper with the fable of the Ambassador of Bantam whose mission to England is an utter failure because he interprets the forms of politesse in their literal meaning, becoming offended in proportion as he becomes offensive. At its simplest, Tillotson's sermon supports the conventional distinction between English bluntness and French ceremony, between the sincerity of natural manners and the hypocrisies of fine breeding. Addison thanks God he was born an Englishman, able to inherit a language 'wonderfully adapted to a Man who is sparing of his Words, and an Enemy to Loquacity' (No. 135). The character of Sir Roger de Coverley exhibits the honesty, innocence, oddity and shortness of speech that belongs to an unselfconsciously good man, one who has maintained 'an Integrity in his Words and Actions' in spite of all the snares put in the way of simplicity. As we would expect Sir Roger is ignorantly English in the theatre, very good at 'Natural Criticism' (No. 335), and his conversation consists of a 'blunt way of saying things, as they occur to his Imagination, without regular Introduction, or Care to preserve the Appearance of Chain of Thought' (No. 109). In Addison's scale of singularity Sir Roger's comes somewhere in the middle, for his contradiction of social forms is not complete or systematic, but only 'as he thinks the World in the wrong.' A combination of country living and a club of thoughtful city friends keeps him well protected from social acerbities like city wits and roving Mohocks, and to this extent he is like Toby, Trunnion, or Bramble whose withdrawals from society are tempered with a limited sociability consisting of family, friends or the traditions of an armed service. At the extremes singularity turns into either madness or heroism, and this is when the contradiction of social forms becomes absolute. At one end is a man like Cato who, refusing to pass his whole life in opposition to his own sentiments, ceases to be sociable: 'Singularity in Concerns of this Kind is to be looked upon as heroick Bravery, in which a Man leaves the Species only as he soars above it' (No. 576). At the other end is the unhappy gentleman in the same paper who has a commission of lunacy taken out against him for having followed, in all departments of his life, the dictates of reason at the expense of fashion, form and example. Whether considered heroic or mad, Don Quixote is the literary archetype of this extreme singularity, and his descendents in the eighteenth century novel are those like Parson Adams or Parson Yorick who carry their singular selves into the world's view and risk society's retaliations. But at all points on the scale, singularity argues some sort of opposition to society and an integrity which is irregular in terms of the social forms it ignores but which is consistent and coherent in terms of private values. This 'more than ordinary Simplicity' represents for Tillotson 'true Greatness of Mind.' Tillotson's own sincerity is, for Steele, sublimely self-consistent. For Addison it is potentially heroic.

The confrontation between the singular individual and society at large, whether it is the mild and peaceable pursuit of integrity or the more ostentatious process of self-exemption from social forms, sets up a conflict between a private and the public schemes of value that is echoed in satire as well as in fiction. For the Augustan satirists one of the most vexing problems (and their difficulties with epic are an aspect of it) is that in the very act of defending the common forms and values of their society they see innovative irregularity in such vast array that those forms and values dwindle before their eyes into singularity. Starting from what seem to be the opposite assumptions of the humorist, the satirist ends up in precisely the same confrontation; and it is no wonder that the anecdotes of Swift, Pope and Johnson reveal them in the attitudes of humorists, cherishing modes of eccentric behavior as if to emphasize that their qualities of mind are no longer representative of the society they live in. However, satire offers a major resource to its agents who find themselves in this predicament, and that is its own irregular form. In an Horatian mood Pope confesses,

> I love to pour out all myself, as plain
> As downright *Shippen*, or as old *Montagne*.

As an ingenuous private man, indulging the casual habits of self-revelation, Pope can use the pane in his breast as window and as mirror:

> In this impartial Glass, my Muse intends
> Fair to expose myself, my Foes, my Friends.[5]

Imitating the humorous singularity of the French essayist is, of course, another way of imitating Horace who uses an ambling and indirect method of exhibiting folly, 'sometimes an Epicurean, sometimes a Stoic, sometimes an Eclectic.'[6] By placing Montaigne, Shippen or Erasmus as middle terms in this sort of Horatian exercise, Pope can claim all the integrity he wants ('My Head and Heart thus flowing thro' my Quill') from the very irregularities which make his satire unobtrusively effective. Simultaneously he defines the characteristics of isolated singularity and he exposes the forces which have driven him to it. And while the 'present age' he is publishing mistakes him for verse-man, prose-man, papist, protestant, Whig and Tory, he derives the double benefit of being consistent with himself at the same time as continuing a satirical tradition, quietly reconciling a private and public ideal. Swift makes a similar set of extremes coincide in *A Tale of a Tub* by impersonating the singularity of the very latest writers. His narrator points proudly to the central item in the catalogue of modern irregularities, 'the great *Modern* Improvement of *Digressions*,' and he compares it with improvements in cookery such as '*Soups* and *Ollio's*, *Fricassées* and *Ragousts*.' He goes on:

> 'Tis true, there is a sort of morose, detracting, ill-bred People, who pretend utterly to disrelish these polite Innovations: And as to the Similitude from Dyet, they allow the Parallel, but are so bold to pronounce the Example it self, a Corruption and Degeneracy of Taste. They tell us, that the Fashion of jumbling fifty Things together in a Dish, was at first introduced in Compliance to a depraved and *debauched Appetite*, as well as to a *crazy Constitution*.[7]

As usual in the *Tale*, the narrator's metaphors have a literal satiric meaning and his literal statements make metaphorical sense as satire. The 'Similitude from Dyet' is not a similitude at all but the etymological derivation of the name of satire itself, the *satura lanx* or dish of mixed meats which make up that '*olla*, or hotchpotch, which is properly a satire.'[8] Not only does the narrator write satire unconsciously, here he defines it in what he thinks is a novel metaphor. As he pursues the analogy according to the letter, listing all the physical ills that might induce a taste for such food, he loses his grasp on the two senses of *taste*, which in any case suggested merely that bad literature caters for bad sensibilities, and insensibly makes room for the real suggestion, which is that satirical mixtures are produced not to flatter debauched appetites and crazy constitutions but to correct them. By a scheme of subversive, witty necessity observable throughout the *Tale*, what the narrator proposes in the way of idle nonsense resolves itself into specific antagonism to just that sort of nonsense. In this conclusive instance his modern formlessness provides the classically loose form of satire, the illustration of the one being the definition of the other, and Swift's own Horatian integrity finds an inverted image of itself in the glass of modern literary incompetence. To put it another way, the reader experiences simultaneously the cause and effect of satire, the irregularity of dunces and the irregularity of wit which converts the conversions of a crippled imagination back into a consistency that 'a great majority among the Men of Taste' (a fairly small club judging by the tone of the 'Apology') will enjoy. Like Pope, Swift reconciles his own internal consistency – wit and taste – with the need for public correction by deploying a two way mirror that allows us to glimpse the one while we see the reflection of public folly that calls for the other. It is a combination of 'the very *bottom* of all the *Sublime*' with *'the noblest and most useful gift of humane Nature.'*[9]

The authorized irregularity of satire means that the satirist is free not only to shadow the follies of the age in the wild dancing light of his own wit, but also to parody other forms of literature. Dryden mentions the *cento* of Ausonius 'where the words are Virgil's, but by applying them to another sense, they are made a relation of a wedding-night.'[10] Butler's burlesque and Dryden's mock-epic open the road to many experiments in the art of 'using a vast force to lift a *feather*,'[11] as Pope calls it, a calculated transgression against the rules of mechanics and proportion. This sort of satire still reflects and even reproduces the ridiculous disparities and inflated assumptions in the behavior of knaves and fools, but its constant use of great literary models puts the possibility of serious imitation of them at a greater remove. It is a two-sided disqualification that the satirists invite: on the one hand they prove that the social values which belong to the production of epic no longer exist, and on the other they develop irregular habits which satire can happily sustain but not the more regulated forms of epic and tragedy. These habits narrow their social circle into the tight circumference of a club, defined by enemies and founded upon literary tastes which can only be satisfied in practice by parody. One of the results, already obvious in Pope, is to establish extra affiliations with literary irregulars like Montaigne. Prior finds much to admire in Montaigne too; while Swift, much to Pope's incomprehension, takes a great delight in Rabelais. Samuel Johnson develops a strong taste for the irregularities of Burton's *Anatomy of Melacholy*, and less notable readers begin to consume macaronic and booby literature. *Don Quixote* exerts a fascination over the minds of satirists and novelists alike. Here we have defined, almost in its full extent, the literary tradition and resources of Laurence Sterne.

Since Cervantes' appeal is so wide, and therefore likely to be representative of irregularities in style and in heroes that the eighteenth century finds so much satisfaction in, it is best to begin with him. 'The use of pompous expression for low actions or thoughts is the *true Sublime of Don Quixote*,' says Pope.[12] One of Swift's ironic impersonations, according to Pope, is of 'Cervantes' serious air.' Pope is speaking for many readers who relished the effects Cervantes is able to produce from the distance he sets between himself and the action of the story, those fictional contributors to the narrative whom he makes responsible for its faults, elisions, lies, bombast and parodic historiography. A mock-epic propriety, which matches collisions in style with collisions in dialogue between the knight and the squire and which makes the parodic encounter of high and low styles reflect and mimic the encounters between Quixote's dream and the world, is bound to invite admiration from an age skilled in concocting this sort of heterogeneous mixture. But it isn't simply a compendium of mock-epic devices and a mad hero that *Don Quixote* offers its eighteenth-century readership. Stuart Tave puts the date of critical revaluation at about the same time as the performance of Fielding's farce *Don Quixote in England* – 1738.[13] After this it is more common to regard Quixote as a humorist, not a madman, and to study the narrative complexity of the story less as a vehicle of satire than as an enquiry into the theory and practice of writing fiction. Even before this, however, the analogy between Quixote's defence of a literary ideal and the efforts of the Tory satirists to preserve something similar must have been evident and have developed the sort of covert sympathy with the knight that exists between him and his chronicler Cid Hamet Benengeli. Swift's outrage at Bentley's attempt to lessen the authenticity of classical texts is not unlike that Quixote feels when Cardenio blackens the name of Queen Madasima; and the way Swift and Pope seem consciously to interpret their lives in terms of Horace's bears comparison with the way Quixote models his career on that of Amadis. *Don Quixote* dramatizes the odd or heroic dependence on books which is to become a major theme of the British comic novel, already apparent in Addison's examples of singularity, one of whom is suspected of madness for reciting Homer out of his window and the other for quoting Milton in his bedroom. Quixote represents that particular sort of integrity which is defined by literary activity, an idealism expressed as a practical demonstration of the neo-classical theory of imitation so that life itself becomes the realization of a literary model. The growing tendency to call attention to the nobility of Quixote's character allows and enshrines this idealism, and when Sterne's Tristram entertains the 'highest idea' of the 'spiritual and refined sentiments' he finds in *Don Quixote*, or when a critic like Beattie can refer to the 'sublimity of Don Quixote's mind,' it is clear that the knight's *intentions* can be held to be of a high and even a sublime order, even if his adventures are comic disappointments.[14] This is not to go as far as Romantic critics like Coleridge and Leigh Hunt who abstract the Quixotic humorist from the complex social and literary forces which he reflects and embodies, but it is to acknowledge that 'true Greatness of Mind' which Tillotson and *The Spectator* had praised as the accompanying quality of 'more than ordinary Simplicity.'

As for the Cervantic style and structure, Pope offers some very intriguing comments in his 'Postscript.' The context is his consideration of Longinus' criticism that by the *Odyssey* Homer's genius had passed its meridian heat and that the sublimity of the *Iliad* had been replaced by narrative and dream. So Pope has in mind the epic, the sublime and Longinus as he pauses in his praise of the beautiful variety of the *Odyssey* to commend *'the true Sublime* of *Don Quixote.'* It is strange that he uses the phrase 'the true Sublime' instead of 'mock-sublime' or 'mock-epic' since the sublime can scarcely be said to exist where there is not some proper and manifest connection between objects, feelings and words. It is possible that Pope was thinking of a part of *Don Quixote* very relevant to his defence of the *Odyssey* as a kind of comic epic. The Canon of Toledo's description of a comic epic in prose is not only applicable to the narrative variety of *Don Quixote* but is also remarkably close to Pope's description of the same thing in the *Odyssey*: the fable may be as various and the hero as diverse as an author chooses to make them, and if the whole is rendered

> in a grateful style, and with ingenious invention, approaching as much as possible to truth, he will doubtless compose so beautiful and various a work, that, when finished, its excellency and perfection must attain the best end of writing, which is at once to delight and instruct, as I have said before: for the loose method practised in those books, gives the author liberty to play the epic, the lyric, and dramatic poet, and to run through all the parts of poetry and rhetoric; for epics may be writ in prose as in verse.[15]

For his part Cervantes, through his Arabian deputy, exploits every opportunity offered by the chivalric epic and this formal interpretation of its real epic potential to invent a mixed fable, mixed hero and mixed narrative style in order to achieve the maximum variety. In the same terms that Cervantes is offering his novel to the public as a comic epic in prose, Pope is defending the variety of the *Odyssey* as belonging to comic epic (the same terms, incidentally, that Fielding will use to found his genre of comic epic poem in prose in *Joseph Andrews*). The phrase 'true Sublime' suggests on Pope's part a half-conceived connection between Cervantes' arts of variety and Homer's: 'Let it be remember'd, that the same Genius that soar'd the highest, and from whom the greatest models of the *Sublime* are derived, was also he who stoop'd the lowest, and gave to the simple *Narrative* its utmost perfection' ('Postscript,' p. 389). He seems to want to say that there is as much sublimity in Homer's stooping as in his rising, but it is to Cervantes he pays the compliment of having discovered a new and yet true sublime. Because Pope is trying to rid the term 'sublime' from connotations of action, vigour, fire, and sustained flight he invokes Horace's characteristic preference for the *Odyssey*, and it is likely he is also thinking of other definitions and illustrations of it that Longinus offers. Unfortunately for him and us those portions of sections XXX and XXXI of *On the Sublime* are missing in which Longinus discusses the positive applications of mock-epic, 'dressing up a trifling Subject in grand and exalted Expressions.'[16] All that remains are two examples from Herodotus to show how vulgar terms can be used in such a way as to have far from vulgar meanings. He returns briefly to the subject in his discussion of hyperboles where he notes their double-edged quality: 'they enlarge, and they lessen' (*OS*, p. 91). It is as if Pope, unwilling to start a controversy about a new definition of the sublime, makes Cervantes supply an example of what is missing from Longinus' treatise. What he proposes quite specifically, however, is the question 'how far a Poet, in pursuing the description or image of an action, can attach himself to *little circumstances*, without vulgarity or trifling?' Like his *Preface to the Iliad* this 'Postscript' exhibits Pope's fascination with circumstantiality and how far it is reconcileable with the faculty of invention and with propriety of expression. Again, Cervantes offers him a fine example of 'the *low actions of life* . . . put into a figurative style'; and again Longinus is being glanced at, who says that an accurate and judicious choice of 'adherent Circumstances . . . and an ingenious and skilful Connexion of them into one body, must necessarily produce the Sublime' (*OS*, p. 27). Pope is wondering at what point the feather can be cut between the circumstantiality of 'stooping' and that of mock-epic, pondering, no doubt, the paradoxical way in which the extremes of burlesque and mock-epic on the one hand and sublimity and propriety on the other seem to meet.

Cervantes offers his English readers a narrative that explores some of the range and effects of comic epic, one which Pope regards in some way as the perfection of mock-epic, its 'true sublime'; he also gives them a hero who combines the nobility, or sublimity, of intention with a ridiculous public figure and who therefore represents in its plainest form the mixture of private integrity and public oddity that belongs to the singular or irregular man of sincerity. I want to consider a little more closely the sublime possibilities of this sort of character and to examine how these might be realized when the character becomes an author. Montaigne is the outstanding example of a man whose irregularity of self is expressed in the irregular form of his essays. His rhapsodic style of writing ('without any certain Figure, or any other than accidental Order, Coherence, or Proportion')[17] has the moral value of being utterly devoid of art and, like Sir Roger's irregular conversation, opens a window on to an ingenuous heart. Diderot says of Montaigne that 'the licence of his style is practically a guarantee to me of the purity of his habits'[18] and it is that sort of honest casualness that Shaftesbury seeks to represent in his 'random essays' or which David Hartley aims for in the introduction to his

Observations on Man by writing 'frequently without any express Design, or even any previous Suspicion of the Consequences that might arise.'[19] We have already seen how in the *Spectator* the 'true Greatness of Mind' that singularity manifests and protects is given high praise – Steele even compares the natural modesty of 'a great Spirit' with the propriety of expression that belongs to the 'just and sublime' in literature (No. 350). Addison also considers literary irregularity, and talking of Seneca and Montaigne as originators of loose and immethodical writing he affirms that if it is undertaken by men of learning or genius to read it is like being 'in a Wood that abounds with a great many noble Objects, rising among one another in the greatest Confusion and Disorder' (No. 476). In the following paper he realizes the metaphor by describing the irregularity and variety of a humorist's garden where plants 'run into as great a Wildness as their Natures will permit.' This is called 'Gardening . . . after the *Pindarick* Manner.' These images look forward to those in which Pope will praise Homer ('a wild paradise') and to Johnson's defence of Shakespeare, so that it is no surprise to find Addison using Longinus and Shakespeare in order to praise the exuberant irregularity of genius that cannot be constrained and which bursts its bounds to produce 'what we call the Sublime in Writing' (No. 592). By no stretch of the imagination might Addison be suspected of thinking Montaigne's *Essays* sublime. In another paper he laughs at him as 'the most eminent Egotist that ever appeared in the World' (No. 562) and considers him diverting in proportion as he is absurd. But Longinus' own standards are more flexible, and he praises warmly those orations of Demosthenes where 'Order seems always disordered' and where 'he makes Excursions into different Subjects, and intermingles several seemingly unnecessary Incidents' (*OS*, pp. 56, 59). Indeed under the figures of *asyndeton* and *hyperbaton* Longinus includes almost every irregularity, from digression to syntactic breakdown, as aspects of the sublime. As long as they are warranted by pressure of feeling any failure in the order of words, even speechlessness itself, may be powerfully expressive. It is not difficult to see that an author like Sterne, already consciously imitating and incorporating the irregularities of Montaigne's and Burton's prose, is aware of the permission he gets from Longinus to make digressions, apostrophes, starts and gaps. Yorick and Eugenius have both read Longinus, and we are expected to read him too. In a chapter where Tristram irritably dispenses with all rules and the cold conceits they beget, he says, 'O! but to understand this, which is a puff at the fire of Diana's temple – you must read Longinus – read away – if you are not a jot the wiser by reading him the first time over – never fear – read him again' (*TS*, pp. 281–82).

It is worth taking Tristram's advice to find out to what degree sublimity can be supported without a splendid or lofty object for the feelings to work on. From Addison to Kames there seems to be an agreement that the sublime belongs to what is eminent, bold, and huge (as well as irregular) so that, in Burke's definition, 'the mind is so entirely filled with its object, that it cannot entertain any other.'[20] Yet Longinus is not so prescriptive and insists rather on the largeness of soul than the largeness of object, that capacity for 'Boldness and Grandeur in the Thoughts' which mean and ungenerous minds can never arrive at. So although the sublime is often the result of considering something immense, like the Creation, it can also be evident in Alexander's quip to Parmenio. What Longinus does expect is a concentration of the faculties which will need no assistance from verbal 'Pomp and Garnish' (*OS*, p. 14) and which will convey an apparently unmediated impression of the 'Flux and Reflux of Passion.' This representation may be so pure and intense that the *cause* of the feelings expressed is reproduced in the audience's imagination. Thus you display 'the very Action before the Eyes of your Readers' and mimic the very blows of the assault you are talking about (*OS*, pp. 63, 56). It is a sort of natural propriety that results from and in a naked apprehension of what is experienced, the very opposite of irony. In this sense the mind is indeed filled with its object and the words used to represent this fullness will have an immediacy and propriety because they will be implicated in the very experience they are describing. Montaigne had not heard of Longinus, but with the help of Horace and Plutarch he manages to achieve these sorts of effects (in a domestic way) by associating his mind to his feelings and actions. Free of any allegiance to art Montaigne evolves what he calls 'naturalized art' by representing in his irregular essays all the oddities that accident and custom invite him to contemplate. 'Grandeur of Soul,' he says, 'consists not so much in mounting and proceeding forward, as in knowing how to govern and circumscribe itself. It takes every thing for great, that is enough' (III, 456). He limits his faculties to what he is doing and concentrates them on that; so when he dances, he dances; when he sleeps, he sleeps – he even dreams that he dreams – and whatever action or feeling he finds himself experiencing, 'I do not suffer it to dally with my Senses only, I associate my Soul to it too' (III, 459). These circumscriptions and associations close the gap between Montaigne's observed and observing self almost to nothing, and they are expressed in words that are entirely fit and apt. In one of his best essays Montaigne discovers, for instance, that the naturalized arts of making love and writing about it are practically the same: 'the Action and the Description should relish Theft' ('Upon Some Verses of Virgil,' III, 131), hence the sweetest sexual pleasures and the best amorous writing result from obliquity and indirection. The pattern of circumscription is completed with his removal of any difference between what he does and what he writes: 'I write of my self and of my Writings, very near as I do of my other Actions; and let my Theme return upon my self' (III, 397). Far from ensnaring himself in baroque tangles of infinite regression, Montaigne's circumscriptions indicate how closely his soul attends to his experience and how faithfully in his 'loose and unknit Articles' he represents that attendance. In two ways, then, the *Essays* can be considered as having sublime qualities: Montaigne's capacity for absorption in an experience, no matter how insignificant; and the oblique, digressive and unfinished form in which he renders this absorption. And these qualities both stem from what Montaigne himself chooses to call grandeur of soul.

The mind filled with its object is what Sterne, in his sermon 'Search the Scriptures,' considers to be the hallmark of the Biblical sublime. Invoking Longinus ('the best critic the eastern world ever produced') he distinguishes between classical poetry which relies for its effects on 'the sweetness of the numbers, occasioned by a musical placing of words' and the 'beautiful propriety' of the Bible which arises more from 'the greatness of the things themselves, than . . . the words and expressions.'[21] When Yorick derides the French sublime he uses the same standard: 'The grandeur is *more* in the *word*; and *less* in the *thing*.'[22] It is an important idea that is aired throughout the century and often in a context where the primitive sublime of the Old Testament is being preferred above the classical one. For instance 'John Lizard' in *Guardian* No. 86 compares Homer's and Virgil's descriptions of horses with the praise of the war-horse in Job 39, and he says, 'I cannot but particularly observe, that whereas the classical poets chiefly endeavour to paint the outward figure, lineaments, and motions; the sacred poet makes all the beauties to flow from an inward principle in the creature he describes.' He believes this imparts such spirit and vivacity to the images and style 'as would have given the great wits of antiquity new laws for the sublime, had they been acquainted with these writings.' William Smith, who translated Longinus and who is as partisan as the *Guardian* correspondent in preferring examples of scriptural sublime, praises its 'majestic Simplicity and unaffected Grandeur' which consists 'not in Ornament and Dress' but in the unmediated confrontation between even 'low and common Objects' and what he calls *spirit* (*OS*, pp. 130, 168). This produces a natural propriety in the expression which may seem very close to burlesque but which is in fact the very opposite: 'He saith among the trumpets, Ha, ha; and he smelleth the battle afar off.' In his *Inquiry* Burke tries to distinguish between refined language, which lacks force in proportion as it is descriptive and exact, and the power of primitive language which gives very imperfect but strong ideas of objects; and he concludes that there are certain natural arrangements of words which are much more apt at conveying the experiences of objects:

> Uncultivated people are but ordinary observers of things, and not critical in distinguishing them; but, for that reason, they admire more, and are more affected with what they see, and therefore express themselves in a warmer manner. If the affection be well conveyed, it will work its effect without any clear idea, often without any idea at all of the thing which has originally given rise to it.
>
> (*Inquiry*, p. 180)

It is a short step from this sort of reasoning to Wordsworth's ideas about language in the *Preface to the Lyrical Ballads*. There Wordsworth poses again Pope's question about how far an author may attach himself to little circumstances; and he answers it by saying that as long as there is a natural force linking sensibility to object, language which is necessarily 'dignified and variegated' will result. Indeed what occasions the central disagreement between him and Coleridge is his belief in the primitive and constitutive nature of language; for in low and rustic life 'men hourly communicate with the best objects from which the best part of language is originally derived . . . a more permanent and a far more philosophical language than that which is frequently substituted for it by poets.'[23] In his note to *The Thorn* Wordsworth enforces the distinction between the language of conventional signs (including poetic diction) and this much more philosophical language (he uses the term precisely, I think, as a synonym for what was also known as 'universal language') by turning, as 'John Lizard,' Smith, Sterne, and Burke do, to the orientalisms of the Bible for examples of majestic simplicity that might be mistaken by refined critics as embarrassing tautologies and repetitions, as disorder without any braveness. Much more confident than Pope (who feels it necessary to excuse Homer's attachment to low circumstances of cookery and bedmaking in the *Iliad*) these critics identify a kind of sublime which can attach itself very freely to low circumstances and render them in an irregular style, provided the mind is full enough of those objects to guarantee a primitive and natural propriety in the representation of them.

It is ironic that Pope, one of the first to establish Longinian tenets in English criticism, should have received from one of his major critics and apologists, Joseph Warton, so little credit for snatching graces beyond the reach of art. But by looking at the critical debate surrounding Pope and ideas of sublimity we can arrive at some standards for measuring the comic sublime in fiction. It is Warton's view that 'Pope's close and constant reasoning had impaired and crushed the faculty of imagination'[24] and out of delicacy he makes his point by quoting Voltaire on Boileau: 'Incapable peut-être du sublime qui élève l'âme, et du sentiment qui l'attendrait . . . laborieux, sévère, précis, pur, harmonieux, il devint, enfin, le poète de la raison' (*EGWP*, I, xi). Yet those lines of the *Essay on Criticism* which exhibit so well that 'liberal and manly censure of bigotry' Warton is supposed to approve of, he selects as an example of a mixed metaphor: 'how can a *horse* "snatch a grace" or "gain the heart"?' (*EGWP*, I, 136–67). Despite this he goes to some lengths to redeem Pope from Addison's 'partial and invidious' comparison between the *Essay* and Horace's *Art of Poetry*, asserting that Pope avoids the irregularity of the Roman by proceeding with 'just integrity, and a lucid order' (*EGWP*, I, 101). Just who is being invidious and partial is not quite clear, and Warton manifests most clearly the double vision of the age, able rationally to identify what belongs to the sublime and yet not able to enjoy it: he likes Pope for not being distracted by the warmth and vigour of imagination and yet feels obliged to devalue him precisely because he is bereft of that 'acer spiritus ac vis' which mixes metaphors and moves irregularly. Not surprisingly he draws the same distinction between expressive and descriptive poetry that is drawn by Sterne, Burke, and the others when he imagines how Pope's epic might have turned out: 'he would have given us many elegant descriptions, and many GENERAL characters, well drawn; but would have failed to set before our eyes the REALITY of these objects, and the ACTIONS of these characters' (*EGWP*, I, 290–91). However, Warton's double vision provides valuable assistance in analysing the qualities of poetry which *he* enjoys while thinking they are unsublime but which Pope and others felt had sublime potential.

Wit, and particularly mock-epic wit, is approached by Warton with the theory of imitation in mind to show that what is admirable in it is also what is unheroic. Like Addison and Pope, Warton reckons that all that is left to a modern poet is novelty of expression, 'to shine and surprise' by the manner in which he imitates the just models of classical literature, those changeless repositories of the common sense of mankind. Although Johnson quarrels with Pope's definition of true wit as one which 'depresses it below its natural dignity, and reduces it from strength of thought to happiness of language,' his own definition of wit as 'at once natural and new'[25] merely proposes the problem as a solution since Nature is already the province of Homer and Virgil and, with nothing naturally new under the sun, all that remains is imitation, as Warton points out (*EGWP*, II, 54). One of the advantages Warton sees in modern novelty, however, is its fidelity to real life; and he instances Pope's contribution to the imitation of Horace (Satires, II, vi), Swift's *City Shower*, Gay's *Trivia*, and Hogarth's prints as pieces 'describing the objects as they really exist in life . . . without heightening or enlarging them, and without adding any imaginary circumstances' (*EGWP*, II, 51–52). His preference for this sort of realism blinds him to the mock-epic and burlesque distortions which allow low and ordinary things to be magnified in this way; and it is such a solid preference that he carries it into a variety of areas, praising Montaigne for giving 'so strong a picture of the way of life of a country gentleman in the reign of Henry the Third' and drawing attention to the naturalism of *Don Quixote*: 'MADNESS is a common disorder among the Spaniards at the latter part of life, about the age of which the knight is represented' (*EGWP*, II, 152; I, 133). He even goes so far as to adduce the lively, dramatic and interesting parts of the *Iliad* from the 'innumerable circumstances' that are included in the narrative. Nevertheless he means to draw a sharp line between the circumstantiality that arises from an heroic inability to generalize and those 'DOMESTICA FACTA' which are the proper objects of modern writing and which render the man 'skilful in painting modern life . . . THEREFORE, disqualified for representing the ages of heroism, and that simple life, which alone epic poetry can gracefully describe' (*EGWP*, I, 291). At one blow Warton demolishes the careful speculations of Pope's 'Postscript' aimed at finding the point at which moderns, like ancients, might attach themselves to little circumstances without vulgarity or trifling.

Even if Warton ignores the part played by mock-epic techniques in highlighting the small circumstances of modern life, when he turns his attention to this kind of wit he defines very neatly the ironic element in it that will always inhibit the unmediated encounter of sensibility and object: 'As the poet disappears in this way of writing, and does not deliver the intended censure in his own proper person, the satire becomes more delicate, because more oblique' (*EGWP*, I, 211). Indeed he is right to emphasize the part played by reason in the theory and practice of eighteenth century poetry and wit, because thanks to Locke much of it is directed at the faculty of discrimination. Ideas are united and occult resemblances discovered on the basis of their real incongruity with the purpose of having the rational or moral difference perceived clearly by the reader. Francis Hutcheson points out that it is the *contrast* 'between ideas of grandeur, dignity, sanctity, perfection, and ideas of meanness, baseness, profanity, [which] seems to be the very spirit of burlesque, and the greatest part of our raillery and jest is founded upon it.'[26] Pope's editor

Warburton, glossing the lines on true wit, argues that the image given back to the mind is Fancy's homage to the Judgment and an invitation for the latter's approval of her work.[27] When wit is fully embarked on mock-epic or burlesque associations of ideas, the obliquity and irony of the resemblances is often properly understood insofar as the reader knows the basis upon which they are rationally distinct. To read the fourth book of *Gulliver's Travels*, for example, is to re-master one of the common propositions of logic: that a man is not a horse. The moral function of most mock-epic confusions is to promote the discovery that they ought not to exist in good heads and to prompt the separation of ideas which wit, mimicking the fantasies and misconceptions of fools and dunces, has allied. Burke, who can see the strength of minds 'not critical in distinguishing' things, shows that Locke's supposed distinction between wit and judgment which forms the basis of so many theories of wit in this century, is not a distinction at all: 'There is no material distinction between the wit and the judgment, as they both seem to result from different operations of the same faculty of comparing' (*Inquiry*, pp. 58–59). Whether wit depends on the resemblance or (as Addison and Hutcheson feel is sometimes the case) the contrast or opposition of ideas, it is the perception of the difference between them, the final and decisive act of the judgment, which determines the ironic value of the union. To the extent that mock-epic and burlesque pursue these judgmental distinctions they have little to do with the sublime possibilities of irregularity.

Yet Warburton picks out an example of what looks like mock-epic contrast in Pope's *Essay on Man* but which behaves in a very different way and to which he gives the name sublime. They are the lines about Newton:

> Superior beings, when of late they saw
> A mortal Man unfold all Nature's law,
> Admir'd such wisdom in an earthly shape,
> And shew'd a NEWTON as we shew an Ape.
>
> (II, ll. 31–34)

To pay a compliment to Newton by comparing him with an ape is to bring it almost within the verge of ridicule, yet a curious encounter between the emotions of pride and humility takes place by means of the comparison. In his note Warburton says:

> And here let me take note of a new species of the Sublime, of which our poet may be justly said to be the maker; so new, that we have yet no name for it, though of a nature distinct from every

> other poetical excellence. The two great perfections of works of genius are Wit and Sublimity. Many writers have been witty, several have been sublime, and some few have possessed both these qualities separately: but none that I know of, besides our Poet, hath had the art to incorporate them; of which he hath given many examples, both in this Essay and his other poems, one of the noblest being the passage in question. This seems to be the last effort of the imagination, to poetical perfection: and in this compounded excellence the Wit receives a dignity from the Sublime, and the Sublime a Splendour from the Wit; which, in their state of separate existence, they both wanted.
>
> (III, 50–51 n.)

Warburton's linkage of the terms 'wit' and 'sublime' recalls Hutcheson's terms 'grave wit' and 'serious wit,' but they stand for opposite ideas; for Hutcheson believes that 'In this serious wit, though we are not solicitous about the grandeur of the images, we must still beware of bringing in ideas of baseness or deformity, unless we are studying to represent an object as base and deformed' ('Reflections,' p. 109). But there is no doubt that Pope has brought in a base and deformed idea without any intention of demeaning Newton and has succeeded, as Warburton points out, in a 'compounded excellence' from which it is impossible to abstract the idea of grandeur from the low circumstances in which it is conceived. In fact Pope seems to have answered the query from the 'Postscript' by calculating to a nicety an attachment to little circumstances which is neither vulgar nor trifling and discovering how much real beauty there can be in a low image by uniting it with a sublime but otherwise inexpressible conception. All the negative feeling that might have been aroused by picturing Newton as a showground monkey and the angels as pitchmen and mountebanks is converted into a positive and ascending feeling which is nevertheless contained within the hierarchical limits imposed by the image. The difference between this sublime wit and the mock-epic it resembles is that the analogical relation of the lower and higher ideas is not separable into the constituent resembling ideas, partly because one of them is sublimely imprecise and partly because it is only apprehended with the aid of the low image. It is as it were a vertical arrangement from which neither idea can be abstracted or distinguished without entirely losing the effect of their association, and when the reader has climbed by 'ape' to 'angel' the 'ape' can no more be removed than the rung of a ladder one is standing on. Nor would Pope want it to be, since this sort of sublimity is founded quite deliberately on the qualities of the 'isthmus of our middle state' from whose limitations not even Newton is exempt.

As a scholar of ancient wisdom and letters Warburton is well placed to discover what Pope is doing. Having understood the necessity of Ovid's delivering on 'the most sublime and regular plan, A POPULAR HISTORY OF PROVIDENCE' amidst the superficial irregularities of his *Metamorphoses*, and having grasped the political truths couched by Virgil under Aeneas' descent into the shades,[28] Warburton can discover in Pope's lines a modern version of that sort of necessity where the sublime idea *demands* a primitive vehicle on which to be conveyed. It is as if the wheel has come full circle and out of the ironical contrasts of mock-epic Pope discovers a form responsive to just this kind of necessity, a kind of transcendent burlesque. In a sense all primitive metaphors are a form of burlesque since what is almost beyond conception and expression is fixed in a sensible, material shape that allows it to be thought of and uttered but which is necessarily of a lower order than the mystery it conveys. Thus in Bacon's interpretation of myth, upon which Warburton is modelling his interpretations, the hairy figure of Pan represents the secrets of the universe just as Newton as ape represents the reach of a human mind in establishing the principles of universal motion.

It is significant that two other examples of the sublime selected by Warburton from the *Essay on Man* are chains of imagery that look like arguments but which are designed to embarrass rational inquiry. In lines 35–42 of the first epistle Pope has, says Warburton, 'joined the beauty of argumentation to the sublimity of thought' (III, 7 n.), but the argument consists of 'the harder reason' which poses a series of unanswerable questions. In the same epistle (ll. 157–60) Pope answers questioning man by referring him to God whom he apostrophizes as the contradictions the questioner wishes to be resolved, making 'the very dispensation objected to, the periphrasis of his Title' (III, 23 n.). In both cases Pope is using the rhythms of argument and the strategy of tautology by accommodating himself to Longinus' definition of the apostrophe where the periphrasis turns 'what was naturally a Proof into a soaring Strain of the Sublime and the Pathetic' (*OS*, p. 47). In none of these examples does wit assemble ideas on any principle that the judgment can approve. They are overlaid and inseparable and, in the case of Newton, present a mixture of the great and the mean that does not have the effect Hutcheson predicts: 'no other effect but to separate what is great from what is not so' (*Reflections*, p. 114). According to Pope's version of Longinus, he has managed to snatch a grace beyond the reach of argument and reflection 'without passing thro' the judgment.' It is in celebration of this sublime illogic that Warburton pillories some French critics who had accused the *Essay* of being a rhapsody: 'It is enough just to have quoted these wonderful Men of method, and to leave them to the laughter of the public' (*DLMD*, III, 167 n.).

Since I have suggested that in the 'Postscript' Pope was considering Cervantes as in some way an exponent of what Warburton calls the witty sublime, I want to take a scene from *Don Quixote* which conforms to its standards, and then compare it with a scene from *Joseph Andrews* and one from *Tristram Shandy*. The first takes place during Quixote's troublesome sojourn at the castle of the Duke and Duchess, just after Sancho's departure for Barataria and immediately before Altisidora begins her practical jokes. The knight is worried by many things: his numberless obligations to his hosts, a feeling that his fidelity to Dulcinea is under threat, an unease about the way adventures are occurring, and most of all the loss of Sancho. In this melancholy state he goes off to bed:

> He therefore shut the door of his chamber after him, and undressed himself by the light of two wax-candles. But oh! the misfortune that befell him, unworthy such a person. As he was straining to pull off his hose, there fell not sighs, or anything that might disgrace his decent cleanliness, but about four and twenty stitches of one of his stockings, which made it look like a lattice-window. The good Knight was extremely afflicted, and would have given then an ounce of silver for a drahm of green silk; green silk, I say, because his stockings were green.
>
> (II, 280–81)

Then Benengeli makes an apostrophe to poverty ('O poverty! poverty! what could induce that great Cordova poet to call thee a Holy Thankless Gift! . . .') in which he lists all the miserable shifts impoverished honour is driven to in order to disguise its penury. It follows the pattern of many ridiculous incidents in the novel by juxtaposing the two narrative styles Benengeli is so famous for, his careful delivery of 'every minute particular distinctly entire' (II, 251) and his talent of 'launching into episodes and digressions' (II, 276). It is a perfect example of using pompous expression for a low action and ought to make us laugh at the contradiction between Quixote's chivalric pretensions (mimicked in the high style) and his abject circumstances (minutely chronicled in the low style). Yet the scene does not excite this sort of laughter nor did Benengeli think it would: he predicts that it will not make us laugh outright but that it 'may chance to make you draw in your lips and show your teeth like a monkey' (II, 278). One of the reasons for this is that the chapter reminds us of the correspondence that often exists between the narrator and the knight, for it begins with Benengeli's deep regret that he has confined his fancy and parts to the single design of this bare history and it contains an account of why Quixote begins bitterly to regret the constraints his profession is laying him under. In a sense both narrator and knight are lamenting the control now being exercised over the story by the inventions of the Duke and Duchess which keeps them both from a liberty they had previously enjoyed. The laddered stocking and Benengeli's apostrophe are not so remote from each other as might at first appear: the accident represents an aspect of the knight's loss of liberty and the apostrophe represents feelings about that loss which may seem to be in excess of the trivial circumstance but which both the knight and the narrator are experiencing. The connexion between the minor humiliation and Benengeli's commentary on it is made even less burlesque because it is stated that 'these melancholy reflections are renewed in Don Quixote's mind, by the rent in his stocking.' More than that the green silk gathers other parts of the story together, like the green ribbons Quixote adorned his helmet with, the sneers of the gentry who deride him as one of 'your old-fashioned country squires that . . . darn their old black stockings themselves with a needleful of green silk' (II, 18), and the nets of green thread that Quixote will get entangled in as soon as he has left this enchanted castle. The colour green, the thread, the stocking all combine to make an image expressive of Quixote's vulnerable idealism, and the little circumstance is given an unobtrusive figurative function which, far from contradicting or being contradicted by the sublime address to poverty, supports, defines and weights it to the point where it conveys a genuine flavor of the pain being felt. Stocking and apostrophe, like 'ape' and 'angel' in Pope's analogy, offer a new notion of Quixote's heroism; they invite us to consider him as a man whose aspirations are bounded by natural frailties which at once frustrate and ennoble them. In showing our teeth like monkeys at this mixture we respond both to the comedy and the nobility and don't allow one idea (of indignity or nobility) to predominate over the other. The one is crucial to the other.

Parson Adams' entertainment at the joking squire's recalls the indignities Quixote is subjected to at the castle; and when he stands up to vindicate his dignity in front of his tormentors we are presented with a similar case of heroism whose limited range provides a foundation for larger ideas of it:

> 'My Appearance might very well persuade you that your Invitation was an Act of Charity, tho' in reality we were well provided; yes,

> Sir, if we had had an hundred Miles to travel, we had sufficient to bear our Expenses in a noble manner.' (At which Words he produced the half Guinea which was found in the Basket.) 'I do not shew this out of Ostentation of Riches, but to convince you I speak the Truth.'[29]

Although Adams is speaking in his own voice and is therefore free of the burlesque diction that Fielding gives himself permission to use, he provides his own mock-epic inflations by using words like 'noble,' 'riches' and 'truth.' The coin and the ample gesture with which it is produced do not, as he expects, contradict his appearance as an impoverished naif or warrant the truth of what he says. But they indicate the other values of spontaneity, simplicity and odd integrity which Adams' hosts equally despise and which he is too unselfconscious to estimate. In this respect the production of the half-guinea and words like nobility and truth have, within the limits of the situation, an applicability and a meaning that is not as grand as Adams thinks they have or which they normally possess but which is well above the measurements being made by the squire and his companions. The coin, like Quixote's stocking, functions both as a little circumstance and as an image upon which thoughts of relative sublimity can be built. Once again, the lower and higher ideas must be taken together, for any attempt to abstract one at the expense of the other would make too little or too much of Adams' qualities.

Sterne refers to his version of the mock-epic as his 'Cervantick humour . . . of describing silly and trifling Events with the circumstantial Pomp of great Ones,'[30] and probably he conceived of it initially as a means of satire, having enjoyed great success with his imitation of *Le Lutrin*, *A Political Romance*, and thinking his talents lay that way. The remark is made about the description of Slop's arrival, and it is at that very point in Tristram's narration we see quite clearly how the device has been transformed into a pair of Hogarthian scales on which the *poco più* and the *poco meno* – the insensible more or less – are subtly balanced in order to celebrate the universal 'triumph of slight incidents over the mind' (*TS*, pp. 100, 322). Sterne is different from Cervantes and Fielding to the extent that his use of mock-epic and burlesque inflations is never designed to separate ideas by ironic assessments of their comparative value. He has already learned what they discover, and so when uncle Toby gives up the siege of Dendermond to go and help the dying Le Fever, and his nephew avers that it was to his 'eternal honour' that he did so and that the 'kind BEING, who is a friend to the friendless' (*TS*, pp. 423–24) shall recompense him for his sacrifice, we would be obtuse not to understand the relative but still real value of the sacrifice and the complex significance of Toby's bowling-green campaigns. Since circumstances alone determine the value of things in the Shandean circle, and since every object within its circumference has at least two handles by which it may be grasped, slight incidents and little circumstances very often have large reverberations and little effort is needed on Tristram's part or ours to see constant analogies between the miniature and the grand. Sterne's study of the Bible revealed how 'minute circumstances' can be 'truly affecting'[31] and what a great pressure they can exert on our feelings and our minds, so he already assumes that little ideas, and even little volumes, can stand for greater ones. But like Cervantes and Fielding, Sterne is careful to control the process so that no falsely sublime ideas supplant those that are anchored in the little circumstances which provide the conditions as well as the images on which the higher ideas can rest. At no point should the comic sublime be mistaken either for sentimentalism or realism because it absolutely depends upon a continuous traffic between high ideas and low circumstances that modifies them both in terms of one another. And always this traffic originates in or is directed towards a peculiar cast of mind which is making no common or logical sense out of the world it perceives.

It is likely that in *Tristram Shandy* the range of devices attributable to the comic sublime will be extensive because the narrative is fully and continuously sensitive to the sorts of character and situation that produce this vertical arrangement of associated or analogous ideas. There is no space to explore all of the range properly, but I want to emphasize those parts which are most prominent and which link Sterne firmly with his Augustan predecessors. First of all it should be plain that his irregular narrative is authorized by Longinus and that all his apparent departures from the rules of formal rhetoric, except for the experiments with typography and idiogram, are classified in *On the Sublime*. Although these irregularities are directed towards comic ends, they are designed to convey the full weight and pressure of Tristram's experience. His ambition to 'so manage it, as to convey but the same impressions to every other brain, which the occurrences themselves excite in my own' (*TS*, p. 337) is a plan to generate that corresponding excitement in the reader which Longinus reckons as the acid test of the sublime, that swelling of the mind to the point where it seems 'as if what was only heard had been the Product of its own Invention' (*OS*, p. 15). By every means in his power Tristram seeks to banish that impersonality of the narrative voice which Warton says is characteristic of mock-epic, and every invitation extended to the reader to participate in the production of his story is to heighten the sympathy and to dull the judgment. The idea of critical distance is so antipathetic to Tristram (and his author) that the

Preface is introduced quite purposely into the body of the text not for any systematic or theoretical statement about the work in hand but simply to 'speak for itself.' What it speaks is an associationist defence of associationist wit which *illustrates* why there is no need to pass through the judgment to gain its end. It is a contradiction by enactment of Locke's influential counter-definitions of wit and judgment that manages, without any arguments, set dissertations or definitions, to make Burke's point about the judgmental affinities of wit which compares its ideas instead of associating them. It is hard to think of a piece of prose in English which imitates so well Montaigne's skill at thinking in metaphor and analogy, that tautological shifting from illustration to illustration that Tristram calls *dialectick induction* and for which he claims Rabelais' authority too.

I have tried to show in this essay how, with similar social and cultural forces producing the humorist and the mock-epic, ideas of irregularity and sublimity can be attached to both. It is in Sterne's novel that a narrative style which emerges directly from Cervantes' 'true Sublime' fits most closely and necessarily round the humorists of the Shandy family so that the hobbyhorse itself, that idol of the cave and image of integrity, becomes the vital tool of narrative representation, better than fame, voice, brush, evacuation or *camera obscura* (*TS*, p. 77). By taking this step Sterne confronts some of the apparently intractable problems which the singular man presents admirers and narrators with. The prime one is that he is likely to be socially invisible or socially unacceptable in proportion to his sincerity; for if irregularity stands in some sort of ratio to integrity then, like Sir Roger de Coverley, he will be hard to understand and yet be insufficiently prepossessing to incline an audience to patience. As a breed he is rare, either because (as Fielding suggests) once discovered the lucky naturalist keeps his habitat a secret or because (the more common explanation) he is especially vulnerable to predators. So the first job is to find the specimen, and the second is to make him speak. Tristram therefore establishes a circle four miles in diameter as his *world* and locates three humorists within its boundaries who can thrive immune from metropolitan knavery. Yet there remains the problem of language and representation. Addison suggests that God alone can understand the language of a thoroughly good and private man:

> There are many Vertues, which in their own Nature are incapable of any outward Representation: Many silent Perfections in the Soul of a good Man, which are great Ornaments to Humane Nature, but not able to discover themselves to the Knowledge of others; they are transacted in private, without Noise or Show, and are only

> visible to the great Searcher of Hearts. What Actions can express the entire Purity of Thought which refines and sanctifies a virtuous Man? That secret Rest and Contentedness of Mind . . . These and the like Vertues are the hidden Beauties of a Soul, the secret Graces which cannot be discovered by a mortal Eye, but make the Soul lovely and precious in his Sight, from whom no Secrets are concealed.
>
> (*Spectator*, No. 257)

If Addison says there is no language fit for these perfections, Tillotson in his sermon on sincerity defines the predicament of such a man as linguistic isolation. He will need 'a Dictionary to help him to understand his own Language' (I, 7) because current words have turned into the paper money of compliment, 'running into a Lie' to participate in conversation which 'is little else but driving a Trade of Dissimulation.' Expressed in Tillotson's exchange metaphor, the good and sincere man can neither buy nor sell, and his perfections are indeed silent ones. It is a theme Sterne returns to frequently in his sermons. His favorite heroes in the Bible are Joseph, who makes himself known to his brothers in an eloquent silence (II, 232), and Job, whose heroic cast is revealed both in his own verbal restraint and in his patience in the face of the misconstructions his friends place on the few words he utters. Addison's opinion that words and actions, however innocently uttered and performed, are deceitful mediums and 'apt to discolour and pervert the Object' (*Spectator*, No. 257) is illustrated in the story of Yorick's life and death. His career is a painful example of how the actions and words of a good man can be either misunderstood or wilfully misinterpreted when they pass through the medium of opinion and prejudice which 'so twists and refracts them from their true directions – that, with all the titles to praise which a rectitude of heart can give, the doers of them are nevertheless forced to live and die without it' (*TS*, p. 23). Nevertheless Sterne has devoted his novel to the business of describing the characters of men who have these silent or inaccessible virtues, and he chooses to sensitize us to the language of inarticulateness and dumbness in which this sort of character speaks. It is a double lesson in morality and linguistics.

In *Tristram Shandy* there is an alphabet of hobbyhorsical signs that matches the variety of primitive linguistic devices which Warburton classifies and discusses in *The Divine Legation of Moses*. These are the same devices which critics like Warton, Kames and Burke associate with the sublime, and which Sterne associates with the consistency of hobbyhorsical virtue. First of all there is silence, the primitive muteness of what Longinus calls 'a naked Thought without Words'

(*OS*, p. 18). It is this sort of silence which in *Tristram Shandy* can be certain proof of pity or can weave dreams of midnight secrecy into the brain. Silence is usually made intelligible by some sort of gesture, what Warburton calls 'the voice of the sign,' and so the silent disposition of limbs, or the handling of a pipe, or the glance of an eye will often carry the meaning of a hobbyhorsical dialogue. A refinement of the language of gesture is what Warburton calls the speaking hieroglyph, and that takes place when action forms itself into a statement and not just a response. Bridget communicates with Trim by this method. But a subtler form of argument by action is to perform what one is questioned about. Toby proves his hobbyhorse is a hobbyhorse by 'getting on his back and riding him about' and Yorick's journeys through his parish are an explanation in the action of why he rides the sort of horse he does. When Toby whistles *Lillabulero* or when Yorick reads the account of Gymnast's fight with Tripet, they are offering examples of this sort of parabolic delivery of a message by gesture. Sometimes these expressive arrangements of the body are accompanied by words, as in Toby's setting the fly free or in Trim's gesture of dropping the hat while reciting a self-evident truth. In the domain of pure language, the primitive belief in the performative function of words is held by Walter Shandy who constantly exhibits his faith in the power of naming and for whom the most expressive sign of the fall of empires is the fact that their *names* 'are falling themselves by piece-meals into decay' (*TS*, p. 354). Walter's theory of the auxiliary verbs, which he steals from Obadiah Walker's *Of Education*, is in fact a primitive syntactic basis for a universal language scheme in which, if the word is already known, the thing is known too. In Toby's case we hear another primitive use of the word, which is the extension of its reference by catachresis. For Toby the origin of language is in military science, and that provides him with a fund of literal terms which, when applied to other phenomena such as *trains* of ideas, a *mortar* and pestle, the *bridge* of a nose etc., imitate the process of early language growth by figurative applications of literal words. As for Yorick's puns, they are figurative uses of words that remind us how ideas are formed out of the body's sensations and activities by establishing instant etymologies.

The primitive nature of hobbyhorsical language offers a variety of ways of determining in some detail the characters of the men who use it. Like all primitive language, it both conceals and reveals meaning, and it will offer up its secrets only to those with enough patience and candor to decipher it. Once that effort is made, the hobbyhorse speaks the consistency of its rider and the audience can become as familiar with that consistency as if a Momus glass were placed in the breast. In a comic way certain valuable truths are revealed that were thought to be inexpressible and we learn a tongue that may not be the language of the gods but which God understands. Sterne finds a compendious store of these comic sublimities in Rabelais, and that he regarded them as versions of the sublime is likely from the name he gives to one of his earliest characters. 'Longinus Rabelaicus' is the leading figure in Sterne's *Fragment in the Manner of Rabelais* where he is busy producing a *Kerukopaedia*, or institute of sermon-making, that will pay as much attention to the *tune* of the sermon as its content. It will take into account the constitution of the preacher, the disposition of his limbs, the intonation of his voice and all the physical and spiritual accompaniments that belong to saying something with that natural propriety that sincerity demands. Rabelais himself adapts much of his wit from the Bible, and he sees 'voices of the sign' and punning as fit vehicles for the carnivalesque union of body and mind which he loves because it is the opposite of hypocrisy and insincerity. Sterne has no tradition of carnival, but he makes moral assumptions about the totality of the human constitution ('the soul and body are joint-sharers in every thing they get' – *TS*, p. 616) of which the hobbyhorse is the odd emblem. Along with the Latitudinarian divines he was so fond of borrowing from, like Tillotson, Clarke, Stillingfleet and Tenison, he sees in Newtonian science a variety of physical proofs of this assumption, and in the work of Cheyne and Hartley he finds physiological accounts of the close relationship between the soul, or mind, and the body. This is the central unifying concept of 'sensibility' and the common property of the age, but Sterne typically insists that there is a language appropriate to this union. So the comic sublime is not only the natural language of sincerity, or the constant exchanges between gestural, literal and metaphorical sense that Rabelais passes on; it is also the language of science itself which is supplying the lower, material component of meaning to words like *spirit, inspiration* and *gravity* and unconsciously creating the sort of pun Sterne and Rabelais enjoy so much.[32]

In his narrative Tristram reproduces all the primitivism of his characters' language, even adding primitive cries, parable, metaphor and the literary equivalent of gesture in the form of hieroglyphs. Since I have defined the comic sublime as mounting a higher idea upon a little circumstance or image in order to give a unified expression of a higher truth that has lower relations, I want briefly to strengthen the links between Tristram's narrative and certain effects of Pope and Montaigne by way of insisting on the great difference between Sterne's wordplay and Swift's. If the comic sublime is a response appropriate to the mixed condition of man, where little circumstances provide the impressions that make his elevated ideas, where mind and body are mutually dependent in making sense of things, and where there is a moral as well as physical relation between what is done and what is thought, it follows that it will affirm the inseparability of the ideas it joins, be they in a pun, a gesture, or a metaphor, because they are already linked in the joint activity of the body and mind. It will also follow that in any account of these reciprocal activities, words will tend to reproduce that reciprocity, not merely describe it or, as in mock-epic, establish an ironic distance between the account and the activity, and between the upper and lower elements of the activity itself. Any pun which announces the equilibrium of physical and mental experience *reflects* or *enacts* the very process it is applied to by making the two senses apparent but inextricable:

> In all distresses (except musical) where small cords are wanted, – nothing is so apt to enter a man's head, as his hatband: – the philosophy of this is so near the surface – I scorn to enter into it.
> (*TS*, p. 165)

The puns on 'cord' *quasi* 'chord' and on 'enter a man's head' (as meaning both the conception of an idea and the pressure of a hatband) are a lowly but thoroughly appropriate illustration of the comic sublime. The one sense is necessary to the other both as explanation and as utterance of Obadiah's 'feelings.' The causal relation between circumstance and idea is announced by words which proclaim in themselves the inevitable ambiguity of meaning that is made in this way. At first hearing this sort of wordplay sounds frivolous and unnecessary, but it is a testimony to Sterne's solid and coherent faith in sensationism and associationism. And as enactive prose this punning is cousin to some impressive relations. Addison praises Pope and Boileau praises Longinus for having managed to write about the sublime sublimely. Addison has in mind Pope's clever adjustments of the sound to the sense in the *Essay on Criticism*, and Boileau is referring to the famous seventh section of *On the Sublime*. Addison calls it exemplifying 'precepts in the very Precepts themselves' (*Spectator*, No. 253). It is the result of the idea of the object becoming so powerful and exclusive that the quality of the object invades the expression or representation of it. As Demosthenes becomes moved as he talks about an assault, he reproduces the blows in the rhythms of his oration. There is an example of this in the famous attack on Sporus in the *Epistle to Dr. Arbuthnot*. Pope's horror at his enemy's ambiguous qualities mounts with each antithetical example of them until finally he calls Sporus himself 'a vile Antithesis,' as if the nastiness of Sporus is so perfectly adapted to that rhetorical technique that it becomes infected with his evil and its inoffensive name is converted by association into the most opprobrious epithet Pope can think of.[33] Less impassioned but of the same nature is Montaigne's discovery in 'Upon Some Verses of Virgil' that action and description must imitate one another. In constantly elaborating the indissoluble connexions between his mind and his body Montaigne evolves a style that perfectly represents the reciprocity of thought and action, idea and sensation, by slipping with a natural metaphorical ease between them until the book and Montaigne become, as he says, consubstantial, mutually illustrative. The circumscription of Montaigne's experience (dreaming that he dreams, writing that he writes) comes of bending his mind habitually to his body's experience and intensifying the natural relation of the two. Consequently it is pointless in reading his *Essays* to consider his mind as distinct from his body or his style as distinct from the unions it is imitating. In *Tristram Shandy* there are several examples of this sort of circumscription which belong, as the puns do, to the comic sublime. When Tristram plagiarizes an attack on plagiarism, invokes Cid Hamet Benengeli's Invocation, or makes a digression in the very process of writing about digressions, he is comically filling his mind with his object to the degree that description becomes part of the thing described. This tautological reflection in the very prose of the object referred to repeats the effect of puns and literalized metaphors: that of the circumstanced idea, the thing that must always attend the thought it provokes.

Although so much of Swift's wit seems to play up and down the same vertical scale as Sterne's, it always establishes differences, never identities or natural relations. In a discussion of Swift's literalized metaphors, Maurice J. Quinlan points out that it is contrast, and not association, that he is aiming for 'in order to reveal an ironic disparity between the two meanings.'[34] The apparent resemblance between the two writers (one which Sterne claims along with the common source of Rabelais) is due perhaps to Swift's constant mockery of primitive forms of language, or at least of Baconian approaches to interpreting or imitating those forms. Whatever belongs to type, symbol, analogy, heiroglyph, sign, or mystery is a symptom of dullness and an opportunity for wit to destroy the silly symmetries and literalized notions that foolish minds invent and enjoy. And no matter how cleanly the satirical idea fits over the dunsical one (for example the modern improvement of digressions and the definition of the *satura lanx*), the test presented to the reader is to see and know the difference, and so mount to the disembodied region of the middle air whence wit makes its attacks on the dunces who sprawl in the *matter* of bathos, bombast, and bad magic. Rising properly, in *Tale of a Tub* at any rate, is the condition of having no lead at one's heels and of being free from material considerations. St John of Revelations, Panurge and Jack consume holy texts in order to prophesy, but for sensible folk that sort of bibliophagy is no longer appropriate.

Although this sets Swift at a further remove than the 'due distance' Sterne mentions (*Letters*, p. 76), it offers a clearer idea of Sterne's real connections and affiliations. In narrative technique they are with those, like Montaigne, who learn the naturalized art of irregularity, and with Cervantes who both invents a mock-epic narrative and superintends its conversion into the comic sublime. In morality he is close to the genial and masculine sentimentalism of Fielding, who likewise appoints the upper and lower limits in which incorporated minds think and feel. Sterne's interest in the humorist as a figure of real integrity, and in the means by which such a figure expresses himself, is closely involved with his interest in narrative and has much the same line of development, beginning with Cervantes and strengthened by the eighteenth century interest in humorism and irregularity. His physiological interest in the interaction of mind and body places Sterne quite definitely among Newtonians, and quite far from innovators of sublime styles like Chatterton, Smart and Blake whose primitivism has a more mystical basis that is, in Blake's case, profoundly opposed to the mechanist tradition. His interest in language links Sterne with those who were exploring the growth of languages and the structure of ideas, like Warburton, Hartley and Hume; and he owes a good deal less to Locke in this respect than is often supposed. Finally, in his pursuit of the subtler forms of irregularity, a mixture of associationist wit and 'sensible' language, Sterne has Longinus to instruct him in how to break rules and find others.

Notes

1. See E. P. Thompson, 'The Crime of Anonymity,' in *Albion's Fatal Tree: Crime and Society in Eighteenth-Century England*, by Douglas Hay (*et al.*) (London: Allen Lane, 1975), pp. 255–344.
2. See Frye's 'Towards Defining an Age of Sensibility,' in *Eighteenth Century English Literature: Modern Essays in Criticism*, ed. James L. Clifford (New York: Oxford University Press, 1960), pp. 311–18.
3. See *Tristram Shandy*, ed. James A. Work (New York: Odyssey Press, 1940), p. 85; and *Joseph Andrews*, ed. Douglas Brooks (London: Oxford University Press, 1971), p. 9. I am indebted to many critics and scholars, chiefly to Stuart M. Tave, *The Amiable Humorist: a Study in the Comic Theory and Criticism of*

the Eighteenth and Early Nineteenth Centuries (Chicago: University of Chicago Press, 1960); Ronald Paulson, *The Fictions of Satire* (Baltimore: Johns Hopkins Press, 1967) and *Satire and the Novel in Eighteenth-Century England* (New Haven: Yale University Press, 1967); and Lionel Trilling, *Sincerity and Authenticity* (Cambridge, Mass.: Harvard University Press, 1967).

4. *The Works of the Most Reverend Dr John Tillotson, Late Lord Archbishop of Canterbury*, 2 volumes (London: Ralph Barker, 1712), I, 7.

5. Alexander Pope, 'The First Satire of the Second Book of Horace,' in *Imitations of Horace*, ed. John Butt (London: Methuen and Co. Ltd., 1939), II, 51–52, 57–58.

6. John Dryden, 'A Discourse Concerning Satire,' *Of Dramatic Poesy and Other Critical Essays*, ed. G. Watson (London: J. M. Dent, 1962), II, 123.

7. Jonathan Swift, *A Tale of a Tub*, ed. A. C. Guthkelch and D. Nichol Smith (Oxford: Clarendon Press, 1958), pp. 143–44.

8. John Dryden, 'A Discourse Concerning Satire,' II, 146.

9. Jonathan Swift, *A Tale of a Tub*, pp. 18, 44.

10. John Dryden, 'A Discourse Concerning Satire,' II, 103.

11. Alexander Pope, 'Postscript,' *The Odyssey of Homer, Books XIII–XXIV*, ed. Maynard Mack (London: Methuen and Co. Ltd., 1967), X, 387.

12. Ibid, X, 388. Further references to the 'Postscript' will be incorporated, in parenthesis, into the text.

13. See Stuart M. Tave, *The Amiable Humorist*, p. 157.

14. See *Tristram Shandy*, p. 22; and James Beattie, 'An Essay on Laughter and Ludicrous Composition,' *Essays* (Edinburgh: Printed for William Creech, 1776; rpt. New York: Garland Publishing Inc., 1971), p. 603. Further references to *Tristram Shandy* will be incorporated, in parenthesis, into the text under the abbreviation *TS*.

15. Miguel de Cervantes Saavedra, *The Life and Achievements of the Renowned Don Quixote de la Mancha*, trans. Peter le Motteux, ed. J. G. Lockhart (London: J. M. Dent, 1906; rpt. 1970), I, 393–94.

16. Dionysius Longinus, *On the Sublime*, trans. William Smith (1739; rpt. New York: Scholar's Facsimiles and Reprints, 1975), p. 71. Further references to *On the Sublime* will be incorporated, in parenthesis, into the text under the abbreviation *OS*.

17. Montaigne, *Essays of Michael Seigneur de Montaigne*, trans. Charles Cotton (London: 1711), I, 253.

18. Diderot, *Jacques the Fatalist*, trans. Robert J. Loy (New York: Collier Books, 1962), p. 211.

19. David Hartley, *Observations on Man, His Frame, His Duty, and His Expectations* (1749; rpt. Florida: Scholar's Facsimiles and Reprints, 1966), I, vi.

20. Edmund Burke, *A Philosophical Inquiry into the Origin of our Ideas of the Sublime and Beautiful, The Works of Edmund Burke* (London: George Bell & Sons, 1902), I, 88. Further references to *A Philosophical Inquiry* etc. will be incorporated, in parenthesis, into the text under the abbreviation *Inquiry*.

21. Sterne, *The Sermons of Mr Yorick* (Oxford: Basil Blackwell, 1927), II, 230.

22. Sterne, *A Sentimental Journey*, ed. Gardner D. Stout (Berkeley: University of California Press, 1967), p. 159.

23. Wordsworth, 'Preface to Lyrical Ballads,' *The Prose Works of William Wordsworth*, ed. W. J. B. Owen and Jane Worthington Smyser (Oxford: Clarendon Press, 1967), I, 137.

24. Joseph Warton, *Essay on the Genius and Writings of Pope* (1782; rpt. Farnborough: Gregg International Publishers, 1969), 1, 291. Further references to *Essay on the Genius*, etc. will be incorporated, in parenthesis, into the text under the abbreviation *EGWP*.

25. Samuel Johnson, *Johnson's Lives of the Poets: A Selection*, ed. J. P. Hardy (Oxford: Clarendon Press, 1971), p. 12.

26. Francis Hutcheson, 'Reflections upon Laughter,' *An Inquiry Concerning Beauty, Order, Harmony, Design*, ed. Peter Kivy (The Hague: Martinus Nijhoff, 1973), p. 109. Further references to 'Reflections upon Laughter' will be incorporated, in parenthesis, into the text under the abbreviation 'Reflections.'

27. See *The Works of Alexander Pope*, ed. William Warburton (London: 1753), I, 104n.

28. William Warburton, *The Divine Legation of Moses Demonstrated* (London: 1837), I, 468; I, 251. Further references to *The Divine Legation* will be incorporated, in parenthesis, into the text under the abbreviation *DLMD*.

29. Fielding, *Joseph Andrews*, p. 220.

30. *Letters of Laurence Sterne*, ed. Lewis Perry Curtis (Oxford: Clarendon Press, 1935; rpt. 1965), p. 77. Further references to *Letters of Laurence Sterne* will be incorporated, in parenthesis, into the text under the abbreviation of *Letters*.

31. See 'Self Knowledge,' in *The Sermons of Mr Yorick*, I, 41.

32. See Donald Davie, *The Language of Science and the Language of Literature 1700–1740* (London: Sheed and Ward, 1963); and Margaret C. Jacob, *The Newtonians and the English Revolution 1689–1720* (Hassocks: Harvester Press, 1976), who establishes interesting and, in this context, significant links between Newtonian science and Biblical exegesis.

33. See *The Poems of Alexander Pope*, ed. John Butt (London: Methuen and Co. Ltd., 1963), p. 608.

34. Maurice J. Quinlan, 'Swift's Use of Literalization as a Rhetorical Device,' *PMLA*, 12 (Dec. 1967), 516–21.

7 *A Sentimental Journey*: Purposeful Play

Carol Kay

Carol Kay's *Political Constructions* proposes what I have called a 'liberal' model for reading the ideological significance of the eighteenth-century novel (see Introduction to *The English Novel Volume I: 1700 to Fielding*, pp. 17–19). As I have argued in the Introduction to this volume (see especially pp. 15–20), so Kay argues that Sterne's playfulness represents a period within which the constitutional anxieties of an earlier period have waned, so that the novelist now has leisure to enquire into the peculiarities of individual sensation and whim, as well as to cultivate the resulting arts of politeness. This allows Kay to propose an idea to some extent reflected in Starr's essay above, but which has been influential in its own right: 'remasculinization' is the successful appropriation by men like Yorick of feminine softness, modesty, and delicacy.

At the end of *Tristram Shandy*, Walter, who has had early warning of Widow Wadman's 'secret articles which had delayed the surrender,' holds forth on the evils of women's lust to Yorick and Mrs. Shandy, asserting 'that every evil and disorder in the world, of what kind or nature soever, from the first fall of *Adam*, down to my Uncle *Toby*'s (inclusive) was owing one way or other to the same unruly appetite' (IX, 32, 644).[1] Yorick tries twice to speak, once to bring 'my father's hypothesis to some temper,' then to 'batter the whole hypothesis to pieces' when Walter claims that engendering takes place in the dark because 'all the parts thereof – the congredients – the preparations – the instruments –, and whatever serves thereto, are so held to be conveyed to a cleanly mind by no language, translation, or periphrasis whatever' (IX, 33, 645).

Yorick is interrupted the first time by the appearance of Toby with his look of 'infinite benevolence and forgiveness.' Toby's modesty, which has been in the past a refutation of Walter, is here not sufficient to halt Walter on his course of condemnation; in fact, Walter is impelled by resentment on Toby's behalf. The second time, when Yorick is even more determined to speak, Obadiah breaks in with a complaint opposite to Walter's resentment of lust. The Shandy bull has not lived up to his duties and is in danger of losing the reputation of a 'town bull.' Yorick is allowed to read a lesson in the last words of the book, but it is a lesson against lessons, his praise of the cock-and-bull story. What he might have said to 'temper' an attack on lust could not be said in *Tristram Shandy*, even though the display of extremes raises hope for an agreeable middle.

In *A Sentimental Journey* Yorick comes out from the margins into the center of the book, and it is a coming out for Sterne as well. With the publication of four volumes of his sermons as the *Sermons of Mr. Yorick*, Sterne underlined his identification with the character. To bring Yorick into *A Sentimental Journey*, set in 1762, is to make clear that this Yorick is even closer to Sterne than the one in *Tristram Shandy*, who is supposed to have died in 1748.[2] Although Yorick is not to be seen in the pulpit in *A Sentimental Journey* any more than in *Tristram Shandy*, he does remind us at the outset of the kind of coat he wore and that he was not going to leave it behind when he went to France: 'The coat I have on, said I, looking at the sleeve, will do' (65).[3] Gardner Stout appropriately links this passage to a letter in which Sterne answers the criticism of a friend. After reading a draft of the first two volumes of *Tristram Shandy*, the friend urged Sterne to avoid gross allusions and remember his character as a clergyman.

Sterne replied, 'A Very Able Critick and One of My Colour too – who has Read Over tristram – Made Answer Upon My saying I Would consider the colour of My Coat, as I corrected it – That that very Idea in My head would render My Book not worth a groat – still I promise to be Cautious – but I deny I have gone as farr as Swift – He keeps a due distance from Rabelais & I keep a due distance from him – Swift has said a hundred things I durst Not Say – Unless I was Dean of St. Patrick's'.[4] Although Sterne had not become Dean of Saint Patrick's by the time of *A Sentimental Journey*, he had enjoyed preferment in the church, popularity in the best circles of London and Paris society, and a good deal of literary recognition (even if much of it controversial), so it is reasonable to suppose that there were now some things he did dare say, even if they took him yet farther from Swift than he was in *Tristram Shandy*. He was on his way to exploring the latitude in latitudinarianism.

Sterne's developed sense of literary authority takes him on a different novelistic path from Richardson's or Fielding's, since it led him to write a much shorter book than his first. In the perspective of *A Sentimental Journey*, the enormous length and learned wit of *Tristram Shandy* look more elaborately defensive than Toby's fortifications; the insistent play, the nagging of the reader, seem like the strategies of a late bloomer to persuade the company of his unprecedented precocity. With the learned wit pared away, what remains is an astonishing rapidity, a remarkably flexible modulation between reflection and exemplary action. The encumbered narrative of *Tristram Shandy* constantly falls behind, or at least grows backward; in *A Sentimental Journey* Yorick is always ahead of himself. From the beginning his words precipitate him into scenes for which he is not quite prepared. It is not surprising, then, that Yorick should reach the point sooner, more clearly, and more often than Tristram does. He is not totally different from the characters of *Tristram Shandy*, since he is also propelled by defensiveness into somewhat aimless self-extension, but he scores points in this process rather than merely falling into it. *A Sentimental Journey* begins in the middle of an argument because Yorick wants to win it, or at least credential his opinions, by his journey. Yorick in *Tristram Shandy* fell rather thoughtlessly into controversies and contempt, but he did not try to defend his reputation.

Perhaps it is the much-criticized Yorick-Sterne of *Tristram Shandy* and the *Sermons* that the Yorick-Sterne of *A Sentimental Journey* wishes to defend. When we consider the typical English associations with France that might make one speak of things being better ordered there, certain freedoms in the relations of the sexes and freedoms to relate things about the sexes come to mind. Well-mannered flirtation, flattery, frankness about bodily functions, sexy jokes, and cuss words (as well as French maids and adultery) strike the English as very French, and it makes sense that Sterne should take us to France to win his argument against the critics of his bawdry. What results is an unprecedented, and in its own way highly courageous, defense of sex in the head.

Of all the mixed up things that make up the motley pages of *Tristram Shandy*, the mixture of chastity and concupiscence is the most confounding. If the reader tries to clean up a bawdy reference, it spreads the dirt. In a chapter about Walter's learned collection of books on noses, Tristram warns the embarrassingly female reader: 'Now don't let Satan, my dear girl, in this chapter, take advantage of any one spot of rising-ground to get astride of your imagination, if you can any ways help it; or if he is so nimble as to slip on, – let me beg of you, like an unback'd filly, to *frisk it, to squirt it, to jump it, to rear it, to bound it*, – and to kick it, with long kicks and short kicks, till like *Tickletoby*'s mare, you break a strap or a crupper, and throw his worship into the dirt. – You need not kill him' (II, 36, 226). It turns out that getting it off is very like getting it on, but the reader can't get out of it and get on with other things. Like so much of the particolored jesting in *Tristram Shandy*, these embarrassments remind us of a human weakness, but not too severely. Nevertheless, the narrator, who has offered to 'halve this matter amicably' (II, 11, 109), so as to allow the reader 'something to imagine in his turn,' seems especially anxious to blame the reader for immodest thoughts. It is because such thoughts are the natural concomitant of censorship. In 'the fragment' on the Queen of Navarre, *whiskers* becomes an indecent word, and it could happen to anything, when 'the *extreams* of DELICACY, and the *beginnings* of CONCUPISCENCE' come together: 'Chastity, by nature the gentlest of all affections – give it but its lead – 'tis like a ramping and roaring lion' (V, 1, 348).

In 'Slawkenbergius' Tale' Strasbourg falls because the citizens are absorbed in their curiosity about Slawkenbergius's nose, but in the first story 'fragment' in *A Sentimental Journey*, Abdera is saved by sex in the head. The satiric laughter of Democritus has no power of reform, but, it is suggested, only adds 'libels and pasquinades' to other kinds of violence, 'poisons, conspiracies, and assassinations.' Yet the Abderites are converted to love and friendship by the passage from the *Andromeda* of Euripides celebrating the obsessive (even tyrannical) power of Love: 'O, Cupid, prince of gods and men.' It sexualizes the mind: 'nothing operated more upon their imaginations, than the tender strokes of nature which the poet had wrought up in that pathetic speech of Perseus' (131). In this 'fragment' Sterne decisively rejects (rather than merely ignoring, as in *Tristram Shandy*) the formative power of satire, and he equally rejects the madness that his source, Burton's *Anatomy of Melancholy*, found in this example of infectious love discourse. The quicksand of sexy thoughts in *Tristram Shandy*, where chastity and immodesty bog down together, has become a scene from a golden age of cooperation and reconciliation: 'Friendship and Virtue met together, and kiss'd each other in the street.' The men play on their pipes while the women listen 'chastly.'

The narration has been sent off into Abdera by Yorick's reflections on his newly hired servant La Fleur, a former soldier who practices the utopian morality of making love not war. When the landlord who had recommended La Fleur to Yorick confesses 'he is always in love,' Yorick replies:

> I am heartily glad of it, said I, – 'twill save me the trouble every night of putting my breeches under my head. In saying this, I was not making so much La Fleur's eloge as my own, have been in love with one princess or another almost all my life, and I hope I shall go on so, till I die, being firmly persuaded, that if I ever do a mean action, it must be in some interval betwixt one passion and another: whilst this interregnum lasts, I always perceive my heart locked up – I can scarce find in it, to give Misery a sixpence; and therefore I always get out of it as fast as I can, and the moment I am rekindled,

I am all generosity and good will again; and would do any thing in the world either for, or with any one, if they will but satisfy me there is no sin in it.
– But in saying this – surely I am commending the passion – not myself.

(128–29)

Yorick asserts his state of continual arousal (or at least frequent arousal) as an ideal condition of charitable responsiveness that leads to moral acts and is clearly bounded by the fences of the moral law. We are not teased with questions about the possible moral ambiguity of being 'in love with one princess or another almost all my life.' By contrast Tristram always nags us to worry about his relation to his dear, dear Jenny. Is she his wife, mistress, daughter, or friend? The defense of the French sentimental friendship he winds into is too casual and ironic to serve as a moral defense. 'Sentiment' here is a set of false alternatives, the pure or the delicious:

Surely, Madam, a friendship between the two sexes may subsist, and be supported without – Fy! Mr. *Shandy*: – Without any thing, Madam, but that tender and delicious sentiment, which ever mixes in friendship, where there is a difference of sex. Let me intreat you to study the pure and sentimental parts of the best *French* Romances; – it will really, Madam, astonish you to see with what a variety of chaste expression this delicious sentiment, which I have the honour to speak of, is dress'd out.

(I, 18, 49)

We may well wonder which are 'the sentimental parts' of book or reader. The reader's intercourse with a book is suggested by the range of meaning of the term *sentiment*: it can be an opinion or an idea, a physical or emotional feeling, but it may also be, according to Johnson's dictionary, 'a striking sentence in a composition,' or according to the Oxford English Dictionary, an epigram or toast. A passage in Sterne's letters which anticipates Yorick's praise of infatuation complains of the vagueness of the term *sentiment*, which he has taken to himself from the French. In the context it is clearly associated with filling up an empty mind:

I am glad that you are in love – 'twill cure you (at least) of the spleen which has a bad effect on both man and woman – I myself must ever have some dulcinea in my head – it harmonizes the soul – and in these cases I first endeavour to make the lady believe so, or rather I begin first to make myself believe that I am in love

> – but I carry on in my affairs quite in the French way, sentimentally – *l'amour* (say they) *n'est rien sans sentiment* – Now notwithstanding such a potter about the *word*, they have no precise idea annex'd to it –
>
> (*Letters*, 256)

Sentimentality is linked to persuasion, which is a kind of make-believe; it does not necessarily make you believe. Sterne quotes his French adage about the necessity of sentiment in the letter La Fleur brings to Yorick to help him to write to the engaging Fleming, Mme. de L***. It is full of 'sentiments,' that is, good sentences that anyone might find useful ('vive la bagatelle' as well as 'vive l'amour'). The particular sentiments of the sender can remain veiled in these good turns of phrase, especially because Yorick removes the one line that specifies a time for one's 'turn.' We can say about Yorick's sentimentality what he says about the 'French sublime' of the wigmaker: 'The French expression professes more than it performs' (159).

The kind of sentimental sex liberation Yorick defends is not geared to performance. The episodic structure maintains an ethos of not going all the way with anyone. It seems odd that so many critics linger over the supposed sexual ambiguity of 'the conquest,' since Yorick is quite clear that he defends only feeling 'the movements which rise' and intends to 'govern' them by morality.[5] Judgments of tone may differ. In this rather grave, preacherly passage about divinely created nature, I find the sexual references neither snickering nor ironic. They assert a freedom of fantasy and feeling that is bounded by laws governing action:

> If nature has so wove her web of kindness, that some threads of love and desire are entangled with the piece – must the whole web be rent in drawing them out? – Whip me such stoices, great governor of nature! said I to myself – Wherever thy providence shall place me for the trials of my virtue – whatever is my danger – whatever is my situation – let me feel the movements which rise out of it, and which belong to me as a man – and if I govern them as a good one – I will trust the issues to thy justice, for thou hast made us – and not we ourselves.
>
> (237–38)

We might take this freedom of feeling to be modeled on the Hobbesian and Anglican freedom of conscience. Thought and feeling are private; actions are the matters that concern the commonwealth.

But Sterne goes farther than advocating tolerance; he advocates enjoyment of erotic sentiment, which is the greater because of a recognition of limits: 'There is a sort of pleasing half guilty blush, where the blood is more in fault than the man – 'tis sent impetuous from the heart, and virtue flies after it – not to call it back, but to make the sensation of it more delicious to the nerves – 'tis associated' (234). In the scene of brinksmanship with the *fille de chambre* Yorick would have pleased Hobbes in the readiness with which he takes the coward's role and avoids heroic moral combat. Sentimentality operates as a prophylactic against passion. Because Yorick has Eliza's image in his heart and around his neck, he avoids pursuing the affecting Mme. de L***. The sentimental letter he takes from La Fleur is really a kiss-off.

Yorick's morality is very far from Clarissa's: she struggles to get thoughts as well as actions in line with a high standard and suffers over the slender strand of a 'conditional liking' for a man of whom she does not entirely approve. Sterne's monk tells Yorick, ''Twas too late to say whether it was the weakness or goodness of our tempers which had involved us in this contest' (100), and Yorick compels the gentle traveller to give something to the beggars of France, with the reassurance that 'he need not be so exact in setting down his motives for giving them – they will be register'd elsewhere' (132). Yorick's easy conscience, his lack of perfectionism, can be a welcome antidote to Richardson's rigors. Moreover, it is not hard to see that Clarissa, for all her suffering, is a much more dangerous character than Yorick. Yorick, as he tells us, is willing to 'give up the triumph, for security' (235).

Coming to France in 1762, before peace has been declared, may not seem the best route to security, but Yorick has come like so many other travelers to perfect the peaceable virtue of compleasance, or as it is more usually called in the context of French culture, 'politeness.' Smooth, polished manners that enable people to get along, the arts of elegant conversation and compliment, were thought to be the flower of the French court. In his important exploration 'Of the Rise and Progress of the Arts and Sciences' (1741), David Hume weighed the value of 'modern politeness' and 'modern gallantry,' both 'the natural produce of courts and monarchies'.[6] These cultural values arise in modern monarchies rather than in the ancient or modern republics, because in a monarchy the people 'must turn their attention upward, to court the good graces and favour of the great,' and to be prosperous a man must 'render himself *agreeable*, by his wit, complaisance, or civility' (*Essays*, I:186–87).

Hume understands that these court values are not confined to the court, but are diffused throughout a monarchical society, for 'a long train of dependence from the prince to the peasant . . . beget[s] in every one an inclination to please his superiors, and to form himself upon those models, which are the most acceptable to people of condition and education' (*Essays*, I:187). So it is not surprising that Yorick need not go to court to find politesse. We might consider the extremely civilized beggars who impress Yorick in Montreuil. As one steps aside, bowing in deference to the female beggars, Yorick exclaims, 'Just heaven! for what wise reason hast thou order'd it, that beggary and urbanity, which are at such variance in other countries, should find a way to be at unity in this?' (132). Another beggar offers snuff to those beside him, and Yorick honors him more by taking snuff than by the charity. A soldier's loyalty to the king takes Yorick's fancy. Two more of the beggars are good at compliments ('Mon cher et tres charitable Monsieur,' and even better, 'My Lord Anglois'). Finally, a man too proud to beg stirs Yorick's charity the most. One female beggar, however, seems outside the circle of politeness and begs only for 'the love of God': her dislocated hip disqualifies her for gallantry.

Hume defends gallantry as an extension of politeness. Rather than a degeneracy in masculine virtue, Hume explains gallantry as a civilized form of authority exercised by a modern male over a modern female, 'a studied deference and complaisance for all her inclinations and opinions' (*Essays*, I:193). The sexes did not mingle in company in the ancient world, and therefore they lacked the refinement of modern society. We should remember that Hume boasted in his posthumously published autobiography of his own popularity among 'modest' women. In the early essay he continues, 'what better school for manners, than the company of virtuous women; where the mutual endeavour to please must insensibly polish the mind, where the example of the female softness and modesty must communicate itself to their admirers, and where the delicacy of that sex puts everyone on his guard, lest he give some offense by any breach of decency' (*Essays*, I:194)

Wanting to look good to a woman is an acceptable motive for moral development in the sociology of refinement and politeness, so Yorick's improvement in manners to the monk is not ironized by our perception that he is showing off to a lady; that is the way it is supposed to work. The lady teaches him a further lesson in politesse: he should not call nervous, English-style attention to the special circumstances of politesse, such unchaperoned settings as the remise, where the sexes hold intercourse. But we cannot really expect (and perhaps we would not want) an Englishman to learn politesse perfectly, as Yorick shows in his final discomfiture in the bedroom of an inn alone with a female traveler and her maid.

Yorick, as I have said, does not want to go very far down the road with a woman. There is usually not much conversational intercourse, and it is usually interrupted. Expressive silences and Yorick's skill in translating faces and gestures mean that he does not have to learn much from the woman herself. He cannot attend to the directions of the grisette in the glove shop. Since he has read the love story of Maria as told by Tristram Shandy, he does not need to ask Maria about it; indeed, given her disordered wits, he knows more about it than she does, though she does remember the 'pale, thin' Tristram Shandy pitying her and that he 'half-promised' to see her again (272). Perhaps Yorick does not need very much sentimental education at the hands of a woman, because he already has all the valuable attributes of a woman. By the process I am calling remasculinization, Sterne has appropriated softness, delicacy, and modesty for his male character.

Yorick's graveyard tears show that he is 'as weak as a woman' and deserving of pity (103); his Shandyesque taste for double entendres is interpreted as a strategic cover for extreme modesty: 'I have something within me which cannot bear the shock of the least indecent insinuation: in the sportability of chit-chat I have often endeavoured to conquer it, and with infinite pain have hazarded a thousand things to a dozen of the sex together – the least of which I could not venture to a single one, to gain heaven' (217). So Yorick does not need to spend very much time or become very intimate with women. If he did, he might be in danger of crossing over some frontier. The danger of too much intercourse between the sexes may be sexual intercourse, but it may also be the effeminacy of men.

Hume admits that modern politeness, 'which is naturally so ornamental, runs often into affectation and foppery, disguise and insincerity' (*Essays*, I:191), but he claims that every social habit contains a negative potential. Yorick of course learns the great secret of flattery from a successful beggar who approaches only women, and with it he keeps his 'places' at the tables of people of rank, until he grows ashamed and feels this 'dishonest reckoning' is the 'gain of a slave' and a 'vile prostitution of myself to half a dozen different people' (266).

Perhaps Montesquieu in *The Spirit of the Laws* (1748) is the farthest-reaching analyst of the sociology of politeness under monarchy. A deep moral ambivalence about modern society comes through his defense of modern difference from ancient republican virtue. The guiding principle of a monarchy for Montesquieu is competitive honor, egoistic concern for other people's opinions, rather than the altruistic love of public good which was the virtue of republics. Politeness may lead people to sociable pleasure in one another, but it is a form of the competitive wish to 'distinguish oneself from others'.[7] Delicacy of taste develops in the scene of luxury where a multiplicity of goods and constantly varying values make fine discriminations possible (IV, ii, 199). The intercourse of men and women in French society draws Montesquieu out of his philosophic neutrality into a defensive, partisan 'we': 'If only we could be left as we are' (XIX, vi, 271). The mingling of men with women, their desire to look good in one another's eyes, motivates the increase of taste, 'which is the source of the nation's wealth,' and the increase of politeness, 'which attracts so many visitors to its shores' (XIX, v, 271).

But this sociability that inspires taste and commerce deteriorates the morals. In the *Discourse on the Origin of Inequality* Rousseau's revulsion from the social and political system of the court is tracked all the way back to an early stage of tribal society, when by spending time together and by looking at each other with erotic preferences men and women evolve corrupting principles of competition in honor, along with the arts of singing, dancing, and civility. Inequality originates in politeness even before the invention of private property.

The character type many modern historians think of as bourgeois man, a calculator of advantages, a restless consumer of new values, a competitor above all, turns out to be in Montesquieu primarily the political subject of a monarchy, a participant in commercial culture only secondarily. More recently Norbert Elias has argued that the social psychology of calculating, competitive, polite, and self-controlled individuals appeared first as a 'courtly rationality' of the early modern absolutist state before the urban-commercial ethos became culturally important, and then for a long time worked along with it to form the modern personality.[8] Elias is as sympathetic to the 'courtly art of human observation' (*Power and Civility*, 274) in Saint-Simon and others as I am to the more abstract theory of Hobbes and Hume. The marketlike model of competitive desire and esteem is never afflicted with the mystifications of 'bourgeois individualism': 'the individual is always seen in his social context, *as a human being in his relations to others, as an individual in a social situation*' (*Power and Civility*, 274).

It therefore makes sense for Sterne to send Yorick to absolutist France in order to bring to prominence in his fiction what could strike us as a bourgeois sense of the personality as engaged in 'a sentimental commerce.'[9] In Yorick's trip we find bourgeois commerce continually resolved into the forms of honor. Yorick's purchases (except for the indispensable French wig) have the quality of gifts that show, in spite of his modest means, his generosity and superiority to need and his intention to give honor as well as to receive it. He hires a larger carriage than he needs, pays wages to a servant untrained but graceful and decorative, buys gloves he cannot wear and ruffles he does not want. The scenes of salesmanship are extremely polite. The grisettes display their gloves and laces quietly and patiently without puffing them. M. Dessein is as adept at compliment as Yorick and foils him in a gentlemanly 'duel' of wishing each other well, garnished by courteous bowing. Yorick wishes to relieve M. Dessein of the pain of seeing the ramshackle (and doubtless cheap) *désobligeant* (a kind of carriage), but M. Dessein assures him that the pain of hiring out an unworthy vehicle to 'a man of honour' would be worse pain (88).

The scenes not only exemplify Hume's long chain of dependence, which diffuses politeness everywhere; they also point up the peculiar status of the bourgeoisie in an aristocratic society. The people in trade are often in a 'client economy' rather than a free market; that is, they are tied to a deferential relation with their aristocratic patrons and forced by their situation to extend large, long-term credit (as well as politesse).[10] Yorick, as a tourist who pays as he goes, has less of this sort of local political power, but the deferential manners of the grisette in the glove shop (and of her husband) suggest the usual attitude toward authority. We might compare the adventure recorded in Boswell's *London Journal*, in which on a 'trial of civility' he sallies forth, an unknown Scot, into a London shop and persuades the tradesman to trust him for the price of a sword because he looks like a gentleman. Boswell sententiously reads the moral of the story to the man: 'Sir . . . if you had not trusted me, I should not have bought it from you.'[11] Like Yorick, Boswell likes to delude himself that his class privilege is a set of highly personal attributes, so he warns the sword cutter, 'Pray don't do such a thing again. It is dangerous.' In fact, however, a dealer in such gentlemanly merchandise must adapt his manners to his patrons.

That commerce itself involved agreeable manners was a hopeful article of faith for the new economics of the mid-eighteenth century. We have seen Montesquieu's connection of the polite intercourse of the sexes, taste, fashion, and consumption. Hume's *Political Discourses* (1752), his most popular book, especially in France, asserted, with even fewer hesitations than Montesquieu had expressed, the social values of what had previously been condemned as luxury. 'Refinement in the Arts' – that is, the development of industry, commerce, and consumption – ushers in the cultural superiority of people in modern Europe:

> They flock into cities; love to receive and communicate knowledge; to show their wit or their breeding; their taste in conversation or living in clothes or furniture. Curiosity allures the wise; variety the foolish; and pleasure both. Particular clubs and societies are

> everywhere formed: Both sexes meet in an easy and sociable manner: and the tempers of men as well as their behaviour, refine apace. So that, beside the improvements which they receive from knowledge and the liberal arts, it is impossible but they must feel an encrease of humanity, from the very habit of conversing together, and contribute to each other's pleasure and entertainment.
>
> (*Essays*, 1:301–2)

The growth of demand in eighteenth-century England for just such items as wigs and gloves and books has been judged the basis for 'the birth of a consumer society,'[12] but how far down the social scale the demand reached has been a matter for speculation. Hume clearly believes that commerce has strengthened the political power of the 'middling rank of men.' Statistics on the increase of wages in the second half of the eighteenth century and on increased industrial output both suggest an increase in consumption; reports of travelers and complaints of social critics such as Fielding suggest that emulation in fashion reached far down the social ladder, although the largest increases came only in the last quarter of the century. However many plebeian readers might eventually sympathize with Yorick's consumer adventures, in these passages Sterne does not seem to emphasize the democratic potential of commercial sociability.

Two of the most memorable accounts of commerce in *A Sentimental Journey* treat it as a respectable lapse from gentlemanly status. The Chevalier de St. Louis sells pates 'without solicitation' (210) near the gates of the palace at Versailles. To all who inquire, he tells the story of his service at the head of a company in war and his impoverishment at the conclusion of the peace, and he refers courteously to the king as 'the most generous of princes.' As a result, word gets round to the king, so that, without solicitation, the officer is rewarded with a pension that 'broke up his little trade' (211). This episode leads into the next story of 'the sword.' Unlike other French provinces, the special laws of Brittany allow a member of the nobility to suspend his noble rank if he wishes to engage in commerce and to resume it when he declares to a court that he has desisted from this nonnoble activity. The Marquis de E**** resigns his sword and spends nineteen or twenty years of successful application to business in Martinique, yet nonetheless also requires 'bequests from distant branches of his house' to enable him to reclaim his nobility and to support it. The characters in these stories do not exactly 'earn' a living by commerce; it helps 'support' their social dignity, but in indirect ways.

Sterne is surprisingly favorable in these sections to aspects of French polity which for Englishmen typified the tyranny of French government. The officer's roundabout approach to the king suggests the dangers of public criticism or petition. Even the liberal regulations of Brittany show the high legal walls between the aristocratic and commercial class. The social and political segregation of classes was not reinforced by such legal restrictions in England. But the sentimental journey of Sterne, by contrast to the satirical criticism of Smollett, extends sympathy to things French, even to French styles of authority. At the opera Yorick eagerly places himself beside 'a kindly old French officer.' The officer reminds him of Captain Toby Shandy, but this is not the Toby who wanted to go on fighting in 1761; *A Sentimental Journey* was written well after the Treaty of Paris in 1763. Yorick's predilection for veterans is a sentimental affection for finding philanthropy in surprising places: 'I love the character . . . because I honour the man whose manners are softened by a profession that makes bad men worse' (170). When Yorick's philanthropy is aroused by the sight of a dwarf crowded out by a tall, corpulent German, the sympathetic officer directs a sentinel to attend to it, the German is brought back at musket point, and Yorick claps and cries out, 'This is noble.' He is only a little embarrassed when the officer reminds him of the political significance of the act: 'and yet you would not permit this . . . in England' (179). Perhaps Sterne, like Hume, would have longed for better police control of the crowds during the Wilkite riots. The use of standing armies to control the urban population was one of the hallmarks of French absolutism and the bugbear of English politics, but sentimental philanthropy draws Yorick to approve of it.

The most astonishing extension of Yorick's political sympathies is his imaginative approach to Catholicism. Yorick's typical Protestant attack on monkish sloth and ignorance is not far from the attack on papistry that Sterne issued from the pulpit and in *Tristram Shandy*, but in *A Sentimental Journey* Yorick comes to feel it is bad manners to a 'courteous figure.' Inspired by his civilized wish to impress a lady, he makes his apologies to the monk with an exchange of snuffboxes. The monk's horn snuffbox then becomes for Yorick an object of superstitious, Catholic-style veneration, a holy relic: 'I guard this box, as I would the instrumental parts of my religion, to help my mind on to something better; in truth, I seldom go abroad without it; and oft and many a time have I called up by it the courteous spirit of its owner to regulate my own, in the justling of the world' (101).

Yorick's sentimental practice is to invest the world with superstition, to perform miraculous acts of transubstantiation with holy relics and rituals. The emblematic chapter titles, 'The Desobligeant,' 'The Remise,' lead to 'The Supper,' and finally to the daring of 'The Grace,' where Yorick sees religion mixing in the simple peasant dance. But like the sexual liberation of the book, the affection for French authority and religion are an indulgence of personal fantasy and feeling that goes out on a short limb. Yorick never does give money to the monk's convent, and he considers that the monk 'took sanctuary, not so much in his convent as in himself' (102). He does not join in Catholic ritual; Catholics join him in sentimental ritual, potentially a subtle vindication of the authority of individual conscience.

The peaceful, ecumenical religious sentiment, like the nostalgia for picturesque philanthropic soldiers, does not obliterate the differences that a war could exacerbate. Yorick's fear of the Bastille, Sterne's best sop to the anti-French prejudices of the English, shows the limits of sentimental fantasy. When he is warned of the dangers of traveling without a passport, Yorick first remembers his joke with Eugenius about getting clapped into the Bastille and living there 'a couple of months entirely at the king of France's expense' (196). He tries to extend the spirit of fun in a debunking and reassuring reduction of the Bastille to a word for a tower, and he walks himself easily downstairs, stripping it of its terrors. But the cry of a starling, 'I can't get out – I can't get out,' and his ineffectual struggle to release it from its cage call back his 'dissipated spirits' to reason (198). He walks heavily upstairs exclaiming against slavery and addressing himself to liberty. In his room he exercises his imagination on the plight of one captive, which makes him burst into tears and run off to beg a passport.

The reaffirmation of anti-French politics is not the end of the story, however. The starling, trained by a young English groom, sings a 'song of liberty' that is an 'unknown language at Paris.' So the bird is readily sold to Yorick, but back in England the song of liberty has almost as little credit as in Paris:

> In my return from Italy I brought him with me to the country in whose language he had learn'd his notes – and telling the story of him to Lord A – Lord A begg'd the bird of me – in a week Lord A gave him to Lord B – Lord B made a present of him to Lord C – and Lord C's gentleman sold him to Lord D's for a shilling – Lord D gave him to Lord E – and so on – half round the alphabet – From that rank he pass'd into the lower house, and pass'd the hands of as many commoners – But as all these wanted to *get in* – and my bird wanted to get out – he had almost as little store set by him in London as in Paris.
>
> (204–5)

In the end the enslaved bird with its desire for liberty finds a resting place as the crest of Yorick's coat of arms, which happens to be the coat of arms used by Sterne, decorated with a starling, or 'stern.'

I began by saying that in some senses Sterne comes out in *A Sentimental Journey*. As Yorick takes on more teacherly responsibility than Tristram did, he comes out as an advocate for certain freedoms of thought and feeling, and these entail advocacy of certain freedoms and powers of art to move readers. His spokesmanship for religious and sexual tolerance, however hedged about, probably took courage and a considerable degree of the sort of self-criticism allegorized in his episode with the monk. But perhaps most significant, Sterne comes out as someone who can't get out, who cannot sing along with a groom a song for English liberty, because he has been too busy getting in. The vagueness in *Tristram Shandy* about Yorick's 'war,' which was in that book quickly buried in funereal oblivion, is illuminated in *A Sentimental Journey* by the translation of the starling.

Sterne as a cleric and author is part of the clique of aristocratic rulers, someone who 'tells,' who gives and seeks favors, and he is also himself a token of honor, a fashionable object of consumption – like a well-hung woodcock passed from one gentleman's larder to another.[13] It is not only in France that he has become good at circulating, and perhaps this recognition of his subjection at home makes him sympathetic to the way they order things in France. Yorick tells the Comte de B**** that the French are polite 'to an excess,' or at least more polished than he would like to see the English. He takes as his illustration of complaisance that leaves no rough edges the example of much-circulated coins: 'by jingling and rubbing up against one another for seventy years together in one body's pocket or another's, they are become so alike you can scarce distinguish one shilling from another' (232). By contrast Yorick claims that Englishmen 'keep more apart' than Frenchmen and so preserve a character that is franker, more easily visible, and therefore perhaps more valuable. But the coins Yorick chooses for illustrating the smoothness of the French are 'King William's shillings,' English coins that have rubbed up against one another so much that they have worn away the features of the defender of English liberty.

Notes

1. This and subsequent parenthetical references are to volume, chapter and page number of James Aiken Work, ed., *The Life and Opinions of Tristram Shandy, Gentleman* (New York: Odyssey Press, 1940).

2. Michael Seidel draws the opposite conclusion about the resurrection of Yorick in *A Sentimental Journey* after his death in *Tristram Shandy*. Instead of coming closer to Sterne as I have said, Yorick in Seidel's view becomes more and more clearly literary, illustrating that 'the powers of the narrative and dramatic imagination are never quite ready to give the *coup de grâce* to successful inventions.' See 'Narrative Crossings: Sterne's *A Sentimental Journey*,' *Genre* 18 (Spring 1985):7. Seidel's account of the creation of narrative space in *A Sentimental Journey* resembles in some ways my account of the mechanisms of protraction in *Tristram Shandy*, but I see in the later work a significant change in the management of narrative authority.

3. This and subsequent parenthetical numbers refer to Gardner D. Stout, Jr., ed., *A Sentimental Journey through France and Italy by Mr. Yorick* (Berkeley: University of California Press, 1967).

4. Perry Curtis, ed., *The Letters of Laurence Sterne* (Oxford: Clarendon Press, 1935), p. 76. Hereafter cited in the text as '*Letters*'.

5. In *The Journal to Eliza* Yorick complains to his surgeons about the diagnosis of venereal disease, 'for I have had no commerce whatever with the Sex – not even with my wife, added I, these 15 years.' Is it the duty of a critic to disbelieve him? The *Journal* itself suggests Sterne's preference for the diffusive pleasures of literary fantasy. See lan Jack, ed., *A Sentimental Journey . . . to which are added 'The Journal to Eliza' and 'A Political Romance'* (London: Oxford University Press, 1972), p. 141.

6. David Hume, *Essays Moral, Political and Literary*, ed. T. H. Green and J. H. Grose (London: Longmans, Green 1875), I: 191. Hereafter cited in the text as '*Essays*'.

7. Melvin Richter, ed., *The Political Theory of Montesquieu* (Cambridge: Cambridge University Press, 1977), IV, ii, 198. Further references are to this edition and are cited in the text.

8. Norbert Elias, *Power and Civility* (1939), trans. Edmund Jephcott (New York: Pantheon, 1982), p. 281.

9. Arthur Hill Cash, *Sterne's Comedy of Moral Sentiments: The Ethical Dimension of the 'Journey'* (Pittsburgh: Duquesne University Press, 1966), chap. 1.

10. John Brewer, 'Commercialization and Politics,' in Neil McKendrick, John Brewer, and J. H. Plumb, *The Birth of a Consumer Society: The Commercialization of Eighteenth-Century England* (Bloomington: Indiana University Press, 1982), p. 198.

11. Frederick A. Pottle, ed., *Boswell's London Journal, 1762–1763* (New York: McGraw-Hill, 1950), p. 60.

12. Neil McKendrick, 'The Consumer Revolution,' in *The Birth of a Consumer Society*, pp. 31–32.

13. According to Douglas Hay, 'Pheasants and hares and sides of venison were . . . so many tokens of social position; game was a special currency of class based on the solid standard of landed wealth, untainted by the commerce of the metropolis.' See 'Poaching and the Game Laws on Cannock Chase,' in Hay *et al.*, *Albion's Fatal Tree: Crime and Society in Eighteenth-Century England* (New York: Pantheon, 1975), p. 246.

Part IV

Walpole

8 Time and Family in the Gothic Novel: *The Castle of Otranto*

Ian P. Watt

Because of the spectacular success of his book *The Rise of the Novel*, Ian Watt is arguably the most famous of all critics of the eighteenth-century novel (see Introduction to *The English Novel Volume I: 1700 to Fielding*, pp. 1–5). In this essay, he asks why *The Castle of Otranto* began a rage for the genre we now call the gothic novel. Watt points to two major features of the gothic imagination that mark Walpole's novel, and which become habits in later gothic novels. The first is the relation of the present to the past: the dynamics of some truly distant world determine those of the present – the gothic betokening for example a Catholic world in which the supernatural plays a stronger role than in modern, eighteenth-century life. Second, the power of the past is not only a way of figuring the unconscious, but a way to talk about our implication in our family histories.

Long ago Matthew Arnold, confronting what Darwin had recently demonstrated to be our common ancestor – 'a hairy quadruped furnished with a tail and pointed ears, probably arboreal in his habits' – was moved to wonder how 'this good fellow' could ever have 'carried in his nature, also, a necessity for Greek.'[1] It was even longer ago that an unpromising stripling named Conrad was dashed to pieces by some archaic military hardware in the courtyard of the Castle of Otranto; and even today we still hardly know how it was that this 'enormous helmet, a hundred times more large than any casque ever made for human being, and shaded with a proportionable quantity of black feathers'[2] also carried in its nature an evolutionary necessity for Emily Brontë's Heathcliff and Faulkner's Thomas Sutpen.

Two aspects of that necessity are the subject of the present enquiry. What gave *The Castle of Otranto* – at first sight the most sensationally unpretentious novelette that can well be imagined – its power to bring into being a whole new fictional mode that has been characteristic of the last two centuries? What was the essential imaginative matrix which struck off, not only the nine hundred odd works that are listed – however dubiously – in Montague Summers' *A Gothic Bibliography*

(1941), but also many later novels that are often placed in the Gothic tradition? I will suggest that two elements in that matrix, the function of time and the treatment of the family, provide a set of particular characteristics in the very miscellaneous literary phenomena to which the label 'Gothic' is currently applied.

The very word 'Gothic' suggests that the genre has got something to do with time. It is hardly too much to say that etymologically the term 'Gothic Novel' is an oxymoron for 'Old New.' When Horace Walpole subtitled *The Castle of Otranto* 'A Gothic Story' in the second edition, to him the term 'Gothic,' as he had already made clear in the original Preface, meant 'the darkest ages of Christianity,' or, more generally, merely 'very old.' 'Novel,' on the other hand, originally meant the 'new'; and such were the contemporary subjects of what, in 1764, were beginning to be called novels. Walpole himself was aware that the essential originality of *The Castle of Otranto* depended on this temporal dichotomy of past and present:

> It was an attempt to blend the two kinds of romance, the ancient and the modern. In the former all was imagination and improbability: in the latter, nature is always intended to be, and sometimes has been, copied with success.[3]
>
> (p. 7)

A closer scrutiny reveals that the relation of ancient and present time in Walpole's narrative is somewhat more specific and complex in nature; obviously all the events take place in Gothic times, but that past itself has considerable depth, and the psychological present in which the characters live is only the immediate surface on which the power of a long anterior past is manifested.

The distant pastness of the whole tale is insisted on in Walpole's title-page and Preface. The original Italian version, he asserts, was printed in black letter – what we now call Gothic type – in 1529; but internal evidence points to a much earlier date of composition; and the actual period of the action, we are told, must go further back still, to some time between 1095 and 1243, the dates of the first and last crusades, 'or not long afterwards.' This defines what we may call the period both of the narrative present of the story and of its anterior past.

The events of the plot, in what the reader experiences as the narrative present, take only three days. The action begins on Conrad's fifteenth birthday, which is supposed to be the day of his wedding to Isabella – a wedding which will strengthen the position of his father, Manfred, Prince of Otranto; but it is in fact the day of Conrad's death. From the opening of the temporal sequence is a progression whose intervals are related to calendar time by signals in the narrative – sunset, moonshine, dawn, etc.

The plot, in five chapters like the acts of a tragedy, is equally linear, logical, and concentrated. In the first chapter, Conrad is crushed by the gigantic helmet. Then a handsome young peasant announces that this helmet is 'exactly like that on the figure in black marble of Alfonso the Good . . . in the church of St. Nicholas' (p. 18). Almost immediately that particular helmet is reported missing: an ominous coincidence. Meanwhile, Manfred resolves that he must cast aside his wife, Hippolita, and marry Conrad's intended, Isabella. Horrified, Isabella attempts to escape and in her flight through a subterranean passage sees a ghostlike figure who turns out to be the handsome peasant, called Theodore. He tries to help her but in the process is discovered by Manfred, who is on the point of sentencing Theodore to death when the news comes that an armed giant – or at least an awfully big leg and foot – has been seen lying in the long gallery.

The remaining chapters work out these puzzles. The next day Father Jerome, a priest at the convent near the church of St. Nicholas, announces that Isabella has taken sanctuary there. Theodore is once again on the point of being executed when a birthmark on his neck luckily reveals that he is really Father Jerome's son. Then a great procession arrives, with a gigantic sword that is carried by a hundred knights. (This echo of the 'hundred times' larger scale of the helmet illustrates Walpole's rough and ready use of numbers to indicate the supernatural dimension of his narrative.) The leader of the knights, who remains masked, eventually proves to be Isabella's father, the Marquis of Vicenza. He found the sword in the Holy Land; and on its blade is written

> Wher'er a casque that suits this sword is found,
> With perils is thy daughter compass'd round:
> Alfonso's blood alone can save the maid,
> And quiet a long-restless prince's shade.
>
> (p. 79)

We surmise that the matching accessory which 'suits this sword' must be the huge casque that landed on Conrad. As to 'who alone can save the maid' (presumably Isabella), it must surely be Theodore, who must therefore be of Alfonso's noble blood. As for 'quieting' the 'long-restless prince's shade' we are given many clues as to what person may own the 'shade.' The first and most obvious comes very early: 'ancient prophecy which was said to have pronounced, "That the castle and lordship of Otranto should pass from the present family, whenever the real owner should be grown too large to inhabit it"' (pp. 15–16). Manfred has shown no sign of abnormal growth; and so he cannot be 'the real owner,' and eventually proves to be the grandson of Richard, Alfonso's false chamberlain, who long ago poisoned his master and made himself the owner of Otranto by a forged will. We must, then, wait until someone's shade gets big enough to wear the helmet; that shade, of course, proves to be Alfonso's own. He is literally a shade – a ghost – and when he throws the castle down according to the prophecy, Manfred is frightened into abdicating, and Alfonso's grandson, Theodore, is restored to the rule of his rightful principality.

The essence of *The Castle of Otranto*, then, is the progressive revelation of the secrets of the two family pasts; but its interest for the reader depends not on this in itself – the disclosure of the rather murky genealogies of the descendants of Alfonso and Richard – but on the excitement generated by how the ghostly survivors of the anterior past operate on the affairs of the fictional present, which wholly preoccupies them. Past and present are, it seems, locked together; the living characters are the captives of the past, while the characters of the past – notably Alfonso – live on as spirits only to be their vigilant captors. The anterior past has all the power. Whenever the present generation attempts to avoid its fate, as when Manfred attempts to marry off his son, its effort is wholly ineffectual. The only imperative causality in the life of the present, apparently, is to complete what was done long ago; only when the helmet, sword, armor, and the giant hands and feet are finally reconstituted can Theodore succeed to Otranto, and the perturbed spirit of his ancestor leave its sublunary caves and rise in apotheosis through the clouds to be received into the arms of his patron St. Nicholas.

The history of the word 'gothic' supplies one basic clue to the meaning of the power and the appeal of the past. The *Oxford English Dictionary* informs us that in the sense of medieval, 'gothic' was early used with the pejorative connotation expressed by Dryden: 'all that has something of the Ancient gust is called a barbarous or Gothique manner'[4] (1695). Such reprobation continued well into the eighteenth century, partly because no reasonably precise architectural or chronological meaning was as yet attached to 'gothic.'[5]

But long before there was any genuine understanding of what we call Gothic architecture, there arose the fashion for imitations of Gothic buildings and ruins. Walpole's own house, Strawberry Hill (begun 1749), was the most celebrated of many early examples; and literature, in Richard Hurd's *Letters on Chivalry and Romance* (1762), for example, reflected a parallel counter-movement to the previous prejudice against the barbarism of the gothic. 'Gothic,' in Walpole's day, was exchanging the disgrace of being old-fashioned for the distinction of being antique.

The Augustan nostalgia for its antithesis was itself dependent on the new sense that the present was radically separate from the past. This historical awareness began in the Renaissance, which looked back at the classical world through the darkness of the Gothic period; but both the increasing body of historical knowledge (to which Walpole himself made many contributions), and the conscious Augustan effort to follow Roman models, developed historical consciousness much further. Anachronism in Renaissance painting or drama seems unconscious; in Walpole it is a conscious fashion which also reflects his spiritual and aesthetic needs.

The new need for conscious anachronism brings us to the psychological basis of the tension in Gothic between past and present – the individual's awareness of the quotidian dullness of the present and the consequent longing for something totally different. This contrast was to lead the rich, and later their humbler imitators,[6] to cover the land with castles and mansions, suburban villas, and country cottages – all in the Gothic manner – and the same contrast was to become a great theme of the Romantic poets. But the spiritual appeal of the Gothic past is already explicit in Walpole. Thus he writes in a letter to George Montagu (5 January 1766):

> Visions, you know, have always been my pasture, and so far from growing old enough to quarrel with their emptiness, I almost think there is no wisdom comparable to that of exchanging what is called the realities of life for dreams. Old castles, old pictures, old histories, and the babble of old people make one live back into centuries that cannot disappoint one.
>
> (*Corr.*, 10:192)

In earlier ages there had been nothing picturesque about wearing swords or going into gloomy dungeons;[7] their appeal to the imagination depended on a social order based on life insurance rather than carrying swords; on *habeas corpus*, the rule of law and the beginnings of an organized police force. As Thomas Blackwell put it in his contrast between Homeric times and his own: 'The marvellous and wonderful is the nerve of the epic strain: but what marvellous things happen in a well-ordered state? We can hardly be surprised.'[8] Or Walpole, speaking of the modern novel: 'the great resources of fancy have been dammed up, by a strict adherence to common life' (p. 7).

Escaping the milieu of the common life, Walpole's title proclaimed as the chief protagonist in his novel what was to become the most characteristic symbolic element in Gothic fiction generally, the castle. The 'dramatised decay' of the ruin, as Kenneth Clark terms it (*Gothic Revival*, p. 30) inspired fascination and awe, and the later part of the century saw ruins become a major preoccupation of art, architecture, and landscape. And in the Gothic novel, the castle becomes connected with the family because it is essentially the material survivor of a powerful lineage, a symbol of the continuing life of its founder. Only, therefore, when Otranto's living heir, Theodore, is safely in the courtyard can 'the walls of the castle' be 'thrown down by a mighty force,' and the form of its founder, Alfonso, 'dilated to an immense magnitude,' appear 'in the centre of the ruins' (p. 108). Within the walls the most common material objects are likenesses – either portraits or sculptures – which, like ancient documents, attest the continuing presence of the dead. The portrait of Alfonso, his statue, even the helmet, armor, and sword – all assert his paternal power. So do the ancient prophecy and the riddling quatrain.

From likenesses of the dead to the world of the supernatural is no great leap for Walpole's liberated 'resources of the fancy' – as Alfonso presumably discovers when he steps down out of his picture frame. Walpole was at some pains to excuse the element of superstition in his story on the grounds that it was typical of the times depicted, and that he had in any case much restricted its operation, as compared to earlier writers of romance, where 'the actors seem to lose their senses the moment the laws of nature lose their tone.' So in general his motive for seeking the greater imaginative freedom of the supernatural must be seen as yet another aspect of how Gothic was a reaction to the intellectual temper of the century. Walpole liked *The Castle of Otranto* most among his works, he wrote to Madame du Deffand, because there alone he had given 'reign to . . . imagination. . . . I am even persuaded that in the Future, when taste will be restored to the place now occupied by philosophy, my poor *Castle* will find admirers.'[9] His own time, alas, wanted 'only cold reason,' which had established a rigid distinction between the natural and the supernatural after Newton had cast light on nature's laws, and definitively depersonalized and demythologized the physical world.

The systematizing of this division between the natural and the supernatural orders inevitably affected general attitudes to the past and to the unseen world. By the time of Pope the supernatural had become to the enlightened a dubious and rather fanciful rival order, like the sylphs in *The Rape of the Lock*; and by the middle of the century such beliefs were becoming a sign of religious archaism, as in John Wesley and Parson Adams. To give the occult power of the past a real existence in fiction it was now necessary to set the narrative back in time into the Gothic past, to the times before the Reformation when Roman Catholic superstition held sway, and to the countries – most notably Italy – where it was still rampant.

To an Enlightenment sceptic like Walpole, of course, religious superstition was equally repulsive to political liberty and scientific reason; but it remained congenial to the aesthetic imagination. Hence Walpole compromised with his times both by setting the events back in times and places where credulity was universal, and by presenting his supernatural interventions in a selective way.

Walpole's supernature is entirely populated with beings who, for all their monstrous size and power, are essentially historical beings with rational human aims. This is typical of the Gothic novel in general; supernature is both secularized and individualized. Alfonso the Good, or whichever of his unseen adjutants is currently on duty to ruffle the helmet's plumes at the appropriate time, seems to be wholly concerned with bringing about a more satisfactory state of affairs in the secular world of his genealogical descendants; and when this rectifying mission has been accomplished, he can be trusted to hand Otranto back to the custody of Newtonian physics.

There are other orders of experience besides the supernatural which exist outside time as it is viewed by natural science: there is the sacred time of myth and ritual and the mystics; and – much more important for the Gothic tradition – there are the special kinds of time in which dreams and the unconscious have their being; and both are peculiarly open to the irruptions of the forces of the past.

In dreams, time is intensely real in the sense that we are immersed in a series of scenes which follow each other with hallucinatory vividness: it is very much a question of now, and now, and now. The connection of these scenes is not causal; the fragments are real, but they have their own kind of temporal order which is unconscious or imaginative, rather than consecutive in any logical way. The specific time-setting of the dream is typically unlocalized or shifting; but when we recall the dream later we often realize that we have revisited various scenes of our long-past life, though not in their chronological order. What initially provokes the dream, though, is normally some present occasion; and this provides a basic structural analogy to the symbiosis of past and present in Gothic.

The closeness of the two kinds of mental representation – dreams and Gothic fiction – is reflected in two well-known facts. First, dreams, particularly nightmares, are common in Gothic novels; many of the best are like nightmares – *Frankenstein* or 'The Fall of the House of Usher.' Second, many Gothic novels apparently began as actual dreams. In her Preface, Mary Shelley, for instance, says *Frankenstein* did, and so does Walpole in a letter to William Cole (9 March 1765):

> Shall I even confess to you what was the origin of this romance? I waked one morning in the beginning of last June from a dream, of which all I could recover was, that I had thought myself in an ancient castle (a very natural dream for a head filled like mine with Gothic story) and that on the uppermost bannister of a great staircase I saw a gigantic hand in armour. In the evening I sat down and began to write, without knowing in the least what I intended to say or relate. The work grew on my hands, and I grew fond of it – add that I was very glad to think of anything rather than politics . . .
>
> (*Corr.*, 1:88)

We can be fairly confident, I think, that Walpole's dream was a transposition of sights familiar to him partly from Strawberry Hill and particularly, as he wrote, from the great court of Trinity College, Cambridge.[10] We can also see how the symbolic meanings of these images reflect the unconscious life.

The unconscious shares with Gothic the characteristic that anything (we are credibly informed) can happen there, and that its psychological spectrum reflects the extremes of what we seek and what we fear much more dramatically than is common either in the novel or in real life. There is a further parallel: both dreams and the unconscious share with Gothic fiction the tendency to deal with present problems through a special reliving of the past. As Auden puts it in his elegy for Sigmund Freud, 'He wasn't clever at all: he merely told / the unhappy Present to recite the Past.'

This particular aspect of Gothic – the unhappy present reciting the past – is clearest, I suppose, in the later Gothic tradition, in Dickens, with Miss Havisham immobilised in the posture of frustration, or in Ibsen's *Ghosts* and *John Gabriel Borkman*, where the past has irrevocably foreclosed the possibilities of the present. In all these, once again we have a double past; for the crucial events of the past, whether betrayal, theft, murder, rape, or incest, were themselves the residue of an infinitely earlier past, which lived on in the archaic violence of the unconscious.

The unconscious, as we have all learned, is very like a Gothic castle: not the clean, well-lighted and cellarless place of the modern single-family residence, but a many-tiered vertical maze – and a dark and dirty one at that. Its many levels connect only through narrow, turning staircases and concealed trapdoors; and its towers, vaults, caverns, and dungeons are both the natural scene of death and terror and rape, and established symbols for our unconscious drives. Their sexual symbolism is now an open book to a normally contaminated mind; but it may be worth suggesting how the facts that, as Freud put it, 'We are not masters in our own house,' and that there are rooms in it that we may never really see, both supply an enduring psychological basis for the appeal of the Gothic genre, and help explain its frequent concentration on family relationships.

Melodrama and Gothic are not always clearly distinct genres, but the reader's responses to their characters usually differ. In melodrama, we hiss at the villain. In Gothic our attitude is more complex; the villain nearly always excites some degree of identification, whether he is predominantly evil, like Mrs. Radcliffe's Montoni in *The Mysteries of Udolpho*, or predominantly sympathetic, like Ambrosio in *The Monk*,[11] Melmoth, or Heathcliff. Most typically the reader has a divided sympathy, and this ambivalence seems to follow the division between the id and the superego.

Here, too, Walpole is a precursor. His hero, Manfred, is on one hand a cruel and tyrannical usurper whose mind often turns, in Walpole's phrase, 'to exquisite villainy'; yet on the other hand, something in us finds much to admire and to envy in his cunning and self-confident resolution to pursue his aims; Walpole's own unconscious sympathy is made clear very early when he gives Manfred so firm a command of irony at the expense of superstition and sentimental pretence. Like Walpole, we know we ought to condemn Manfred, but we find we cannot; he appeals to a division in us between the conscious and the unconscious, between the public and the private, between the day and night side of the personality. These tensions provide a complexity which does something to atone for the thin psychological characterization of *The Castle of Otranto*, and is also typical of Gothic fiction. When there is character development in the Gothic, as in *The Monk*, it is a morally emblematic series of accelerating villainies rather than a psychologically cumulative process; more typically, the Gothic character is sustained by a labile balance between the past and the present, between the unrestrained impulses of the id and the controls of reason and normality.

Perhaps it is this unconscious irresolution that explains one puzzle about so many Gothic novels. At times Manfred and Montoni seem so potently and enviably demonic that we see no reason whatever that their victims, or their whole social order, should survive at all. Yet we also find these Gothic supermen having occasional spasms of normality – moral qualms, moments of kindness, ordinary muddled human sympathy. Their destructive power is apparently not limitless, and oddly defeats our expectation. This contradiction becomes more apparent in the nineteenth century, when the Gothic theme becomes psychologically internalized in such characters as Ahab and Heathcliff: they seem much more terrifying persons than their actions turn out to be.

It may be that the essential explanation of why Gothic villains never realized their full destructive potential is in the Freudian view of the relation between parents and children. Perhaps Manfred, for instance, alternates between the demonic and the normal because Walpole was torn between deep admiration for his father, and an equally deep fear of his father's power. Of course Horace Walpole knew that he was no more likely to continue the family's greatness than was Conrad; and so the dread giant hand on the bannister belonged to the paternal authority that was both desired and hated. But it also had its limits – Sir Robert was now dead.[12]

In any case it is surely within the nucleus of the family that the basic conflicts of the Gothic take place; and for at least three reasons. First, that the most universal of man's social and moral regulations all concern the interplay of power, property, marriage, and sex within the family; second, that these regulations, and the forces which oppose them, are internalised in the unconscious; and last, that these conflicts directly and continuously affect the relationships of the past and the present in the individual's experience. Here again Walpole anticipated later developments; the moral of his work, he wrote in the Preface to the first edition, was 'that *the sins of fathers are visited on their children to the third and fourth generation*' (p. 5).

The psychological contradictions concerning character and the family, it should perhaps be added, work both ways: Freudian theory can itself be seen as a Gothic myth. It presents the individual, much as Gothic does, as essentially imprisoned by the tyranny of an omnipotent but unseen past. The oedipal situation, or more generally, the terrible authority of the parents in the unconscious, is the Freudian equivalent of the supernatural or demonic power of the Gothic protagonist. The parallel is strengthened by the prevalence of paternal incest in Gothic fiction (of which Manfred's passion for Isabella, the girl who was to have been his daughter-in-law, is an example).[13] There is a further parallel in that tradition of Gothic which goes from *The Castle of Otranto* to 'The Fall of the House of Usher' and *The House of the Seven Gables*, where the supreme power is the patriarchal authority of the long-dead lineal ancestor, who is still the real, though invisible, master of the house and its occupants.

More generally, we can conclude that although a sense of the mysterious and immobilising power of the past is one of the characteristic features both of psychoanalysis and Gothic fiction, that power is normally humanised as far as our quotidian experience is concerned. In this respect it seems that characterization in the Gothic novel has a somewhat similar function to that allotted the individual ego in psychoanalytic theory: to mediate between the conflicting demands of two sides of the unconscious, the superego and the id.[14]

So much for the psychology of the Gothic. I have obviously not been attempting a complete account either of *The Castle of Otranto* or of its genre. Such an account would have to concede that it is often forced, sometimes dull, and stylistically Walpole's worst piece of prose writing – with hardly a suggestion of the brilliance and understanding of the letters or the memoirs, for instance. *The Castle of Otranto,* in fact, very largely lacks the courage of its Gothic convictions; and yet its basic structure contains enough of the essential features of the later Gothic tradition both to explain its historical importance in establishing the new form, and to help us understand some of its characteristic elements.

Walpole himself shared much of the optimism of the Enlightenment; in his Gothic tale, therefore, the past is fairly benign: Manfred repents, and Theodore is returned to his rightful place. For the most part Mrs. Radcliffe followed this comfortable ideological perspective. After the end of the eighteenth century, however, the Gothic tradition took a darker turn. Gothic was still the world of the ancient romance, in the sense that it was a kind of fiction in which all the most violent and destructive extremes of human possibility could be realised, as opposed to the novel, which habitually confines its characters and events within the more normal quotidian spectrum of action and motive. But whereas Walpole had allowed the more affirmative forces of justice and virtue to vanquish evil, Monk Lewis and Charles Maturin and later Gothic writers operated more and more within the darker shades of the moral spectrum; the past is evil and tends to triumph; the fate of both the Monk and of Melmoth is eternal damnation.

Whether the balance of power in the world of the Gothic novel is held by good or evil, however, it is typically – though not always – a world where, in a variety of forms, the redoubtable past haunts the impotent present; it is the past which holds the key.

The Gothic tradition in its specialised historical sense is usually agreed to end with *Melmoth the Wanderer* in 1820: more precisely, perhaps, we might say that one branch of it continues in an increasingly sub-literary and specialised tradition about vampires and werewolves, while the other branch continues to deepen the main moral perspectives of Gothic in works which in other respects come closer to the main tradition of the novel.

The immediate setting in an historical past, and the use of the supernatural, became rarer in this later and looser version of the

Gothic; and at the same time it incorporates many of the interests and techniques of the main fictional tradition. With the Brontës,[15] for instance, it assimilates the fuller psychological characterization and the denser presentation of the environment of the Victorian novel in general.

On this issue the roles of time and the family offer an interesting contrast in two acknowledged classics of the Gothic in its wider sense. In *Wuthering Heights*, for instance, the most memorable part of the narrative – from chapters 3 to 17 – deals with events of a generation ago (between 1771, the arrival of Heathcliff at Wuthering Heights, to the deaths of Catherine and Hindley Earnshaw in 1784); Lockwood learns of them after his calls at Wuthering Heights in 1801. To that extent the story enacts a double plunge backwards into time: to the days of Cathy's marriage, and then further back to her childhood with Heathcliff; and this backward movement itself takes us even further back symbolically to an unconscious world of eternal primitive possession. On the other hand the optimistic conclusion of the novel – Heathcliff's death and the marriage of Catherine and Hareton – occurs in the present tense of the novel, in 1802 and 1803. This contrast suggests an inherent contradiction in the book. One way of looking at it would be as a working out of the dual role of the Gothic hero: the dark powers of the id have their way for a time, but they succumb to the attrition of moral and social norms in the end. As Thomas Moser has argued,[16] the later parts of the book really amount to a final denial of Emily Brontë's initial psychological premises: the bad, exciting past is not omnipotent; the demonic Heathcliff, of all people, goes soft; Cathy and Wuthering Heights cease to be haunted by him; and the Gothic world fades into the dull domestic Victorian one almost without a protest.

On the other hand Hawthorne's *The House of the Seven Gables* (1851), is much closer to the *Otranto* pattern. There is – first of all – the Gothic present embodied in the colonial house itself which has survived into the eighteen-fifties. The movement back in time reveals the secrets of two anterior pasts: that of one generation back, when Clifford Pyncheon was sentenced to prison, thirty years before, for the alleged murder of his uncle, Jaffrey Pyncheon; and that of about two centuries before, when Colonel Pyncheon had originally seized the land from Matthew Maule, and has him executed as a wizard. In the narrative present, Judge Pyncheon, sitting beneath the portrait of the founder of his lineage, Colonel Pyncheon, dies choked with blood according to Maule's curse, the same fate that had befallen the original Colonel Pyncheon and his descendant, Jaffrey Pyncheon. The past is beginning to be expiated, and the present must now be reconstituted. The old deed to the Indian lands is discovered by the lodger, Mr. Holgrave, who turns out to be a descendant of Matthew Maule, and of his son, Thomas, who had built the house; and time can start going forward once again, instead of back, when Holgrave, now called Maule, gives his family name to Phoebe, the only representative of the Pyncheon lineage who has a future.

In the twentieth century, certainly, there has been no inclination to underestimate the extent to which we are haunted by the past and the family; and so the Gothic theme has surfaced in many new, concealed, or unexpected forms. In Faulkner's *Absalom, Absalom!*, for instance, the central pattern is very clear; the two generations which haunt Sutpen's Hundred are traced back to the intractable brutalities and the mysterious inheritance of Thomas Sutpen: the densely layered family history of the Sutpens, cannot, any more than the past of the South, be altered; Quentin Compson, and other defeated survivors of history, can only attempt to understand its multifarious power. One could also argue that the tradition continues in the literature of the mindless molecular now, and even that, the present times being what they are, contemporary fiction in general is rapidly becoming more and more indistinguishable from the Gothic novel – in Thomas Pynchon, Joyce Carol Oates, or Kurt Vonnegut, for example.

In general, we can be reasonably certain that, unlike the Gothic language, the Gothic novel is unlikely to disappear. As long as we are ambivalent about our incomparable modernity; as long as our political sky gets blacker daily with chickens coming home to roost; as long as children have parents, and so do parents; as long as we continue to experience boredom, night, sleep, and fear; as long as we fail to experience freedom and happiness; the past, alas! will continue to haunt us, and see to it that we spend much of our lives on Gothic time.

Notes

1. 'Literature and Science,' *Philistinism in England and America*, ed. R. H. Super (Ann Arbor: University of Michigan, 1974), p. 64. The Darwin citation is from *The Descent of Man*, Part III, ch. 21, p. 7.
2. Horace Walpole, *The Castle of Otranto: A Gothic Story*, ed. W. S. Lewis (London: Oxford University Press, 1964), p. 17. Later quotations are from this edition.
3. Walpole said much the same thing in a 16 March 1765 letter to Joseph Warton, where he wrote that he wished to 'blend the marvellous of old story with the natural of modern novels' (W. S. Lewis, ed., *The Yale Edition of Horace Walpole's Correspondence* (New Haven: Yale University Press, 1937–83), 40:377. Subsequently cited as *Corr.*
4. s.v. Gothic, 4.

5. Renaissance usage, as in Giorgio Vasari (1551), merely connected the term with the *maniera tedesca* of the Goths who had sacked Rome and destroyed the classical orders of architecture. Our less derogatory and more historical classification awaited François Blondel the Younger, who in 1771 established the distinction between *architecture gothique ancienne* – the 6th to the 11th c. (the word 'romanesque' wasn't to appear until 1819) – and the *architecture gothique moderne*, from the 12th c. to 1515, the accession of François Premier. In 18th-c. England, although many of his contemporaries made a vague equation between 'Gothic' buildings and the Saxon period, Walpole in general equated 'Gothic' with the pointed arch and perpendicular ornamentation (Kenneth Clark, *The Gothic Revival* [N.Y.: Holt, 1962], pp. 46–65), although the issue is not raised in *The Castle of Otranto*.

6. As Ernest Fischer puts it, 'The bourgeois wanted to disguise his capital in fancy dress' (*The Necessity of Art* [Harmondsworth, Middlesex: Penguin, 1971], p. 208).

7. Walpole was delighted with a dungeon at Hurstmonceaux, an elaborate 15th-c. castellated mansion, because it 'gives one a delightful idea of living in the days of soccage and under such goodly tenures' (*Corr.*, 37:138, to Bentley, 5 Aug. 1752).

8. *Enquiry into the Life and Writings of Homer* (London, 1735), p. 26.

9. Letter dated 13 March 1767 (*Corr.*, 3:260), trans. from the French by the author.

10. As Warren H. Smith showed in a letter to the ed., *Times Literary Supplement* (23 May 1936), p. 440.

11. In *The Monk* the literal haunting of the narrative present by an anterior past mainly occurs in the subplots (the legend of the bleeding nun, e.g.). As far as the protagonist is concerned, it is his own atavistic passions that are gradually revealed, to the astonishment of his admirers (including himself), and that lead to rape, murder, and his own damnation.

12. The relationship of the Gothic novel to the archetypal and primordial structures of psychological development have been illuminatingly explored, in Leslie Fiedler's *Love and Death in the Americal Novel* (Cleveland: Meridian, 1962), for instance, and Frederick Crews' *The Sins of the Fathers* (N.Y.: Oxford University Press, 1966); while more recently, Maurice Lévy, in his *Le Roman Gothique Anglais 1764–1824* (Toulouse: Faculté des Lettres et Sciences Humaines, 1968), has investigated those aspects of the Gothic novel which appealed to the French surrealists, notably to André Breton and Paul Eluard. See also *The Female Gothic*, ed. Juliann E. Fleenor (Montreal: Eden, 1983).

13. Walpole's play, *The Mysterious Mother*, contains a double incest: the mother sleeps with her son, and later kills herself when he marries their joint offspring. The Freudian aspect of *The Castle of Otranto* is treated in Martin Kallich's *Horace Walpole* (N.Y.: Twayne, 1971), pp. 101–4.

14. The implications of this for characterization have been well demonstrated in Francis Russel Hart's essay 'The Experience of Character in the English Gothic Novel.' Hart argues that we must not make the common assumption that the Gothic protagonists are merely flat emblematic portrayals of the demonic in the non-representational world of the romance; they are that, and they are also human beings; and so the central mystery in Gothic novels is one where 'autonomous natural existences – characters – come to assume demonic roles' and this is the 'terrifying truth in an enlightenment context . . . that the demonic is no myth, no superstition, but a reality in human character

or relationship, a novelistic reality' (*Experience in the Novel: Selected Papers from the English Institute*, ed. Roy Harvey Pearce [N.Y.: Columbia University Press, 1968], p. 99).

15. See especially Robert B. Heilman, 'Charlotte Brontë's "New Gothic",' in *From Jane Austen to Joseph Conrad*, ed. Robert C. Rathburn and Martin Steinmann, Jr. (Minneapolis: University of Minnesota, 1958), pp. 118–32.

16. '"What is the Matter with Emily Jane?" Conflicting Impulses in *Wuthering Heights*,' *Nineteenth-Century Fiction* 17 (1962): 1–19.

Part V

Burney

9 *Cecilia*: Money and Anarchy

JULIA EPSTEIN

Alluding to a number of critics and theorists influenced by Bakhtin, among them Terry Castle, Peter Stallybrass and Allon White (see *The Politics and Poetics of Transgression*), Julia Epstein argues that in *Cecilia*, Burney engages on a newly hardheaded critique of class relations. This critique is set within a general attack on the market-place which infects the entire world of the book, and is figured in the phantasmagoric quality of carnival and masquerade.

Cecilia; or, Memoirs of an Heiress was published in 1782 by a far more publicly self-conscious author than had produced the surreptitiously composed *Evelina* in the 1770s. An expectant audience with preconceived notions of what a Burney heroine would be like and familiarity with the mechanisms of ironic narration presented through Burney's comic narrative voice awaited this second work of fiction. Like Evelina 'Anville,' Cecilia Beverley is bereft of kin and alone in the social world she enters. While Evelina enters a hostile and complicated world that periodically encloses her in a mesh of social ideology metaphorized by Burney as physical or psychological assault, that world remains ringed by a comedic subtlety and its dangers are finally transcendable, though at a cost. *Cecilia*'s world, in contrast, bristles with absolute menace. The plethora of wittily drawn characters and abundance of satirically choreographed social scenes cannot mask in this second novel Burney's stark world view: young women live inside an envelope of continual material threat to their individual selfhood and to their social and economic survival.

Cecilia undergoes a triple orphaning in the first pages of Burney's second novel. Both her parents die, her uncle dies, and she is removed from the home of Mrs. Charlton, her 'maternal counsellor.' As the novel's title suggests, she is an heiress, receiving ten thousand pounds a year from her father and another three thousand pounds attached to an estate from her uncle. She is to receive this money when she comes of age at twenty-one, a time she is eight months shy of when the story opens, 'with no other restriction than that of annexing her name, if she married, to the disposal of her hand and her riches' (1:2). This laconically described restriction will be crucial.

Cecilia's world is far more fraught with danger than is the often uncomfortable but ultimately negotiable world of Evelina. As Clarissa Harlowe's grandfather's will had bound her to a conflict between family responsibility and individual desire, so Cecilia's uncle's will binds her to an impossible choice between public obedience and personal happiness, and between private desire and public wealth. The restriction on Cecilia's name in her uncle's will, presented in a dismissive way as minor when it is first introduced, ultimately controls the novel's plot and the tendentious reading of woman's place in the social world that Burney presents through the economic and legal tribulations of her second and most financially independent heroine. Unlike Evelina and the heroine of *The Wanderer*, who answer to the created nonsense words by which they are called, Cecilia Beverley is tied by law to a family name that has no particular meaning for her but which she cannot shed. That surname – Beverley – becomes the 'seal' embedded in Cecilia's given name, and it literally seals her fate.

Witness two key scenes in which Cecilia's problematic name is invoked. In the confrontation between Cecilia's lover, Mortimer Delvile, and his mother concerning his planned marriage to Cecilia, the son argues vigorously that he would not be sinning against any integrity to give up his family name and take on Cecilia's as he takes on her inheritance. 'What honour do I injure that is not factitious?' he asks. 'In the general commerce of the world, it may be right to yield to its prejudices, but in matters of serious importance, it is weakness to be shackled by scruples so frivolous, and it is cowardly to be governed by the customs we condemn.' But when his mother counters that the renunciation of his family name will bring curses on him from his father 'when your name becomes a stranger to your ears, and you are first saluted by one so meanly adopted!' (2:215), he blanches. He and Cecilia pledge never to see each other again, at this, the final blow from Augusta Delvile to her son: 'Heavens! . . . what in the universe can pay you for that first moment of indignity! Think of it well ere you proceed, and anticipate your sensations, lest the shock should wholly overcome you. How will the blood of your wronged ancestors rise into your guilty cheeks, and how will your heart throb with secret shame and reproach, when wished joy upon your marriage by the name of Mr. *Beverley*!' (2:216). The name itself is not repugnant to the Delviles; the Beverley family is respectable. And certainly the money annexed to that name appeals strongly to the Delviles' depleted and crumbling estates. But Burney's precocious theme – that a woman should retain her maiden name upon her marriage – contains the seeds of revolution for a social order that was entering upon a period of chaotic transition at the end of the eighteenth century. The Delviles represent the tenacious *ancien régime* of the landed gentry's patriarchal family structure, and Cecilia's name challenges familial and marital institutions as well as threatening the sanctity of patrimonial succession.

A second narrative crux involving her name occurs when Cecilia's inheritance is stripped in a scene with the lawyer sent by her uncle's next heir. She has indeed by this time married with the intention of giving up her name, but the wedding was secret, and Cecilia plans to remain in her house until her husband returns from the Continent to 'claim' her and to make their union public. Secrets, however, are always dangerous objects in a Burney novel, and, characteristically, they are never well kept. The exchange between Cecilia, now in a nominal limbo but still using the name 'Miss Beverley,' and Eggleston's lawyer ('an entire stranger: an elderly man, of no pleasant aspect or manners') bears lengthy citation because it underlines the metaphoric functions of naming in a Burney novel:

> She desired to know his business.
> 'I presume, madam, you are the lady of this house?'
> She bowed an assent.
> 'May I take the liberty, madam, to ask your name?'
> 'My name, sir?'
> 'You will do me a favour, madam, by telling it me.'
> 'Is it possible you are come hither without already knowing it?'
> 'I know it only by common report, madam.'
> 'Common report, sir, I believe is seldom wrong in a matter where to be right is so easy.'
> 'Have you any objection, madam, to telling me your name?'
> 'No sir; but your business can hardly be very important, if you are yet to learn whom you are to address. It will be time enough, therefore, for us to meet when you are elsewhere satisfied in this point.'
> She would then have left the room.
> 'I beg, madam,' cried the stranger, 'you will have patience; it is necessary, before I can open my business, that I should hear your name from yourself.'
> 'Well, sir,' cried she with some hesitation, 'you can scarce have come to this house, without knowing that its owner is Cecilia Beverley.'
> 'That, madam, is your maiden name.'
> 'My maiden name?' cried she, starting.
> 'Are you not married, madam?'

> 'Married, sir?' she repeated, while her cheeks were the colour of scarlet.
>
> 'It is properly, therefore, madam, the name of your husband that I mean to ask.'
>
> 'And by what authority, sir,' cried she, equally astonished and offended, 'do you make these extraordinary enquiries?'
>
> (2:388–89)

After half a page of further stammering, the attorney, having identified himself and his errand, becomes blunt ('Are you married or are you not?' [2:389]), and Cecilia, while asking for time and being granted a week, is forced into a confession: Eggleston, indeed, now owns the house she is living in, and she owes him money. And it is instructive to remember Mrs. Delvile's threat to Mortimer that he should be 'mortified' (his name suggests that susceptibility to this threat) when called Mr. Beverley. It is, instead, Cecilia who must undergo this trial. When Eggleston writes, her disappointment at his news is 'embittered by shame and terror, when, upon folding it [the letter] up, she saw it was directed to Mrs. Mortimer Delvile' (2:396). It is Cecilia whose powerfully conceived identity is subsumed into that of her husband, just as Evelina's far more fragile 'maiden name' experiences protean shifts from Anville to Belmont to Orville in quick succession.

Naming highlights the issue of class consciousness in Burney's novels. Both Evelina Belmont and Juliet Granville have aristocratic parentage, though they have to struggle for recognition, and both are proud to 'own' the lost names they work so hard to regain. Cecilia differs here, and bears more resemblance to Camilla Tyrold, who comes from a respectable, though not wealthy, landed family. But all Burney's heroines have close ties and repeated dealings with the bourgeoisie, and class distinctions – underwritten by the complex of naming rituals – frequently hold center stage in Burney's fiction. Much has been written about the ways Burney uses comedy and dialect to poke fun at these distinctions, something she does in all her novels (witness the hilarious speech of Cecilia's miserly guardian Briggs) and this has particularly been remarked in the Branghton sequences in *Evelina*. But little attention has been paid to the serious critique of class that Burney's novels embody. This critique is especially crucial for *Cecilia*, a novel in which all the characters struggle to get or keep money, by parsimony and niggardliness (Briggs), by marrying their children advantageously (the Delviles, Mrs. Belfield), by marrying themselves advantageously (Monckton, Sir Robert Floyer, Marriot), by fleecing others or gaming (Harrel), or, finally, that rarity, by working for what they earn (the Hills, and, eventually, Belfield). Cecilia, like

Clarissa before her and Dorothea Brooke after her, wants money only in order to carry out charity work. *Cecilia* participates in a line of novels about philanthropy by women, of which Sarah Scott's 1762 *Millenium Hall* is perhaps the best known.[1] But not for a minute does anyone, from any class, allow her to forget that she is an heiress, and Burney means to make a social point through the irony of this novel's ending, with its titular heiress penniless. In the novel's final lines, we are told that Cecilia 'knew that, at times, the whole family must murmur at her loss of fortune, and at times she murmured herself to be thus portionless, though an HEIRESS' (2:473).

Burney's focus on money as a medium of exchange for her plot and for her materialist social critique is relentless in *Cecilia* and leads to the novel's major achievement: its phantasmagoric metaphor of masquerade develops directly out of the surreal quality Burney gives to money and to financial transactions and their repercussions. Cecilia's economic position is clearly endangered from the outset: the question of where honorably to bestow money (and, behind that question, of how honorably to acquire it) underlies the plot. In the custody of her first guardian, Harrel, Cecilia is inexorably drawn into the household's dissipations, in which the conversation consists of 'comparative strictures upon celebrated beauties, hints of impending bankruptcies, and witticisms upon recent divorces' (1:31), all issues that turn on the marketing of class and gender. Her second guardian, Briggs, is a wonderful proto-Dickensian caricature of avarice, practicing penny pinching as a high art and eliding the first person when he speaks, always breathlessly, as though to conserve words as he conserves shillings. He represents the mirror opposite of the spendthrift Harrel. Trapped between these two extremes, Cecilia resolves to forego 'the frivolous insipidity of her present life, to make at once a more spirited and more worthy use of the affluence, freedom and power which she possessed' (1:51) through charity and intellectual study. Her efforts, however, fail. She becomes, despite herself, the underwriter of aristocratic pretension and waste through her coerced loans to Harrel, her notes from a moneylender, and her most insidious mentor, Monckton, who reminds us of both Villars and Mandlebert, supposedly benign counselors who, perhaps not so inadvertently, endanger their charges. Burney's tag line for Monckton when we first meet him is to tell the reader aphoristically that 'pleasure given in society, like money lent in usury, returns with interest to those who dispense it' (1:5). The financial metaphor pervades the novel.

Harrel bleeds Cecilia of money; Briggs, who controls her cash flow, refuses to advance her any; her third guardian, Compton Delvile, is too proud to interfere in such a vulgar problem. The only expenditure Cecilia makes for herself – bills to a bookseller to provide her with reading that will furnish a mental escape from the implacable materiality surrounding her – draws remonstration. 'Words get no cash,' Briggs scolds her (1:174), and Delvile exhorts her never to 'degrade herself by being put on a level with writers' (1:179). Much more practical than Camilla, who incurs debts through ignorance of marketplace realities as well as through imposition and charity, Cecilia has reason to feel continually frustrated, and Burney may have been using that frustration to convey her own increasingly bitter views on the state of the literary marketplace. Her merciless concern with financial detail – the novel dwells with ledger-book particularity on the elaborate specifications of each exchange of funds and each operation of promissory note collection – marks this as a novel that broke new ground in the eighteenth century. Burney here shines a spotlight on the relations between women and men with a plot that relies on financial complication based on an oddly gynocentric economic foundation.

This foundation supports the novel's reliance on masquerade, carnival, and madness to make its critique of eighteenth-century materialism. The masquerade metaphor in the novel permits Burney to comment on the personal and social toll of shifting class categories that she had begun to analyze comedically with the *ton* and Branghton portraits in *Evelina*. Recent work on the 'carnivalesque' as not merely a category of social history and popular culture but of cultural analysis itself derives from Mikhail Bakhtin's seminal study of Rabelais, a work first translated into English in 1968.[2] The literary studies that build most interestingly on Bakhtin also make use of the anthropological work of Edmund Leach and Victor Turner on carnival and liminality.[3] Most recently, Peter Stallybrass and Allon White have at once extended and critiqued Bakhtin's notion of the carnivalesque in their elaboration of a category of what they have called 'transgression,' a category that focuses on the carnivalesque as an inversion or abrogation of narrative cultural codes leading to 'the recoding of high/low relations across the whole social structure.'[4] Terry Castle has written importantly on carnival and the masquerade in the eighteenth century, and she offers a detailed reading of *Cecilia* in conjunction with an analysis of masquerade as an organizing metaphor in eighteenth-century fiction.[5] *Cecilia*'s insistence on inverting economic hierarchies in such a way that the category of 'heiress' becomes culturally impossible and its Burneyan reliance on figuring locations of public pleasure as discursive sites for the mapping of social classifications can be read in the light of this recent work on carnival. The carnivalesque in *Cecilia* emerges out of the effects of the ever-present possibility of assault and violence on a protagonist for whom no mask can be fashioned, no disguise can disguise adequately, no niche in the class or gender order can be made safe or appropriate.

Early in the novel, and with the aid of incongruous mixes of classes, Burney establishes the slightly out-of-control atmosphere that pervades *Cecilia.* A character named Morrice figures in many of the carnival scenes, beginning at a breakfast held at Monckton's house in the novel's opening pages. A chameleon and self-appointed lackey, Morrice aims to insinuate himself into society by pleasing, and he shifts roles as quickly as he sees the need to make himself useful to people he wants not to offend. An elastic, silly-putty character, Morrice, not overtly evil, triggers much of the disaster in *Cecilia.* At the breakfast, he usurps Monckton's seat next to Cecilia, and Monckton removes him by suddenly suggesting a game of 'move-all' – a sort of hectic musical chairs. Later, in London, a similar scene occurs when Morrice suddenly and loudly leaps over the back of a sofa to sit beside Cecilia, and is again ousted as suddenly and violently by Monckton. Finally, as Cecilia tries to make a quick and clandestine trip to London before her first, aborted wedding, she encounters the ubiquitous Morrice on the road, and he insists not only on accompanying her, but on following her and unearthing her connection with Mortimer Delvile. In the process, he breaks the leg of an already injured pet dog he drops while chasing the disguised Delvile on horseback. Burney is still critiquing manners and social behaviors, but the near-slapstick antics of Morrice go beyond those of a Captain Mirvan or a Lovel and always verge on the chaos of madness, so that when he is present the narrative begins to resemble *Alice in Wonderland.*

The masquerade in book 2, a sequence in which Morrice figures prominently, comprises one of the most extraordinary passages in Burney's fiction, and figures centrally in the atmosphere of baroque carnival permeating this narrative. The question of money – who will pay the workmen? how will the awning over the dessert table for the 'masks' be financed? – hovers over everything. No one retrenches expenses in this novel, though significantly it is at the garishly costly Harrel masquerade that Cecilia meets the novel's hero, Mortimer Delvile, her guardian's son. All the characters appear in disguise in this sequence, and the boundaries between characters and their identities, and between social class and acceptable behaviors, are radically broken by the chaotic presence of 'masks.' Cecilia, in particular, is unable to recognize her companions accurately, at first taking the white domino who protects her to be her friend Belfield and the devil who persecutes her to be her would-be suitor Sir Robert Floyer, though the reader learns that the devil is really Monckton, in a metaphorical revelation of his true self, and the domino turns out to be Mortimer Delvile, the novel's hero. It is a key to the importance of the masquerade in *Cecilia* that the novel's lovers first meet here. Though censorious of the Harrels' extravagance, Cecilia nevertheless looks forward to and relishes the masquerade: 'Cecilia herself, however little pleased with the attendant circumstance of wantonly accumulating unnecessary debts, was not the least animated of the party; she was a stranger to every diversion of this sort, and from the novelty of the scene, hoped for uncommon satisfaction' (1:99). As Terry Castle has pointed out, this set scene is a locus simultaneously of social pleasure and of a moral disapproval engendered by its institutionalization of disorder and sexual theater.[6] Cecilia's response to the evening typifies this paradox.

Events at the masquerade demonstrate an observation made by symbolic anthropologists, that body images, clothing, and rules about the control of bodies and their presentation reflect the distribution of social power in a given culture.[7] Cecilia, indeed, becomes the heroine stripped bare as she decides to attend in ordinary dress, a decision that ironically marks her and makes her unwillingly the center of attention: 'There were so many masks that Cecilia wished she had herself made one of the number, as she was far more conspicuous in being almost the only female in a common dress, than any masquerade habit could have made her' (1:120). As a consequence, she is literally imprisoned by Monckton in his Don Devil costume. He persecutes her for most of the evening and necessitates that she be rescued – she is metaphorically surrounded by his wand and his insistent silence. The evening literally 'breaks up' when Morrice, dressed as a harlequin, pulls down the elaborate awning and colored lights in a failed attempt to impress the company by leaping over the dessert table, a prank that plunges the room into darkness and scatters glass, papier-mâché, lamps, and oil over the screaming crowd.

The Lord of Chaos reigns here: the Harrels' apartments resonate with 'the variety of dresses, the medley of characters, the quick succession of figures, and the ludicrous mixture of groups' and with 'the conceited efforts at wit, the total thoughtlessness of consistency, and the ridiculous incongruity of the language with the appearance' (1:101) in a cacophony of what Mikhail Bakhtin would call 'heteroglossia.'[8] In his study of Rabelais, Bakhtin discusses the revolutionary role of carnival and ritual public spectacle, delineating a multiplicity of styles and languages, sensuousness, and an impulse to play as key elements. 'Carnival,' according to Bakhtin, is neither an art form nor a sphere of life, but inhabits the borderline between life and art: people live inside the carnival, which subsumes all life into it while it lasts. Carnival liberates its participants from social and sexual laws that exist outside it; it breaks down hierarchies of all kinds, obliterating categories of gender, rank, class, age, and profession as it simultaneously frees its actors from norms of etiquette and decency. It represents the mutability of a 'world inside out.'[9]

A plenitude of unreadable signs takes over at the masquerade in *Cecilia*: 'Every room was occupied, and the common crowd of regular masqueraders were dispersed through the various apartments. Dominos of no character, and fancy-dresses of no meaning, made, as is usual at such meetings, the general herd of the company: for the rest, the men were Spaniards, chimney-sweepers, Turks, watchmen, conjurers, and old women; and the ladies shepherdesses, orange girls, Circassians, gipseys, haymakers, and sultanas' (1:102–3). Communication in 'local cant' with '*Do you know me? Who are you?* and *I know you*; with the sly pointing of the finger, the arch nod of the head, and the pert squeak of the voice' (1:102) represents a coded fall into Babel in which categories of sex and class intersect, merge, and explode. This Babel fascinates Burney as a polyphonic symbol of the social world her heroines must learn to decode. In the 'carnival' sequences of *Cecilia* (and there are less acute, less chaotic parallel sequences in the other three novels as well), forbidden incursions of role reversal and a liberating social blasphemy intrude upon the official rules of social life.[10]

The Babel in *Cecilia* continues in the next important sequence: a duel between Sir Robert Floyer and Belfield occasioned by a dispute over rights to Cecilia's arm at the opera, a dispute in which Cecilia becomes a disembodied anatomy, a metonymic arm. Cecilia fails to recognize the semiotic significance of sexual disputes and their resultant duelling: 'all she could find to regret with regard to herself, was wanting the presence of mind to have refused the civilities of both' (1:138). She is misread as Mandlebert had misread Camilla: for Sir Robert, 'her silence he only attributed to admiration, her coldness to fear, and her reserve to shame' (1:145). Unlike Elizabeth Bennet, who is only briefly bereft of words when she encounters Darcy at Pemberley, Cecilia seems unable to speak when she must explain appearances that are against her. When she meets Delvile in Belfield's rooms, 'notwithstanding the openness and purity of her intentions, [Cecilia] was so much disconcerted by this unexpected meeting, and pointed speech, that she had not the presence of mind to call him back and clear herself' (1:206). And she avoids taking the initiative in communications. Later, at his home, she 'chose rather to wait the revival of his own curiosity, than to distress or perplex herself by contriving methods of explanation' (1:232). She also fails to ask Mrs. Delvile if she can remain there rather than return to the Harrels, because 'she knew not how to make her proposal; but from the uncommon partiality of Mrs. Delvile, she hoped with a very little encouragement, she would lead to it herself' (1:235). She does not. Like all of Burney's heroines, Cecilia is beset by misunderstanding, missed connections, plots and subterfuge, and economic nightmares. And like Burney's other heroines as well, Cecilia brings some of her troubles on herself through a combination of ignorance, trustingness, and a too-cautious manner of dealing with the world; quite to her harm, 'she suffered not her affections to triumph over her principles' and made sure 'her passions were under the control of her reason' (1:244). Cecilia's world relies on codes – masks, gestures, games, social regulations, inheritance laws, wills – that control the protagonist's movement.

Moral economy and the economy of morals reign in this coded narrative. Belfield, ashamed of the trade of his father, learns too late that 'though discernment teaches us the folly of others, experience singly can teach us our own!' (1:212). Exhorted by Cecilia to fear imminent financial ruin, Mrs. Harrel only 'assured her *she did nothing but what everybody else did*, and that it was quite impossible for her to *appear in the world* in any other manner' (1:186). Cecilia herself lives in ignorance of the world's arrangements: 'The stations and employments of men she only knew by occasionally hearing that such were their professions, and such their situations in life; but with the means and gradations by which they arose to them she was wholly unacquainted' (1:241). In all the society scenes in *Cecilia*, Burney comments on the idiosyncracies and superficiality of *ton* life, in which high fashion, demonstrated by the 'ennuyé' Meadows, consists of the 'happy art in catching the reigning foibles of the times, and carrying them to an extreme yet more absurd than any one had done before him' (1:270).

Fashionable society and fashionable promenade locations always lead back to 'carnival' of one sort or another in *Cecilia*. At the Pantheon, for example, Morrice again inserts anarchic potential into the action by overturning a teapot that singes Delvile's shoulder when he bends to protect Cecilia from a burn. A more important 'carnival' scene occurs at Vauxhall and leads up to Harrel's suicide. Harrel proposes the Vauxhall expedition 'in a hurrying manner' (1:385) and orders a hackney coach. When his wife and Cecilia both become alarmed, Harrel grows violent. On arrival, he 'made them take several turns in the midst of the company, and walked so fast, that they could hardly keep pace with him' (1:388). Harrel drinks more and more champagne, and begins to assemble a motley crew of fellow revelers, a crew that resembles the mix-and-match assembly of the Harrel masquerade earlier in the novel. Another of Cecilia's would-be suitors, Marriot, joins them, then Morrice, then Harrel's creditors themselves, Hobson ('a fat, sleek, vulgar-looking man, dressed in a bright purple coat, with a deep red waistcoat, and a wig bulging far from his head with small round curls' [1:390]) and Simkins ('a little mean-looking man, very thin, and almost bent double with perpetual cringing' [1:391]). The *ton* crowd also materializes: Meadows with his disdainful yawning, contrived obliviousness, and complaints; Captain Aresby, with his precious insertion of French phrases into every sentence; and Sir Robert Floyer. At a ball held earlier at the Harrels' after their first near miss with bankruptcy, Meadows' cold but accurate remarks had foreshadowed and prefigured Harrel's later public suicide at Vauxhall when he lamented, ''Tis terrible to be under the same roof with a set of people who would care nothing if they saw one expiring!' (1:327).

Harrel's suicide is one of Burney's most extraordinary fictional achievements. Harrel has on several occasions used threats of suicide to bilk Cecilia of her inheritance in scenes that darken and virtually parallel the Macartney sequence in *Evelina*. And like the later and far more admirable Ferdinando Falkland of William Godwin's 1794 novel *Caleb Williams*, Harrel is periodically beset by 'fits of horror' (1:337). While the actual act of suicide, when it finally occurs, takes place just offstage, the narrative does not spare the gory details of Harrel's slow dying. Amid waiters covered with blood and staring spectators, Cecilia herself takes charge of calling for a surgeon and organizing the disposal of the body. Ironically, a scene in which all the difficult work that involves both emotional and physical fortitude is undertaken by a woman (Cecilia soundly lambastes Floyer for allowing his friend to be attended in his dying moments only by servants and strangers) ends with another conflict scene between two men vying to 'protect' Cecilia by seeing her home, Floyer and Mortimer Delvile. Delvile wins this time. But they return to find an execution at the Harrels' house, and the chaos of Harrel's uncontrolled life comes to an end as Cecilia and Mrs. Harrel take refuge with the Delviles for the night.

The carnival atmosphere of *Cecilia* touches every facet of the narrative: first and most obviously in the masquerade scene, then in the two actual and several near and averted duels between rivals for the heroine's affections, then at Vauxhall during Harrel's drunken preamble to his suicide, later in the eventually apoplectic screaming confrontation between Delvile and his mother over his marriage, and finally in the scene that precedes Cecilia's madness and imprisonment. Each society scene along the way also adds to this depraved atmosphere: carriage accidents, mindless conversations with idiotic characters such as Captain Aresby and the vapidly chattering Miss Larrolles, maddening interruptions of important meetings by the intrusion of minor characters. Language in these sequences is cacophonous, coded, and meaningless. Meadows and Morrice, each of whom in his way holds all opinions simultaneously, represent the devaluation of communication and the inability of characters trapped in this social system to forge stable identities for themselves. Characters try continually to be what they are not: Monckton, the novel's villain, reveals his true nature only anonymously at the masquerade in which he wears a devil costume; Belfield, ashamed of his family, tries to pass as a gentleman and then as a peasant; Morrice repeats whatever he thinks anyone wants to hear, always on the lookout for the main chance and holding no real opinions of his own; Meadows spouts whatever he thinks will be most disagreeable; and Harrel insists on an appearance of wealth even when he knows his dissipation has ruined not only himself and his wife but his ward as well. In contrast, Briggs and Compton Delvile grasp too assiduously what they are, and so thoroughly exaggerate their characters with arrogance and miserliness that they become almost intentional self-caricatures.

A number of conclusions can be drawn from the carnivalesque qualities of *Cecilia*. When Cecilia participates in the masquerade, albeit without wearing a mask herself, she simultaneously disapproves of the Harrels' way of life and is excited by it. This is a primary quality of the carnival: it represents in ritual fashion the contiguity and simultaneity of pleasure and disapproval in social life – liberation is always balanced by containment, freedom by restraint. It is worth noting here that one criticism of Bakhtin has been his unwillingness to see the central irony in carnival: it is a fundamentally sanctioned social activity, a permissible blurring of categories and norms.[11] This situation produces the intense narrative tension present in *Cecilia*. The tension comes not from suspense – we can anticipate more or less what will happen, if not next, then eventually – but from an ambience of continual threat: 'What continual disturbance . . . keeps me thus forever from rest!' laments Cecilia. 'No sooner is one wound closed, but another is opened; mortification constantly succeeds distress, and when my heart is spared my pride is attacked, that not a moment of tranquillity may ever be allowed me!' (2:232). The world is forever upside down in *Cecilia*, its hierarchies challenged, its repressed desires erupting when least able to be fulfilled. The scenes play out a perpetual game of gender and class warfare, a theater of masks and cross-purposes.

Cecilia's madness derives directly from these cross-purposes, and from frustration at her own powerlessness in the face of absurd circumstances. In other words, Cecilia goes mad for the same reason Camilla goes mad: there is no sane response to the circumstances she finds herself in. Efforts to enlist others in her aid fail. When, for example, she finally resorts to asking Compton Delvile to intervene for her and disabuse Sir Robert Floyer concerning his presumptions for her hand in marriage, her guardian refuses to debase himself in this way. Cecilia writes to the baronet herself, though not with much effect: 'Provoked and wearied, Cecilia resolved no longer to depend upon any body but herself for the management of her own affairs' (1:304). However, taking action herself not only does not extricate her from misunderstanding or financial disaster, it makes things worse, because every action she takes causes the social world around her to impute to her motives which are either false or base or both.

The point Burney makes in all her novels, but preeminently in *Cecilia*, is that a beautiful heiress cannot possibly remain independently single by choice: such an eventuality would not be credited as plausible in polite society. Mr. Hobson puts it well when he notes: 'As to a lady, let her be worth never so much, she's a mere nobody, as one may say, till she can get herself a husband, being she knows nothing of business, and is made to pay for everything through the nose' (2:411). As Lady Honoria Pemberton, a cousin of the Delviles, remarks, 'Everybody one meets disposes of Miss Beverley to some new person' (1:345). Lady Honoria is a character who performs the same role Camilla's brother Lionel plays in Burney's third novel and the anarchic Morrice plays more brutally in *Cecilia*: she is a disruptive force perpetually amusing herself with practical jokes at the expense of others and of propriety. But Lady Honoria's disruptions are knowing, insightful, and calculated. Her sharp wit refreshingly challenges the staid codes of social behavior in the novel. She recognizes the stakes for women in this society, and she has the novel's last word. When Cecilia chides her on her lack of principles, she responds reasonably, 'Not a creature thinks of our principles, till they find them out by our conduct; and nobody can possibly do that till we are married, for they give us no power beforehand. The men know nothing of us in the world while we are single, but how we can dance a minuet, or play a lesson upon the harpsichord' (2:466). Lady Honoria tries to manipulate this slippery female role and to turn slipperiness itself into freedom.

Cecilia is not, however, as calculating as Lady Honoria, because she is not yet as bitter. Cecilia's madness, like Camilla's, is distilled from the frustration of unbearable powerlessness, the frustration of always having to enlist another's authority. Its first symptoms appear when Delvile and Monckton fight a duel, and Monckton is thought fatally wounded. This duel occurs in a parallel place in the narrative to the duel between Sir Robert Floyer and Belfield, and in the intervening pages occur several other averted duels. Indeed, Cecilia becomes adept at managing the rivals for her affections. Disturbed by the duel occasioned after the opera imbroglio, she maneuvers around the simultaneous offers of lemonade from Delvile and Floyer at the Harrels' ball, and makes an ingenious response to their question, 'Which is to be the happy man?' '"Each, I hope," answered Cecilia, with admirable presence of mind, "since I expect no less than that you will both do me the honour of drinking my health"' (1:322).

At the same time, however, Cecilia begins to be deprived of speech: 'All utterance seemed denied her, and she curtseyed without saying a word' (1:339). Her conversations with Mortimer become monosyllabic and halting; in other situations, Cecilia defends herself vociferously and with self-assurance, but with Mortimer Delvile Cecilia is as tongue-tied as is Camilla with Mandlebert. And as Edgar Mandlebert materializes only when least desired, so Cecilia continually meets Delvile unexpectedly and in inopportune and suspicious-looking circumstances (a favorite technique of Burney's for setting up misunderstanding and misreading as well as tension in the reader – sign systems in her novels are always dangerously booby-trapped). An anticipated duel also opens the novel's climactic sequence, when Delvile unexpectedly turns up in London while Cecilia is making plans to join him abroad, and finds her in the company of Belfield in what look like damning circumstances. What follows builds such incredible tension that the reader herself feels lost; Delvile and his wife each order the other around and draw premature conclusions without any evidence.

First, Delvile commands that Cecilia go in her chair to his father's house in St. James-square, but as soon as she leaves, she jumps out of the chair and returns to the Belfields in Portland-street, because it occurs to her that Mortimer will challenge Belfield, and she wants to prevent bloodshed. The men are gone when she returns, but she follows them to a coffeehouse. They have just left. Now she decides to go to the Delvile house, but by then Mortimer has come, inquired for her, found she had not come, and left again, and Compton Delvile, still not crediting her marriage, refuses to admit her. The lovers chase each other around the city in this way for page after page, returning to both Portland-street and the coffeehouse. Cecilia has taken the cringing Simkins with her, who impedes progress, and she finally loses control when the coachman drunkenly demands to be paid and Simkins disputes his bill. The crisis builds: 'The inebriety of the coachman became evident; a mob was collecting; Cecilia, breathless with vehemence and terror, was encircled, yet struggled in vain to break away; and the stranger gentleman, protesting, with sundry compliments, he would himself take care of her, very freely seized her hand' (2:428). Encircled and 'taken care of,' Cecilia is like Evelina at Marylebone Gardens and like herself at the masquerade, a prisoner of men pretending all around her to be gallant and in fact suffocating her with their 'protection.'

Cecilia is meanwhile convinced that her husband and Belfield have shot each other, and suddenly she screams, 'He will be gone! he will be gone! and I must follow him to Nice!' and 'with a strength hitherto unknown to her, she forcibly disengaged herself from her persecutors' and runs down the street (2:429). The narrator describes Cecilia's mad rush through London in a prose teeming with palpable tension:

> Meanwhile the frantic Cecilia escaped both pursuit and insult by the velocity of her own motion. She called aloud upon Delvile as she flew to the end of the street. No Delvile was there! – she turned the corner; yet saw nothing of him; she still went on, though unknowing wither, the distraction of her mind every instant growing greater, from the inflammation of fatigue, heat, and disappointment. She was spoken to repeatedly; she was even caught once or twice by her riding habit; but she forced herself along by her own vehement rapidity, not hearing what was said, not heeding what was thought. Delvile, bleeding by the arm of Belfield, was the image before her eyes, and took such full possession of her senses, that still, as she ran on, she fancied it in view. She scarce touched the ground; she scarce felt her own motion; she seemed as if endued with supernatural speed, gliding from place to place, from street to street, with no consciousness of any plan, and following no other direction than that of darting forward wherever there was most room, and turning back when she met with any obstruction; till, quite spent and exhausted, she abruptly ran into a yet open shop, where, breathless and panting, she sunk upon the floor, and, with a look disconsolate and helpless, sat for some time without speaking.
>
> (2:429–30)

The reader is inside the disintegrating mind of the heroine in this passage, following her through the streets of London controlled by a maniacal mental image. The narrator neither judges nor sympathizes. In Burney's most important narrative departure in *Cecilia*, she experiments with a vocally rich and multilayered third-person omniscient narrator. While Burney's post-*Evelina* style has been vilified by critics, some have recognized her contribution to the evolution of a storytelling voice for the novel. Burney experiments in *Cecilia* with pre-Austenian irony, and conveys both comedy, melodrama, and serious social satire in a voice that controls the narrative tone with its overripe sense of vitriolic menace. No one had written like this before Burney.

As Cecilia runs, she retains an image of a bleeding Mortimer Delvile before her eyes. This image echoes the earlier ruptured blood vessel of Augusta Delvile, Mortimer's mother and Burney's most overwhelming mother figure. She collapses in a pawnshop called 'Three Blue Balls' where again she is imprisoned, locked into a room while the proprietors place an announcement for her in the *Daily Advertiser*. She has lost her purse to the coachman and Simkins, and the advertisement, entitled MADNESS, mentions the Delviles. For two days, Cecilia remains in the room, refusing food and drink (also a factor in Camilla's madness), and 'though naturally and commonly of a silent and quiet disposition, she was now not a moment still, for the irregular starts of a terrified and disordered imagination were changed into the constant ravings of morbid delirium' (2:433). When her friends find her, 'her dress was in much disorder, her fine hair was dishevelled, and the feathers of her riding-hat were broken and half falling down, some shading her face, others reaching to her shoulder' (2:434). She resembles Madame Duval thrown into the ditch by Captain Mirvan in *Evelina*.

Chillingly, when Delvile first speaks to Cecilia and is not recognized, he asks, 'Is it me or my name you thus disown?' (2:439), making clear the important separate identity of names in Burney's novels. She remains 'senseless, speechless, motionless, her features void of all expression, her cheeks without colour, her eyes without meaning' (2:450) until restorative sleep brings her to herself. Among her first gestures when well is to write an accusing letter to Monckton, signed 'Cecilia Delvile' (2:460). Camilla went mad when she entered a social limbo as a woman inappropriately alone; Cecilia goes mad effectively for the same reason. Both heroines recover into the arms of men who have learned their lessons from this experience: if you are going to 'take care of' and 'protect' a woman in the eighteenth century, you had better not leave her side, not for a minute. Danger lurks in every corner, and in the abstract the love of a good man serves no purpose.

It is this omnipresent sense of danger that most distinguishes *Cecilia* from a novel that, thirty years later and using a title from Burney's second novel's ending, addresses the same basic themes: Jane Austen's *Pride and Prejudice*.[12] The elder Bennets and Delviles each present pictures of conjugal mismatch borne for the purpose of social disguise. Burney's clear portrait of marital strife in the Delvile household is groundbreaking for eighteenth-century fiction. Burney and Austen discuss the accommodations these couples have made to their infelicity in strikingly similar fashion. Family pride controls both Mortimer Delvile and Fitzwilliam Darcy, and both first propose to the heroines after prolonged distance and cold behavior, and only when their efforts to give up their feelings have failed. Both offend their chosen women when they make their first declarations, as both focus on their failed attempt to overcome what they see as a damaging and unfortunate prepossession, and Delvile exacerbates this offense with a proposal of secrecy. In both cases, especially in the characters of Compton Delvile and Lady Catherine de Bourgh, immovable pride and prejudice are shown to be duping mechanisms whereby social rules thwart individual desire and the possibility of individual happiness. In both novels; hedonistic people bring ruin on themselves and those close to them: Mr. and Mrs. Harrel; Wickham and Lydia. In both novels, frustrated society women hone their tongues on sarcasm: Lady Honoria Pemberton and the Bingley sisters.

Cecilia is, nevertheless, ultimately a far darker and far more troubling novel than is Austen's *Pride and Prejudice*. The central houses in the two works symbolize this difference. Delvile Castle is surrounded by a moat with its drawbridge drawn up and 'no taste was shown in the disposition of the grounds, no openings were contrived through the wood for distant views or beautiful objects' (2:1) – this is a gloomy and entombing place. In Compton Delvile's pompous, self-important, and haughty house, 'every thing had an air of state, but of a state so gloomy, that while it inspired awe, it repressed pleasure' (1:93). Delvile Castle is the antithesis of *Pride and Prejudice*'s Pemberley – 'dark, heavy, and monastic' (2:1); an austere and decaying object. Pemberley, in bright contrast, stands 'on rising ground' and is situated in order to maximize the distance and beauty of its prospects.[13] Delvile Castle, like Burney's novels, lacks space for 'views': it is as claustrophobic as the text which encloses it. Elizabeth Bennet's world is indeed 'light and bright and sparkling'; Cecilia Beverley's world is a dim and narrow passageway.

While no one is as evil as Monckton or as frightening as Briggs or Compton Delvile in the pages of *Pride and Prejudice*, the entailed situation of Longbourn and the diminution of Cecilia's inheritance turn both novels to an underlying emphasis on money and its concomitant, class. Collins and Morrice resemble each other as characters whose limbo-like residence in the middle class makes them anxious to curry favor with those above them, and they become absurd in their efforts to please. The practicality of Charlotte Lucas is similar to that of Lady Honoria, though the latter is more outspokenly bitter. Charlotte, at least, gets a 'manageable' husband, albeit an insufferable one. Balls and dances figure prominently as the loci of social hierarchy and social rule-making in both novels, and both rely almost entirely on dialogue and conversation to forward their plots. Burney's experimental use of a third-person narrator prefigures Austen's own ironic narrative voice. The dominant difference between these two thematically parallel novels concerns the difference in style between Burney's graphic materiality and Austen's ironic subtlety.

Burney believed the key scene in *Cecilia* to be that in which Mrs. Delvile responds apoplectically to her son's passion for the heroine. Samuel Crisp had objected vociferously to this explicitly bloody confrontation, but Burney defended her narrative in a letter dated 15 March 1782:

> The conflict scene for Cecilia, between the mother and son, to which you so warmly object, is the very scene for which I wrote the whole book, and so entirely does my plan hang upon it, that I must abide by its reception in the world, or put the whole behind the fire. . . . I meant in Mrs. Delvile [*sic*] to show how the greatest virtues and excellences may be totally obscured by the indulgence of violent passions and the ascendancy of favourite prejudices.
>
> (*DL* 1:418)

This was one time that Burney did not allow a 'daddy' to censor her, and it explains her version of the 'pride and prejudice' theme and its treatment in *Cecilia*.

While Cecilia is still ill and incarcerated in the pawnshop, Dr. Lyster speaks the lines from the novel's last pages that provided Jane Austen with her well-known title and summarized the plot of Burney's second novel:

> The whole of this unfortunate business . . . has been the result of PRIDE and PREJUDICE. Your uncle, the Dean, began it, by his arbitrary will, as if an ordinance of his own could arrest the course of nature! and as if *he* had the power to keep alive, by the loan of a name, a family in the male branch already extinct. Your father, Mr. Mortimer, continued it with the same self-partiality, preferring the wretched gratification of tickling his ear with a favourite sound, to the solid happiness of his son with a rich and deserving wife. Yet this, however, remember; if to PRIDE and PREJUDICE you owe your miseries, so wonderfully is good and evil balanced, that to PRIDE and PREJUDICE you will also owe their termination: for all that I could say to Mr. Delvile, either of reasoning or entreaty, – and I said all I could suggest, and I suggested all a man need wish to hear, – was totally thrown away, till I pointed out to him his *own* disgrace, in having a *daughter-in-law* immured in these mean lodgings.
>
> (2:462)

At the end of Jane Austen's novel, both Darcy and his aunt Lady Catherine are effectively chastened: neither will ever again behave with such inhuman arrogance. But Dr. Lyster's treacly moral notwithstanding, only more of the same converts her dreadful father-in-law to Cecilia's side. She and any children she may have (and, we suspect, she had better produce at least one male heir after all this trouble) are to suffer even more greatly in the Delvile pride because now they themselves must participate in it.

In order to achieve the fulfillment of privatized desire, Cecilia gives up a great deal: a name, a fortune, and the ability to act independently. To gain a husband, she loses a self, and it is not at all clear in the novel's denouement that Burney believes this to be a good bargain. The flighty Lady Honoria Pemberton has, perhaps, the last word, given the entrapped helplessness Cecilia has endured until her marriage could be acknowledged: 'You can do nothing at all without being married; a single woman is a thousand times more shackled than a wife; for, she is accountable to everybody; and a wife, you know, has nothing to do but just to manage her husband' (2:465). The vision of Cecilia 'immured' in Delvile Castle – despite all that propriety and a loving husband can offer – remains a grim vision. Though in the end Burney's lovers begin to take possession of something like happiness, in a Burney novel 'happiness' simply means the calm possession of mutual knowledge, the lifting of the veil of secrecy and misunderstanding.

Notes

1. Margaret Anne Doody remarks on this lineage in *Frances Burney: The Life in the Works* (New Brunswick, N.J.: Rutgers University Press; Cambridge: Cambridge University Press, 1988), chap. 5.

2. Mikhail Bakhtin, *Rabelais and His World*, trans. Helene Iswolsky (Bloomington: Indiana University Press, 1985).

3. In particular, see Edmund Leach, 'Time and False Noses,' in *Rethinking Anthropology*, ed. E. Leach (London: Athlone Press, 1961), 132–36, and Victor Turner, *The Ritual Process: Structure and Anti-Structure* (Ithaca: Cornell University Press, 1977).

4. Peter Stallybrass and Allon White, *The Politics and Poetics of Transgression* (Ithaca: Cornell University Press, 1986), 19.

5. Terry Castle, 'Eros and Liberty at the English Masquerade, 1710–1790,' *Eighteenth-Century Studies* 17 (1983–84): 155–76; idem, 'The Carnivalization of Eighteenth-Century Narrative,' *PMLA* 99 (1984): 903–16 [reproduced in *The English Novel Volume I: 1700 to Fielding*, chap. 6]; idem, *Masquerade and Civilization: The Carnivalesque in Eighteenth-Century Culture and Fiction* (Stanford: Stanford University Press, 1986). This work represents a major contribution to eighteenth-century studies, and my own reading of *Cecilia* is indebted to Castle's analysis.

6. Terry Castle, 'Carnivalization of Eighteenth-Century Narrative,' 903–16.

7. Carroll Smith-Rosenberg discussed this distribution in 'Mis-Remembering Richardson: Representations of the American Middle Class,' unpublished paper discussed at the 'Language, Culture, Gender, and Power' group at the University of Pennsylvania on 28 May 1986, 35.

8. See Mikhail Bakhtin, 'Discourse in the Novel,' the final essay in *The Dialogic Imagination*, ed. Michael Holquist (Austin: University of Texas Press, 1981), 263 and *passim*.

9. Bakhtin, *Rabelais and His World*, 5–11.

10. See Wayne Booth, 'Freedom of Interpretation: Bakhtin and the Challenge of Feminist Criticism,' *Critical Inquiry* 9 (1982): 45–76, for a discussion of the ways recent critics have employed Bakhtin's idea that there is no neutral language and that the self is dialogic rather than monologic.

11. For this criticism, see Terry Eagleton, *Walter Benjamin: Toward a Revolutionary Criticism* (London: Verso, 1981), 148; Roger Sales, *English Literature in History, 1780–1830: Pastoral and Politics* (London: Hutchinson, 1983), 169; and Stallybrass and White, *Politics and Poetics of Transgression*, 12–16.

12. Judy Simons comments on the parallels between *Cecilia* and *Pride and Prejudice*, though she concludes that Austen 'developed and substantiated the realist vision that Fanny Burney introduced' and argues that Burney's approach is more 'tentative' than Austen's. See Simons, *Fanny Burney* (Totowa, N.J.: Barnes & Noble Books, 1987), 65–66.

13. *The Novels of Jane Austen*, 3d edn, ed. R. W. Chapman, 5 vols. (Oxford: Oxford University Press, 1982), 2:245.

Part VI

Wollstonecraft

10 Mary Wollstonecraft: The Gender of Genres in Late-Eighteenth-Century England

MARY POOVEY

Author of important feminist and cultural-materialist books on late-eighteenth-century and nineteenth-century culture, Mary Poovey here turns her attention to the problem of why Wollstonecraft's *Maria* is both fragmentary and internally conflicted. Poovey argues that the very structure of sentimentalism was bound to create ambivalences for Wollstonecraft, since it both served to arouse female desire, and to lead women to the single institution within which it was legitimate but which also sought to control and sublimate it. Wollstonecraft turned her hand to writing novels for generic reasons: political theory – a genre in which Wollstonecraft felt at ease – was insufficiently associated with the realm of feeling, and its public nature made it seem an improper enterprise for a woman. Wollstonecraft is aware of the feminist potential of criticizing sentimental norms, but is also unable to escape their allure.

Today, Mary Wollstonecraft is best remembered for her forays into that most 'masculine' of all late-eighteenth-century genres, political disquisition. But her two vindications suggest that, while that genre allowed her to voice her considerable intellectual insights, it did not accommodate her equally adamant emotions – or, to use eighteenth-century terminology, her 'sentiments.' Moreover, partly because her two political vindications were considered both 'unladylike' and politically volatile, Wollstonecraft may have feared that her message would not reach those who most needed to hear it. In *Maria, or the Wrongs of Woman*, Wollstonecraft set out to remedy both of these problems, to reformulate the insights of *A Vindication of the Rights of Woman* in a genre she felt certain could articulate her own emotion and attract a female audience – the sentimental novel. But the attempt to fictionalize 'the peculiar Wrongs of Woman' afflicted Wollstonecraft, for perhaps the first time in her life, with what seems very like writer's block. Whereas she had composed *The Rights of Men* in less than a month and *The Rights of Woman* in six weeks, she spent a year working on *Maria* – only to leave the manuscript less than a third finished when she died. Godwin's description of the composition of *Maria* reveals that the work induced insistent anxiety:

> She began it in several forms, which she successively rejected, after they were considerably advanced. She wrote many parts of the work again and again, and, when she had finished what she intended for the first part, she felt herself more urgently stimulated to revise and improve what she had written, than to proceed, with constancy of application, in the parts that were to follow.[1]

Almost any passage from the text of this much belabored first part reveals that the hesitation which afflicted *Maria*'s composition haunts its prose as well. Syntax is frequently disjunctive, narratives are broken off literally in mid-sentence, and, most troubling of all, the relationship between the narrative consciousness and that of the heroine Maria is inconsistent. All of the hesitations in composition and in achievement culminate, in fact, in a conspicuous failure to establish a consistent or purposeful attitude toward the subject under consideration. Even though *Maria* is an unfinished novel, then, both the time Wollstonecraft devoted to this work and the problems which prove to be characteristic suggest that she was having even more difficulty with this project than with the genre we might have expected to be daunting.

The problem is not simply that Wollstonecraft could not construct a successful narrative; both her first novel *Mary* and the story of Jemima, contained within *Maria*, argue for Wollstonecraft's competence as a storyteller. Rather, the problem seems to lie in the difficulty Wollstonecraft had in reconciling her intended 'purpose' with the genre, which here shapes the 'structure,' of the work.[2] According to her sketchy preface, Wollstonecraft's purpose was political, to show 'the peculiar Wrongs of Woman.' And her structure, like those of what she considered 'our best novels,' was intended to delineate 'finer sensations' rather than *'stage-effect,'* 'passions rather than manners.'[3] (Her implied model is Rousseau's *Julie*; the effects she denigrates belong, on the one hand, to improbable gothic romances like *The Mysteries of Udolpho* and, on the other, to social comedies such as *Evelina*.) But, as she was to discover in the process of composing *Maria*, Wollstonecraft's political insights and the sentimental structure through which she hoped to develop 'finer sensations' were dangerously at odds. For those 'finer sensations' – and the sentimental genre in which they were characteristically enshrined – were deeply implicated in the very values of bourgeois society which Wollstonecraft wanted to criticize. It is Wollstonecraft's recognition of this incompatibility and – equally to the point – her resistance to this recognition that account for both the hesitations of composition and the contradictions that mark the text. In her final work, Wollstonecraft identified one aspect of what she held to be the tyranny of eighteenth-century bourgeois institutions, yet because her own values – indeed, her own self-definition – were inextricably tied up with the values of these institutions, she was unable to pursue her revolutionary insights to their logical conclusion. *Maria*, in other words, chronicles one determined woman's struggle to get outside ideology – to 'advance,' to use her words, 'before the improvement of the age' – and her failure to make that advance sets us brooding on the curious complicity of gender and genre in the late eighteenth-century sentimental novel.

Wollstonecraft's dilemma is epitomized by the uncertain perspective of the novel's omniscient narrator. In chapter four, for example, which traces Maria's emotional surrender to a fellow inmate, the narrator moves from judgmental observer to unreflecting sympathizer. Maria has been imprisoned in a madhouse so that her avaricious husband can gain control of the independent fortunes of both Maria and their infant daughter. At the beginning of the chapter, the narrative voice comments authoritatively on Maria's situation. 'Pity,' this voice observes,

> and the forlorn seriousness of adversity, have both been considered as dispositions favourable to love, while satirical writers have attributed the propensity to the relaxing effects of idleness; what chance then had Maria of escaping, when pity, sorrow, and solitude all conspired to soften her mind, and nourish romantic wishes, and, from a natural progress, romantic expectations?
>
> (48)

The most pressing question here is the narrator's attitude toward Maria's 'romantic expectations.' The rhetoric of imprisonment suggests that, at the very least, Wollstonecraft understands such wishes to originate in deprivation and confinement. An adjacent passage, moreover, underscores the insight that 'romantic expectations' are actually projections of unanswered desire. 'Having had to struggle incessantly with the vices of mankind,' the narrator continues,

> Maria's imagination found repose in pourtraying the possible virtues the world might contain. Pygmalion formed an ivory maid, and longed for an informing soul. She, on the contrary, combined all the qualities of a hero's mind, and fate presented a statue in which she might enshrine them.
>
> (49)

The 'statue' is Maria's fellow prisoner, Henry Darnford, who soon emerges from featureless obscurity to become a vital force in Maria's drama. But the narrator remains curiously ambivalent about the precise nature of his role. Her description of Maria's emotional surrender, for example, culminates in a question which seems to announce the narrator's shrewd awareness that 'romantic expectations' often do not correspond to real possibilities. And yet the ambiguous origin of the sentiments expressed in the first part of this passage suggests that the narrator still harbors the hope that such romantic expectations might be fulfilled. As the two lovers embrace, 'Desire was lost in more ineffable emotions, and to protect her from insult and sorrow – to make her happy, seemed not only the first wish of his heart, but the most noble duty of his life. Such angelic confidence demanded the fidelity of honour; but could he, feeling her in every pulsation, could he ever change, could he be a villain?' (50) Is this question the narrator's ironic reminder of the possible delusion of 'romantic expectations'? Or is it the narrator's desperate attempt to resist the 'ineffable emotions' that already seduce Maria? By the end of this brief chapter the distance between the narrator and Maria almost wholly disappears; even allowing for ironic overtones – as some modern editors do – the honorific language of this passage suggests that the narrator shares Maria's 'romantic wishes' and perhaps her 'romantic expectations' as well. 'So much of heaven did they enjoy, that paradise bloomed around them; or they, by a powerful spell, had been transported into Armida's garden. Love, the grand enchanter, lapt them in Elysium, and every sense was harmonized to joy and social extacy' (51).

I've spent so long on this chapter because the progression of the narrator here – from detached, critical observer to emotional participant – recapitulates the movement which constitutes the organization and, theoretically, the target of criticism of the novel. The movement is the 'fall' into female sexuality, or, more precisely, the fall into that susceptibility to romantic expectations which eighteenth-century bourgeois society annexed to female sexuality. The problem here is that the narrator – and, by implication, Wollstonecraft herself – has just fallen victim to the very delusion which it is the object of this novel to criticize.

This seduction of the narrator constitutes the third occurrence of this pattern, and, from the three taken together, we begin to glimpse both Wollstonecraft's insight and her dilemma. As if to emphasize the importance of this pattern, the novel opens *in medias res*, precisely at the moment at which Maria is about to fall into romantic love for the second time. Just as Maria was initially confined in a loveless, repressed youth, so she is now confined in a madhouse. Just as she was then 'liberated' into a loveless marriage, so she is soon to be 'released' into the ambiguous, but decidedly dangerous, embrace of Darnford. And – most telling from the perspective of the narrative – the pander in each case is sentimentality – or, more precisely, a sentimental story. Maria's imagination was originally 'animated' or aroused by her uncle's sentimental history; now Rousseau's *Julie* fuels her fantasies about Henry Darnford and encourages her to receive him 'as her husband' (138). Clearly Wollstonecraft senses danger in this pattern, which is endemic to the sentimental genre. And yet at every point at which the narrator could underscore this danger, she hesitates, and the point is lost. Instead of shaping her 'structure' to her 'purpose,' Wollstonecraft repeatedly struggles – not very convincingly – to resolve the paradox she has introduced. 'We see what we wish, and make a world of our own,' she acknowledges of Maria's wishful projection, 'and, though reality may sometimes open a door to misery, yet the moments of happiness procured by the imagination, may, without a paradox, be reckoned among the solid comforts of life' (139).

In order to understand fully the implications of these narrative hesitations we need to examine Wollstonecraft's fundamental insights about the relationship of sentimentalism to both female sexuality and the bourgeois institution of marriage. For *Maria*'s central subject is really the way in which female sexuality is defined or interpreted – and, by extension, controlled – by bourgeois society. The primary institution of this control is marriage, which is, as Tony Tanner has recently reminded us, the fundamental 'mythology of bourgeois society.' With its institutionalization of kinship distinctions and alliances, its harnessing of individual sexual desire to the economic unit of the nuclear family, marriage is the basis of 'all the models, conscious and unconscious, by which society structures all its operations and transactions.'[4] Because of the particular legal and economic practices of late-eighteenth-century England, the power of this mythology was particularly strong in Mary Wollstonecraft's society. According to eighteenth-century bourgeois conventions, female sexuality could only be legitimately expressed – indeed, only existed as a positive cultural sign – within the institution of marriage. This was true partly because confining female sexual expression to marriage served to control that appetite which some men feared would 'devour them alive' sexually.[5] But even more importantly, it also insured that the transfer of property from one generation to the next would be legitimate. In the late eighteenth century, as what Dr. Johnson called England's 'fixed, invariable external rules of distinction and rank' increasingly gave way before incursions of new wealth, the prestige and political power of an individual (and his family) was frequently established through the twin practices of marrying for money and strict settlement, a legal arrangement which kept the family estate intact for the eldest son of each generation.[6] Given the rigid provisions of strict settlement and the importance of property, the chastity of a woman was especially critical, for if her fidelity was in question, so too was the integrity of the family. Jean-Jacques Rousseau underscored the severity of this transgression when he called it 'treason': when the faithless wife

> gives her husband children who are not his own, she is false both to him and them, her crime is not infidelity but treason. . . . Can any position be more wretched than that of the unhappy father who . . . is haunted by the suspicion that this is the child of another, . . . a thief who is robbing his own children of their inheritance. Under such circumstances the family is little more than a group of secret enemies, armed against each other by a guilty woman. . . .[7]

Even when family estates did not hang in the balance – that is, even when one's suitor was not the eldest but a younger son – the morality upon which strict settlement depended prevailed. Women were characteristically treated as counters in an economic exchange; they were valued as much for what they represented as for who they were. 'Men have a property in their wives and daughters,' Gilbert Burnet flatly stated.[8] Once married, the property of their fathers which young girls represented became the property of their husbands. And, under the Roman law which still governed late-eighteenth-century English women, so did they. As Maria recognizes, a married woman is 'as much a man's property as his horse, or his ass' (107). In England in the eighteenth century, a married woman had no independent legal rights: she could not sue her husband for divorce, she could not visit her children if her husband took them from her, and, most importantly, she could not act upon her own desires if they conflicted with those of her husband. Within marriage, as Maria phrases it, the feeling woman is 'required to moralize, sentimentalize herself to stone' (102).

This last observation reminds us of one role played in this system of morality by the late-eighteenth-century ideology of sentimentalism, and by sentimental novels in particular. For because the kind of economically advantageous marriages which frequently took place in this period often entailed the objectification of women, their reduction to symbols of property rather than their recognition as individuals, it had to be enforced not only by laws, but by a set of values that could make inequality seem 'right' or even 'natural.' Wollstonecraft recognized that one of this system's most effective guardians was the internalized set of values which encouraged women to sublimate their potentially anarchic desire, a system of values that was identified in the late eighteenth century with sentimentalism. Paradoxically, sentimentalism served both to arouse female sexuality and to control it.[9] In the first of these two functions, exemplified in this novel by Maria's adolescence, sentimental stories arouse a young woman's imagination (and, by extension, her potentially promiscuous erotic desire)[10] by engaging her vicariously in thinly disguised sexual exploits. But because the young girl is protected (or confined) by both ignorance and inexperience, the expectations generated by reading romantic stories lead her to project her desire uncritically onto an individual man, a 'hero,' with whom she then seeks to realize her imaginative and sexual desires through marriage.

The irony (and tragedy) of this situation is that, as often as not, the desire so aroused was in excess of the gratification offered women through marriage. Precisely because one effect of marriage was to limit desire and, more perniciously, to strip women of their status as autonomous subjects, sentimentalism theoretically generated a clash between female desire and male will. For, once imprisoned within marriage, a woman existed in the same state of confinement that characterized her adolescence. The desire threatened to begin again, to lead a woman to seek fulfillment outside the marriage bed. But the second effect of sentimental novels curtailed this threat. Despite the ominous spectres of adultery and seduction in eighteenth-century sentimental novels, the function of such flirtations with transgression was actually to sublimate female desire, to provide vicarious gratification which compensated for the diminished fulfillment of marriage. One function of sentimental novels, then, was actually to reinforce the institution which the desire they aroused could theoretically have subverted.

This was not, of course, the only or even the most explicit function of sentimental novels. As the etymological kinship suggests, 'sentimental' was closely associated with both 'sentiments' and 'sensibility,' and thus implied both an initial physiological sensation and the quality of response that sensation produced.[11] During most of the eighteenth century, 'sentimental' did not carry the pejorative connotations we now often assign it; instead, it suggested feelings which were not only strong but rational. The values associated with sentimentalism were therefore moral as well as aesthetic, and, especially in the second half of the century, sentimental theories were advanced to support many humane programs – from justifications for the American revolution and the freeing of enslaved Negroes to arguments for the humanitarian treatment of the poor.

Yet despite Mary Wollstonecraft's adamant support of these political causes, she repeatedly voiced grave reservations about the 'sensibility' that was cultivated by sentimental novels. For, as we will see, the very 'sensibility' which might temper men's acquisitive impulses could easily simply overwhelm women, who were neither encouraged to discipline feelings by reason nor provided with constructive outlets for their aroused emotions. By such reading, Wollstonecraft complained in *The Rights of Woman*, women's 'senses are inflamed, and their understandings neglected, consequently they become the prey of their senses, delicately termed sensibility, and are blown about by every momentary gust of feeling. . . . All their thoughts turn on things calculated to excite emotion; and feeling, when they should reason, their conduct is unstable, and their opinions are wavering. . . .'[12] The fact that such weakness is considered one of women's most 'feminine,' hence attractive, qualities, Wollstonecraft argued in *The Rights of Woman*, indicates the extent to which men are anxious to perpetuate their power at the expense of women's self-realization.

This recognition of the sentimental ways and means of marital tyranny is the heart of Wollstonecraft's insight in *Maria*. Yet despite the clarity of many of Maria's statements about marriage, the heroine remains ominously attracted to the very sentimentalism that has twice ensnared her. 'True sensibility,' she calls it, 'the sensibility which is the auxiliary of virtue, and the soul of genius, is in society so occupied with the feelings of others, as scarcely to regard its own sensations' (126). Even after the scheming brutality of Venables theoretically opens her eyes to the naïveté of such sentiments, Maria continues to extoll the purported selflessness of this '*active* sensibility' and to encourage her infant daughter to perpetuate the mother's mistakes: 'Whilst your own heart is sincere,' she writes in the memoirs she intends for her daughter, 'always expect to meet one glowing with the same sentiments' (77).

This returns us, of course, to the central problem; for what is confusing here is how Wollstonecraft intends for us to take the character of Maria. Do Maria's repeated lapses into the very sentimental jargon Wollstonecraft denounces constitute an ironic presentation? And, if so, does the irony extend to Maria's insights about marriage? Or is Wollstonecraft herself prey to the same delusive 'romantic expectations' that she shows crippling Maria? And, if so, what does this tell us about the tyrannical complicity between marriage and sentimentalism that Wollstonecraft is trying to expose?

The most telling argument for reading the characterization of Maria ironically is Wollstonecraft's juxtaposition of Maria's first-person narrative with another first-person narrative, that of Jemima, Maria's warder in the madhouse. Jemima's story is decidedly *un*-sentimental. Her history begins not with romantic expectations but with sexual violation ('My father . . . seduced my mother'), and it details the events of a continuing victimization: Jemima is raped by her master when she is sixteen, and the ensuing pregnancy drives her into the streets. After a self-inflicted abortion, poverty forces Jemima into prostitution. But as a self-sufficient prostitute, Jemima experiences an unorthodox, if momentary, freedom, a freedom which, no matter how qualified, Wollstonecraft says Jemima 'values': 'my independence,' Jemima calls it. Such subversive independence cannot be tolerated, however; night watchmen, jealous of her autonomy, soon drive Jemima to seek refuge in institutionalized prostitution – first in a whorehouse, then in a relationship with a 'worn-out votary of voluptuousness.' This sexual exploitation marks Jemima's entry into bourgeois society: the old man teaches her to read and confines her in a monogamous relationship. Upon her lover's death, Jemima learns the other face of bourgeois security: along with her freedom she has squandered her rights. Left penniless, Jemima is reduced, in rapid order, to a washerwoman, a thief, and a pauper, before she finds employment in the madhouse to which Maria is confined.

From her history of persecution, however, Jemima has developed both intellectual resolution and emotional resilience. 'The treatment that rendered me miserable,' she comments, 'seemed to sharpen my wits' (53), and with these 'sharpened wits' she learns how to survive in bourgeois society; Jemima endures by 'despis[ing] and prey[ing] on the society by which she had been oppressed' (31). Despite the fact that she is a victim, Jemima is also a survivor – and potentially a new kind of heroine as well.

For if Jemima's experiences have taught her to despise men, they have not wholly frozen her to a more radical expression of feminine feeling: Jemima retains the capacity to love – not men, significantly, but women. Jemima's only childhood wish was for a 'mother's affection,' her only feelings of guilt stem from her having made another woman suffer, and she is quick to respond to Maria's anguish. Moreover, Jemima's 'feminine emotions' are more resilient than Maria's nurtured, middle-class sensibility. When the two women finally escape the madhouse, Jemima goes first; and when they are confronted by a last, menacing male, the terrified Maria throws 'her arms round Jemima, and crie[s], "Save me!"' (141). In the most developed of the projected conclusions to the novel, Wollstonecraft has Jemima save Maria once more, this time from an attempted suicide, by restoring to Maria her lost daughter and then ushering her into the female world just glimpsed at the end of the passage.

This genuinely radical, indeed, feminist story has the potential to call into question both the organizational principles of bourgeois society and the sentimentalism that perpetuates romantic idealism. For the anarchy implicit in Jemima's brief exploitation of female sexuality combines with the stark realism of the narrative to explode the assumptions which tie female sexuality to romance and thereby to the institutions men traditionally control. But Wollstonecraft does *not* develop the revolutionary implications of Jemima's narrative. Instead, her story is quickly, ostentatiously, suppressed. Jemima's history occupies only one of the seventeen completed chapters of *Maria*, and it is suspended prematurely by an unspecified 'indistinct noise' whose only function is to curtail this narrative. The effect of this narrative on her auditors (two captives in a madhouse) is only to give rise to 'the most painful reflections on the present state of society' (not to effective actions), and, after their escape, Jemima insists only on being Maria's 'house-keeper' (not her equal). The abrupt manner in which Jemima's story ends and the thoroughness with which her tough attitude is reabsorbed into Maria's sentimentalism suggest that Wollstonecraft is not willing to consider seriously such a radical alternative to women's enslavement. For such a solution would entail renouncing not only the bourgeois institution of marriage, but also the romantic expectations that motivate Maria and, we must conclude, the narrator as well.

For, despite the strong suggestions that Maria's incorrigible romanticism is being presented ironically, despite Wollstonecraft's emphasis on the pernicious effects of sentimentalism, the narrator herself repeatedly lapses back into sentimental jargon and romantic idealism. At such moments, the theoretical wisdom of the narrator simply collapses into the longing of the character. These repeated collapses are characteristically marked by Wollstonecraft's insistence on semantic distinctions where substantial differences do not exist. 'The real affections of life,' Wollstonecraft comments in a typical passage, 'when they are allowed to burst forth, are buds pregnant with joy and all the sweet emotions of the soul. . . . The substantial happiness, which enlarges and civilizes the mind, may be compared to the pleasure experienced in roving through nature at large, inhaling the sweet gale natural to the clime' (143–44). Wollstonecraft wants happiness to be 'substantial,' 'real,' physically possible. But the explicitly metaphorical language she uses to depict that happiness ('buds pregnant with joy') calls attention only to the fictiveness, the literariness, the patent immateriality of this ideal. Despite her anxious assertions that such happiness is 'substantial' and that the 'real affections of life' and 'true sensibility' somehow differ from the romantic delusions that twice ensnare Maria, Wollstonecraft actually reveals only that her own ideals are insubstantial – figments, in fact, of the very romantic idealism they are meant to transcend.

Repeatedly, then, the narrator falls victim to the same sentimental idealism that cripples Maria. Wollstonecraft continues to cherish the belief that, by fidelity to personal feelings kept pure of the taint of self-interest and the 'grossness of sensuality,' an individual can express a sensibility 'true' in the metaphysical – and physical – sense of that word. And yet even Wollstonecraft knows that something is wrong. In the crucible of her novel, things just don't work out that way: Darnford's love is 'volatile,' Maria's happiness is less substantial than the bars of her madhouse cell. And the fiction that Wollstonecraft believed 'capable of producing an important effect' repeatedly threatens to fall out of grace and into just another sentimental novel.

Wollstonecraft is aware that there is a critical gap between the realism of her isolated political observations and the idealism of her sentimental paradigms. And, as if searching for an antidote for her own susceptibility, Wollstonecraft repeatedly aborts the sentimental structure of *Maria* in order to reassert her political purpose. At virtually every point at which the characters' stories begin to elicit the reader's identification, Wollstonecraft ruptures the narrative either by the interjection of non-dramatic political commentary, by simply severing the dramatic action, or by ejecting characters out of the novel altogether. The hiatuses in the novel are frequent and obtrusive – even in those chapters Godwin describes as finished. Yet these ruptures are not expressions of a telling ambivalence on Wollstonecraft's part toward sentimental *feeling*. Rather, they constitute one expression of a crisis in self-confidence not uncharacteristic of eighteenth-century women writers. Instead of questioning the validity of sentimental feeling, Wollstonecraft limits her suspicion to one particular aspect of feeling – the creative, self-expressive imagination.

According to sentimental theory, the imagination is a faculty whose characteristic activity is projection, both salutary and harmful. The imaginative projection of feeling, according to Adam Smith and David Hume, is the root of sympathy; yet the imaginative projection of desire, Dr. Johnson warned, is the heart of human vanity.[13] Because this latter propensity is so tied up with the former, the imagination is for Wollstonecraft a highly ambiguous faculty, the 'characteristic of genius,' on the one hand, the self-filled boudoir of desire, on the other. And, for her, *women's* imaginations are particularly suspect because women, lacking both personal experience and practical opportunities, are especially tempted to project their desires into fiction *instead* of into the real world. How many, Wollstonecraft wonders in *Maria*, of women's imaginings are vain – vain, not only in the sense of self-centered, but in the root sense of that word, *vanus*, empty, ineffectual?

Thus Wollstonecraft's ambivalence about feeling focuses most consistently on the very enterprise in which she, as an imaginative artist, is engaged. And this ambivalence about the creative imagination becomes both a theme of *Maria* and a repeated agitator of the narrative structure. Wollstonecraft is wary of the products of the creative imagination because she fears they will have the effect on readers that Rousseau's *Julie* has on Maria: engaging their readers' imaginations, fictions *dis*engage those readers from life; eliciting imaginative identification, they feed wishful fantasies instead of initiating political action. Wollstonecraft breaks off the various narratives of *Maria* at their most affecting moments at least partly because she senses that the narrative contract is drawing the reader into stories that are patently not true, and whose very aesthetic closure would artificially resolve whatever politically effective emotions the stories might arouse.

By the same token, Wollstonecraft is ambivalent about the process of imaginative creation. For women especially, this opportunity for self-expression is particularly tempting – but also particularly dangerous. For without political or economic opportunities to put their ideas into effect, women's imaginings threaten to become merely escapes from, not engagements with, reality. In the madhouse, both Maria and Darnford become artists, but while Darnford's compositions are primarily political, Maria becomes a sentimental writer. Her first compositions are 'rhapsodies descriptive of the state of her mind' (30–31), and, as she begins to compose her own history, she finds herself embarked on an escapist, sentimental journey: 'She lived again in the revived emotions of youth, and forgot her present in the retrospect of sorrows' (31).

Wollstonecraft shows, however, that such imaginative escape is really no escape at all. Maria's art is, in fact, an expression – perhaps even a cause – of her political impotence. The composition and effect of Maria's manuscript is virtually a paradigm of female sentimental authorship, with the writer confined in a prison of 'disproportioned' passion, the intended beneficiary (her absent daughter) cut off from the purported moral, and the major reader (Darnford) aroused by the story only to that 'transporting' passion with which he soon seduces Maria. Despite Maria's determination to plot a real escape, her schemes produce only this romantic – and escapist – narrative. Her liberation comes only at the instigation of Darnford's male guards, and, outside the madhouse, Maria remains completely ineffectual. Just as she had earlier been outschemed by the crafty George Venables (who is the novel's consummate artist, with the power to deploy as well as imagine plots), so Maria is now outdone by the obdurate masculine logic of the courts. In the last chapter of the novel, Maria is tried for adultery, but her written defense is as easily disposed of as any mere piece of paper. Feminine logic – the argument based on feeling – has no authority among the men who author laws with the patriarchal fiat of their all-powerful Word.

In this final chapter of the novel, Wollstonecraft – through Maria's written defense – attempts one last time to fuse 'purpose and structure,' to find a form which will betray neither her political insights nor her feeling heart. Whereas the preceding sixteen chapters, whether narrated in first or third person, tended to be dramatic narratives, and to highlight subjective responses, in this chapter Wollstonecraft tries to 'restrain [her] fancy,' to avoid such unreliable, because escapist, flights of the creative imagination. Here Wollstonecraft summarizes objective events rather than feelings in order to diminish the personal aspect of Maria's history, to specify those events which are the universal 'Wrongs of Woman.'

But Maria's final plea does not solve the problem of women's ineffectualness. For the heart of the problem is not, as Wollstonecraft supposed, finding the proper form of expression for the feeling heart. Rather, the real problem lies in the bourgeois concept of the autonomous feeling heart itself. Basically, all Maria's argument does is to privilege this feeling heart: she justifies her flight from Venables by an appeal to her own subjective judgment and urges the jury to consult their own feelings in deciding her case. Moreover, Maria's defense, for all its insight, simply strives to institutionalize feminine feeling as a new rationale for the old covenant of marriage. Even as she pleads for freedom from Venables, Maria calls Darnford her 'husband' and declares that what she really wants is only a new marriage in which to better fulfill 'the duties of a wife and mother' (148). We are not really surprised that Maria's attempt to generalize and institutionalize feeling has no effect on the court, for in her argument Wollstonecraft fails once more to take her own insights to their logical conclusions. Just as she turned from exploring the radical implications of Jemima's narrative, so Wollstonecraft now stops short of exposing the tyranny of the marriage contract itself. Instead, the defiant Mary Wollstonecraft clings to that bedrock of bourgeois society – the belief in individual feeling – and in so doing her fledgling voice hesitates, and finally falters into silence.

Wollstonecraft does not develop the hybrid form which might have fused 'purpose and structure' largely because she refuses to relinquish the values tied up with sentimental structure itself. But Wollstonecraft's dilemma was not unique. Indeed, it is only one example of a philosophical as well as a social problem that beleaguered men as well as women in the late eighteenth century. For the fundamental desire which makes her retain those values and which informs not only this work but all of Wollstonecraft's literary productions (and her turbulent life as well) is a longing to identify – or assert – a reliable relationship between phenomenal reality and that intimation of transcendent meaning which the imagination so doggedly, so teasingly, projects. Wollstonecraft's refusal to abandon the ideal of 'true sensibility,' in other words, even when recognizing that the romantic expectations endemic to such sensibility were agents of bourgeois tyranny, reflects her yearning for some connection between spiritual values and real, everyday experience. What might seem to us to be the artificial vocabulary of sentimentalism expresses – and attempts to satisfy – this longing. Wollstonecraft's sentimentalism, then, is another expression of what Hegel called the 'nostalgia for transcendence'; it constitutes one more desperate attempt to construct a myth of the autonomous self and of Presence – here, now, in this world. Although such may very well be the eternal aspiration of imaginative literature, the particular intensity of this longing at the end of the eighteenth century signals the inadequacies of empiricism and rationalism to fill the vacuum left by Enlightenment challenges to orthodox religion. Other contemporary literary expressions of the same desire include not only the novels of Richardson and Rousseau, but also the wishful conclusion of Johnson's 'Vanity of Human Wishes' and the entire aesthetic program of Wordsworth's natural supernaturalism.

The sentimental narrative, then, must be understood as more than just an effete sibling in the otherwise hardy literary lineage that includes Tom Jones and Huck Finn. Rather, the sentimental novel is a logical development of the secularized realistic novel: it is the cry for transcendent meaning in a profane world; it is social realism nostalgic for the absolutism of romance narratives. But by the end of the eighteenth century, the cultural quest which formed the nucleus of the first romances had become a quest of the individual heart, and the grail had become the private treasure of romantic love. Late-eighteenth-century sentimentalism, in other words, is the secular romance of individualism – and therein lies the dilemma. For in a society constituted upon *economic* individualism, upon marketplace competition, the feeling heart cannot compete with cash. And, even more critically, that myth of personal autonomy perpetuated by sentimentalism – like the myth of bourgeois individualism itself – tended to blind its adherents to the way in which the individual romance is 'written' by the social text of which it is, in fact, only one episode. Sentimentalism was no more an effective solution to the spiritual impoverishment of bourgeois society than it was to the continuing political and economic injustices of the class system. For to believe that an individual could achieve personal happiness within an enlightened marriage – as Maria and Wollstonecraft continue to do – was to ignore the systemic oppression integral to the legal and economic institution of eighteenth-century marriage. And to believe that, despite this institution, personal happiness could be hoarded up, like private property, within the storehouse of the human heart, was to underestimate the complex social and economic factors that delineated the opportunities for, even the forms of, happiness available. Maria's celebration of the 'humanizing affections' of the individual actually constitutes Wollstonecraft's retreat from that insight to which she was so close in *The Rights of Woman* – the recognition that the individual's 'situation,' his or her position within class, gender, economics, and history – really delimits freedom and effectively defines the 'self.'

No doubt the problem of sentimentalism loomed large for any late-eighteenth-century liberal (Rousseau is a case in point), but for women the dilemma was particularly acute. For women both had a special investment in sentimentalism and were its particular victims. Not only did the 'humanizing affections' theoretically natural to women and privileged by sentimentalism give the fair sex an important function in a society increasingly dominated by economic competition, but sentimentalism was also effectively the only genre in which women were allowed legitimate self-expression. A woman's only 'business,' as Wollstonecraft recognized in *The Rights of Woman,* was the 'business' of the heart; for her, sentiments constituted the only 'events.'[14]

The consequences of this social and cultural position were far-reaching indeed, for it set the stage for sentimentality's particular victimization of women. Instead of having access to the Enlightenment myth of self-determination, instead of having opportunities to 'make' themselves professionally, women were defined strictly by their sexuality. 'The male is only a male now and again,' as Rousseau phrased it; 'the female is always a female . . . ; everything reminds her of her sex. . . .'[15] Because women were so defined, they were actively encouraged to envision emotional and even spiritual fulfillment in sensual terms and yet, at the same time, because their sexuality had to be susceptible to the control of marriage, they were enjoined to sublimate, to desexualize, their literal sexuality into highly euphemistic terms. Bourgeois ideology simultaneously shackled women's aspirations to the fatal parabola of physical desire and denied them either free sexual self-expression or a cultural myth of female sexual transcendence. The fusion of 'self' with sexuality, in other words, enslaved a woman to the ineluctable fact that the apparently illimitable longing of physical desire inevitably finds death in satisfaction. And because female sexuality was not accorded the same symbolic significance that man's theoretically more abstract, less material sexuality has traditionally been granted, women were not encouraged to value even the momentary pleasure accorded by literal sexual self-expression. Indeed, given the restrictions placed upon the expression of female sexuality in eighteenth-century society, women were encouraged to view their sexuality as a function of *male* initiative, a response to present and future relationships, not as self-expression at all. This is the murderous paradox sentimental novels expounded for women in particular: they encouraged women to formulate both social definition and transcendent meaning only in sexual terms, yet they denied female sexuality autonomous, much less transcendent meaning.

The twist given female sexuality by bourgeois society is the heart of darkness Mary Wollstonecraft never identified. Yet it helps explain why sentimentalism was so appealing and so fatal to her as well as to many less thoughtful eighteenth-century women. Mary Wollstonecraft could not renounce 'true sensibility' because it was the only form her society allowed her to express either her sexuality or her craving for transcendent meaning. Yet retaining that form of expression – indeed, that self-definition – prohibited her from disentangling her femaleness from male institutions or control. And it also helps explain Wollstonecraft's self-contradictory presentation of sexuality in *Maria*. For, on the one hand, Wollstonecraft insists in this novel – to a degree remarkable for any eighteenth-century novelist – on the importance of female sexual expression. Yet, on the other hand, despite Wollstonecraft's insistence that sexual fulfillment is not only necessary but possible, every sexual relationship she depicts is explicitly dehumanizing and graphically revolting. Descriptions of sexuality are virtually the only descriptions in this novel with any degree of physical specificity, and they – like Venables' 'tainted breath, pimpled face, and blood-shot eyes' – suggest grotesqueness, violence, and contamination.

Wollstonecraft's own sexual betrayal by the American Gilbert Imlay might seem to explain her ambivalence toward sexuality, but the language of her tortured letters to Imlay indicates that Wollstonecraft's personal ambivalence was shaped by this distortion of sexuality by sentimentality which I have just described.[16] The problem, I think, was a general dilemma for women of this period. I want to suggest that the way in which sentimentalism, on the one hand, allowed female desire legitimate expression and, on the other, harnessed that expression to the prerogatives of bourgeois society, made it virtually impossible for a woman to disentangle her desire – whether it be the desire for sexual expression or creative expression – from the central assumptions and institutions of society. 'True sensibility' – and the sentimental genre that best expressed this feeling – was implicated at nearly every level in the values by which eighteenth-century society made and interpreted itself. And women, at the heart of the heart of those values, were the most bound and gagged of all society's prisoners.

Late-eighteenth-century moralists were virtually unanimous in pointing out both the appeal of the sentimental novel for women[17] and its dangers.[18] Certainly, the genre seems to have posed nearly insurmountable problems for most of its practitioners. Perhaps, in fact, the only effective way a woman who thought as well as felt could successfully deal with the problem of feeling was to satirize 'true sensibility,' as Jane Austen did in her juvenilia and in *Northanger Abbey*. The irony Austen was to perfect in her mature works can even be seen as a second and more sophisticated handling of feminine feeling, for the distance irony affords enables Austen to explore her characters' 'romantic expectations' – and delusions – without committing herself definitively to the same desires. Austen's relationship to bourgeois assumptions remains protectively opaque – implicitly critical in isolated phrases at the same time that the narrative privileging of marriage seems to ratify the central bourgeois institution.

Yet despite Austen's aesthetic 'solution' to what is really a cultural dilemma, Mary Wollstonecraft's frustration remains the characteristic gesture of a woman writer of her period. And we should not forget that hers was simply the first of many complaints about the inadequacies of genre to gender. In our own century, for example, Virginia Woolf dreamed of a 'play-poem' that could fuse the protective objectivity of drama with the expressive subjectivity of lyric.[19] And, nearer to Wollstonecraft's own day, the American Margaret Fuller lamented that 'for all the tides of life that flow within me, I am dumb and ineffectual, when it comes to casting my thoughts into a form. No old one suits me. . . . I love best to be a woman; but womanhood is at present too straightly-bound to give me scope.'[20] Too 'straightly-bound' by patriarchal definitions, Fuller might have added. And by the genres of feeling and self-expression that are women's legacy from the era of 'true sensibility.'

Notes

1. William Godwin, *Memoirs of Mary Wollstonecraft*, ed. W. Clark Durant (London and New York: Constable, 1927), p. 111.
2. Godwin states that Wollstonecraft believed the 'purpose and structure of the . . . work . . . capable of producing an important effect' (Preface to *Maria,*

or the Wrongs of Woman [New York: Norton, 1975], p. 5). Mitzi Myers also explores the difficulty Wollstonecraft had in reconciling purpose and structure in 'Unfinished Business: Wollstonecraft's *Maria*,' *The Wordsworth Circle*, 11, no. 2 (Spring 1980), pp. 107–114.

3. *Maria, or the Wrongs of Woman* (New York: Norton, 1975), pp. 7, 8. All future references, cited in the text, are to this edition.

4. Tony Tanner, *Adultery in the Novel: Contract and Transgression* (Baltimore: Johns Hopkins University Press, 1979), p. 15.

5. From Joseph Swetnam, *Araignment of Lewd, Idle, Froward, and vnconstant women*. Quoted by David J. Latt, 'Praising Virtuous Ladies: The Literary Image and Historical Reality of Women in Seventeenth-Century England,' in Marlene Springer, ed., *What Manner of Women: Essays on English and American Life and Literature* (New York: New York University Press, 1977), p. 43.

6. The standard discussion of this subject is H. J. Habakkuk, 'Marriage Settlements in the Eighteenth Century,' in *Transactions of the Royal Historical Society*, 32 (4th series) (London: Royal Historical Society, 1950).

7. *Émile*, tr. Barbara Foxley (New York: Dutton, Everyman, 1974), pp. 324–25. To Samuel Johnson, the transgression was equally serious. 'Consider,' Johnson advised Boswell, 'of what importance to society the chastity of women is. Upon that all the property in the world depends. We hang a thief for stealing a sheep; but the unchastity of a woman transfers sheep, and farm and all, from the right owner.' James Boswell, *Journal of a Tour to the Hebrides*, ed. Allan Wendt (Boston: Houghton Mifflin, Riverside, 1965), p. 250.

8. *The Earl of Rochester* (1680). Cited in Christopher Hill, *Milton and the English Revolution* (New York: Viking Press, 1977), p. 120.

9. Rousseau discusses this paradox in his *Letter to d'Alembert*.

10. The connection between the aroused imagination and aroused female sexuality is made explicit in the admonitions of eighteenth-century moralists against novel-reading. Thomas Gisborne, for example, describes the lust for novels as arising from and stimulating 'appetite': 'The appetite becomes too keen to be denied. . . . The contents of the circulating library, are devoured with indiscriminate and insatiable avidity. Hence the mind is secretly corrupted.' *An Enquiry into the Duties of the Female Sex* (1797; London: T. Cadell Jr. and W. Davies, 1799, 4th edn), pp. 228–29. Laetitia Hawkins makes the connection even more precise: sentimental novels, she claims, arouse the 'irrascible passions . . . miscalled *love*' and so threaten both self-control and moral order. *Letters on the Female Mind*, 2 vols. (London: Hookham and Carpenter, 1793), I, 42.

11. In his *Keywords: A Vocabulary of Culture and Society* (New York: Oxford University Press, 1976), Raymond Williams explains that the word *sentimental* was, throughout the eighteenth century, informed by its root affiliation with *sensible* and that it was closely associated with both *sensibility* and *sentiments*. 'The significant development in "sense" was the extension from a process to a particular kind of product: "sense" as good sense, good judgment, from which the predominant modern meaning of *sensible* was to be derived. . . . *Sensibility* in its C18 uses ranged from a use much like that of modern "awareness" (not only "consciousness" but "conscience") to a strong form of what the word appears literally to mean, the ability to feel. . . . The association of *sentimental* with *sensibility* was then close: a conscious openness to feelings, and also a conscious consumption of feelings." See *Keywords*, pp. 235–38.

12. *A Vindication of the Rights of Woman* (1792; New York: Norton, 1975), pp. 60–61. The ambivalence toward sentimentalism is also discussed by R. F. Brissenden, *Virtue in Distress* (New York: Harper and Row, 1974).

13. As David Hume describes sympathy, it depends upon imaginative projection: 'We have no such extensive concern for society but from sympathy; and consequently, 'tis that principle, which takes us so far out of ourselves, as to give us the same pleasure or uneasiness in the character of others, as if they had a tendency to our own advantage or loss.' *A Treatise of Human Nature*, ed. Ernest Mossner (1739 and 1740; Middlesex, England: Penguin, 1969), p. 630. See also Johnson's 'Vanity of Human Wishes.'

14. *The Rights of Woman*, p. 183.

15. *Émile*, p. 324. Lovelace, in Richardson's *Clarissa*, underscores this definition when he refers to women simply as 'the sex, the sex.'

16. A passage from one of Wollstonecraft's letters to Imlay will suffice. 'Yes, these are emotions, over which satiety has no power, and the recollection of which, even disappointment cannot disenchant; but they do not exist without self-denial. These emotions, more or less strong, appear to me to be the distinctive characteristic of genius, the foundation of taste, and of that exquisite relish for the beauties of nature, of which the common herd of eaters and drinkers and *child-begetters*, certainly have no idea. You will smile at an observation that has just occurred to me: – I consider those minds as the most strong and original, whose imagination acts as the stimulus to their senses.' *Collected Letters of Mary Wollstonecraft*, ed. Ralph Wardle (Ithaca: Cornell University Press, 1979), p. 291. In the last sentence of this passage, Wollstonecraft transfers the impetus of sexual excitation to the imagination in order to rob physical stimulation of its devastating primacy. But such a transfer comes close to purifying 'love' of its physical component altogether.

17. The appeal of these novels is graphically conveyed by Hannah More: 'Such is the frightful facility of this species of composition, that every raw girl, while she reads, is tempted to fancy that she can also write. . . . And as Corregio, on first beholding a picture which exhibited the perfection of the Graphic art, prophetically felt all his own future greatness, and cried out in rapture, "And I too am a painter!" so a thorough paced novel-reading Miss, at the close of every tissue of hackney'd adventures, feels within herself the stirring impulse of corresponding genius, and triumphantly exclaims, "And I too am an author!" The glutted imagination soon overflows with the redundance of cheap sentiment and plentiful incident, and by a sort of arithmetical proportion, is enabled by the perusal of any three novels, to produce a fourth; till every fresh production, like the progeny of Banquo, is followed by

    Another, and another, and another!'

    Strictures on the Modern System of Female Education, 2nd edn, 2 vols. (London: T. Cadell Jr. and W. Davies, 1799), I, 185.

18. Hannah More is equally eloquent on the danger of sentimental novels. Such works, she argues, 'teach, that character is only individual attachment; that no duty exists that is not prompted by feeling; that impulse is the main spring of virtuous actions, while law and religion are only unjust restraints.' *Strictures*, I, 35–36.

19. Virginia Woolf, *A Writer's Diary*, ed. Leonard Woolf (New York: Harcourt Brace, 1953; Signet edn), p. 134.

20. Quoted in Sandra M. Gilbert and Susan Gubar, *The Madwoman in the Attic: The Woman Writer and the Nineteenth-Century Literary Imagination* (New Haven: Yale University Press, 1979), p. 71.

Part VII

Godwin

11 Rhetoric, History, Rebellion: *Caleb Williams* and the Subversion of Eighteenth-Century Fiction

Donald R. Wehrs

In this essay on Godwin's *Caleb Williams*, Donald Wehrs takes issue with Marxist theorists such as Terry Eagleton and Frank Lentricchia (who has since abjured the position he occupied in this essay). Eagleton and Lentricchia represent political critics who propose dyadic oppositions between formal reading and historical criticism, as well as oppositions between hegemonic and counter-hegemonic literature. Partly by appealing to Hans Robert Jauss's reception theory, Wehrs makes a doubly corrective claim: the opposition between rhetorical and historical reading is false; and when we look carefully at Godwin's novel, we find that the relation between hegemonic and counter-hegemonic forces is internally dialectical. Godwin pits empirical and romantic modes of eighteenth-century narrative against each other, revealing the internally conflicted nature of late eighteenth-century ideology, and registering his own ambivalence about the revolutionary option.

Much recent literary theory argues that critics, faced with the complicity of Western literature in false values and baneful social practices, must choose between the alternatives of, as Frank Lentricchia puts it, working 'on behalf of a dominant hegemony by reinforcing habits of thought and feeling that help to sustain ruling power' or working 'counter-hegemonically as a violator, in an effort to dominate and to re-educate' by revealing 'naturalized conventions' to be 'all bourgeois encrustations of consciousness.'[1] The value of counter-hegemonic criticism may be questioned by examining Godwin's *Caleb Williams*. Written by a committed radical, *Caleb Williams* represents the consequences of rebellion while being itself a sustained act of rebellion against the norms and 'lessons' of eighteenth-century fiction. By probing the inconsistencies of Falkland's 'official' story – a story that follows the conventional patterns of eighteenth-century 'realistic' novels – Caleb resists Falkland's domination by means of a form of 'counterhegemonic' criticism, but the freedom he gains remains strangely illusory. Instead of achieving spiritual independence, Caleb grows to identify with his persecutor/victim and ends by doubting the propriety of resistance. Both internally, as a vehicle for persuading readers of certain positions, and externally, as an event in literary history, *Caleb Williams* challenges central premises underlying current 'political criticism.'[2]

Like many contemporary Western Marxists, Lentricchia insists that any critical stance is always already a political stance while rejecting the base/superstructure model underlying traditional Marxism.[3] His position does not depend upon 'Marxism or any other philosophy rest[ing] on the foundations of reality or history' (p. 12). Instead, Marxist theory 'is itself a kind of rhetoric whose value may be measured by its persuasive means and by its ultimate goal: the formation of genuine community' (pp. 12–13). Justifying Marxism through its abstract goal, Lentricchia makes the experience of Marxist government irrelevant to the theory's truth as rhetoric.

One might reply to Lentricchia by recalling Edmund Burke: 'Abstractly speaking, government, as well as liberty, is good; yet could I, in common sense, ten years ago have felicitated France on her enjoyment of a government . . . without enquiry what the nature of that government was . . . ? Can I now congratulate the same nation upon its freedom?'[4] Burke's observations bear upon the 'persuasive means' of a goal of 'genuine community' because the power of such rhetoric cannot be evaluated apart from the history of such rhetoric. Both Lentricchia and Eagleton distinguish rhetorical from formalist criticism, but to the extent that the effectiveness of rhetorical modes is viewed separately from the history of their effects, rhetorical analysis becomes formalism. Lentricchia's determination to keep Marxism as 'rhetoric' isolated from 'reflectionist' theories leads him to neglect historically created imperatives to get beyond pleasant abstractions (who wants an un-genuine community?) if, after the French Revolution, a rhetoric of radical social change is to be persuasive. In its portrayal of rebellion, *Caleb Williams* challenges Lentricchia's rhetorical justification for counter-hegemonic activity at the same time that it undercuts his theory of rebellion.

Lentricchia argues that '[o]ur identities are very nearly hopelessly complicated . . . by a hegemonic process that would enroll us in a range of corporate identities, some concentric, others in conflict,' but nonetheless, the 'shifting forces of hegemonic authority' are pregnant with 'structural instability' because every age is 'transitional' and because language is intrinsically 'undecidable' (pp. 78–80). If freedom lies in resistance to cultural formation, then literature, by promoting a sense of cultural continuity, abets hegemony. But a pedagogy designed to neutralize influence by historicizing text and critic risks producing de-historicized students, students who find cynicism and indifference preferable to what Foucault calls 'the endlessly repeated play of dominations.'[5] Sensing the danger of a quietism he associates with Paul de Man, Lentricchia insists that counter-hegemonic criticism should call attention to 'the historically stubborn story of resistance, whose marks continue to be made within those very mechanisms that reproduce existing, stratified power relations' (p. 143). However, Godwin's novel suggests that the division of literature into two opposed traditions is no more tenable than the segregation of rhetoric from history. Revealing the *literary* origins of Caleb's rebellion, Godwin delineates an interplay between literature's twin roles as 'story of resistance' and enforcer of 'sociocultural conservation and continuity' (p. 140); similarly, the rebellion of Godwin's novel against the generic tradition it inherits is inseparable from fidelity to the forms and values inscribed within that tradition.

Before turning to *Caleb Williams*, we must consider the objection that to use a novel to evaluate the assertions of a literary theory is to compare apples and oranges. Such an objection assumes that while a novel and theory may consider a common subject – in this case, the origin and consequences of rebellion – their claims belong to different spheres, to literature in the first case and life in the second. But the isolation of literature from life, the relegation of the former to 'pseudo-statements,' is precisely what rhetorical criticism rejects. Godwin's novel, no less than Lentricchia's theory, seeks to persuade readers through distinct rhetorical modes. It is my argument that those modes are shaped by and gain efficacy through their historicity.

When Caleb, fascinated by Falkland's brooding, inconsistent conduct, asks the steward Collins for an explanation, he receives a story that follows the conventions, echoes the themes, and re-stages scenes familiar to any reader of Richardson, Fielding, Goldsmith, and Burney. Falkland's story, taking up the first third of Godwin's novel, is 'official' in several senses: put forth for public consumption, it has been sanctioned by universal assent; woven from patterns typical to eighteenth-century fiction, it draws upon previously established traditions of interpretation; the story is thrice attenuated from a speaker (Caleb recounts in the third person Collins's account of Falkland's account). However, once Caleb begins, in the manner of a counter-hegemonic critic, to question the 'official' version, he places in doubt the 'naturalized conventions' that underlie Falkland's representation of himself.

But deconstruction alone does not foster successful rebellion. Though Caleb discovers the fraudulence of eighteenth-century fictional norms as they operate in Falkland's 'cover story,' he cannot conceive of his own 'story' in their absence. Godwin pursues, through Caleb's 'memoirs,'[6] a deconstruction similar to his hero's, exposing the unwillingness of eighteenth-century 'realistic' fiction to trace the 'practical effects' of 'the existing constitution of society'[7] by writing a novel that shows the 'true' consequences of social circumstances reversing and rendering ironically implausible the standard patterns of fiction from Richardson to Burney. Just as Falkland's descent from nobility to murder inverts *Sir Charles Grandison*, so Caleb's story, orginally conceived as a tale of persecution and pursuit ending in the hero's madness, reverses the 'virtue rewarded' scheme of *Pamela*.[8] However, the novel's irony toward novels emerges from its generic consistency, from its insistence that novels should really present the true, unadulterated consequences of actual conditions. Godwin's revolt, like Caleb's, never moves beyond dependence upon what it reveals to be duplicitous: *Caleb Williams* remains an anti-eighteenth-century novel that is not yet a nineteenth-century novel.

Falkland's 'official' story corresponds to distinct fictional conventions. However opportune, the apparently 'chance' murder of Falkland's adversary, Squire Tyrrel, stands within a tradition of 'providential' resolutions for the heroes of eighteenth-century novels, extending from Mr. B.'s proposal of marriage to Mr. Burchell's transformation into Sir William Thornhill. After seemingly intractable problems, grounded in social circumstances, are placed before a protagonist, and after the protagonist bears up under their weight, the problems simply disappear through sudden conversions (Mr. Square's repentence), the discovery of mistaken identity (Joseph Andrews, young Wilson in *Humphry Clinker*), or strokes of fortune (Lord Orville proposes to Evelina; Amelia recovers her stolen inheritance). Falkland intends, as a young gentleman of means early imbued by his 'favorite authors' with 'the love of chivalry and romance' (p. 10), to use his privileged social position to cultivate politeness, inspire rectitude, and render moral service. In effect, he expects to imitate Sir Charles Grandison. As with Grandison, his generosity and nobility bring him the respectful affection of all his country neighbors – except Squire Tyrrel. Ignorant and boorish, Tyrrel enjoys local pre-eminence through his mastery of 'horseflesh . . . , shooting, fishing and hunting' (p. 17) before he is challenged by someone who, through a 'transvaluation of values,' shifts the basis of merit from the manly arts to the practice of civility and magnanimity.

When Tyrrel's dependent niece conceives an infatuation for Falkland, he seeks to punish her for admiring 'modern' virtues by forcing her to marry 'the uncouth and half-civilised animal' Grimes (p. 47). Tyrrel re-creates the situation of *Clarissa*, but with a difference. Instead of pursuing wealth through coerced wedlock, he seeks, much in the manner of Lovelace, ideological vindication: by proving the superiority of force and pride upon the body of his niece, Tyrrel can enforce a 'story' that will expose the inefficacy of Falkland's values and hence undermine the basis of his character. As with the conflict between Mr. B. and Pamela, Lovelace and Clarissa, the fate of the body is important not for its own sake, but because it provides an index for evaluating the claims of competing worldviews; its destiny discloses the judgment of 'real experience' or Providence upon the assertions of contradictory sets of words. After Falkland's opportune appearance foils Grimes's attempted rape of Emily, Tyrrel imprisons the girl on a trumped-up charge of owing him back rent. Up to this point, Falkland has been able to translate his moral notions into effective action. Just as the approbation he receives recalls similar praise lavished upon Sir Charles Grandison, so his chance rescue of Emily very nearly repeats the circumstances of Sir Charles's rescue of Harriet Byron: in both cases, the young lady struggles against a seducer in a carriage on a lonely road when the hero happens to ride within earshot. Even Tyrrel's imprisonment of Emily repeats a pattern already encoded in eighteenth-century fiction: Lady Booby finds legal means to persecute Joseph in Book IV of *Joseph Andrews*; Squire Thornhill imprisons the Primroses in *The Vicar of Wakefield*.

Whereas Lentricchia makes rebellion contingent upon finding an 'oppositional' story embedded within the 'official' one, Godwin makes the principles implicit in eighteenth-century fiction the source of his critique. By tracing the 'realistic' consequences of legal corruption, Fielding and Goldsmith reveal the 'practical effects' of the 'existing constitution of society' to be unsavory indeed; but instead of pursuing those 'effects' to their logical conclusion, they arrest the implications of their own stories: the accidental discovery of Joseph's true birth frees him from Lady Booby's persecutions; when Mr. Burchell resumes his identity as Squire Thornhill's powerful, benevolent uncle, he rights the wrongs done the Vicar's family. More than faint-heartedness is involved in the eighteenth-century novel's oscillation between realistic circumstances and romance resolutions. The novel would, on the one hand, derive its 'truth' from mimetic accuracy and probable causation, limiting itself to 'natural Means' of sparing the hero lest 'the Truth and Dignity of History' be violated;[9] on the other hand, it would have 'happy endings' reveal a providential guidance or moral logic at odds with immoral probabilities. By freeing the Primroses, Sir William Thornhill institutes essential justice despite social realities; Amelia's rescue from the degradations of London through an unexpected inheritance suggests an *ultimate* rewarding of virtue, even though the dark public world Fielding presents provides little reason to expect one. Godwin exposes the inconsistency of conflating the facts of this world and the principles of a better one by pointedly refusing to dilute the tragic potential of real conditions. Emily contracts a fever and dies in jail before Falkland can save her. Since Falkland 'places' himself within the norms of eighteenth-century fiction, the violation of those norms by Emily's death cannot but threaten his very being: 'He burst away from the spot with a vehemence, as if he sought to leave behind him his recollection and his existence . . . [H]e could not prevent himself from reproaching the system of nature, for having given birth to such a monster as Tyrrel' (pp. 89–80). Tyrrel's success in frustrating Falkland's good intentions suggests that the 'truth' of ordinary experience and the 'truth' of a providential order do not converge in fact, however they may in fiction; if eighteenth-century novels are broken, inconsistent narratives, then the exemplary character Falkland has sought by 'assiduously conform[ing] to [a] model of heroism' (p. 10) might prove illusory and ineffectual.

His fears seem confirmed when, shortly after Emily's death, Tyrrel brazenly enters an assembly. Falkland delivers an eloquent rebuke that forces the villain to retreat in confusion. Tyrrel's embarrassment recalls Mr. B.'s similar embarrassment when challenged by Pamela's articulation of inner nobility. The retreat of vice before virtue, 'full of wildness and horror' (p. 95), suggests that experience really does confirm moral values. But, in an act equivalent to Mr. B. raping Pamela despite her moral superiority, Tyrrel returns, surprises Falkland with a blow, and thrashes him publicly. The assault fuses generic and political implications. By refusing to play under Falkland's rules, Tyrrel reveals the vulnerability of civility to barbarism, underlining, with his fists, the gap between rhetorical power and practical effect.

Once the 'story' Falkland encounters suggests that an eighteenth-century hero may be an imaginary social-linguistic construct, he first longs 'for annihilation, to lie down in eternal oblivion' (p. 98) and then murders Tyrrel in a moment of blind rage. Yet, by constructing an eighteenth-century 'official' version of the event, shifting responsibility for the plot resolution to a convenient third party (Hawkins and son), he would ask others to acknowledge a self he knows to be illusory. Falling back on Tyrrel's methods, Falkland reveals the presence of Tyrrel's instincts within himself as well as the dependence of civilized values upon force in order to prevail. Falkland loses the ability to seek confirmation of his character in the implications of events once he falsifies events to fit a character. In a manner typical of much eighteenth-century fiction, Falkland's story arrests the consequences of the action artificially: he is 'baffled of the vengeance' he would have sought because Tyrrel happens, by chance, to turn up dead immediately after the beating (p. 88).

Whereas the incongruence between realism and romance in Fielding and Richardson reflects genuine opposing conceptions of truth (one based on observation, the other on faith), by the time of Goldsmith and Burney, generic tension dissipates as the inconsistencies of form become conventional. Falkland's 'official' story resembles the subplot of Burney's *Camilla*. Eugenia, a wealthy maiden deformed by smallpox, is kidnapped and forced into marriage by the fortune-hunter Bellamy. While she refuses to 'lower' herself by annulling the marriage, Bellamy plans to extort her family's fortune. Burney resolves the tension between ideal conduct and its practical effects by having Bellamy accidentally shoot himself. The tale Falkland constructs fits the Goldsmith–Burney mold; it is a type of story whose inner inconsistencies and blurred implications reveal less the conflict between two notions of truth than a strained effort to convince others, through worn conventions, of what one can no longer believe oneself.

As Caleb broods upon the story, probing its points of divergence from eighteenth-century norms, its seeming self-evidence grows 'mysterious' (p. 107). The apparent murderers, tenants mistreated by Tyrrel, hardly fit their roles: 'So firm, so sturdily honest and just, as [Hawkins and son] appeared at first; all at once to become . . . murderer[s]!' (p. 107). Tyrrel's convenient death, instead of resolving matters in the hero's favor, leaves Falkland tormented by 'agonies and terrors' (p. 107). Just as Falkland's efforts to oppose Tyrrel's disruption of his 'story' lead him, ironically, to supersede the norms that he would have circumscribe his character, so Caleb's effort to assimilate Falkland's story to a familiar discursive field leads, ironically, to his own estrangement from that field. Instead of rebellion being explicable, as in Lentricchia, only in terms of unstable cultural formation or the 'undecidability' of language, it arises in *Caleb Williams* from the struggle to maintain a form of life and belief. Falkland seeks to erase any ironic gap between experience and the conceptions of self and world he derives from literature. But Tyrrel's murder reinforces the very irony it would abrogate by increasing the distance between self-projection and actuality, between rules of formation and the realities they would order. Caleb's rebellion assumes, ironically, a similar pattern.

Just as Godwin subjects eighteenth-century fiction to irony by adhering to one of its principles (truth derived from observation) at the expense of another (truth as providential order), so Caleb deconstructs Falkland's story by demanding that it achieve the 'realistic consistency' it pretends to. Caleb's rebellion, no less than Falkland's, rests upon a 'self' constituted by eighteenth-century norms. As Falkland expects reality to translate virtue into effective action, Caleb expects reality to reward intellectual inquiry with certain knowledge: 'I could not rest till I had acquainted myself with the solutions that had been invented for the phenomena of the universe' (p. 4). His love of 'natural philosophy' is allied with 'an invincible attachment to books of narrative and romance'; in both he seeks principles that make meaningful sense of experience. Godwin traces the conservative impulse in rebellion, the desire to maintain a form of belief and self-projection through rendering its implications consistent with itself and with external experience.

But Caleb's pursuit of truth and consistency is complicated by a compulsive, pervasive delight that, as with Falkland's susceptibility to instinctual violence, places the character's actions outside his ability to explain them: 'I remembered . . . [Falkland's] terrible looks; and the recollection gave a kind of tingling sensation, not altogether unallied to enjoyment. The farther I advanced, the more the sensation was irresistible' (pp. 107–108). From sadistic games of reminding his master of the murder, Caleb proceeds to reading Falkland's correspondence and breaking into his private trunk. He accuses himself of acting 'contrary to every received principle of civilized society . . . [by] trampling on the established boundaries of obligation' (pp. 137–38). Paradoxically, even as the abstract good of 'truth' leads him into guilt and self-estrangement, Caleb's rebellion remains grounded in admiration and solicitude: 'I feel that my soul yearns for [Falkland's] welfare. . . . I had known [him] from the first as a beneficent divinity' (pp. 137–38).

Jauss's reception theory, not Lentricchia's oppositional criticism, clarifies the connection between admiration and rebellion. Arguing that ideological critics ignore art's 'communicative function,'[10] Jauss maintains that aesthetic communication balances identification and distance: total distance engenders mere curiosity about the 'other'; uncritical identification permits ideological (de)formation. Caleb's freedom of judgment emerges from, and is retained by, viewing Falkland aesthetically, as a hero. Only to the extent that Caleb identifies with Falkland's desire to 'conform . . . to [a particular] model of heroism' (p. 10), only to the extent that he shares Falkland's hope of experiencing life as a consistent story, does his critical sense gain focus. Its historical specificity invests his rebellion with a shape of its 'own': by attempting to replace a defective story with the 'true' one, Caleb would shore up the eighteenth-century norms that Falkland's inconsistencies threaten.

As Caleb's rebellion grows out of admiration, so his actions repeat, inadvertently, Falkland's and his story becomes, like his master's, an ironic subversion of the historical norms his identity demands. Falkland could describe Tyrrel's murder in the terms Caleb employs for describing his forcing open Falkland's trunk: 'In the high tide of boiling passion I had overlooked all consequences. . . . I have always been at a loss to account for my having plunged thus headlong into an act so monstrous. There is something in it of unexplained and involuntary sympathy' (p. 133). Since, at critical moments of transgression, Caleb and Falkland share with Tyrrel a blind, 'involuntary' impulsiveness, their degree of guilt is blurred in a way that makes problematic the relation between an event and its interpretation. Godwin moves, in Caleb's story, from exposing the incongruence between the eighteenth-century novel's dual sources of truth (observation and faith) to challenging the notion that truth may be drawn from observation; in doing so, he undermines the 'character' that Caleb hopes his discourse will 'justify.'

Godwin displays, in *Political Justice*, faith in the irresistible force of truth strangely juxtaposed with skepticism about the ability to determine truth in particular cases.[11] On the one hand, the natural self-validation of truth renders violent revolution unnecessary: 'Who ever saw an instance in which error unaided by power was victorious over truth? . . . Has the mind of man the capacity to choose falsehood and reject truth, when her evidence is fairly presented?'[12] On the other hand, Godwin argues that '[n]o two crimes were ever alike; and therefore the reducing them . . . to general classes . . . is [as] absurd' as making punishment proportionate to a 'degree of delinquency' that 'can never be discovered.'[13] But how can a character prove his merit if the evaluation of individual acts becomes uncertain? Moreover, if an individual's conduct is shaped by outer circumstances and 'involuntary' compulsions, how can one distinguish between deeds that display character and deeds that disclose its (de)formation? While Caleb would justify himself through the self-validation of a realistic story, Godwin's novel portrays truth as neither irresistible nor certain – nor is its diffusion necessarily moral.

Like Falkland, Caleb expects his story to adhere to rules of formation derived from eighteenth-century fiction. His 'memoirs' should vindicate the writer by having 'that consistency, which is seldom attendant but upon truth' (p. 3). Caleb would reduce his life to the morally unequivocal pattern of pursuit by an enemy 'inaccesible to intreaties and untired in persecution,' a persecution his intrinsic character has 'not deserved' (p. 3). From Pamela and Clarissa on, the distresses of eighteenth-century novelistic heroes and heroines arise from misrecognition. Were Pamela and Clarissa known for what they are, they would have no stories; the evidence of their letters justifies them by showing the ironic gap between how they are perceived and how they are 'really.' For this reason, reading Pamela's journal converts Mr. B. to virtue and Clarissa's letters enforce her posthumous vindication. In *Northanger Abbey* Catherine Morland is possessed by feelings 'rather natural than heroic'[14] when, instead of allowing the Tilneys to misconstrue her character, she immediately explains how the Thorpes tricked her into missing their intended walk. Placing himself inside inherited generic norms, Caleb assumes that his 'meaning no ill' will eventually be transparent to others, keeping any one from being 'seriously angry' with him (p. 108). After he has goaded Falkland into confessing the 'truth' and his attempt to flee his master's oppressive surveillance ends with arrest on a false charge, Caleb expects to be vindicated by a simple relation of the truth: 'Innocence and guilt were, in my apprehension, the things . . . most opposite to each other. I would not suffer to believe, that the former could be confounded with the latter. . . . Virtue rising superior to every calumny, defeating by a plain, unvarnished tale all the strategems of vice . . . was one of the favourite subjects of my youthful reveries' (p. 180).

Having driven Falkland from the refuge of an inconsistent, selfcontradictory Goldsmith–Burney story, Caleb hopes to 'locate' himself within a typical eighteenth-century 'plain, unvarnished tale' of persecution and victimization. Godwin suggests that the dissemination of particular values (in this case, the values encoded in the norms of eighteenth-century fiction) fosters criticism and revolt by constituting specific patterns of identification, specific modes of emulation: Caleb suspects Falkland's 'official' story because it inadequately answers the requirements of the novelistic tradition; he seeks first to construct a 'better' version of Falkland's story and then to construct his own story as an exemplary – and hence convincing – realization of eighteenth-century fiction's assumptions. Caleb's independence of judgment emerges not from instabilities in cultural formation, but from his insistence that inherited norms and principles be realized consistently and universally.

Up to a point, his experience, like Falkland's, seems to confirm the pattern it would realize: he *is* persecuted and misrecognized. After hearing Falkland's charge of robbery, Caleb's old friend Thomas will not listen to his explanation: 'For your sake, lad, I will never take any body's word, nor trust to appearances, tho' it should be an angel' (p. 176). When Caleb applies to an 'amiable old man' for protection, he receives a favorable hearing until he divulges his name, at which the old man retreats in horror (p. 249). In Godwin's original ending, Caleb was to continue the victim of everybody's faith in Falkland's lies until, imprisoned once again, he was to go mad from despair of ever being believed. The 'existing constitution of society' would produce an ironic anti-*Pamela*, leaving intrinsic merit and innocence forever misrecognized and slandered.

Though Godwin retains his indictment of society, Caleb's simple persecution–victim scheme grows increasingly suspect as real persecution and paranoia blend together, bringing Caleb to declare, 'I could almost have imagined that I was the sole subject of general attention, and that the whole world was in arms to exterminate me' (p. 238). Both Caleb's ability to discern truth and the capacity of events to yield univocal interpretation become questionable. His rebellion and insistent distinction between himself and 'the other' notwithstanding, Caleb's fugitive's life resembles Falkland's experience after murdering Tyrrel: either might observe, 'My life was all a lie. I had a counterfeit character to support. . . . I was not free to indulge, no not one, honest sally of the soul' (pp. 255–58). Even the reality of Falkland's persecution grows murky. Released from prison because Falkland fails to appear against him, Caleb later hears his master declare, 'Were you so stupid and undistinguishing as not to know that the presevation of your life was the uniform object of my exertions?' (p. 281). Rendering uncertain the extent to which Falkland's persecution is magnified by Caleb's paranoia, showing Caleb repeat Falkland's 'story' unawares, Godwin creates a narrative that transgresses the rules of formation upon which Caleb's 'character' depends. Indeed, the complexities that subject Caleb's conception of his story and himself to irony also render his pursuit of 'truth' morally ambiguous.

Falkland challenges the 'merit' of allowing any abstract good to determine conduct: 'Is truth . . . entitled to adoration for its own sake . . . ? Will a reasonable man sacrifice to barren truth, where benevolence [and] humanity . . . require that it should be superseded?' (p. 282). While Falkland is, of course, implicated by his own guilty secret, the honest, simple people Caleb meets reinforce his Burkean point. After Laura, an exemplary, charitable country woman, learns of Caleb's reputation, she refuses to hear his 'true' story: 'The good man and the bad, are characters precisely opposite, not characters distinguished . . . by imperceptible shades. The Providence that rules us all, has not permitted us to be left without a clue in the most important of all questions' (pp. 299–300). Collins elaborates on the harm Caleb's 'truth' might do: 'If you could change all my ideas, and show me that there was no criterion by which vice might be prevented from being mistaken for virtue, what benefit would arise from that?' (p. 310). Though Falkland is a murderer, and bringing murder to light is good in the abstract, the practical effects of revealing this particular truth make its disclosure potentially criminal. Collins notes, 'If you even succeed in perplexing my understanding, you will not succeed in enlightening it. . . . Meanwhile for the purchase of this uncertainty I must sacrifice all the remaining comfort of my life' (p. 310).

While Lentricchia may be confident of the rhetorical efficacy of the abstract goal of 'genuine community,' Godwin's novel suggests that by 1794 such modes of persuasion were already suspect. Subjecting their expectations to irony, the events Falkland and Caleb encounter make dubious the prospect of reducing polyvalent experience to univocal patterns; by emphasizing the difficulty of inferring an interpretation from events, Godwin implies that the inherence of ambiguity and unexpectedness in actual experience renders equivocal and potentially reprehensible conduct that abstract idealism would seem to vindicate. Their efforts to realize selfprojections bring Falkland and Caleb to confront 'surprises' (Tyrrel's attack, Falkland's ambiguous persecution–solicitude) which in turn disclose 'surprise' inner depths (Falkland's murderous instincts, Caleb's abiding devotion to his compromised master) that place each character outside the 'self' he would vindicate. Making surprise part of 'a more profound principle of order' that 'frustrate[s] . . . expectations modeled on older conventions,'[15] the very form of Godwin's novel encodes suspicion of a rhetoric that would make an abstract goal the justification of radical action. Not only do Falkland and Caleb harm others, imposing death, injustice, and incertitude in futile efforts to retain selves their stories have already repudiated, they remain locked into the same Lacanian 'imaginary' however much events subject it to irony.[16]

Caleb Williams begins with the intent of exposing the frauds of eighteenth-century fiction but ends by questioning the moral consequences of unmasking them for the sake of abstract 'truth.' The rewritten conclusion, in which Caleb, moved by Falkland's sad decrepitude, changes his intended accusation into a self-accusation only to have Falkland so 'penetrated' by 'grief and compunction' (p. 323) that he announces his own guilt, has often been seen as an example of the selfless morality Godwin urges in *Political Justice*.[17] It might also be viewed as the vindication of 'a plain, unvarnished tale' after all. But Falkland's confession, no less than Caleb's selfaccusation, exchanges one feverishly unreliable reading of events for another. When Caleb declares, 'I proclaim to all the world that Mr. Falkland is a man worthy of affection and kindness, and that I am myself the basest and most odious of mankind!' (p. 323), his 'sincerity' provokes an equally extreme assertion by Falkland: 'My name will be consecrated to infamy, while your heroism, your patience and your virtues will be for ever admired' (p. 324).

Caleb and Falkland would see themselves as villains rather than allow ambiguity of conduct and responsibility to set them outside eighteenth-century fiction's range of 'the true.'[18] No more willing than Laura and Collins to recognize as 'truth' the problematic implications of Godwin's story, both expect moral clarity from experience and believe – as good eighteenth-century readers – that stories are about the 'vindication of character,' describing either triumphant virtue (Grandison, Amelia) or the gradual recognition of misjudged merit (Pamela, Tom Jones, Primrose, Evelina). To the extent that Godwin portrays outer circumstances and inner compulsions shaping individuality, he anticipates the nineteenth-century novel's concern with character formation.[19] But since Caleb and Falkland place themselves within eighteenth-century norms, they experience vulnerability to 'involuntary' forces as a terrifying lack of autonomy; once their stories fail to affirm the presence of 'intrinsic merit,' being unable to imagine any other basis for character, they are left with none. Caleb concludes his self-justifying 'memoir' by confessing, 'I began . . . with the idea of vindicating my character. I have now no character that I wish to vindicate' (p. 328).

Linked by a common incapacity to imagine any transformation of self that is not a subjugation or annihilation of self, Caleb and Falkland struggle to enclose daily experience within specific rules of formation, to prevent events from casting doubt on certain interpretative models, in part to secure themselves against the threat of change. There is something ultimately reactionary in their resistance to the challenge posed by other people and unanticipated events to the 'stories' they would realize, as though experience could be kept from 'surprising' an established perspective with new circumstances or contrary viewpoints. In the readiness of Falkland and Caleb to condemn themselves in terms of the eighteenth-century novel's rules of formation (rather than acknowledge the inadequacy of those terms), there is a foretaste of the dread of change and uncertainty that Nadezhda Mandelstam found lurking within abstract revolutionary idealism: 'People had been promised that all change was at an end, and further changes were inadmissible. . . . Let time stand still. The stopping of time means peace and stability. They need it so much, the leaders of our age.'[20]

The rhetorical force of Godwin's novel is inseparable from its historicity. Just as Caleb's resistance to Falkland is shaped by his identification with distinct cultural-linguistic norms, so the persuasiveness *for us* of Godwin's portrait of moral revolt degenerating into 'involuntary' tyranny does not simply rest upon its obvious affinities with the Orc cycle and Byronic Prometheanism. Rather, the ambivalence towards rebellion encoded in the form of *Caleb Williams* enters, at a historical moment that Blake, Byron, and Godwin demarcate, the realm of literary expression in response to specific interactions between rhetoric and history in the 'real world' (namely, the French Revolution). Falkland and Caleb attempt to evade their historicity by seeking to render an inherited worldview free from the revision and challenge of particular experience. Similarly, a criticism that would isolate rhetorical analysis from the interplay between history and rhetoric would not historicize literature, but shield itself from the 'subversive' potential implicit in historicity.

Notes

1. Frank Lentricchia, *Criticism and Social Change* (Chicago and London: University of Chicago Press, 1983), pp. 147–48. Further references are to this edition and will be cited parenthetically in the text.
2. In general, Adorno and Marcuse emphasize the liberating function of aesthetic form, its resistance to the rationalizing, normalizing hegemony of consumer culture, while Jameson, Lentricchia, and Eagleton, drawing on the French tradition, emphasize its mystifying function, its promotion of false consciousness. See T. W. Adorno, *Aesthetic Theory*, trans. C. Lenhardt (London: Routledge & Kegan Paul, 1984); Herbert Marcuse, *The Aesthetic Dimension: Toward a Critique of Marxist Aesthetics*, trans. Herbert Marcuse and Erica Sherover (Boston: Beacon, 1978); Frederic Jameson, *The Political Unconscious: Narrative as a Socially Symbolic Act* (Ithaca: Cornell University Press, 1981); Terry Eagleton, *Literary Theory: An Introduction* (Minneapolis: University of Minnesota Press, 1983). Traditional readings of *Caleb Williams* divide between political and psychological approaches. See David McCracken's introduction in *Caleb Williams* (New York: Norton, 1977), pp. vii–xxii; Gerald A. Barker, 'Justice to Caleb Williams,' *Studies in the Novel* 6 (1974): 377–88; John Pesta, '*Caleb Williams*: A Tragedy of Wasted Love,' *TSL* 16 (1971): 67–76. In '*Caleb Williams* and the Attack on Romance,' *SNNTS* 8 (1976): 81–86, C. R. Kropf remarks the novel's critique of eighteenth-century fiction, arguing that Godwin follows Fielding's portrayal of things 'as they are' against Richardson's portrayal of things as they ought to be. Mitzi Myers notes Falkland's resemblance to a 'tragic Quixote' (p. 604) in 'Godwin's Changing Conception of *Caleb Williams*,' *SEL* 12 (1972): 591–628.
3. Just as reflectionist aesthetics (Lukács and Goldmann) are rejected by Marcuse (*The Aesthetic Dimension*, pp. 1–21), Adorno (*Aesthetic Theory*, pp. 326–29, 358–59), and Jameson (*The Political Unconscious*, pp. 43–44), so Jameson and Lentricchia use the doctrine of semi-autonomy to undermine the base's determination of superstructure. See *The Political Unconscious*, pp. 23–43; *Criticism and Social Change*, pp. 122–23. Lentricchia even minimizes Althusser's preservation of economic 'determination in the last instance': 'The stress . . . is not on the metaphysical temptation of the 'last instance' but on semi-autonomous levels, each possessing its own structural and internal necessity' (p. 122). Citing Althusser's 'antiteleological formula for history' (p. 34), Jameson flirts with a 'paradigm' enfolding all literature into a master narrative of Freedom struggling against Necessity (pp. 101–102). Less coy, Lentricchia flatly rejects the 'teleological ideal' underlying 'all traditional Marxist acts of interpretation' (p. 12).
4. Edmund Burke, *Reflections on the Revolution in France* (Harmondsworth: Penguin, 1969), p. 90.
5. Michel Foucault, *Language, Counter-Memory, Practice: Selected Essays and Interviews*, trans. Donald F. Bouchard and Sherry Simon (Ithaca: Cornell University Press, 1977), p. 153.

6. William Godwin, *Caleb Williams* (New York: Norton, 1977), p. 3. Further references are to this edition and will be cited parenthetically in the text.

7. William Godwin, 1794 Preface, *Caleb Williams* (New York: Norton, 1977), p. 1.

8. See D. Gilbert Dumas, 'Things as They Were: The Original Ending of *Caleb Williams*,' *SEL* 6 (1966): 575–97. In his 1832 account, reprinted in *Caleb Williams* (New York: Norton, 1977), pp. 335–41, Godwin notes that he began with a story of persecution, conceiving first Caleb's flight, then Falkland's story.

9. Henry Fielding, *The History of Tom Jones, A Foundling*, ed. Martin C. Battestin (Middletown, Conn.: Wesleyan University Press, 1975), p. 876.

10. Hans Robert Jauss, *Aesthetic Experience and Literary Hermeneutics*, trans. Michael Shaw (Minneapolis: University of Minnesota Press, 1982), p. 20; also see pp. 152–88.

11. Just as Godwin advocates anarchism by conjoining confidence in man's ability to see his individual interest in the general good with a hard-headed analysis of how every form of government opens avenues for moral corruption, so he maintains that the progressive diffusion of reason will allow truth to be apprehended clearly while denying the justice of criminal penalties because the same act may be evaluated variously. See Peter H. Marshall, *William Godwin* (New Haven and London: Yale University Press, 1984), pp. 93–117.

12. William Godwin, *An Enquiry Concerning Political Justice*, ed. Raymond A. Preston, 2 vols. (New York: Alfred A. Knopf, 1926), 2: 82–83.

13. *Political Justice*, 2: 169.

14. Jane Austen, *Northanger Abbey and Persuasion* (London: Oxford University Press, 1975), p. 83.

15. Paul Ricoeur, *Time and Narrative*, trans. Kathleen McLaughlin and David Pellauer, 3 vols. (Chicago and London: University of Chicago Press, 1985), 2: 22.

16. See Wilfried Ver Eecke's discussion of Lacan's account of aggressivity as a means of conserving the imaginary in 'Hegel as Lacan's Source for Necessity in Psychoanalytic Theory,' in *Interpreting Lacan*, ed. Joseph H. Smith and Walter Kerrigan (New Haven and London: Yale University Press, 1983), pp. 113–37, esp. pp. 126–35.

17. See Barker, pp. 377–88; *Political Justice*, 2: 116–27.

18. See Foucault's discussion of speaking 'within the true,' 'The Discourse on Language,' p. 224, in Michel Foucault, *The Archeology of Knowledge*, trans. A. M. Sheridan Smith (New York: Pantheon, 1972).

19. See Anthony Winner's discussion of Balzac's portrayal of character in *Characters in the Twilight: Hardy, Zola and Chekhov* (Charlottesville: University Press of Virginia, 1981), pp. 9–27.

20. Nadezhda Mandelstam, *Hope Against Hope: A Memoir*, trans. Max Hayward (New York: Atheneum, 1970), p. 50.

Part VIII

Austen

12 The Juvenilia and *Northanger Abbey*

Marilyn Butler

Marilyn Butler is a well-known critic of romanticism, and, more specifically, of the literary and cultural consequences of the French Revolution. *Jane Austen and the War of Ideas* is essential reading for those interested in Jane Austen's politics. Combining intellectual history with formal reading, Butler argues that Austen must be seen in the context of the post-revolutionary climate of the 1790s. She has irritated a certain line of feminist critics by arguing – as in this chapter from her book – that Austen's sympathies lie with those who dislike the extremism of the French Revolution, and that, in this sense, she is 'conservative.'

We are often told that Jane Austen's original satirical inspiration was fed by dislike for a literary manner, rather than for a moral idea. The juvenilia are, according to this view, 'burlesques': though definition and re-definition tends to surround the word, since it is by no means easy to see what, precisely, is being burlesqued. Goldsmith's history-writing, in 'The History of England . . . by a partial, prejudiced and ignorant Historian'? Surely not. The conventions of the sentimental novel, variously in 'Volume the First'? The great majority of these short fragments seem meant for nothing more ambitious than to raise a laugh in a fireside circle by that favourite eighteenth-century comic recourse, extreme verbal incongruity. The heroine Alice 'has many rare and charming qualities, but sobriety is not one of them'.[1]

Love and Freindship is another matter. Here there is an unequivocal relationship with the sentimental novel, a tilt at both form and content. Mackenzie had used the letter-novel not as a means of contrasting different characters, but in order to indulge his heroine's propensity for narcissistic self-examination.[2] *Love and Freindship* presents an uninterrupted stream of letters from the heroine, Laura, who dismisses the occasional criticisms of others in favour of a complacent view of her own character. 'A sensibility too tremblingly alive to every affliction of my Friends, my Acquaintance, and particularly to every affliction of my own was my only fault, if a fault it could be called.'[3]

But though this may be parody, it is directed not at manner but at substance: Laura (and Mackenzie's Julia) pretend to a virtue which Jane Austen wishes to deny them. The capacity to feel was presented as the transcendent merit of every sentimental heroine from Julie to Delphine, enough in itself to lift them above the common run of mortals. Laura is placed in a numerous company when she is made to applaud her own refinement and dismiss the more utilitarian or extrovert qualities of others:

> She [Bridget] could not be supposed to possess either exalted Ideas, Delicate Feelings or refined Sensibilities —. She was nothing more than a mere good-tempered, civil and obliging Young Woman; as such we could scarcely dislike her – she was only an Object of Contempt.[4]

The intention in satirizing Laura is above all to expose the selfishness of the sentimental system. Here is a heroine governed by self-admiration, and aware only of those others so similar in tastes and temperament that she can think of them as extensions of herself. Her rejection of the claims of the rest of humanity arises either from hostility to those who try to thwart her, or from unawareness of the claims of anyone outside the charmed circle of sentimental friendship. The co-heroine, Sophia, cannot even visit her beloved, Augustus, in Newgate – '"my feelings are sufficiently shocked by the *recital*, of his Distress, but to behold it will overpower my Sensibility"'.[5] Laura remembers to mention the death of her parents only because it is a factor in making her destitute.[6] Rather more subtle, perhaps, is Jane Austen's mocking observation of the solipsism which may lie behind the sentimentalist's paraded sensitivity to nature:

> 'What a beautiful sky! (said I) How charmingly is the azure varied by those delicate streaks of white!' 'Oh! my Laura (replied she hastily withdrawing her Eyes from a momentary glance at the sky) do not thus distress me by calling my Attention to an object which so cruelly reminds me of my Augustus's blue satin waistcoat striped with white!'[7]

Although Jane Austen's sentimentalists act in a way that is at the very least equivocal, for in practice they appear ruthlessly self-interested, it is no part of her intention to suggest that they are insincere. In her view the contradiction is inherent in the creed: she wants to show that the realization of self, an apparently idealistic goal, is in fact necessarily destructive and delusory. As a formal burlesque rather than a novel, *Love and Freindship* is quite apart from

Jane Austen's later career. Thematically, however, it makes the first chapter of a consistent story.

Of the early work, *Catharine, or the Bower* is the nearest attempt at true fiction: in fact it is the first recognizable effort at the classic Jane Austen form of novel. As in so many works of the period, an inexperienced young girl is on the threshold of life. One source of interest for the reader was clearly to have been Catharine's assessment of 'the world': her eventual discriminations about Camilla Stanley, the girl who offers her false sentimental friendship, and Camilla's brother Edward, who, as a lover, threatens her peace more substantially. In dramatizing this process of growing discernment Jane Austen achieves a technique which already belongs to the era of Maria Edgeworth rather than of Fanny Burney. The dialogue offers the reader direct evidence about the character of the two girls:

> 'You have read Mrs. Smith's Novels, I suppose?' said she to her Companion —. 'Oh! Yes, replied the other, and I am quite delighted with them – They are the sweetest things in the world —' 'And which do you prefer of them?' 'Oh! dear, I think there is no comparison between them – Emmeline is *so much* better than any of the others —' 'Many people think so, I know; but there does not appear so great a disproportion in their Merits to *me*; do you think it is better written?' 'Oh! I do not know anything about *that* – but it is better in *everything* – Besides, Ethelinde is so long —' 'That is a very common Objection, I believe, said Kitty, but for my own part, if a book is well written, I always find it too short.' 'So do I, only I get tired of it before it is finished.'[8]

The characteristic of Camilla's mind as revealed here is carelessness, a habit of exaggeration and inaccuracy. She is not interested in the books they are talking about, though Catharine is. The striking feature of the conversation is its implicit moral frame of reference. Catharine is right to take the issue seriously, because it is a test case, a trial attempt at defining the good, which is the process upon which the moral life depends.

Dialogue of this kind is developed in *Northanger Abbey*, and in far subtler forms in the later novels, beginning with *Pride and Prejudice*. It is always associated with a narrative prose which so closely tracks the heroine's consciousness that it often approximates to 'free indirect speech'. Jane Austen never gives up her option of insinuating comments into her heroine's thought-process that in fact could have emanated only from the author, but in *Catharine* she is still clumsy about such interventions. Catharine's introduction to Camilla is spoilt by the superfluous observation that Camilla 'professed a love of Books without Reading, was lively without Wit, and generally goodhumoured without Merit'. But in the passage that follows, the author's comment, though officious, shows a kindly insight into the heroine's dangerous intellectual isolation:

> . . . and Catharine, who was prejudiced by her appearance, and who from her solitary Situation was ready to like anyone, tho' her Understanding and Judgement would not otherwise have been easily satisfied, felt almost convinced when she saw her, that Miss Stanley would be the very companion she wanted. . . .[9]

Here is the first example of Jane Austen's technique of comparing the evidence given to the mind with the mind's insidious habit of perverting evidence: two planes of reality, the objective and the subjective, respectively presented in dialogue and in a form which approaches internal monologue. Catherine Morland's thoughts about Isabella, Elizabeth's about Mr. Wickham, and Emma's about Frank Churchill, are anticipated in Catharine's self-deceiving trains of thought about Camilla and afterwards about Edward:

> The Evening passed off as agreably as the one that had preceded it; they continued talking to each other, during the chief part of it, and such was the power of his Address, & the Brilliancy of his Eyes, that when they parted for the Night, tho' Catharine had but a few hours before totally given up the idea, yet she felt almost convinced again that he was really in love with her. . . . The more she had seen of him, the more inclined was she to like him, & the more desirous that he should like *her*. She was convinced of his being naturally very clever and very well disposed, and that his thoughtlessness & negligence, which tho' they appeared to *her* as very becoming in *him*, she was aware would by many people be considered as defects in his Character, merely proceeded from a vivacity always pleasing in Young Men, & were far from testifying a weak or vacant Understanding.[10]

If Jane Austen was no more than sixteen when she wrote this, it is something of a *tour de force*; and what makes it more remarkable is that the resourceful use of language supports other appropriate narrative techniques. Catharine's situation is well prepared in the opening pages of exposition. We are shown that she is especially vulnerable because she is solitary: her childhood friends, the Wynnes, have gone away, and she is left in the company of her aunt, Mrs. Percival, who is fussy and prosaic. Catharine likes to indulge her sentimental regret for the Wynnes alone in her 'Bower', a romantic spot which, as the sub-title indicates, was to have been given special symbolic significance. Mrs. Percival, a prototype perhaps for Mrs. Jennings or Miss Bates, objects to her habit of going there, but for valetudinarian reasons which at the moment Catharine finds easy to dismiss. The real threat offered by the Bower was clearly to have been to her moral health, for it encourages her in a dangerously solipsistic reverie; and it is there, appropriately, that Edward Stanley appeals to her emotions by seizing her hand. It is clear even from these short beginnings that the story was to have encompassed both the natural evolution of Catharine's error, and its moral implications, so that in conception and, primitively, in technique, it belongs to the series that culminates with *Emma*.

The first of Jane Austen's novels to be completed for publication, *Northanger Abbey*,[11] makes use of all the same important features. A naïve, inexperienced heroine stands at the threshold of life and needs to discriminate between true friends and false. The evidence she is given are words and the system of value they express; so that the reader, cleverer or at least more cleverly directed than Catherine, is able to make the correct discriminations for himself as the action unfolds. In one important respect the second Catherine is a coarser conception than the first, for she has been crossed with the burlesque heroine of the 'female quixote' variety, so that many of her intellectual errors are grosser and far more improbable. Yet although *Northanger Abbey* is often remembered for its sequence at the abbey, when Catherine is led by her reading of (presumably) Mrs. Radcliffe's *Romance of the Forest*[12] into fantastic imaginings, the central impulse of *Northanger Abbey*, and its serious achievement, has nothing to do with burlesque. Like *Catharine*, it uses the literary conversation not for the sake of the subject, but in order to give an appropriate morally objective ground against which character can be judged.

Catherine Morland has five important conversations about the Gothic novel: with Isabella Thorpe (vol. i. ch. vi); with John Thorpe (i. vii); with Eleanor and Henry Tilney (i. xiv); with Henry Tilney, in his phaeton on the way to Northanger Abbey (ii. v); and with Henry Tilney again, when he uncovers her suspicions of his father, the General (ii. ix). In all of these conversations, as in *Catharine*, the reader is not asked to criticize certain novels, nor the habit of novel-reading,[13] but rather to consider the habits of mind which the different speakers reveal. For example, when Isabella and Catherine first discuss horrid novels together, in chapter six of the first volume, Isabella's knowledge proves superficial: she is dependent on her friend Miss Andrews for all her information, and Miss Andrews knows what is current, but not *Sir Charles Grandison*. From this conversation it emerges that Isabella's mind is not held by novels, for it continually runs after young men, whereas Catherine's comments are characterized by extreme, if naïve, interest. 'I do not pretend to say that I was not very much pleased with him [Henry Tilney]; but while I have *Udolpho* to read, I feel as if nobody could make me miserable.'[14] Again, when Catherine raises the subject 'which had long been uppermost in her thoughts' with John Thorpe, it is to discover that despite his assurance he does not know *Udolpho* is by Mrs. Radcliffe, and that he has got less than half-way in the first volume of the five-volume *Camilla*. On the other hand, the characteristic of the Tilneys which emerges when Catherine raises the subject with them is informed interest. 'I have read all Mrs. Radcliffe's works,' says Henry, 'and most of them with great pleasure.'[15] The mild qualification is important, for the proper attitude of the person who reads is a discriminating exactness – the quality Henry shows when he challenges Catherine's word 'nice', and Eleanor when she emends it to 'interesting'.[16]

After discussing novels the Tilneys move on to the subject of history, just as the earlier Catharine of the juvenilia did. Both topics, together with the Tilneys' choice of landscape, enable Jane Austen to illustrate character at a light and amusing level without imputing triviality. Choice of these as subjects for conversation already implies a certain degree of thoughtfulness and rationality – unlike John Thorpe's topics of horses, curricles, drink, and money, and Isabella's of 'dress, balls, flirtations and quizzes'.[17] Thus far at least the conversations about Gothic novels in *Northanger Abbey* belong to the over-all strategy of the novel, which is concerned first to reveal the character of the heroine, second to contrast the minds of her two sets of friends, the Thorpes and the Tilneys.

The clarity of Jane Austen's conception appears to waver in the second volume. Henry's teasing conversation with Catherine during their drive to the Abbey is, as earlier dialogues were not, a series of observations directed *at* the Gothic mode. What Henry invents is a burlesque Gothic story, compounded of various clichés – ancient housekeeper, isolated chamber, secret passage, instruments of torture, hidden manuscripts, and extinguished candle – though it should also be noticed, since it is typical of the discriminating reader in the period, that he puts as much stress upon verbal blunders as upon extravagances of plot. He imagines Catherine surmounting an '*unconquerable*' horror of the bed, and discovering a secret door through 'a division in the tapestry so artfully constructed as to defy the minutest inspection'.[18] Henry's lively and critical approach to his Gothic material is thus contrasted with Catherine's selection of precisely the wrong aspect to comment on. 'Oh! Mr. Tilney, how frightful! – This is just like a book! – But it cannot really happen to me. I am sure your housekeeper is not really Dorothy.'[19]

The memory of Henry's intelligent detachment in this conversation lingers as an unspoken commentary on Catherine's series of interior monologues at Northanger – while she searches her room, or lies terror-stricken in bed, or concocts wild fantasies concerning the General and the death of Mrs. Tilney. Typically, it is in the 'objective' form of dialogue, where we are equally detached from both parties, and not in subjective thought-processes, that we hear, reliably, the note of rationality. And it is through another speech from Henry that Catherine is brought at last to an understanding of the 'real' world of long-lasting social and religious institutions:

> 'What have you been judging from? Remember the country and the age in which we live. Remember that we are English, that we are Christians. Consult your own understanding, your own sense of the probable, your own observation of what is passing around you – Does our education prepare us for such atrocities? Do our laws connive at them? Could they be perpetrated without being known, in a country like this, where social and literary intercourse is on such a footing; where every man is surrounded by a neighbourhood of voluntary spies, and where roads and newspapers lay everything open? Dearest Miss Morland, what ideas have you been admitting?'[20]

There is clearly a difference in Jane Austen's use of dialogue in the first volume and in the second. In the first, it is the reader alone who is enlightened, by comparable dialogues between Catherine and the Thorpes, and Catherine and the Tilneys. During the same period the heroine neither learns to discriminate between her two groups of friends, nor to be discriminating about them. Although Henry Tilney has been setting her a good example for virtually a full volume, Catherine returns from her walk with him and Eleanor nearly as unenlightened as when she set out:

> It was no effort to Catherine to believe that Henry Tilney could never be wrong. His manner might sometimes surprize, but his meaning must always be just: – and what she did not understand, she was almost as ready to admire, as what she did.[21]

In the second volume the impact on Catherine of Henry's remarks and, negatively, of Isabella's letters, is far greater. Aided no doubt by prosaic external evidence at the Abbey, she is brought sharply to a sense of reality:

> The visions of romance were over. Catherine was completely awakened. Henry's address, short as it had been, had more thoroughly opened her eyes to the extravagance of her late fancies than all their several disappointments had done. Most grievously was she humbled. Most bitterly did she cry.[22]

When she becomes more tranquil, Catherine continues soberly to recognize that 'it had been all a voluntary, self-created delusion, each trifling circumstance receiving importance from an imagination resolved on alarm, and everything forced to bend to one purpose by a mind which, before she entered the Abbey, had been craving to be frightened'.[23] This, then, is the typical moment of *éclaircissement* towards which all the Austen actions tend, the moment when a key character abandons her error and humbly submits to objective reality.

During the period of *Northanger Abbey*'s evolution, before its near-appearance as *Susan* in 1803, Maria Edgeworth was experimenting with similar devices. *Belinda* has precisely the same stylized arrangement of characters, according to their contrasting philosophies of life, and perhaps an even more fully developed sense of the relationship between verbal style and quality of mind. What is very different in *Northanger Abbey*, however, different even from Maria Edgeworth's rather undistinguished execution in *Angelina*, is Jane Austen's reluctance to commit herself to her heroine's consciousness. It is not merely Catherine's emotional distress after she discovers her errors that receives hurried treatment; her actual mental processes are also summarily dealt with. From the consistent *naïveté* of her earlier thinking to her final state of enlightenment is a long step, but Jane Austen is not really concerned to examine it. Ultimately this is because, unlike Maria Edgeworth, she does not value the personal process of learning to reason as an end in itself. What is required of Catherine is rather a suspension of a particular kind of mental activity, her habit of romantic invention; at the moment Jane Austen is not concerned to define positively what kind of regular mental process it is that will keep Catherine sensible. For the naturalistic treatment of an individual's inner history which was promised in the first *Catharine*, here we have to make do with facetious stylization, and allusion to a ready-made inner world acquired from reading other people's books. We are shown that Catherine has learnt a significant general rule, that human nature is worse than she first thought: for, apart from her aberration over the General, she has successively overrated the Thorpes, Frederick Tilney, and perhaps even Henry, with all the sentimentalist's optimism about human nature. The reader is asked to take it on trust that henceforth she will apply more caution, more scepticism, more concern for the objective evidence. Of the actual change in her habits of mind that would make such a revolution possible he sees little or nothing.

Jane Austen was slower to handle the inner life confidently than to deploy dialogue: her next novel with a similar format, *Pride and Prejudice*, also fails to give Elizabeth's train of thought with the same clarity and brilliance with which it presents the dialogue. Yet *Northanger Abbey* is consistent and ingenious in dramatizing the author's point of view, like all Jane Austen's novels to employ a fallible heroine. It establishes the antiphonal role of dialogue and free indirect speech which is to be so important in Jane Austen's career. It deploys characters around the heroine with the kind of antithetical precision that is typical of Mrs. West, but much more amusingly and naturally. Even if Catherine's mind is a somewhat implausible blank, the arrangement of the two pairs of brothers and sisters, the Tilneys and the Thorpes, virtually forces the reader into a series of ethical comparisons between them on the author's terms. However strong his training and his inclination to involve himself uncritically in the heroine's emotions, he is manipulated into undertaking an unfamiliar kind of intellectual activity. Stylistically the novel induces him to value sincerity and accuracy, rather than those emotions which are harder to account for or specify. Formally it requires him to use his judgement and not his feeling.

At the same time *Northanger Abbey* is very much a novel, which is to say that it succeeds in creating and maintaining an autonomous fictional world. The story is not a parody of a novel story, but actually, like *Pride and Prejudice*, employs the common novelist's fantasy of the poor girl who meets, and after a series of vicissitudes marries, the rich young man. Catherine may not be a 'heroine' in the idealized mode of sentimental fiction, but she is a very good heroine at the level which matters. She invites and keeps our sympathy, and she makes us feel that what happens to her matters to us. No wonder, indeed, that in the famous passage in chapter five Jane Austen ironically refuses to condemn the novel: for *Northanger Abbey* is quite as much a novel as *Udolpho* is.

It is perhaps because Catherine is so pleasing, even when she blunders, that some recent critics have felt that Jane Austen ends *Northanger Abbey* by reversing its whole moral tendency; that she turns her irony on the good sense advocated by Henry Tilney, and at least in part vindicates Catherine's intuition. The central piece of evidence cited is that the General, Montoni-like, turns Catherine out of Northanger Abbey, and thus proves to be a villian after all. But an act of rudeness is not villainy. It is not even, to use Andrew Wright's term, 'violence'.[24] It arises from the ill-tempered pique of a snobbish man who has just discovered that Catherine is a person of no social account. There is plenty of evidence throughout the novel that Henry and Eleanor are aware of their father's bad temper, as well as of his snobbery and formality: Eleanor's instant obedience on all occasions, for example, suggests that she has learnt to fear the General's anger. His treatment of Catherine comes nearer to confirming their view of him than hers, although it is perhaps not fully in keeping with either.[25]

Again, after Catherine returns home her romantic feelings are opposed to Mrs. Morland's worthy moralizing, and here at least Jane Austen appears to be on Catherine's side: 'There was a great deal of good sense in all this; but there are some situations of the human mind in which good sense has very little power; and Catherine's feelings contradicted almost every position her mother advanced.'[26]

But it is only by taking this observation out of context that we can read into it a serious meaning which relates to the whole book. The nice little vignette of Catherine's relations with her mother after her return home is surely yet another literary borrowing, this time from Fanny Burney's *Camilla*. Camilla's parents think that Camilla has been spoilt by high life, when really she is pining for the loss of her lover, Edgar Mandlebert; and Mrs. Morland is mistaken in just the same way. Had she really tried to cure a case of true love by fetching down a volume of *The Mirror* (containing 'a very clever Essay . . . about young girls that have been spoilt for home by great acquaintance'[27]), the incident might indeed suggest that Jane Austen was after all merely balancing the merits of feeling and sense. In fact Mrs. Morland's error is no more than a joke designed to reintroduce the hero in the lightest and least emotional manner possible.

Northanger Abbey is a novel, and it works as a novel, while at the same time it subjects the conventional matter of the merely subjective novel to consistently critical handling. Ideologically it is a very clear statement of the anti-jacobin position; though, compared with other anti-jacobin novels, it is distinctive for the virtuosity with which it handles familiar clichés of the type. Very pleasing, for example, is the cleverly oblique presentation of the subject under attack.

Most anti-jacobin novels include characters who profess the new ideology, and are never tired of canvassing it in conversation. In *Northanger Abbey* there is no overtly partisan talk at all. ('By an easy transition [Henry] . . . shortly found himself arrived at politics; and from politics, it was an easy step to silence.'[28]) But in *Northanger Abbey* Jane Austen develops, perhaps from the prototypes the Stanleys in *Catherine*, her version of the revolutionary character, the man or woman who by acting on a system of selfishness, threatens friends of more orthodox principles; and ultimately, through cold-blooded cynicism in relation to the key social institution of marriage, threatens human happiness at a very fundamental level. Isabella Thorpe, worldly, opportunist, bent on self-gratification, is one of a series of dangerous women created by Jane Austen. Lucy Steele, Lady Susan, Mary Crawford, all like Isabella pursue the modern creed of self, and as such are Jane Austen's reinterpretation of a standard figure of the period, the desirable, amoral woman whose activities threaten manners and morals. Moreover, already in *Northanger Abbey* the opportunists find allies where they should properly be most vigorously opposed – among those who uphold only the forms, and not the essence, of orthodoxy. The pompous but mercenary General is as much implicated as John Thorpe in the pursuit of Catherine's mythical fortune. In the same vein, Henry and Mary Crawford meet no resistance, but encouragement, when they threaten to introduce anarchy into Mr. Rushworth's ancestral estate. And William Walter Elliott finds an easy dupe, even an ally, in the empty figure-head he despises, Sir Walter.

That Jane Austen is perfectly clear what she is doing can be demonstrated by identifying the same cluster of themes and characters in *Sense and Sensibility*. Inheriting a set of conservative dogmas, and some impossibly theatrical characters – notably the revolutionary villain – already in her first two full-length novels she produces a more natural equivalent, on a scale appropriate to comedy. Her villains are not only better art than her rivals'; they are also better propaganda. The tendency among the routine anti-jacobins was to create Satanic demon–villains who were dangerously close in the temper of the times to being heroes. Jane Austen's intelligence, like Burke's, is more subtle. Her selfish characters are consistently smaller and meaner than their orthodox opponents, the heroines; they are restricted within the bounds of their own being, and their hearts and minds are impoverished. Jane Austen's achievement, the feat of the subtlest technician among the English novelists, is to rethink the material of the conservative novel in terms that are at once naturalistic and intellectually consistent.

Notes

1. *Minor Works*, ed. R. W. Chapman, Oxford, rev. edn, 1963, p. 23. But for the argument that literary burlesque is pervasive in the juvenilia, cf. B. C. Southam, *Jane Austen's Literary Manuscripts*, Oxford, 1964, p. 9 and *passim*.
2. See the account of Henry Mackenzie's *Julia de Roubigné* in Marilyn Butler, *Jane Austen and the War of Ideas* (Oxford: Clarendon Press, 1975), pp. 26–7.
3. *Minor Works*, p. 78.
4. *Ibid.*, pp. 100–1.

5. *Ibid.*, p. 89.
6. *Ibid.*, pp. 89–90.
7. *Ibid.*, p. 98.
8. *Ibid.*, p. 199.
9. *Ibid.*, p. 198.
10. *Ibid.*, pp. 235–6.
11. To discuss *Northanger Abbey* before *Sense and Sensibility* is a somewhat arbitrary decision. In conception *S. & S.* is the earlier: the letter-version, 'Elinor and Marianne', dates from 1795, while the novel as we know it was begun in Nov. 1797. In structure and theme *S. & S.* is a typical novel of 1795–6, while *N.A.*, which in part reacts to the rage for Gothic of 1796–8, belongs historically a little later. And yet *N.A.*, which was accepted for publication by Cadell under its title of *Susan* in 1803, was probably ready by then in substantially its present form. Cf. Alan D. McKillop, 'Critical Realism in *Northanger Abbey*', *From Jane Austen to Joseph Conrad*, ed. R. C. Rathburn and M. Steinmann, Jr., Minneapolis, 1958; and B. C. Southam, *Jane Austen's Literary Manuscripts*, 1964, p. 62.
12. It was Adeline, heroine of that novel, who stayed at a ruined abbey and found a secret chamber behind the arras, containing a rusty dagger and a roll of paper which told the story of the man kept prisoner there.
13. One of the commonest misconceptions about *Northanger Abbey* is that Isabella leads Catherine astray by introducing her to a world of horror and make-believe. But Catherine's worst error, to be taken in by Isabella, occurs before she has begun to read popular novels. Cf. Kenneth L. Moler, *Jane Austen's Art of Allusion*, Nebraska, 1969, pp. 19–20.
14. *Northanger Abbey*, ed. R. W. Chapman, Oxford, 3rd edn, 1933, p. 41.
15. *Ibid.*, p. 106.
16. *Ibid.*, p. 108.
17. *Ibid.*, p. 33.
18. *Ibid.*, p. 159.
19. *Ibid.*, p. 159.
20. *Ibid.*, pp. 197–8.
21. *Ibid.*, p. 114.
22. *Ibid.*, p. 199.
23. *Ibid.*, pp. 199–200.
24. Professor Wright is one of the most influential critics to hold that Catherine's view of the General is not altogether illusory (*Jane Austen's Novels: A Study in Structure*, London, 1954, pp. 106–7). Among others who have taken the same line, with incidental variations, are John K. Mathison, '*Northanger Abbey* and JA's Conception of the Value of Fiction', *ELH* xxiv (1957), 138–52; Lionel Trilling, *The Opposing Self*, 1955, p. 217; Frank J. Kearful, 'Satire and the Form of the Novel: the Problem of Aesthetic Unity in *Northanger Abbey*', *ELH* xxxii (1965), 511–27; Henrietta Ten Harmsel, *Jane Austen: a Study in Fictional Conventions*, The Hague, 1964, pp. 25–6; and A. Walton Litz, *Jane Austen: A Study of her Artistic Development*, London, 1965, p. 63. But cf. Kenneth L. Moler, *op. cit.*, pp. 38–40.

25. The General's behaviour was so out of line with gentlemanly standards in the period that early readers found it incredible. Maria Edgeworth called it 'out of drawing and out of nature' (letter to Mrs. Ruxton, 21 Feb. 1818: Mrs. Edgeworth, *Memoir of Maria Edgeworth*, privately published, 1867, ii. 6). Hitherto we have thought of him as over-formal, and there is no room to modify his character sufficiently.
26. *Northanger Abbey*, p. 241.
27. *Ibid.*, p. 239.
28. *Ibid.*, p. 111.

13 The Juvenilia and *Northanger Abbey*: The Authority of Men and Books

CLAUDIA L. JOHNSON

Claudia Johnson has made a speciality of writing about the 1790s and their importance for women novelists. Employing much the same methods as Marilyn Butler, namely a combination of intellectual history with close reading of literary texts, she places Austen in a different location on the map of the post-revolutionary world than Butler. Describing the typical concerns and anxieties of anti-Jacobin novelists, Johnson argues that if Austen gains anything from 'conservative' thinkers such as Edmund Burke, she does so with a critical edge, which places her outside the conservative camp.

Jane Austen's earliest literary productions are the fruit of unparalleled self-assurance. With very little ado, Austen proclaims the dignity of her genre as well as the authority of her own command over it – both at a time when such gestures were rare. Unlike her predecessors, Austen pointedly refuses to apologize for novels. By contrast, Fielding's efforts to elevate his own fiction by affiliating it with the classical tradition bespeak his nagging doubts about its status, not to mention his own status in dealing in it; Richardson's prefaces and editorial pronouncements reflect uneasiness about the moral tendency of his work; and women novelists irked Austen no end by marginalizing their work and having their own heroines deny reading anything so frivolous as novels at all: '"Do not imagine that *I* often read novels,"' Austen mimicks, '"– It is really very well for a novel." – Such is the common cant. – "And what are you reading Miss — ?" "Oh! it is only a novel!" replies the young lady' (*NA* 38).[1] Regarding herself and her colleagues as 'an injured body' plagued not simply by reviewers' cant, but even worse, by their own self-defeating habits of internalizing and reproducing it, Austen counters for the first and final time in her career, that novels are works 'in which the most thorough knowledge of human nature, the happiest delineation of its varieties, the liveliest effusions of wit and humour are conveyed to the world in the best chosen language' (*NA* 38). Never again would similar gestures of self-justification appear necessary. Austen's readiness to assume her qualifications to vindicate fiction is more than an outpouring of youthful enthusiasm. It bespeaks a profound confidence which no previous novelist of either sex possessed. Because the acuity and independence of Austen's mature social criticism emerge from her authorial confidence and self-consciousness, it is worth considering closely the first stirrings of both.

From the earliest writings on, Austen's confidence took a remarkably assertive form. Virginia Woolf was one of the first to observe that Austen's early work, generally viewed as precocious diversions for the family circle, was *not* amateurish and contentedly unaspiring, undertaken solely to entertain adored parents, cousins, and siblings. Honoring the 'rhythm and shapeliness and severity' that mark even the earliest of Austen's sentences, Woolf finds that 'Love and Freindship,' for example, was 'meant to outlast the Christmas holidays.' To Woolf, Austen was from the very start a committed artist 'writing for everybody, for nobody, for our age, for her own,' and the most salient quality of her artistry is the unnerving effrontery of its laughter: 'The girl of fifteen is laughing, in her corner, at the world.'[2]

To sit in amused judgment upon the world requires a degree of audacity we do not generally associate with girls of fifteen looking on from their corners.[3] But Austen did not confine the keen presumption of her laughter to the snobs, hypocrites, and bumblers who constitute 'the world.' Like most eighteenth-century novelists and poets, Austen initiated her career by parody. Austen's parodic juvenile writings are exercises in authority which announce both a superiority of judgment which entitles her to authorship and a determination to level that judgment against predominating literary conventions – conventions which would soon be conspicuously freighted with political urgency. Throughout the juvenilia Austen derives her vitality from systematically exploring and dismantling the conventions that governed the literary form available to her. Her fiction of the late 1780s – and later the 1790s – was, in other words, more than a playpen where a precocious girl poked fun at silly fads and people. It was also a workshop, where the would-be artist first set hand to the tools of her trade, identifying operative structures and motifs, and then turning them inside out in order to explore their artificiality and bring to light their hidden implications. 'Jack and Alice,' for example, shocks us into the recognition of how little innocent our acts of reading are, for virtually every sentence of this tour de force turns uproariously on itself to disrupt expectations we had no idea we were nursing to begin with. The temporal displacement of the opening sentence irreverently mocks what George Eliot more soberly called 'the make believe of a beginning':

> Mr. Johnson was once upon a time about 53; in a twelvemonth afterwards he was 54, which so much delighted him that he was determined to celebrate his next Birthday by giving a Masquerade to his Children & Freinds.
>
> (*MW* 12)[4]

Like all parody, Austen's sentence here is hyperconventional and anti-conventional at one and the same time, unfolding a series of codes which first appears unitary, only then to diverge into confounding incongruity. Austen thus begins with the predictable 'once upon a time,' the ostensible purpose of which is to situate us in the narrative present. But much to our bewilderment, by mid-sentence we are transported with no discernible purpose not one but two years before – or is it after? – the 'beginning.' Only after a few double takes will we be able to orient ourselves. And even then the process of reexamination will turn up doubts generated by the word 'about' which we did not notice when reading the passage through for the first time, and which threaten the import of the entire sentence. By concluding with an allusion to masquerade, among the most hackneyed motifs in eighteenth-century fiction, Austen placidly resumes the conventionality that began with 'once upon a time,' only now that conventionality has been undermined. Austen's sentence thus prohibits us from reading naively, as Catherine Morland does at first, for her style continually makes itself subject to doubt. Here it has rendered us wary of the formulas which introduce fiction, but in *Mansfield Park* similar kinds of techniques will be deployed more ambitiously to make us wary of Burkean discourse itself.

But throughout the juvenilia, Austen does more than debunk novelistic formulas and have done. As a rule her treatment of them obliges us instead to slow down and to consider more carefully the realities they conceal. In 'Jack and Alice,' Austen, following Swift and Johnson, intrudes upon the rarefied pastoral atmosphere of sentimental fiction a variety of embarrassing objects that pastoral generally contrives to exclude: 'A few days after their reconciliation Lady Williams called on Miss Johnson to propose a walk in a Citron Grove which led from her Ladyship's pigstye to Charles Adams's Horsepond' (*MW* 18). When Austen, by such techniques as reduction, reversal, literalization, or hyperbole, seems most to 'make strange' the conventional elements of fiction, she often only alerts us to how strange they were before they were tampered with. The understatement in Laura's description of the parameters of her experience in 'Love and Freindship,' for example, turns out to be all too slight:

> Our neighbourhood was small, for it consisted only of your mother. . . . Isabel had seen the World. She had passed 2 Years at one of the first Boarding schools in London; had spent a fortnight in Bath & had supped one night in Southampton.
>
> (*MW* 78)

Here stock phrases are transformed by reduction into nonsense: a neighborhood becomes virtually one person; the 'World' is diminished to a provincial girl's boarding school. And yet in a manner that looks forward to the mature Austen's polyvalent irony, the laughter here turns back on itself. Once we have had our laugh, it becomes clear that Austen has not so much reduced stock phrases such as 'the world' as she has taken them at their face value in certain situations. Emma Woodhouse's 'neighbourhood' is quite as small, hardly affording her a single friend, and far from having seen the 'world,' she has never even seen the sea. Thus if first we are struck by the difference between a young lady's world and the real world, next it is likely that their sameness will appear equally unsettling. Such syntactical child's play may not appear to merit sustained attention, but Austen in fact refined patterns and rhythms very similar to these throughout her career, as the following excerpt from *Persuasion* attests:

> Be it known then, that Sir Walter, like a good father, (having met with one or two private disappointments in very unreasonable applications) prided himself on remaining single for his dear daughter's sake. For one daughter, his eldest, he would really have given up any thing, which he had not been very much tempted to do.
>
> (*P* 5)[5]

Austen's irony typically functions like a Mobius strip, first setting up two clear and discrete planes, and later showing them on the contrary to be coextensive. As in the juvenilia, the reader here hurries along only at her or his own risk, for the second half of Austen's statement will not really make 'known' what the first half says it will – that is, how Sir Walter is a 'good father' – but will rather double back to belie a professed design. Sir Walter's self-sacrifice in remaining single is subverted by parenthetical information relating his attempts to remarry, while the claim that he would 'really' give up anything for a daughter is shaken by the assurance that he has never been so disposed. Rather than appearing as a 'good father,' then, Sir Walter appears to be a poor father indeed.[6]

It is important that we see Austen's early work as exercises in stylistic and generic self-consciousness and not principally as expressions of personal belief, if we are to appreciate what is distinctive about her mature productions. 'Love and Freindship,' for example, is typically read as a fledgling *Sense and Sensibility*, a scathing satire on the unseemliness of excessive feeling. But Austen's parody, here as elsewhere, is never so essentially prescriptive nor so unitary. 'Love and Freindship' parodies the destinies inscribed by sentimental fiction, not the perniciousness of sentiment, and to overlook this layer of detachment in the sketch is to miss many of its most hilarious jokes. Here characters themselves are sometimes bewildered to discover that their very status as sentimental characters dictates otherwise gratuitous courses of action. Edward Lindsay, for example, is roused to manly opposition even when his father plights him to a woman he adores: 'No never exclaimed I. Lady Dorothea is lovely and Engaging; I prefer no woman to her; but know Sir, that I scorn to marry her in compliance with your wishes. No! Never shall it be said that I obliged my Father' (*MW* 81). Edward has no reason to defy his father, just as Laura has no reason to conceal his name 'under that of Talbot' (*MW* 80), except for the fact that both characters live in a fictive world which requires that they do.

In the juvenilia, as in the mature works, we will look in vain for unqualified and securely embedded norms that enable and oblige us to conclude that Austen is simply 'against' impetuous feeling, for example, and 'for' the authority of parents. As George Steiner has observed, Austen's 'radically linguistic' style makes such 'assured reading' difficult because it is always encoding reality in a 'distinctive idiom,' an idiom which, I would emphasize, we are always given specifically to understand is only an idiom.[7] Austen does not target feelings because the characters in 'Love and Freindship' are selfish any more than she targets landowners because in 'Henry and Eliza: A Novel' they behave like slavedrivers: 'As Sir George and Lady Harcourt were superintending the Labours of their Haymakers, rewarding the industry of some by smiles of approbation, & punishing the idleness of others, by a cudgel, they perceived . . . a beautifull little Girl not more than 3 months old' (*MW* 33). And surely she is not against either of these any more than she is against morality itself when she exposes the unfeeling pomposity and self-interest of homiletic discourse: 'We all know that many are unfortunate in their progress through the world, but we do not know all that are so. To seek them out to study their wants, & to leave them unsupplied is the duty, and ought to be the Business of Man' (*MW* 71). In each of these instances, Austen's enterprise is not to scold her characters as, say, West or More would, but rather to expose the perspectivity of various discourses and to demonstrate how stock figures, expressions, and paradigms are not faithful or innocuous representations of reality, but rather themselves are constructions, which promote certain agendas and exclude others. From the age of fifteen on, Austen, sceptical and unawed, refuses to be lulled by her medium and is determined to illuminate the interests served by its broadest structural outlines down to the subtlest details of its words, rhythms, and cadences. As we shall see, the achievement of the juvenilia would serve Austen particularly well once the stakes became higher – when the discourse she would challenge claimed to represent political truth, and when authorial audacity was more of a risk.

When Austen began to compose her full-scale parody *Northanger Abbey* sometime in the mid-1790s, the gothic novel had already been thoroughly imbued with political implications.[8] As Ronald Paulson has put it, 'By the time *The Mysteries of Udolpho* appeared (1794), the castle, prison, tyrant, and sensitive young girl could no longer be presented naively; they had all been familiarized and sophisticated by the events in France.'[9] Paulson's short catalogue of gothic images would seem implicitly to serve the progressive agenda to protect the powerless and the feminine from the abuses of a decaying but still powerful patriarchy, and some progressive novelists, such as Eliza Fenwick in *Secresy, or, The Ruin on the Rock* (1795) or Wollstonecraft in *The Wrongs of Woman, or Maria*, did employ the form or much of its imagery for precisely such purposes. Charlotte Smith, of course, combined politics and gothicism most regularly, as in *The Old Manor House* (1793) and *Marchmont* (1796). In the overtly polemical *Desmond*, in fact, her own heroine calls attention to how gothic 'excesses' figure forth realities which young girls ought to know about. Coming to gothic fiction only after her unhappy marriage, she reports how she now devoured

> the mawkish pages that told of damsels, most exquisitely beautiful, confined by a cruel father, and escaping to a heroic lover, while a wicked Lord laid in wait to tear her from him, and carried her off to some remote castle – Those delighted me most that ended miserably. . . . Had the imagination of a young person been liable to be much affected by these sorts of histories, mine would, probably, have taken a romantic turn, and at eighteen, when I was married, I should have hesitated whether I should obey my friends [sic] directions, or have waited till the hero appeared. . . . But, far from doing so, I was, you see, 'obedient – very obedient . . .'[10]

Would that Geraldine *had* had the benefit of gothic fiction to show her how to be disobedient and teach her what to suspect from her protectors. The distresses she reads about, alas, are now her own: her family commanded her unsuitable marriage for money, her husband is plotting to sell her to a rich duke, her treacherous family, entrapping her with words like 'duty' and 'obedience,' is now confining her because they suspect that her 'hero' – the progressive Desmond – will rescue her. To Smith, as to other reform-minded novelists, the gothic was not a grotesque, but in some ways a fairly unmediated representation of world 'as it is,' if not as 'it ought to be.'

But in Radcliffean gothic, the focus of Austen's parody, the political valence of gothicism is not so clear, and this despite the conservatism of Radcliffe herself. True, *The Mysteries of Udolpho* affirms a Burkean strain of paternalism by reiterating negative object lessons in the need for regulating violently subversive passional energies, lessons which apply equally to Emily, Valencourt, and Montoni.[11] But when one shows how father-surrogates like Montoni wield legal and religious authority over women in order to force marriages and thereby consolidate their own wealth, one is describing what patriarchal society daily permits as a matter of course, not what is an aberration from its softening and humanizing influences. The cozy La Vallée, presided over by the benevolent father St. Aubert, and the isolated Udolpho, ruled by the brooding and avaricious Montoni, can be seen not as polar opposites, then, but as mirror images, for considered from the outside, protectors of order and agents of tyranny can look alarmingly alike. Struck by the same double message in turn-of-the-century architecture, Mark Girouard relates the Gothic revival in English country houses specifically to the 'spectre of the French Revolution' and subsequent reassertion of authority: 'Country houses could project a disconcerting double image – relaxed and delightful to those who had the entrée, arrogant and forbidding to those who did not.'[12]

Radcliffe's novels present the double image Girouard elucidates, for they provide a Burkean rationale for repression, as well as describe the grounds for rebelling against it. In *The Italian* (1797) especially, stock characters, images, and situations veer almost entirely out of control, and a conservative agenda is maintained only by pacing the action of the novel so rapidly as to hinder reflection on politically sensitive issues intrinsic to the material – such as the extent of familial authority, the tension between private affections and public obligations, and the moral authority of the church and its representatives. The movement of the novel as a whole is to cover up. We needn't be alarmed at the ease with which fathers *could* murder daughters, because Schedoni turns out not to be Ellena's father after all; we needn't worry about the lengths to which aristocratic families go to prevent their sons from marrying beneath them, because Ellena turns out to be nobly born; we needn't protest the corruption of religious institutions, for the officers of the Inquisition, after a few perfunctorily gruesome threats of torture, finally acquit themselves as responsible ministers of truth and justice. As if unwilling herself to follow through with the potentially radical implications of her material, Radcliffe opens creaking doors to dark and dreadful passages only to slam them shut in our faces.

It has seemed to many readers that Austen's parody in *Northanger Abbey* debunks gothic conventions out of an allegiance to the common-sense world of the ordinary, where life is sane and dependable, if not always pleasant.[13] But by showing that the gothic is in fact the inside out of the ordinary, that the abbey does indeed present a disconcerting double image, particularly forbidding and arrogant to one who, like Catherine Morland, does not have an entrée, *Northanger Abbey* does not refute, but rather clarifies and reclaims, gothic conventions in distinctly political ways. Austen's parody here, as in the juvenilia, 'makes strange' a fictional style in order better to determine what it really accomplishes, and in the process it does not ridicule gothic novels nearly as much as their readers. Clearly the danger for a reader like Henry Tilney, too often mistaken for an authorial surrogate, is to dismiss gothic novels as a 'good read' – as a set of stock situations and responses to them which need not trouble us with a moment's serious reflection after we have put the book down. He is, in fact, a perfect reader for Radcliffe's particularly evasive brand of escapist thrills about the horrors that occur in safely remote Catholic countries. By contrast, the danger for a reader like Catherine is to mistake gothic exaggerations for unmediated representation, to fail to recognize their conventional trappings. Thus while Henry categorically denies the gothic any legitimately mimetic provenance, Catherine imagines that no more or less than the literal imprisonment and murder of an unhappy wife is the only crime a bad man can be charged with. By making the distrust of patriarchy which gothic fiction fosters itself the subject for outright discussion, Austen obliges us first to see the import of conventions which we, like Henry perhaps, dismiss as merely formal, and then to acknowledge, as Henry never does, that the 'alarms of romance' are a canvas onto which the 'anxieties of common life' (*NA* 201) can be projected in illuminating, rather than distorting, ways. Austen may dismiss 'alarms' concerning stock gothic *machinery* – storms, cabinets, curtains, manuscripts – with blithe amusement, but alarms concerning the central gothic *figure*, the tyrannical father, she concludes, are commensurate to the threat they actually pose.

In turning her powers of parody to a saliently politicized form, Austen raised the stakes on her work. Imperious aristocrats, frowning castles, dark dungeons, and torture chambers were safe enough before 1790, and sometimes in the juvenile sketches, such as 'Henry and Eliza' and 'Evelyn,' they surface in uproariously telescoped fashion. But once social stability was virtually equated with paternal authority, gothic material was potent stuff, and in *Northanger Abbey* Austen does not shy away from it. If anything, she emphasizes the political subtext of gothic conventions: her villain, General Tilney, is not only a repressive father, but also a self-professed defender of national security. To Catherine, the General seems most like Montoni – that is, 'dead to every sense of humanity' – when he, 'with downcast eyes and contracted brow,' paces the drawing room gloomily, pondering political 'pamphlets' and the 'affairs of the nation' (*NA* 187). By depicting the villain as an officious English gentleman, publicly respected on the local as well as national level, and 'accustomed on every ordinary occasion to give the law in his family' (*NA* 247), *Northanger Abbey*, to use Johnsonian terms, 'approximates the remote and familiarizes the wonderful' in gothic fiction, and in the process brings it into complete conjunction with the novel of manners. This conjunction is reinforced by the two-part format of the novel. The world which Catherine is entering for the first time comprises Bath and Northanger Abbey, both of which are menacing and 'strange' – Catherine's recurrent expression – to one whose 'real power,' as Eleanor Tilney says of herself, 'is nothing' (*NA* 225).

Just as conspicuously as *Mansfield Park, Northanger Abbey* concerns itself explicitly with the prerogatives of those who have what Eleanor calls 'real power' and the constraints of those who do not. Henry Tilney is far from believing that women in general, much less Catherine or his own sister, have no 'real power.' To him, women's power – in marriage, in country dances, in daily life generally – is limited, but very real: '[M]an has the advantage of choice, woman only the power of refusal' (*NA* 77). Henry's aphorism describes the conditions of female propriety as they had been traditionally conceived, and as they were reasserted throughout the 1790s by conservative advocates of female modesty. Women, by such accounts, are not initiators of their own choices, but rather are receivers of men's. If the 'power of refusal' seems detrimental or frustrating in its negativity, it is still better than nothing, for it does not leave women without any control of their destinies: women may not be permitted to pursue what they want, but they may resist what they do not want. But in Austen's novels, as in so much eighteenth-century fiction about women, women's power of refusal is severely compromised. Many Austenian men – from Collins to Crawford to Wentworth – cannot take 'no' for an answer.

In *Northanger Abbey*, bullying of various sorts is rampant, and Tilney's confidence in the feminine power of refusal is put to the test. Indeed Catherine's own friends have no scruples about lying in order to force her to comply with them rather than keep her own engagement with the Tilneys, and when caught in his lie, John Thorpe, with the apparent concurrence of Catherine's brother, 'only laughed, smacked his whip . . . and drove on,' overbearing her refusal: 'angry and vexed as she was, having no power of getting away, [Catherine] was obliged to give up the point and submit' (*NA* 87). When mere lying and abduction are not apropos, James and the Thorpes join forces to compel Catherine to surrender her power of refusal. Together, they 'demand' her agreement; they refuse her 'refusal', they 'attack' her with reproach and supplication; and they resort to emotional manipulation ('I shall think you quite unkind, if you still refuse'), fraternal bullying ('Catherine, you must go'), and eventually even to physical compulsion ('Isabella . . . caught hold of one hand; Thorpe of the other' [*NA* 98–100]). So little is Catherine's brother inclined to respect woman's 'only' power, refusal, that he defines, if not feminine, then at least sisterly virtue as a sweet-tempered yielding of her will altogether to his: 'I did not think you had been so obstinate . . . you were not used to be so hard to persuade; you once were the kindest, best-tempered of my sisters' (*NA* 99–100). The moral and physical coercion of powerless females which figures so predominantly in gothic fiction is here transposed to the daytime world of drawing room manners, where it can be shown for the everyday occurrence it is, but no less 'strange' for all that.

Against the selfishness of James Morland and the bluster of John Thorpe, Henry Tilney stands out, not in opposition, but if anything in clearer relief, for his unquestioning confidence in his focality and in the breadth of his understanding prompts him to preempt not only the female's power of refusal but indeed even her power of speech in analogous ways, without doubting the propriety of his doing so. Brothers are treated with great respect in Austenian criticism, certainly with much more than they deserve if *Northanger Abbey* and *The Watsons* are considered with due weight. Because it is assumed that Austen's feelings for her brothers – about which we actually know rather little – were fond and grateful to the point of adoration, the sceptical treatment brother figures receive in her fiction has been little examined. Between Thorpe's remark that his younger sisters 'both looked very ugly' (*NA* 49) and Tilney's reference to Eleanor as 'my stupid sister' (*NA* 113), there is little difference, for in each case, the cool possession of privilege entitles them to disparaging banter, not the less corrosive for being entirely in the normal course of things.

On most occasions, however, Tilney's bullying is more polished. A self-proclaimed expert on matters feminine, from epistolary style to muslin, Tilney simply believes that he knows women's minds better than they do, and he dismisses any 'no' to the contrary as unreal. On the first day he meets Catherine, for example, he tells her exactly what she ought to write in her journal the next morning – the entry he proposes, needless to say, is devoted entirely to the praise of himself. Female speech is never entirely repressed in Austen's fiction, but instead is dictated so as to mirror or otherwise reassure masculine desire. But when Catherine protests, 'But, perhaps, I keep no journal,' Henry, flippantly but no less decisively, does not take her 'no' for an answer: 'Perhaps you are not sitting in this room, and I am not sitting by you. These are points in which a doubt is equally possible' (*NA* 27). That, it would appear, is that, if for no other reason than that Henry himself has said so. But – for all we know to the contrary – Catherine does *not* keep a journal, and this will not be the first time that Henry, believing, as he says here, that reality itself is sooner doubted than the infallibility of his own inscriptions, will with magisterial complacence lay down the law. The effect for a woman like Catherine, 'fearful of hazarding an opinion' of her own 'in opposition to that of a self-assured man' (*NA* 48), is silencing, even when she knows she is right. Catherine would no more dream of opposing Henry here than she would the General himself when he announces that even his heir must have a profession, for as Austen makes clear, silence is exactly what he wishes: 'The imposing effect of this last argument was equal to his wishes. The silence of the lady [Catherine] proved it to be unanswerable' (*NA* 176).

Henry too, then, takes away the feminine power of refusal, simply by turning a deaf ear to it. In this respect, he is more graceful, but he is not essentially different from the General, who asks Eleanor questions only to answer them himself, or from John Thorpe, who declares that his horses are unruly when they are manifestly tame. The characteristic masculine activity in *Northanger Abbey* is measurement, a fiatlike fixing of boundaries – of mileage, of time, of money, and in Henry's case, of words. Although these boundaries turn out to be no less the projection of hopes and fears than are the overtly fanciful stuff of gothic novels, they are decreed as unanswerable facts, and the self-assurance of their promulgators enforces credence and silences dissent. Because Henry dictates the parameters of words, the kind of control he exercises extends to thought itself, the capacity for which he describes in explicitly sexual terms. Appearing to consider his respect for 'the understanding of women' a somewhat unwarranted concession, Henry quips, 'nature has given them so much [understanding], that they never find it necessary to use more than half' (*NA* 114). A great stickler for words, he bristles at any loosening of strict definition – such as relaxing the terms 'nice' and 'amazement' – and he is in the habit of 'overpowering' offenders with 'Johnson and Blair' (*NA* 108) when their usage transgresses prescribed boundaries. But when Catherine and Eleanor get entangled in their famous malentendu concerning 'something very shocking indeed, [that] will soon come out in London' (*NA* 112), linguistic looseness has served them where Henry's correctness could not. To Catherine, of course, what is shocking, horrible, dreadful, and murderous can only be a new gothic novel; to Eleanor it can only be a mob uprising of three thousand. Henry regards the interchangeability of this vocabulary as proof of a feminine carelessness of thought and language which is regrettable, laughable, and endearing at the same time, and he enlightens them by vaunting his manliness and his lucidity: 'I will prove myself a man, no less by the generosity of my soul than the clearness of my head' (*NA* 112).

Henry may be bantering again, but politically speaking the linguistic and intellectual superiority he boasts is no joke. During the 1790s in particular, privileged classes felt their [linguistic and political] hegemony [was] seriously challenged by radical social critics – some of them women, and many of the men self-educated; and as one scholar has recently demonstrated, conservatives met this challenge by asserting that the superiority of their language rendered them alone fit for participation in public life. Tilney's esteemed Dr. Johnson played a posthumous role in this process, for those 'aspects of Johnson's style that embodied hegemonic assessments of language' were 'developed and imitated' as proper models.[14] With the authority of Johnson and Blair behind him, then, Henry is empowered to consider feminine discourse – conversation or gothic novels – as either mistaken or absurd, and in any case requiring his arbitration. The course of the novel attests, however, that the misunderstanding between Catherine and Eleanor is plausible and even insightful: political unrest and gothic fiction are well served by a common vocabulary of 'horror' because they are both unruly responses to repression. Such, however, is not how Henry reads gothic novels, nor how he, in effect, teaches Catherine to read them. Indeed, the reason Catherine assents to ludicrously dark surmises about the cabinet is not that her imagination is inflamed with *Radcliffean* excesses, but rather that she trusts *Henry's* authority as a sensible man, and does not suspect that he, like John Thorpe but with much more charm, would impose on her credulity in order to amuse himself. 'How could she have so imposed on herself,' Catherine wonders. But soon she places the blame where it belongs: 'And it was in a great measure his own doing, for had not the cabinet appeared so exactly to agree with his description of her adventures, she should never have felt the smallest curiosity about it' (*NA* 173). This exercise of power by 'the knowing over the ignorant' is, as Judith Wilt has argued, 'pure Gothic,' and it is structured into the system of female education and manners.[15] In 'justice to men,' the narrator slyly avers that sensible men prefer female 'ignorance' to female 'imbecility' – let alone to the 'misfortune' of knowledge – precisely because it administers to their 'vanity' of superior knowledge (*NA* 110–11). Catherine's tendency to equate the verbs 'to torment' and 'to instruct' seems less confused given the humiliating upshot of her lesson in the gothic at Henry's hands.

But Henry, as we have seen, does not know everything. And what he does not know about gothic fiction in particular is explicitly related to his political outlook. Even though Austen spares us Tilney's 'short disquisition on the state of the nation' (*NA* 111) – delivered in part to bring Catherine to 'silence' – she does not hesitate to caricature his conservative tendency to be pollyannaish about the status quo. Catherine is a 'hopeful scholar' not only in landscape theory but also in gothic novels, and her sensitivity to the lessons they afford far surpasses the capacity of her tutor, because her position of powerlessness and dependency give her a different perspective on the status quo. Gothic novels teach the deferent and self-deprecating Catherine to do what no one and nothing else does: to distrust paternal figures and to feel that her power of refusal is continuously under siege. While still in Bath, Catherine does not feel completely secure with the attentiveness of Mr. Allen's protection; she feels impelled 'to resist such high authority' (*NA* 67) as her brother's on the subject of John Thorpe's powers of pleasing ladies; and though she finds it almost impossible to doubt General Tilney's perfect gentility, she cannot ignore the pall he casts on his household. Further, gothic novels teach Catherine about distrust and concealment, about cruel secrets hidden beneath formidable and imposing surfaces. Before she goes to Northanger, she expects to find 'some awful memorials of an injured and ill-fated nun' (*NA* 141), and what she eventually turns up there about the injured and ill-fated Mrs. Tilney is not that wide of the mark. If these were to be the 'lessons' inculcated to flighty young girls, it is small wonder conservatives should feel that they should be expunged. Writing as late as 1813, the high Tory Eaton Stannard Barrett considered gothic fiction still dangerous enough to warrant savage burlesquing in his own novel *The Heroine*. His anti-heroine's first and most heinous offense is to take gothic novels seriously enough to doubt her good father's paternity, and with that to resist his authority. From such delusions, it is only a short step to the three volumes of utter dementia that finally land her in a lunatic asylum. As the sensible Mr. Stuart patiently explains to her at the end, novels like *Coelebs* and *The Vicar of Wakefield* 'may be read without injury,' but gothic novels 'present us with incidents and characters which we can never meet in the world,' and are thus 'intoxicating stimulants.'[16]

Such of course is precisely the lesson Henry would impress upon Catherine, and it is a lesson he himself believes. When Henry Tilney learns that Catherine has suspected his father of murder, he is stupefied by a 'horror' which he has 'hardly words to —' (*NA* 197). Evidently, Johnson and Blair do not supply Henry with words adequate to what gothic novels describe all the time, and the reason the manly and 'clear-headed' Henry never read gothic fiction sensitively enough to realize this is that it insists on a doubleness which he finds semantically, as well as politically, imponderable. Because he considers England as a uniquely civilized nation, where church, education, laws, neighborhoods, roads, and newspapers make heartless husbands and their crimes rare, improbable, almost unknown, the gothic 'horror' Catherine intuits is as preposterous and even as subversive as the earlier malentendu about the 'shocking' news from London. But gothic fiction represents a world which is far more menacing and ambiguous, where figureheads of political and domestic order silence dissent, where a father can be a British subject, a Christian, a respectable citizen, *and* a ruthless and mean-spirited tyrant at the same time, one who, moreover, in some legitimate sense of the term can 'kill' his wife slowly by quelling her voice and vitality. When General Tilney sacrifices decency to avarice and banishes the now reluctant gothic heroine into the night, he proves that 'human nature, at least in the midland countries of England' *can* in fact be looked for in 'Mrs. Radcliffe's works' and those of 'all her imitators' (*NA* 200). We are never informed of Henry Tilney's reflections on this occasion, and have no reason to suppose him cognizant of the need to revise his lecture to Catherine and to acknowledge the accuracy of her suspicions. But by the end of the novel, Catherine at least is capable of reaching this conclusion on her own: 'in suspecting General Tilney of either murdering or shutting up his wife, she had scarcely sinned against his character, or magnified his cruelty' (*NA* 247).

Given the political ambience of British fiction during the 1790s, it is not surprising that of all Austen's novels, *Northanger Abbey*, arguably her earliest, should be the most densely packed with topical details of a political character – enclosure, riots, hothouses, pamphlets, and even anti-treason laws authorizing the activities of 'voluntary spies'

(*NA* 198).[17] The political contemporaneity of *Northanger Abbey* does not stop with these allusions and with its critical treatment of paternal authority, but indeed extends to another, related theme: the status of promises. The obligation to abide by promises is an important moral rule in the history of political thought, especially since it underlies the contract theory of Locke as well as older natural law theories. At the end of the century, however, the very idea of promises had been radically criticized by Godwin as one of many possible kinds of socially mediating agencies of human decision and practice which cramp the judgment of the individual subject. Debates about the value and violability of promises figure prominently in turn-of-the-century fiction. In anti-Jacobin novels, pernicious or merely benighted characters philosophize as they break their words and betray their trusts left and right. In *The Modern Philosophers*, for example, Hamilton presents the attack on promise keeping as one of the centerpieces of 'new philosophy': Vallaton reasons that the 'nobler' intervening purpose of spending money with which he has been entrusted absolves him from the prior obligation to deliver it to someone else, as he had promised; Mr. Glib releases himself from marriage – 'the mistake he has so happily detected' – quoting Godwin and decrying matrimony as 'an odious and unjust institution'; and the ugly Bridgetina urges a man to break his engagement to another women by ranting 'Who can promise forever? . . . Are not the opinions of a perfectible being ever changing? You do not at present see my preferableness, but you may not be always blind to a truth so obvious.'[18]

Since social stability depends in large part on keeping one's word, it is not surprising that Godwin's critique of promises and trusts proved upsetting to conservative readers. But for reform-minded novelists, keeping promises is more likely to promote cynical and sterile legalism than social cohesiveness. Stopping well this side of Godwin's radical critique of promises, they expose how the sanctity of promises is something for underlings always to observe and for perfidious overlords to omit whenever it suits their interests. Without trumpeting its political relevance, Inchbald shows in *A Simple Story* that breaches of promise are countenanced by the powerful all the time. When Dorriforth's wife breaks her marital vows, she is justly banished into shameful oblivion. Yet Dorriforth, formerly a Catholic priest, had reneged on his vow of celibacy with the full approval of his confessor and the community because doing so enabled him to inherit an immense fortune and thus to enhance the worldly power of the Church. When expedience dictates, powerful characters routinely break their promises – of celibacy, fidelity, secrecy – with complete impunity, and in fact without as much as acknowledging such acts as breaches, while sustaining other promises, particularly punitive ones against subordinates, with inhumane strenuousness. In *Northanger Abbey* Austen, like Inchbald, dramatizes the implications of promise breaking and keeping as a function of the power of the characters concerned.

Breaking engagements and words of honor of all sorts is the predominant activity in *Northanger Abbey*. Instances may vary in intensity, but they all amount to the same thing: Isabella's 'engagement' to marry James Morland; Catherine's 'engagement' to walk with the Tilneys; Henry's 'promise' to wait and read *The Mysteries of Udolpho* with his sister; General Tilney's pompously worded assurance 'to make Northanger Abbey not wholly disagreeable' (*NA* 140) to Catherine, to name only a few. The issue of promise breaking, of course, predates the social criticism of the 1790s, and can thus illustrate the polarization that took place as the reaction wore on. Richardson's Grandison can criticize fashionable lying on generally accepted grounds, but in the 1790s, the topic is marked as radical. An eighteenth-century reader would have recognized as a breach of trust General Tilney's order to deny Catherine at the door when he and his daughter were really at home. Much to the annoyance of the conservative Issac Disraeli, social reformers in their typical way made far too much of this, the domestic prerogative of every gentleman, and thus in *Vaurien*, he has the Jacobin windbag, Mr. Subtile, denounce the practice of 'denying yourself when at home. I would not commit such a crime if a bailiff demanded admittance. It is a national system of lying and impudence.'[19] Catherine could have read in her mother's copy of Richardson's novel that Grandison scorns the practice, and with his example in mind, Lady Williams in 'Jack and Alice' pronounces it 'little less than downright Bigamy' (*MW* 15), a simile which highlights the promissory character of civility and monogamy. It is no accident that manners in Bath seem as 'strange' to Catherine as the behavior in gothic fiction, for in both nothing is predictable and no one can be depended upon, least of all the figures one has been taught to trust. When the deceived Catherine meditates on 'broken promises and broken arches; phaetons and false hangings, Tilneys and trap-doors' (*NA* 87), her associations betray a seepage of the gothic into the quotidian that begins to localize her anxieties. Henry, as we have seen, discredits gothic novels because he believes that English 'law' itself, as well as the pressure of 'social and literary intercourse' (*NA* 197), enforces decency. But in depicting a strange world of broken promises and betrayed trusts, Catherine's gothic novels and *Northanger*

Abbey alike denude familiar institutions and figures of their amiable facades in order to depict the menacing aspect they can show to the marginalized.

Henry Tilney explicitly raises the issue of promises, and his famous conceit jocularly likening marriage to a country dance is striking for the anxiety it persistently evinces about infidelity:

> 'We have entered into a contract of mutual agreeableness for the space of an evening, and all our agreeableness belongs solely to each other for that time. Nobody can fasten themselves on the notice of one, without injuring the rights of the other. I consider a country-dance as an emblem of marriage. Fidelity and complaisance are the principal duties of both; and those men who do not chuse to dance or marry themselves, have no business with the partners or wives of their neighbours. . . . You will allow, that in both, man has the advantage of choice, woman only the power of refusal; that in both, it is an engagement between man and woman, formed for the advantage of each; and that when once entered into, they belong exclusively to each other till the moment of its dissolution; that it is their duty, each to endeavour to give the other no cause for wishing that he or she had bestowed themselves elsewhere, and their best interest to keep their own imaginations from wandering towards the perfections of their neighbours, or fancying that they should have been better off with any one else.'
>
> (*NA* 76–77)

Frederick Tilney's subsequent interference with the dancing, as well as marital plans, of Isabella Thorpe and James Morland engages the serious subjects Tilney flippantly raises here. Given the centrality of illicit sexuality to the fiction of the time, Henry's disquisition rings with special significance, especially since it is always attempting to forestall the threat of faithlessness. In comparison to that of her contemporaries, Austen's fiction is exceedingly discreet. Though she never excludes the illicit entirely, she displaces it onto the periphery of her plots. But from there it exercises considerable influence. Henry's speech is the closest Austen gets to commentary on the subject of fidelity until *Mansfield Park*, and even there the topic is integrated into the dramatic fabric of the plot, rather than isolated and discussed as an abstract issue, as it is here. To Catherine, of course, Henry's comparison is absurd, since an engagement to dance merely binds people 'for half an hour,' while '[p]eople that marry can never part' (*NA* 77). Catherine feels this difference acutely, and her failure to appreciate Henry's humor is another instance of the wisdom she unwittingly articulates throughout the novel. After all, the deceased Mrs. Tilney and her gothic avatar, the 'injured and ill-fated nun' (*NA* 141) whose memorials Catherine expects to find at Northanger, both epitomize the lot of females immured in remote abbeys who would not have the power to leave even if they were not bound by indissoluble vows. To be sure, Austen is emphatically not recommending the passage of divorce laws, as had novelists such as Imlay, Godwin and Holcroft. But neither does she here or anywhere else in her fiction overlook the desolation experienced by those who have more than enough 'cause for wishing that [they] had bestowed themselves elsewhere' (*NA* 77).

Few characters in *Northanger Abbey* have kept promises as faithfully as Mrs. Tilney, not even Henry who, as we have seen, is not above imposing on Catherine's credulity for the sake of a joke. Henry finds the formulation 'faithful promise' ludicrous. The self-appointed monitor of Catherine's language, he rather atypically sputters at some length about its redundancy: 'Promised so faithfully! – A faithful promise! – That puzzles me. – I have heard of a faithful performance. But a faithful promise – the fidelity of promising!' (*NA* 196). Henry naturally disapproves of the phrase because in one very important matter at least he is so eminently faithful: at the end of the novel, Henry feels himself so 'bound as much in honour as in affection to Miss Morland,' that nothing the angry General does can 'shake his [Henry's] fidelity,' and nothing can justify the General's 'unworthy retraction of a tacit consent' (*NA* 247). A faithful subject in a civilized land, Henry, despite what the ingenuous Catherine considers his satirical turn, is too sanguine to acknowledge the aptness of the phrase in a world where almost all promises are not faithful. Isabella Thorpe, of course, is the most conspicuous promise breaker in the novel: 'Isabella had promised and promised again' (*NA* 201) to write, Catherine exclaims, as yet unaware that Isabella's promises – of friendship or love – routinely give way to interest. But Isabella's faithlessness is so foregrounded that it is possible to overlook how it functions to implicate promise breakers like the General and others who, because they possess power, breach trust with impunity. Conservative novels, such as *A Gossip's Story*, counterbalance the moral instability of selfish and flighty females with the sobriety and responsibility of firm father figures, and thus provide a benign rationale for paternal repression. But in *Northanger Abbey* these two tropic figures are mutually illuminating, for in every respect except the position of authority, General Tilney and Isabella Thorpe are similar characters who cause disorder because they never mean what they say.

Already thinking about dropping James Morland in favor of Frederick Tilney, Isabella remarks, 'What one means one day, you know, one may not mean the next. Circumstances change, opinions alter' (*NA* 146). The mutability Isabella describes does release people from some engagements. After Catherine is apprised of Isabella's duplicity, she admits, 'I cannot still love her' (*NA* 207), without appearing to realize how her behavior here exemplifies the pertinence of Isabella's earlier observation on the justness of dissolving certain promises. But Isabella's faithlessness, like the General's, results, not from a change of heart, but from a choice of policy favoring wealth. Just as Isabella chooses Frederick Tilney solely because he, as the General states, 'will perhaps inherit as considerable a landed property as any private man in the county' (*NA* 176), General Tilney courts Catherine solely because he believes her to be heiress to Mr. Allen's large estate. Thus the two figures who most belittle the advantages of wealth also, to Catherine's bewilderment, pursue it the most greedily and unscrupulously. In Isabella's case, of course, this means, as Eleanor Tilney puts it, 'violating an engagement voluntarily entered into with another man' (*NA* 205–6). In the General's case, this means, in effect, stealing Catherine from another man who had at the time 'pretty well resolved upon marrying Catherine himself' (*NA* 244).

The self-interest which prompts Isabella to deploy her charms in order to secure Captain Tilney is surely no more dishonorable than that which prompts the General 'to spare no pains in weakening [Thorpe's] boasted interest and ruining his dearest hopes' (*NA* 245). In very important respects it is less so, for the General's superior position obligates him to consider the care of dependents, let alone invited guests, more conscientiously. Unlike Captain Tilney, Catherine is an unsuspecting party to brute self-interest, and as a woman is wholly dependent upon the good will and guidance of superiors. As it turns out, however, Catherine's trust that the General 'could not propose any thing improper for her' (*NA* 156) is sorely misplaced. Having strong-armed Catherine into Northanger Abbey, 'courting [her] from the protection of real friends' (*NA* 225) and encouraging her sense of 'false security' (*NA* 228), he just as authoritatively thrusts her out, without any qualms about violated trust, and without 'allowing her even the appearance of choice' (*NA* 226). While the pledges made to dependents ought to be observed with, if anything, greater attention, General Tilney appears to believe that they do not matter and can therefore be flouted without inviting the embarrassments of social reproach which Henry believes, in Burkean fashion, restrain the insolent from abusiveness. Indifferent to the 'patriarchal hospitality' which a conservative novelist like West associated with men of his position, the General banishes Catherine from his house precisely *because* he considers her beneath the imperatives of common civility: 'to turn her from the house seemed the best, though to his feelings an inadequate proof of his resentment towards herself, and his contempt of her family' (*NA* 244). To depict the respectable country gentleman not as one who binds himself benevolently and responsibly to inferiors, but who on the contrary behaves as though his social superiority absolved him from responsibility to inferiors, is to cross over into the territory of radical novelists, whose fictions expose petty tyrants of General Tilney's ilk. Not until *Persuasion* would Austen again arraign a figure of his stature so decisively.

For Isabella, the matter stands quite differently. Merely mercenary herself, she is outmatched by Frederick Tilney. A permutation of the gothic villain, he appears on the scene with no other purpose than to gratify his vanity of dominion by breaking a preexisting engagement. Backing away from the depiction of the violation of vows within marriage, Austen nevertheless imputes to a representative of the ruling class – an oldest son, heir, and guardian of national security – an activity which conservative novelists impute to the minions of Robespierre. If Henry's earlier speech on marriage and country dances is a reliable guide, then Isabella does not bear sole responsibility for the jilting of James Morland. At that time Henry, annoyed by Thorpe's ostensible civilities to Catherine, argues, 'He has no business to withdraw the attention of my partner from me . . . our agreeableness belongs solely to each other, and nobody can fasten themselves on the notice of one, without injuring the rights of the other' (*NA* 76). Remembering this, Catherine questions Henry closely about his brother's brazen interference and until the end of the novel finds it impossible to believe that Captain Tilney would connive at breaking others' promises and knowingly injure 'the rights' of her brother. Whatever her own inattention, Isabella believes that Frederick Tilney is attached to her: 'he would take no denial' (*NA* 134), and in this novel refusing the denials of women is a very common activity, no matter how pleasing Isabella may have found it in the present case. Because Captain Tilney not only 'fastens' himself on her attention, but pledges an intention to marry where none exists – in Catherine's words he 'only made believe to do so for mischief's sake' (*NA* 219) – Isabella's breach of promise to Morland looks less self-willed. If she has acted only to secure her own interest, she in turn has been acted upon by Frederick only to destroy James's. Ever the defender of the status quo, Henry does not consider Frederick's trespasses to bespeak any remarkable fault. But when he imputes the whole affair to Isabella's heartlessness, the unconvinced Catherine replies with a scepticism that marks the beginning of her detachment from Tilney's judgment and her awareness of its partiality: 'It is very right that you should stand by your brother' (*NA* 219).

As garrulous and high-spirited as it is, *Northanger Abbey* is an alarming novel to the extent that it, in its own unassuming and matter-of-fact way, domesticates the gothic and brings its apparent excesses into the drawing rooms of 'the midland countries of England' (*NA* 200). With the exception of Isabella, who is herself betrayed, the agents of betrayal are figures from whom Catherine has every right to expect just the opposite. James Morland, hardly a sage or exemplary figure, is not only an eldest son, but is also destined for the Church, as Austen repeats; and yet he considers promises of so little importance that he countenances and even participates in abusive attempts to compel his sister to break her engagements. More formidable personages – General Tilney and his son – with insolent abandon flout agreements basic to civility. Depicting guardians of national, domestic, and even religious authority as socially destabilizing figures, *Northanger Abbey* has indeed appropriated the gothic, in a distinctively progressive way. Catherine, unencumbered by the elaborate proprieties that tie the hands of gothic heroines, is free to make blunt declarations and to ask embarrassing questions that expose the duplicity and the deficiency of those on whom innocence such as her own ought to rely. Whether she is thanking her brother for coming to Bath to visit her, asking Henry what Captain Tilney could mean by flirting with an engaged woman, or trying to reconcile the General's claims of liberality with his anticipated objections to Isabella's poverty, she is discovering – unwittingly perhaps, but with stunning accuracy – the betrayals of paternal figures and the discourse they wield. It is no accident, then, that Austen can back gracefully out of the impasse to which she brings Catherine at the end only by resorting to an authorially underscored *surplus* of the conventions she parodies. Alluding to the 'tell-tale compression of the pages before them' which can only signal that 'we are all hastening together to perfect felicity' (*NA* 250), and declining to describe Eleanor's newfound husband because 'the most charming young man in the world is instantly before the imagination of us all' (*NA* 251), Austen turns Radcliffean conclusions, which labor to undo disturbing and subversive implications, back on themselves: the General's 'cruelty,' we are assured, was actually 'rather conducive' (*NA* 252) to the felicity of Henry and Catherine, since it provided them with the occasion to get to know each other. But carrying over the practice of her juvenilia into her mature work, Austen draws attention to the artificiality, rather than the *vraisemblance*, of her conclusion, and implies in the process that the damage wrought by the likes of General Tilney is in fact not resolvable into the 'perfect felicity' of fiction, and that the convention of the happy ending conceals our all-too-legitimate cause for alarm.

A fitting sequel to the juvenilia, *Northanger Abbey* considers the authority of men and books, women's books in particular, and suggests how the latter can illuminate and even resist the former. Having been 'ashamed of liking Udolpho' (*NA* 107) herself, Catherine regards novels as a preeminently feminine genre which men are right to pooh-pooh as they do: 'gentlemen,' she explains, 'read better books' (*NA* 106). Henry pounces with a characteristically conclusory retort: 'The person, be it gentleman or lady, who has not pleasure in a good novel, must be intolerably stupid' (*NA* 106). Here, as elsewhere, Henry's position is more glib than acute, because Austen herself claims a value for fiction that goes well beyond the pleasure of suspense which Henry appears to think is the only thing gothic novels have to offer: 'when I had once begun [*The Mysteries of Udolpho*], I could not lay down again' (*NA* 106). But *Northanger Abbey* is a dauntlessly self-affirming novel, which Austen undertakes to place alongside *Cecilia*, *Camilla*, and *Belinda* as likewise displaying 'the greatest powers of the mind' and 'the most thorough knowledge of human nature' (*NA* 38).

Of course *Northanger Abbey* stands beside *The Italian* and *The Mysteries of Udolpho* as well, since parodies are acknowledgments of respect, as well as acts of criticism. Austen's display of human nature in *Northanger Abbey* is necessarily coupled with Radcliffe's, and is executed by showing the justification for gothic conventions, not by dismissing them. Continuously sensitizing us to the mediating properties of gothic conventions, Austen provides the readers of her own as well as Radcliffe's novels with the distance necessary to see the dark and despotic side of the familiar and to experience it as 'strange' rather than as proper and inevitable. *Northanger Abbey* accomplishes its social criticism, then, not only by what it says, but also by how it says it, for Austen creates an audience not only able but also inclined to read their novels and their societies with critical detachment.

Notes

1. *Northanger Abbey* in R. W. Chapman (ed.), *The Novels of Jane Austen* (London: Oxford University Press, 1980–82). In the text, the title is abbreviated as *NA*.
2. Virginia Woolf, *The Common Reader*, First Series (New York: Harcourt, Brace, 1953), p. 139.
3. A recent biographer considers Austen's self-confidence here too intense to belong to an 'unpublished novelist' and so argues that the passage is an insertion dating from 1816; see Jane Aiken Hodge, *Only a Novel: The Double Life of Jane Austen* (London: Hodder and Stoughton, 1972), p. 178.

4. *Minor Works* in Chapman (ed.), *The Novels of Jane Austen*. In the text the title is abbreviated as *MW*.

5. *Persuasion* in Chapman (ed.), *The Novels of Jane Austen*. In the text the title is abbreviated as *P*.

6. Austen's irony will appear more volatile if we consider the controversy over the placement of the apostrophe in 'daughter's.' The first edition has 'daughter' in the singular. But Chapman notes that the following sentence makes sense only if 'daughter' is plural, and many editors of widely read paperbound editions accordingly emend the word to 'daughters'' (*P* 292). If Sir Walter 'prides himself' in making sacrifices like 'a good father' to all his daughters, the passage cries out against him even more. Among the few financial cutbacks he actually approves is the elimination of gifts for Anne, and later, readily forgetting Mary's existence altogether, he alludes to Anne as his 'youngest daughter' (*P* 143).

7. See George Steiner, *After Babel: Aspects of Language and Translation* (New York: Oxford University Press, 1975), pp. 8–11.

8. The compositional history of *Northanger Abbey* is still widely debated. For a clear summary of hypotheses see A. W. Litz, *Jane Austen: A Study of Her Artistic Development* (New York: Oxford University Press, 1965), pp. 175–6, and B. C. Southam *Jane Austen's Literary Manuscripts* (London: Oxford University Press, 1964), pp. 60–62. While Cassandra Austen's Memorandum dates the novel at 'about the years 98 & 99,' C. S. Emden has argued that *Northanger Abbey* evolved as early as 1794, a conjecture which would anchor the novel even more firmly to political controversies; see '*Northanger Abbey* Re-Dated?,' *Notes & Queries* 105 (September 1950): 407–10.

9. Ronald Paulson, *Representations of Revolution, 1789–1820* (New Haven: Yale University Press, 1983), p. 221.

10. Charlotte Smith, *Desmond* (London, 1792), 3 vols., vol. 2, p. 174. For a discussion of the radical character of Smith's novel, see Diana Bowstead, 'Charlotte Smith's *Desmond*: The Epistolary Novel as Ideological Argument,' in Mary Anne Schofield and Cecilia Macheski (eds.), *Fetter'd or Free? British Women Novelists, 1670–1815* (Athens: Ohio University Press, 1986), pp. 237–63. For a general essay on the relation of Smith to Austen – which does not, however, make an issue of the former's radical sympathies – see William H. Magee, 'The Happy Marriage: The Influence of Charlotte Smith on Jane Austen,' *SNNTS*, 7 (1975), 120–32.

11. See Paulson, *Representations of Revolution*, pp. 225–27, and Mary Poovey, 'Ideology and *The Mysteries of Udolpho*,' *Criticism* 21 (1971): 307–30.

12. Marc Girouard, *Life in the English Country House: A Social and Architectural History* (New Haven: Yale University Press, 1978), p. 242.

13. Critics who have argued that *Northanger Abbey* shows 'ordinary' life to be safe and fundamentally 'a-gothic' include Marilyn Butler, *Jane Austen and the War of Ideas* (Oxford: Clarendon Press, 1975), pp. 178–79; Kenneth Moler, *Jane Austen's Art of Illusion* (Lincoln: University of Nebraska Press, 1968), pp. 38–40; and most recently P. J. M. Scott, who contends that much of this neither 'profound' nor 'even fairly interesting' novel is devoted to exposing a gap between 'the worlds of art and the life outside them' which is doomed to triviality because the heroine 'is simply not intelligent enough' to make her adventures interesting; in *Jane Austen: A Reassessment* (New York: Barnes & Noble, 1982), pp. 37–39. Most other readers feel that while *Northanger Abbey* does discredit the gothic, it nevertheless prohibits us from trusting too unsuspiciously in 'common life,' as represented by General Tilney. Such

critics include Lionel Trilling, *Opposing Self* (New York: Viking Press, 1955), p. 207; A. W. Litz, *Artistic Development*, p. 63; Barbara Hardy, *A Reading of Jane Austen* (New York: New York University Press, 1976), pp. 130–31.

14. Olivia Smith, *The Politics of Language 1791–1819* (Oxford: Clarendon Press, 1984), p. 19. I am much indebted to this important study.

15. Judith Wilt, *Ghosts of the Gothic* (Princeton: Princeton University Press, 1980), p. 138. My views on the gothic have also been greatly influenced by George Levine, '*Northanger Abbey*: from Parody to Novel and the Translated Monster' in *The Realistic Imagination: English Fiction from Frankenstein to Lady Chatterley* (Chicago: University of Chicago Press, 1981), pp. 61–80; and by William Patrick Day, *In the Circles of Fear and Desire: A Study of Gothic Fantasy* (Chicago: University of Chicago Press, 1985), pp. 22–67.

16. Eaton Stannard Barrett, *The Heroine* (London, 1813), 3 vols., vol. 3, pp. 288–89. Austen reports that she was 'very much amused' by this novel, and that it 'diverted' her 'exceedingly.' See R. W. Chapman (ed.), *Jane Austen's Letters to her Sister Cassandra and Others* (Oxford: Oxford University Press, 1959, 2nd edn), p. 376 (2 March 1814).

17. My discussion owes much to Robert Hopkins, 'General Tilney and Affairs of State: The Political Gothic of *Northanger Abbey*,' *Philological Quarterly* 57 (1978): 213–25, and B. C. Southam, 'General Tilney's Hot-Houses,' *Ariel* 2 (1971): 52–62.

18. Elizabeth Hamilton, *Memoirs of Modern Philosophers* (London, 1800), 3 vols., vol. 3, pp. 56, 105.

19. Isaac Disraeli, *Vaurien; Or, Sketches of the Times* (London, 1797), 2 vols., vol. 1, p. 82.

Notes on Authors

JOHN BARRELL teaches English at the University of York. Alongside various editions, his books include *The Idea of Landscape and the Sense of Place, 1730–1840: An Approach to the Poetry of John Clare* (1972), *The Dark Side of the Landscape: The Rural Poor in English Painting, 1730–1840* (1980), *English Literature in History, 1730–1780: An Equal, Wide Survey* (1983), *The Political Theory of Painting from Reynolds to Hazlitt: 'The Body of the Public'* (1986), *Poetry, Language, and Politics* (1988), *The Infection of Thomas de Quincey: A Psychopathology of Imperialism* (1991), and *The Birth of Pandora and the Division of Knowledge* (1992).

MARILYN BUTLER is Rector of Exeter College, Oxford. Her books include *Maria Edgworth: A Literary Biography* (1972), *Jane Austen and the War of Ideas* (1975), *Peacock Displayed: A Satirist in his Context* (1979), *Romantics, Rebels, and Reactionaries: English Literature and Its Background, 1760–1830* (1981), and *Literature as a Heritage: Or Reading Other Ways* (1988). She has also edited *Burke, Paine, Godwin and the Revolution Controversy* (1984).

MARGARET ANNE DOODY is Andrew W. Mellon Professor of Humanities and Professor of English at Vanderbilt University, Nashville, Tennessee, where she also directs the Comparative Literature Program. Her books include *A Natural Passion: A Study of the Novels of Samuel Richardson* (1974), *The Daring Muse: Augustan Poetry Reconsidered* (1985), *Frances Burney: The Life in the Works* (1988), and *The True Story of the Novel* (1996). She is currently working on a book on Apuleins, as well as a book on hymns and sacred songs.

JULIA EPSTEIN is Professor of Comparative Literature at Haverford College, Pennsylvania, and, in 1997–98, Distinguished Visiting Scholar at the Women's Leadership Institute at Mills College. She is author of *The Iron Pen: Frances Burney and the Politics of Women's Writing* (1989), and *Altered Conditions: Disease, Medicine, and Storytelling* (1995), and (with Kristina Straub) has edited *Body Guards: The Cultural Politics of Gender Ambiguity* (1991).

ROBERT FOLKENFLIK, Professor of English at the University of California, Irvine, is the author of *Samuel Johnson: Biographer* (1978), and has edited, amongst other volumes, *The Culture of Autobiography: Constructions of Self-Representation* (1993). He is currently working on a book entitled *Criticism and Literary Theory from Sidney to Johnson* (also for Longman) – for which he held a fellowship at the Rockefeller Study Center (Bellagio). He has recently completed an edition of *Sir Launcelot Greaves* for the Georgia Edition of the Works of Tobias Smollett.

CLAUDIA L. JOHNSON is Professor of English at Princeton University. She is author of *Jane Austen: Women, Politics, and the Novel* (1988), and *Equivocal Beings: Politics, Gender, and Sentimentality in the 1790s: Wollstonecraft, Radcliffe, Burney, Austen*

(1995). She has recently completed the Norton Critical Edition of *Mansfield Park*, and is currently working on the history of novel studies, entitled *Raising the Novel*.

CAROL KAY has taught at Princeton University, Amherst College, Washington University, and New York University, and now teaches English at the University of Pittsburgh. She is the author of *Political Constructions: Defoe, Richardson, and Sterne in Relation to Hobbes, Hume, and Burke* (1988). She is presently working on a book about Hume.

RICHARD KROLL is Associate Professor of English and Comparative Literature at the University of California, Irvine. He is author of *The Material Word: Literate Culture in the Restoration and Early Eighteenth Century* (1991), and co-editor of *Philosophy, Science, and Religion in England, 1640–1700* (1992). He is currently working on a book on Restoration drama provisionally entitled *The Circular Economies of Restoration Drama*.

JONATHAN LAMB is Professor of English at Princeton University. He is the author of *Sterne's Fiction and the Double Principle* (1989), and *The Rhetoric of Suffering: Reading the Book of Job in the Eighteenth Century* (1995).

MARY POOVEY is Professor of English and Director of the Institute for the History of the Production of Knowledge at New York University. Her books include *The Proper Lady and the Woman Writer: Ideology as Style in the Works of Mary Wollstonecraft, Mary Shelley, and Jane Austen* (1984), *Uneven Developments: The Ideological Work of Gender in Mid-Victorian England* (1988), and *Making a Social Body: British Cultural Formation, 1830–1864* (1995). Her latest book, *A History of the Modern Fact: Problems of Knowledge in the Sciences of Wealth and Society*, will appear in 1998.

GEORGE STARR is Professor of English at the University of California, Berkeley. His books include *Defoe and Spiritual Autobiography* (1965) and *Defoe and Casuistry* (1971). He has a wide range of interests outside eighteenth-century literature, including American literature (Mark Twain, Bret Harte, Joaquin Miller, Ernest Hemingway), architectural history, and Hungarian Calvinist art.

IAN WATT, Professor Emeritus of English at Stanford University, is the author of the classic study *The Rise of the Novel: Studies in Defoe, Richardson and Fielding*, originally published in 1957, but reprinted many times since. Apart from numerous editions of essay collections and novels, primarily by Austen and Conrad, his other books include *Conrad in the Nineteenth Century* (1979), and *Myths of Modern Individualism: Faust, Don Quixote, Don Juan, Robinson Crusoe* (1996).

DONALD WEHRS is Associate Professor of English at Auburn University, Alabama. He has written both on eighteenth-century fiction and on French African fiction, and is presently engaged on a long project bringing together his interest in African literature and novel theory.

Further Reading

I have divided the books and articles listed here into eight categories, to reflect the structure and concerns of this anthology. Some of these, or their main theses, are discussed in my introduction, or are summarized by a key article or chapter included in the collection above. To some extent, any reading list will be arbitrary, but I have tried to present the student with some sense of the standard historiography on each topic or author, as well as with pieces that try new things.

General anthologies of essays

RICHETTI, JOHN (ed.). *The Columbia History of the British Novel*. New York: Columbia University Press, 1994.

RICHETTI, JOHN, *et al.* (eds). *The Cambridge Companion to the Eighteenth-Century Novel*. Cambridge: Cambridge University Press, 1996.

General studies of sentimentalism and the gothic

BARKER-BENFIELD, G. J. *The Culture of Sensibility: Sex and Society in Eighteenth-Century Britain*. Chicago: University of Chicago Press, 1992.

BRAUDY, LEO. 'The Form of the Sentimental Novel.' *Novel* 7 (1973): 5–13.

BREDVOLD, LOUIS I. *The Natural History of Sensibility*. Detroit: Wayne State University Press, 1962.

BRISSENDEN, R. F. *Virtue in Distress: Studies in the Novel of Sentiment from Richardson to Sade*. London: Macmillan, 1974.

CRANE, R. S. 'Suggestions towards a Genealogy of the "Man of Feeling".' *ELH* 1 (1934): 205–30.

FRYE, NORTHROP. 'Towards Defining an Age of Sensibility.' In James L. Clifford (ed.), *Eighteenth-Century English Literature: Essays in Modern Criticism*. London: Oxford University Press, 1959, pp. 311–18.

HAGSTRUM, JEAN. *Sex and Sensibility: Ideal and Erotic Love from Milton to Mozart*. Chicago: University of Chicago Press, 1980.

KAY, CAROL. *Political Constructions: Defoe, Richardson, and Sterne in Relation to Hobbes, Hume, and Burke*. Ithaca: Cornell University Press, 1988.

KIELY, ROBERT. *The Romantic Novel in England*. Cambridge, MA: Harvard University Press, 1972.

MULLAN, JOHN. *Sentiment and Sociability: The Language of Feeling in the Eighteenth Century*. Oxford: Clarendon Press, 1988.

SEDGWICK, EVE KOSOFSKY. 'The Character in the Veil: Imagery of the Surface in the Gothic Novel.' *PMLA* 96 (1981): 255–70.

TOMPKINS, J. M. S. *The Popular Novel in England, 1770–1800*. Lincoln: University of Nebraska Press, 1961.

TODD, JANET. *Sensibility: An Introduction*. London: Methuen, 1986.

VAN SANT, ANN JESSIE. *Eighteenth-Century Sensibility and the Novel: The Senses in Social Context*. Cambridge: Cambridge University Press, 1993.

Women novelists in the later eighteenth century

BALLASTER, ROS. *Seductive Forms: Women's Amatory Fiction from 1684 to 1840*. Oxford: Clarendon Press, 1992.

GALLAGHER, CATHERINE. *Nobody's Story: The Vanishing Acts of Women Writers in the Marketplace, 1670–1820*. Berkeley: University of California Press, 1994.

GONDA, CAROLINE. *Reading Daughters' Fictions, 1709–1834: Novels and Society from Manley to Edgworth*. Cambridge: Cambridge University Press, 1996.

JOHNSON, CLAUDIA. *Equivocal Beings: Politics, Gender, and Sentimentality in the 1790s: Wollstonecraft, Radcliffe, Burney, Austen*. Chicago: University of Chicago Press, 1995.

POOVEY, MARY. *The Proper Lady and the Woman Writer: Ideology as Style in the Works of Mary Wollstonecraft, Mary Shelley, and Jane Austen*. Chicago: University of Chicago Press, 1984.

SPACKS, PATRICIA M. *Desire and Truth: Functions of Plot in Eighteenth-Century English Novels*. Chicago: University of Chicago Press, 1990.

TURNER, CHERYL. *Living by the Pen: Women Writers in the Eighteenth Century*. London: Routledge, 1992.

Smollett

BARRELL, JOHN. *English Literature in History, 1730–1780: An Equal, Wide Survey*. London: Hutchinson, 1983.

BASKER, J. *Tobias Smollett, Critic and Journalist*. Newark: University of Delaware Press, 1988.

DOUGLAS, AILEEN. *Uneasy Sensations: Smollett and the Body*. Chicago: University of Chicago Press, 1995.

PAULSON, RONALD. 'Satire in the Early Novels of Smollett.' *Journal of English and Germanic Philology* 59 (1960): 381–402.

ROUSSEAU, G. S. *Tobias Smollett: Essays of Two Decades*. Edinburgh: Clark, 1982.

SEKORA, JOHN. *Luxury: The Concept in Western Thought, Eden to Smollett*. Baltimore: The Johns Hopkins University Press, 1977.

Sterne

BROWN, MARSHALL. 'Sterne's Stories.' In *Preromanticism*. Stanford: Stanford University Press, 1991.

BURCKHARDT, SIGURD. '*Tristram Shandy*'s Law of Gravity.' *ELH* 28 (1961): 70–88.

CASH, ARTHUR H. *Laurence Sterne: The Early and Middle Years*. London: Methuen, 1975.

—— *Laurence Sterne: The Later Years*. London: Methuen, 1986.

LAMB, JONATHAN. *Sterne's Fiction and the Double Principle*. Cambridge: Cambridge University Press, 1989.

TRAUGOTT, JOHN. *Tristram Shandy's World: Sterne's Philosophical Rhetoric*. Berkeley: University of California Press, 1954.

Burney

CASTLE, TERRY. *Masquerade and Civilization: The Carnivalesque in Eighteenth-Century English Culture and Fiction*. Stanford: Stanford University Press, 1986.
DEVLIN, D. D. *The Novels and Journals of Fanny Burney*. New York: Peter Lang, 1987.
DOODY, MARGARET ANNE. *Frances Burney: The Life in the Works*. New Brunswick: Rutgers University Press, 1988.
Eighteenth-Century Fiction 3 (1991) [special *Evelina* issue].
EPSTEIN, JULIA. *The Iron Pen: Frances Burney and the Politics of Women's Writing*. Madison: University of Wisconsin Press, 1989.
HEMLOW, JOYCE. *The History of Fanny Burney*. Oxford: Clarendon Press, 1958.
ROGERS, KATHERINE M. *Frances Burney: The World of 'Female Difficulties.'* New York: Harvester Wheatsheaf, 1990.

Radcliffe

Most work on Radcliffe appears as a part of more general studies of women authors, the gothic novel, and the novels of the 1790s.

BUTLER, MARILYN. 'The Woman at the Window: Ann Radcliffe in the Novels of Mary Wollstonecraft and Jane Austen.' *Women and Literature* 1 (1980): 128–48.
CASTLE, TERRY. 'The Spectralization of the Other in *The Mysteries of Udolpho*.' In Felicity Nussbaum and Laura Brown (eds), *The New Eighteenth Century: Theory, Politics, English Literature*. London: Methuen, 1987, pp. 231–52.
DURANT, DAVID S. *Ann Radcliffe's Novels: Experiments in Setting*. New York: Arno, 1980.
MILES, ROBERT. *Ann Radcliffe: The Great Enchantress*. Manchester: Manchester University Press, 1995.
POOVEY, MARY. 'Ideology and *The Mysteries of Udolpho*.' *Criticism* 21 (1979): 307–30.
SPACKS, PATRICIA M. 'Female Orders of Narrative: *Clarissa* and *The Italian*.' In J. Douglas Canfield and J. Paul Hunter (eds.), *Rhetorics of Order / Ordering Rhetorics in English Neoclassical Literature*. Newark: University of Delaware Press, 1989, pp. 158–72.

Austen

BUTLER, MARILYN. *Jane Austen and the War of Ideas*. 1975; rev. edn. Oxford: Clarendon Press, 1987.
DUCKWORTH, ALISTAIR M. *The Improvement of the Estate: A Study of Jane Austen's Novels*. Baltimore: The Johns Hopkins University Press, 1971.
EHRENPREIS, IRVIN. *Acts of Implication: Suggestion and Covert Meaning in the Works of Dryden, Swift, Pope, and Austen*. Berkeley: University of California Press, 1980.
EVANS, MARY. *Jane Austen and the State*. London: Tavistock, 1987.
FERGUS, JAN S. *Jane Austen: A Literary Life*. New York: St. Martin's, 1991.
GARD, ROGER. *Jane Austen's Novels: The Art of Clarity*. New Haven: Yale University Press, 1992.
HARDY, BARBARA NATHAN. *A Reading of Jane Austen*. London: Owen, 1975.
HARRIS, JOCELYN. *Jane Austen's Art of Memory*. Cambridge: Cambridge University Press, 1989.
JOHNSON, CLAUDIA. *Jane Austen: Women, Politics, and the Novel*. Chicago: University of Chicago Press, 1988.

KAPLAN, DEBORAH. *Jane Austen among Women*. Baltimore: The Johns Hopkins University Press, 1992.
KIRKHAM, MARGARET. *Jane Austen: Feminism and Fiction*. Brighton: Harvester, 1983.
LITZ, A. WALTON. *Jane Austen: A Study of her Artistic Development*. New York: Oxford University Press, 1965.
NOKES, DAVID. *Jane Austen*. New York: Farrar, Strauss, Giroux, 1997.
TANNER, TONY. *Jane Austen*. Cambridge, MA: Harvard University Press, 1986.
TAVE, STUART M. *Some Words of Jane Austen*. Chicago: University of Chicago Press, 1973.
THOMPSON, JAMES. *Between Self and World: The Novels of Jane Austen*. University Park: Pennsylvania State University Press, 1988.

Index